Islamicate Sexualities

HARVARD MIDDLE EASTERN MONOGRAPHS

XXXIX

Islamicate Sexualities

Translations across Temporal Geographies of Desire

EDITED BY

Kathryn Babayan and Afsaneh Najmabadi

WITH CONTRIBUTIONS BY

Dina Al-Kassim, Sahar Amer, Brad Epps,
Frédéric Lagrange, Leyla Rouhi,
Everett K. Rowson, Valerie Traub

DISTRIBUTED FOR THE
CENTER FOR MIDDLE EASTERN STUDIES
OF HARVARD UNIVERSITY BY
HARVARD UNIVERSITY PRESS
CAMBRIDGE, MASSACHUSETTS
LONDON, ENGLAND

Copyright © 2008 by the President and Fellows of Harvard College
All rights reserved.
Printed in the United States of America

Library of Congress Cataloging-in-Publication Data

Islamicate sexualities : translations across temporal geographies of desire /
edited by Kathryn Babayan and Afsaneh Najmabadi.

p. cm. — (Harvard Middle Eastern monographs ; 39)

"This anthology emerges from a seminar sponsored by the Radcliffe Institute
for Advanced Study in May 2003"—Pref.

Includes bibliographical references and index.

ISBN 978-0-674-03204-0

1. Homosexuality—Islamic countries—History—Cross-cultural studies.
2. Homosexuality in literature. 3. Literature, Comparative—European and
Arabic. 4. Literature, Comparative—Arabic and European. 5. Literature,
Comparative—European and Persian. 6. Literature, Comparative—Persian
and European. 7. Arabic literature—History and criticism. 8. Persian
literature—History and criticism. 9. Literature, Medieval—Islamic influences.
10. Cervantes Saavedra, Miguel de, 1547–1616. Don Quixote—Criticism,
Textual. I. Babayan, Kathryn, 1960– II. Najmabadi, Afsaneh, 1946–
III. Harvard University. Center for Middle Eastern Studies. IV. Radcliffe
Institute for Advanced Study.

HQ76.3.I75I75 2008

306.770956—dc22

2008007240

Contents

Preface

Kathryn Babayan and Afsaneh Najmabadi[1]

DISCIPLINARY DESIRES

This anthology emerges from a seminar sponsored by the Radcliffe Institute for Advanced Study in May 2003. We organized the seminar under the title of "Crossing Paths of Middle Eastern and Sexuality Studies: Challenges of Theory, History, and Comparative Methods." The metaphor of travel across two fields reflected our unsatisfied and perhaps unattainable desire to counter the insularity of Middle Eastern Studies by "queering" Islamic historiography. To explore different genealogies of sexuality, we began to question some of the theoretical emphases and epistemic assumptions affecting our knowledge of the history of sexuality. The methods of queering and traveling were not wholly satisfying for reducing this traditional insularity (for reasons explained in the anthology), but we remain confident that the initiatory dialogues across cultural deployments of sexuality inscribed in the following pages are an important contribution to the broadening of gender and sexualities studies.

To make that crossing of paths possible, we invited discussants (Dina Al-Kassim, Brad Epps, Carla Petievich, and Valerie Traub) from outside Middle Eastern studies and within the fields of comparative literary studies and queer theory. We formulated our invitation as a gesture to complicate the Foucauldian model that too often is translated into a binary that juxtaposes a West-

ern *scientia sexualis* (which produced subjects endowed with
certain scientifically classifiable sexualities) with its imagined
opposite of an Eastern *ars erotica* (an unmitigated desire and
practice of pleasure transmitted from master to disciple through
secrets).[2] We hoped that the workshop would address the need
for materially localized readings of past sexualities represented
within Islamicate textual milieus—whether religious, literary, or
legal. These papers, we envisaged, would begin to draw the contours of Islamicate discourses on practices of both female and
male sexual desires by focusing on kindred histories (from different times and places) of power relations expressed through
words and acts. Concerned with the dynamic interplay between
cultural constructions of gender and sexuality in Islamicate discourses, we wanted to "travel" adventurously across disciplinary fields, integrating literary criticism with social and cultural
history. The dialogue between historians (Kathryn Babayan,
Frédéric Lagrange, Afsaneh Najmabadi, and Everett K. Rowson) and comparative literary scholars (Sahar Amer and Leyla
Rouhi) has now come to inform our diverse interpretations of
texts and contexts, words and acts, across a vast geocultural
domain—Iberian, Arabic, and Iranian—and an equally challenging temporal field, from the tenth century to the medieval
and the modern.[3]

The seminar's success exceeded our expectations. The conversations generated over three invaluable days engaged and challenged the questions we posed in our invitation. We came away
with new queries, revised terms, and an intense desire to carry
on with our discussions, which we did through soliciting and re-
vising the initial papers for publication. What had been envisaged as comments by our discussants—Dina Al-Kassim, Brad
Epps, and Valerie Traub—evolved into contributing papers that
frame the volume from its introduction to its body and epilogue.
We cannot thank our discussants enough for their intellectual
generosity. A productive seminar exchange with Carla Petievich
on the representations of female intimacy (Doganas and Zana-

khis) in Urdu poetry does not appear in this anthology but will instead form part of her forthcoming book.

TERMS AND METAPHORS

The limitations of the term *Middle East* in the seminar's title soon became evident. Two of our participants focused on Iberia and South Asia, regions historically excluded from the boundaries of the Middle East but including Muslim societies. Beyond its cultural and historical shortcomings, the term *Middle East* was a geopolitical and military designation coined by European cartographers at the turn of the twentieth century when oil explorations and naval access were being strategically arranged and delimited in the Persian Gulf region. For the title of this book, we wanted to move away from such a geopolitical category and its attendant Western ethnocentrism, which carries the additional burden today of the disciplinary politics of area studies. Instead, we chose Marshall G. S. Hodgson's coinage, *Islamicate*. Hodgson's term *Islamicate* was intended to highlight a complex of attitudes and practices that pertain to cultures and societies that live by various versions of the religion Islam.[4] *Islamicate*, with its double adjectival ending, was conceived as parallel to the term *Italianate*, which refers not only to what is historically understood as Italian but all that is associated with Italian styles and modes of cultural expression. Although the designation *Islamicate* carries its own limitations for our project, as it tends to reproduce a tradition of equating the Islamic world with its initial Arabo-Persian center, we use it here because of its conceptual movement away from the nineteenth-century universalizing European idea that distinguished between the world's cultures in part on the basis of religious denomination and that had dominated Islamic studies until Hodgson's proposition.

By the end of the seminar, we were being drawn away from the metaphor of traveling through and across times and geo-

graphic regions and were finding ourselves turning to translation as a metaphor for talking about ideas, concepts, terms, and
interpretations and their pertinence to various milieus. Di-
verging from the historiographic tradition that has marginalized
the constructs of gender and sexuality beyond the concerns of
history proper, we began to explore culture through the analytical frame of sexuality. The specificity of "queering" Islamicate
history and culture, we hoped, would also be productive for rethinking European tropes for masculinity and sexual "unmen-
tionabilities." But the unqualified usage of the terms *pederasty*
or *effeminacy*, grounded in the Islamicate world in historically
specific ways, revealed the problematic in "translating" sex and
relevant cultural, linguistic, and epistemological practices from
Islamicate contexts into European and Anglo-American "counterparts." Nevertheless, our translations, which were sometimes
ill-fitting, and our discussions of them gave us insights about the
limitations and possibilities of our project. We asked: What do
the particular processes of normative constructions of sexuality
tell us about the Islamicate past and present? How can we recre-
ate a different usable past? How can we reread our texts mindful
of "sex" and the multitude of practices and attitudes around desire, and what of the variety of homoerotic acts that defy tidy
categorization? What is at stake for gender and sexuality studies
in attributing homosexualities to Anglo-Euro-American culture?
In light of differing Anglo-Euro-American notions of reality,
representation, and knowledge, how do we go about "translating" Islamicate sexualities, based on their own historically determined notions, to English-speaking and -reading audiences?

As translations among disciplinary, geographical, and temporal areas challenged some of the workshop's initial premises,
the participants wondered about the suitability of sexuality as
a lens to interrogate erotic sociabilities and sexual sensibilities
before and beyond the predominant, Foucauldian frame of sexuality. Though Foucault may have correctly claimed that the
nineteenth-century transformations in modes of knowledge and

power-based relations made sexuality the "truth" of our identification and subjectivity, have we scholars unwittingly made
sexuality the "truth" of our historiographies, well beyond the
temporal and geographical confines of Foucault's original proposition? By asking this question, we do not mean to suggest the
invalidity of sexuality as a general topic in historical studies.
Rather, we would like to reflect momentarily on how privileging
and focusing on sexuality in Islamic historiography projects may
overshadow other possible paths of inquiry in the efforts to as-
semble histories.

Our conversations destabilized a range of narratives and rigid
categorizations emanating from geographies with their own
periodizations of time and that have produced various discourses around the body politic and have formulated sexualities
accordingly. The problem of nomenclature—both breaking with
classifications based on acts and types and also naming and understanding same-sex desire—permeated our discussion. What
does the creation of categories and typologies (homosexual, heterosexual, lesbian, queer, effeminate) do for our readings of
texts? Do acts define types? Instead of accumulating a list of
types and acts, should we not explore the contours of regulatory
technologies of gender and sexualities?

Sexuality studies' recent move away from the term *homosexuality* to the phrase *same-sex practices and desires* has attempted to undo some of the cultural burdens of homosexuality.
This analytical shift conforms to the distinction that Foucault
made between those societies that discipline and generate sexualities through typologizing human beings into sexual species
and other societies that punish and regulate practices without
grounding desire onto some inherent self. By adopting the concept of same sex, scholarship on sexuality may have confined us
into thinking about a set of human relations bound by the
"same-sex-ness" of such relationships. Not only have we made
"sex" the truth of these relationships when we attach "same"
onto it, but we may have become participants in regenerating

the binary of male and female biogenital difference as the
defining mark of that truth. Does it matter, for instance, that
two lovers were depicted in medieval Persian or Arabic love poetry with the same androgynous, genderless terms for beauty?
Did they even see themselves in a relationship defined by "sex"
and "*same* sex"? And how does our same-sex assignation dis-
tract us from adequately appreciating the asymmetry in power
and the intricacy of cultural and social webs that endow desire
with meaning? We must tread carefully, for in the process of re-
evaluating the appropriateness of same sex in relationships, we
would be loath to swing unwittingly toward figures such as the
oversexed, lusting woman or the sexless, transcendental mystic
man.

Moreover, *same* sex implies *opposite* sex, which is a modernist notion that has emerged over the last two centuries in tandem
with other notions about the "complementarity of the sexes."
Cultural encounters between Islamicate and European societies,
in part shaped by the forces of colonialism, led to the gradual
abandonment of traditional Islamicate ontologies that specified
one same essence for both man and woman, though the latter
had admittedly been an imperfect version of the former. According to this ontological tradition, as Dror Ze'evi has argued for
the early modern Ottoman context, one could say that all sexual
practices were same-sex practices, some just more perfect than
others.[5] To replace *homosexuality* with *same-sex practices and
desires* overcomes the nineteenth-century sexual burden of mis-
naming and mistyping but leaves us with another burdensome
term—that of binary gender anachronistically applied to earlier
times.

In the spirit of countering dualism, we contested together the
tyranny of our many binaries (such as the facile East-West divide
or the division made by scholars of sexuality between typologizing societies and those concerned with the prohibition of
acts) to recognize that societies that regulate their subjects by
typing them homo- and heterosexual have continued to punish
acts to varying degrees, and societies that discipline dominantly

through the punishment of acts simultaneously tend to categorize people according to types of desire. As a result of the workshop discussions, we recognize the necessity of contextualizing each example within its textual and historical milieu to locate representations of same-sex desire within historically contingent sociopolitical webs of kinship, property, sovereignty, and friendship.

However, "traveling" and "translating" texts and ideas from traditionally European theories and disciplines enabled us to identify for the general study of gender and sexualities the shared problematics and thematics in the relationships between acts and identities, rhetoric and insults, essentialism and constructionism, religion and mysticism. Certain matrimonial economies (such as polygyny) allowed in Islamicate societies alternative relationships of love between women and destabilize the convention of monogamy that bolsters modern fictions about gender, sexuality, love, marriage, and desire. Expanding the cultural boundaries of studies on sexuality prompted us to reconsider the historical periodizations of premodern and modern and to think of "moments" of state-imposed regulations on our bodies as temporal markers between the premodern and modern.

In our conversations, we have resisted a monolithic rendering of Islamicate sexual practices and discourses throughout the ages. One cannot exaggerate the significance of historicizing when it comes to studying gender and sexuality in Islamicate cultures. Islamic studies and the Islamicate world itself continue to be burdened with a scholarly tradition that has all too often situated Islam beyond temporality and geography, thus producing an effect of atemporal uniformity. Despite our best intentions, we often make statements about matters Islamic across vast spans of time and diverse societies. This affects gender and sexuality studies in particularly sharp ways, since it is a relatively new field of scholarship and one is often tempted to make up for the lack of pertinent historical studies by translating from other times and places within and without the larger Islamicate world.

This anthology is focused primarily on literary representations and lacks contributions that draw from other archives that include examples of visual culture or juridical and notarial records to integrate social history extensively. We also recognize the limitations of our geographical scope. We are trying not to be comprehensive in our coverage of the Islamicate world but instead to focus on various texts representing a variety of places, times, and disciplines in the hope that the overall project will generate further scholarship for the field of sexualities studies.

ACKNOWLEDGMENTS

We would like to conclude this preface with a few words of appreciation—first and foremost, for the Radcliffe Institute for Advanced Study, without whose generous support we could not have held this workshop. We would like to thank particularly Drew Faust, Dean of the Institute; Nancy Cott, Director of the Schlesinger Library and Faculty Director for the Humanities Advanced Seminars; and several of the Institute's staff, whose tireless attention to the organization of this seminar made our work possible: Phyllis Strimling, Chung-Un Seo, and Anna Chesson.

NOTES

1. We would like to thank Rima Hassouneh and Sima Shakhsari for their insightful comments on this preface.
2. Michel Foucault, *The History of Sexuality* (New York: Vintage Books, 1990), 1:53–73.
3. We invited Ottomanist scholars to participate in the seminar and contribute to this volume, and we regret that none were able to.
4. Marshall G. S. Hodgson, *The Venture of Islam: Conscience and History in a World Civilization* (Chicago: University of Chicago Press, 1974), 1:57–60.
5. Dror Ze'evi, *Producing Desire: Changing Sexual Discourse in the Ottoman Middle East 1500–1900* (Berkeley: University of California Press, 2006).

ONE

The Past Is a Foreign Country?
The Times and Spaces of
Islamicate Sexuality Studies

Valerie Traub

"The past is a foreign country: they do things differently there."
For many students of history, this epigrammatic sentence with
which L. P. Hartley begins his 1953 novel *The Go-Between* elic-
its a powerful sense of recognition. As Catherine Brown remarks
in an essay exploring medieval reading practices, "[T]he metaphor slips on comfortably, like a well-worn shoe. The past can
feel like a place as much as it does a time—a *foreign* place, outside the doors of the familiar, beyond the gate and the gatekeep-
ers of the *now*."[1] However much we might wish to find in the
past a home, an explanation of our present, or a vision of a possible future, Hartley's yoking of time and space through concepts of difference and distance seems to capture the encounter
with alterity that many scholars associate with the project of historiography itself.

Yet as Brown notes, the "'common-sense' resonance" of Hartley's recourse to implicit binaries of past/present, foreign/home,
they/we, different/similar is worth scrutinizing.[2] Her essay focuses primarily on the way that the practice of reading medieval

1

texts is implicated in dynamics of temporality and comes to the conclusion that "[t]he past is not a foreign country, really."[3] I want to apply pressure to the other side of Hartley's analogy. What are the implications of viewing a foreign country as residing in the past? Since Edward Said's *Orientalism,* we have been aware of the Western penchant for characterizing other cultures, notably those that appear fundamentally "other," as inhabiting a prior time.[4] As Dipesh Chakrabarty reminds us in *Provincializing Europe: Postcolonial Thought and Historical Difference,* there exists a pervasive teleological logic that organizes the relations of East to West—the "'first in Europe and then elsewhere' structure of time."[5] By means of this logic, cultural difference becomes intelligible through tropes of both geographical distance and temporal sequence.

One task of *Islamicate Sexualities* is to disrupt this tendentious mapping of temporal sequence onto cultural geography by putting into play a dialogue—sometimes comfortable, sometimes tense—between contemporary Euro-American lesbian/gay/queer studies and Middle Eastern/Islamicate studies. Apart from the worth of the individual essays included here, the import of this volume as a whole lies in the way it tugs productively in two different directions. On the one hand, it aims to analyze Islamicate sexualities from *within* the field of Middle Eastern studies in a way that attends to the specificity and diversity of cultures that comprise the Islamicate. On the other hand, it seeks to enter into an interdisciplinary dialogue with scholars working on Euro-American lesbian/gay/queer studies, especially queer theory and the history of sexuality.[6] This dual project necessarily raises difficult questions: What cultural and historical baggage accompanies the travel, importation, and translation of lesbian, gay, and queer identities and scholarship into the discursive terrain of the historical and contemporary Middle East? How does the pervasive association of sexual identity with modernity and the West affect the utility of lesbian, gay, and queer discourses for Islamic cultures, past and present? Conversely, how might the geopolitical tensions implicit in these associations productively revise the construction of pre- and early modern histories of Western sexuality?

What emerge clearly from the pages of this volume are the range and complexity of meanings of same-sex desires, practices, and identities, which cannot without simplification be assimilated to Western concepts of heterosexual/homosexual, gay/lesbian, or even queer. Rather than simply apply the analytics of queering to Islamicate texts, the present volume aims to create, through tenacious acts of dialogue, translation, and comparativism, a new field of historical knowledge and site of knowledge production—that of Islamicate sexuality studies.

In describing this collective project as an act of creation, I am not suggesting that the work published here has not been anticipated or the groundwork has not been laid for it by previous studies. Indeed, other scholars, as well as some of the contributors to this volume, have been working on the history of sexuality in the Middle East for years.[7] But as important as these individual contributions have been, no other group of scholars has taken on the responsibility to think capaciously about what it would mean to facilitate the birth of a new field of knowledge. Part of what motivated the convening of the November 2003 seminar at the Radcliffe Institute for Advanced Study—"Crossing Paths of Middle Eastern and Sexuality Studies: Challenges of Theory, History, and Comparative Methods"—was the belief that particular disciplinary configurations (including scholarly training, intellectual commitments, and institutional structures) tacitly hinder as well as enable the investigation of the history of sexuality and its theorization in Muslim cultures of the Middle East. The resulting volume attempts to work through some of the issues posed by the relative weight given throughout the fields of ethnic and area studies, lesbian/gay/queer studies, the history of sexuality, and gender studies to identity politics, institutional location, and what Sahar Amer, following Mirielle Rosello, calls the "national-sexual."[8] Nor, by referring to the creation of a new field of knowledge, do I mean to suggest that something as multifaceted as an academic discipline can be born

overnight. The development of this work, no less than its securing of institutional legitimacy, will no doubt be painstakingly
slow. But just as anthologies such as *Queering the Renaissance*
inaugurated many of the central themes in early modern English
studies,[9] so will *Islamicate Sexualities* set many of the terms of
debate on the history of sexuality in the Islamicate world. In
fact, the effects may be even more far reaching. For pace Chakrabarty, this volume invites us to consider the implications of
"provincializing Europe" for the techniques and methods of historicizing sexuality. If one goal of the volume is to pluralize the
history of sexualities, it does so not only by recognizing the het-
eronomous geographies, ethnicities, and nationalities of the
Islamicate but also by engaging with the effects of asymmetrical
temporalities and divergent periodizations, both within diverse
Islamic locales and between the cultures of the Middle East and
those of the West.

Before detailing the accomplishments of *Islamicate Sexualities*
as well as some of the unanswered questions raised by it, it is important to acknowledge the geopolitical terrain on which any effort to bring Middle Eastern studies and gay/lesbian/queer studies into mutually beneficial dialogue will be enacted. A recently
published essay on the relationship between Arab sexuality and
Western gay discourses of human rights provides one perspective on the lay of the land. Published in *Public Culture* in 2002,
Joseph Massad's hard-hitting "Re-Orienting Desire: The Gay
International and the Arab World" is a deliberate provocation
against what he calls the "Gay International":

> [I]t is the discourse of the Gay International that both produces
> homosexuals, as well as gays and lesbians, where they do not ex-
> ist, and represses same-sex desire and practices that refuse to be
> assimilated into its sexual epistemology. . . . [T]his discourse as-
> sumes prediscursively that homosexuals, gays, and lesbians are
> universal categories that exist everywhere in the world, and based
> on this prediscursive axiom, the Gay International sets itself
> the mission of defending them by demanding that their rights as

"homosexuals" be granted where they are denied and be respected where they are violated. . . . It is precisely [the] perceived
instability in the desire of Arab and Muslim men that the Gay International seeks to stabilize, as its polymorphousness confounds
gay (and straight) sexual epistemology. . . . [T]he assumptions underlying the mission of the Gay International demand that these
resistant "Oriental" desires . . . be re-*oriented* to and subjected by
the "more enlightened" Occident.[10]

Focused on what he calls the Gay International's "missionary
tasks, the discourse that produces them, and the organizations
that represent them,"[11] Massad divides his essay into a critique
of Western publications and a longer exposition of how this
writing has underpinned the "Incitement to Discourse" that, he
argues, has imposed a universalist, identitarian epistemology
onto men who have sex with men in the Arab world. I leave
to others more knowledgeable than I an assessment of the accuracy of Massad's allegations against the missionary and Orientalist presuppositions of particular Western nongovernmental
organizations as well as their alleged coercive effects.[12] My concern is in how his political rectitude finds much of its support by
trafficking in a scholarly strategy—that of erasing difference—
that he explicitly disavows. Noting the "different kinds of
literature—academic studies, journalistic accounts, and human
rights and tourism publications—which are governed by different professional demands, political configurations, markets, and
audiences" that inform his characterization of the Gay International, Massad asserts that he does "not seek to flatten them by
erasing these differences." Yet the effect of his essay is to do just
that.[13] Selectively presenting a small sampling of historical,
pseudo-anthropological, and journalistic work on homosexuality in Muslim cultures as if it comprised a scholarly consensus,
Massad produces a site of critique that has only a tenuous relationship to dominant trends in lesbian/gay/queer studies or the
discipline of the history of sexuality. I do not dispute that those
NGOs that promote the belief that queers in the Middle East
need to be "saved" from repressive regimes may find support for

their views in some of the publications Massad critiques. I do reject his implication that the unreflective Orientalism, "identarian essentialism," and ahistoricism evident there comprises a dominant pattern among scholars working either on Islamicate sexualities or lesbian/gay/queer studies.[14]

Indeed, there is more than a little irony in the fact that much recent scholarship on such topics is informed by theoretical perspectives and methodological commitments that would support Massad's contentions about the complex and historically specific configurations of male-male sex in the Arab world. Social constructionism, for instance, explicitly rejects the possibility of a "prediscursive homosexuality," while queer theory tends to be extremely interested in the "polymorphousness" of erotic desire. But neither social constructivism nor queer theory is much mentioned in "Re-Orienting Desire." Instead, arguing that "supporters of the Gay International's missionary tasks have produced two kinds of literature on the Muslim world: an academic literature of historical, literary, and anthropological accounts . . . and journalistic accounts of the lives of so-called gays and (much less so) lesbians in the contemporary Arab and Muslim worlds,"[15] Massad focuses in the first instance on an anthology of essays edited by Arno Schmitt and Jehoeda Sofer published by Haworth Press in 1992.[16] Much of his argument rests on repudiating the touristic form of anthropology/journalism present in that collection, which indulges in dubious generalizations that would be laughable were they not so invidious.[17] To bolster the broader charge of "errors of historicism,"[18] Massad misinterprets the comments of Everett Rowson, extrapolating from one sentence an entire generalizing method.[19] He also attributes to Bruce Dunne comparisons between the Middle East and the West that he never makes.[20] Connecting the alleged ahistoricism of Rowson (and John Boswell) to that of a passage from Edward Lacey's 1988 introduction to Ahmad ibn Yusuf al-Tifashi's *The Delight of Hearts, or, What You Will Not Find in Any Book*, which celebrates "the constants of human nature, the universal, unvarying qualities of temperament, the unchanged, unchangeable, undying sexual appetites and weaknesses that unite human beings throughout all ages and across all gulfs of religious, cultural, and linguistic difference,"[21] he empties current scholarship of its complexity and nuance and comes close to enacting a universalizing gesture of his own.[22]

Without subscribing to the notion that the appeal of gay identity to Middle Eastern Muslim men is the result of a Western imperialist conspiracy, we nonetheless can recognize that the contradictions exposed by Massad have much to do with the way in which the discourse of gay identity (which inscribes a sexual identity onto modern subjects by means of a taxonomic logic and tends to separate sexuality from gender formations) is part of a conflicted project of modernity.[23] As such, it can only be contradictory and incoherent in all of the ways that Eve Sedgwick detailed over a decade ago.[24] Its problematic repercussions have been amplified in our current political situation wherein neoimperialism, globalization, and the so-called war on terror pit much of the West against much of the East. Massad's critique responds to and partakes in these geopolitical conflicts about the meanings of modernity and tradition, the global and the local, including the role of the contemporary state in regulating the sexuality of its citizens and the state's implication in neoimperial and transnational flows of bodies and capital.[25] Despite flaws in his argument, then, Massad is right that the notion of sexual identity as a function of modernity is implicated in the ideological faultlines between the West and much of the rest of the world.

Massad is not alone in diagnosing a problem of faulty historicism in Western scholarship on Islamic and Arab homosexuality. From a less politicized set of concerns, Will Roscoe and Stephen O. Murray claim in their introduction to *Islamic Homosexualities: Culture, History, and Literature* that "social constructionist accounts still evoke a history of homosexuality as a progressive, even teleological, evolution from pre-modern repression, silence, and invisibility to modern visibility and social freedom."[26] Their volume, on the other hand, argues that "[t]he contrast between 'Western' and 'Islamic' homosexualities is not so much one of visibility versus invisibility or modern freedom versus traditional repression, but of containment versus elaboration, of a single pattern of homosexuality defined and delimited by institutions and discourses closely linked to the modern nation-state versus the variety, distribution, and longevity of same-sex patterns in Islamic societies."[27] How their first contention (the history of homosexuality as a progressive teleology) coheres with "social constructionist accounts" (which typically attempt to avoid developmental narratives) is one question raised by this binarism of invisibility and visibility, repression and progress. A second question is the suitability of applying this binarism to the geopolitical relations of East and West. Simply reversing an ethnocentric presupposition of Western privilege and progress—and thereby reducing the histories of homosexuality to a "single pattern" in the religiously and politically diverse cultures of "the West"—is not conducive to combating either Western exceptionalism or the pull of teleological narratives.[28]

Nonetheless, it is not accidental that arguments coming from such different motivations as those in "Re-Orienting Desire" and *Islamic Homosexualities* each take recourse in *history* to buttress their claims about the epistemic privileging of the West. History, it appears, is a lynchpin in these debates about transnational sexualities and cross-cultural epistemologies. By history, I mean not only the stories a culture tells to itself and others about its modes of sexual existence but the historiographic methods by which such stories are "discovered" and circulated, the textual traces from which such stories are derived, the archives in which scholars seek access, as well as the temporal frameworks (modern, premodern, early modern) in which such stories are situated. Despite their differences, Massad, Roscoe, and Murray would agree that the seemingly canonical narrative of the emergence of homosexual identity as a function of modern discourses, institutions, and practices necessarily positions the non-West as premodern, traditional, anterior, even archeological.[29]

Whether this "present pastness" is lamented as primitive and lacking or, conversely, is celebrated as polymorphously perverse and exotic, the results, they imply, are the same: as sexual categories and epistemologies travel across borders, all efforts at cross-cultural translation and comparison are imbued with politically loaded significations of tradition and modernity.

Within this geopolitical context, white, Euro-American lesbian/gay/queer studies has begun to face the challenges issued by what has come to be called "queer of color critique," which exposes many of the blindspots of lesbian/gay/queer studies while also adopting some of its tools.[30] Increasingly, the field is positioning itself within a postcolonial and race-conscious frame of reference that attempts, in the words of one influential collection, to consider the "interrelations of sexuality, race, and gender in a transnational context"—an effort the editors dub "queer transexions of race, nation, and gender."[31] This growing body of work suggests that certain queer methodologies, when radically refigured according to specific cultural and political exigencies, may offer modes of analysis that enable resistance to those forces that would position a discourse of white, Western sexual identity above, against, and beyond the sexualities of people of color and those of people in other parts of the world.[32] Gayatri Gopinath, for instance, offers a "queer diasporic" orientation that "works in contradistinction to the globalization of 'gay' identity that replicates a colonial narrative of development and progress that judges all 'other' sexual cultures, communities, and practices against a model of Euro-American sexual identity."[33] Such a method—attuned to the effects of dislocation and migration and intent on the performative possibilities of resignification—works, as well, in contradistinction to the anxieties about cultural authenticity that underlie some of Massad's concerns. Finding a way around the epistemological impasse that would necessitate the rejection of all interaction with the "foreign" in the name of authenticity and "home," Gopinath demonstrates that scholars attempting to counter the colonizing effects of first-world/third-world sequence need neither disavow the applicability of Western concepts and methods nor uncritically endorse them.

Gopinath's brief for a queer diasporic method may name a fairly obvious, if nonetheless sophisticated, intersection of queer and postcolonial theory. Arguing that "queerness is to heterosexuality as the diaspora is to the nation," she aims to explode "the binary oppositions between nation and diaspora, heterosexuality and homosexuality, original and copy."[34] Given the different national histories of dislocation across Asia and the Middle East, a method drawn from the experience of South Asian migration may not, perhaps, be the most obvious tool for analyzing Middle Eastern sexualities—unless, that is, one begins to think, as this volume attempts to do, more syncretically about Arab and Islamic diasporas.

Even so, another fruitful point of intersection between queer and postcolonial theory—one that is particularly pertinent to the present volume, insofar as it focuses largely on the pre- and early modern eras—can be found in queer medieval studies. Influenced by postcolonialism, medievalists have argued that the "Middle Ages" tends to be viewed, as modernity's "other."[35] As Catherine Brown notes, there is a "hermeneutic similarity between medievalism and orientalism."[36] Because of this dynamic of othering, medievalists have been particularly attentive to how temporal distance can be spatialized, as well as the effects of relegating the foreign to a premodern past.[37] This awareness has given rise to trenchant analyses of the figures of Jews, Turks, and Muslims in European medieval texts and of the colonizing processes of historiography itself. Queer medievalists, in particular, have demonstrated how conventional historical periodizations privilege not only the modern and the West but also the associated taxonomies that have played a crucial role in the project of sexual modernity. Arguing that the "preposterous historicism" of queer theory could provide a better way of modeling how historical periods, cultural geographies, and sexualities may or may not map on to one another, they advocate queer theory's ability to disrupt modernity's retrospective investment in progress, causality, and supersession—in other words, the coercive sequential requirements of the "pre-" in relation to the "modern."[38]

Given such debates about the applicability of Western logics, temporalities, and methods for non-Western subjects and subjectivities, the publication of *Islamicate Sexualities* is particularly propitious. The volume puts into practice a simple yet easily forgotten notion that, as David M. Halperin put it, "There is more than one strategy for entering into a queerer future."[39] *Islamicate Sexualities* responds, in a more positive key, to Mireille Rosello's contention that "It may be that same-sex attraction cuts across race, gender and class, but I am not sure queers can talk to each other across national borders."[40] Rather than accede to such diminished expectations, *Islamicate Sexualities* explores an alternative route by enacting a cross-cultural, cross-ethnic, cross-linguistic conversation among scholars who work within Arab, English, French, Persian, and Spanish cultural traditions variously located in North Africa, Egypt, Syria, and Iran, as well as Spain, France, and England. The collective strategy, evident in different degrees in each of the essays, is to press against the incommensurate frameworks of analysis that have derived from the cold war–era formation of area studies and post-Stonewall lesbian/gay/queer studies.

There is much to pressure. On one side, until recently, studies of sexuality in the Middle East or Islamicate cultures tended to be written from an Orientalist perspective, which posited sexuality as an essentialized set of beliefs and practices—as well as literary genres—peculiar to Islam. Such beliefs and practices, it was thought, emerged either from the particularities of Islam as a religion or, more generally, from an *ars erotica* associated with the East. For scholars intent on transforming the discipline of Middle Eastern studies beyond its Orientalist origins, there nonetheless has remained an antipathy toward investigations of sexuality, which enforces, in particular, a deliberate forgetting of the homoerotic past. The inhospitability of Middle Eastern studies to the study of sexuality is best addressed by those working

within it, and the defense and further critique of this field will, I
suspect, arise in the course of reviews of this volume.

On the other side is the reluctance of lesbian/gay/queer scholars trained in Euro-American traditions to take on, attempt to
understand, and most of all find their knowledge, terms, and
central concepts challenged and transformed by other cultural
paradigms, models, and questions. The contours of this problem
are congruent with yet not adequately explained by Massad's indictment of a "Gay International."[41] There is, first, the question
of terminology: homo/hetero, gay/lesbian, and queer. As the essays in this volume show, these terms, as well as the concepts
they name, are inadequate to the task of representing the poly-
glot histories that they are made to bear. It is worth noting that
some Western scholars have also argued that such terms and key
concepts (such as coming out and the paradigm of visibility on
which such concepts rely) are inadequate to the task of representing the complexity of Western sexualities, both past and
present.[42] At any rate, these essays remind all of us of the need to
acknowledge the historicity and contingency of our categories of
thought. Second, as I've already intimated, the narrative of the
historical development of homosexual identity remains an obstacle to new theorizations. We thus need to move deliberately
beyond Murray and Roscoe's cautious suggestion that "[t]he
long history and broad distribution of Islamic societies provides
an opportunity for placing the emergence of modern homosexual identity in northern Europe within a broader context."[43] Far
too mild a claim, this stance is complicated and to a certain extent superseded by the demonstration by several essays in this
volume of the historical interarticulation and coimplication of
Eastern and Western bodies, desires, aesthetic traditions, and
analytical paradigms. Thus, it is a matter not so much of bringing to visibility Islamicate texts (interesting as they are in their
own right) or of providing a broader context for the West (important as that is) but of confounding the very terms by which
our understandings of East and West are derived.

One strength of the present volume thus lies in its willingness to tackle some of the epistemological issues that are raised by the contributors' various intellectual and disciplinary positions, while also insisting on a rigorous historical method, linguistic expertise, and theoretical sophistication. Structurally signaled by the editors' inclusion of essays poised in explicit dialogue with the work of other contributors—Dina Al-Kassim's epilogue and Bradley Epps's excursus on competitive comparativism in chapter 4—the volume seeks to reflect metacritically on its own investments, methods, and arguments. This self-reflexive collaboration across national, linguistic, and temporal boundaries produces an interdisciplinary debate about the historicity of erotic desires, practices, and identities in the diverse cultures examined. Such interests partly explain the appeal that various aspects of queer theory, as it has been developed in the European and Anglo-American academy, holds for several of the contributors, for it is one of its more auspicious aspects that queer theory urges us to think as precisely as possible about the intricate dance between erotic desires, acts, and identities. For many (but by no means all) queer theorists, this involves attempting to understand those relations (as well as many other aspects of sexuality) through a recognition of their contingency and historicity. Given the unstable meanings of sexual desires and identities across time and space and given, as well, the opacities of textual representation, the historical question perforce bleeds into an epistemological one. Indeed, as Al-Kassim puts it, the "unanswerable question about the limits of knowing and naming the desire that we moderns hear in the archive" poses insurmountable difficulties: we can never be sure of our ability to recognize, accurately name, and interpret the desires, practices, and identities present in the past. Yet the very obscurity of our knowledge is part of what spurs us on. It provides us with the question that the editors have implicitly foregrounded in structuring the collective conversation that gave rise to this volume: *How* do we know what we (think we) know?

Even as it pursues this question about the means and manner of discernment, *Islamicate Sexualities* seems uncertain—indeed, conflicted—about whether its project is one of "queering" the field of Middle Eastern studies. This ambivalence is, I think, warranted. All of the contributors would oppose the cultural imperialism implicit in any unidirectional importation of a conceptual apparatus derived largely from European and Anglo-American perspectives—as is most obviously thematized in Leyla Rouhi's (chapter 2) and in Brad Epps's (chapter 4) discussions of the debate surrounding the publication of *Queer Iberia*. At the same time, many of them do not eschew Western paradigms but rather analyze and refine their utility for understanding Islamicate texts.

It is worth noting that within the broader field of transnational sexuality studies, the question of whether the strategy of "queering" necessarily imposes an unequal epistemic and methodological privilege is far from decided. Ruth Vanita, for instance, contends in *Queering India: Same-Sex Love and Eroticism in Indian Culture and Society* that "[i]t is significant that it is usually those who have already obtained most of their basic civil rights and liberties in first-world environments who object to the use of these terms [gay, lesbian, queer] in third-world contexts."[44] Noting that all names and terms "are constantly in flux and are only approximations necessitated by and necessary to human communication," she argues that in contemporary India, the political salience of "gay" is far greater than less identitarian discourses.[45] Likewise, Peter A. Jackson, writing about the sexual taxonomies that have developed historically in Thailand, argues that

> we need to be cautious in characterizing the power of external cultural and ethico-religious systems to alter fundamental conceptions of sex and gender in Thailand. Indigenous Thai notions have not only survived a millennium of Buddhism but also show considerable resilience in the face of the recent marketing of Western-styled gay identities via globalizing transport and communication networks.[46]

His study "raises questions about the extent to which the Western conception of gay has, or can be, borrowed within the Thai
context." At the same time,

> the mere existence of the word *gay* in the contemporary Thai lan-
> guage does not indicate that a global gay identity or a transna-
> tional homogenization of human sexuality is a necessary outcome
> of the impact of yet another universalizing world culture. . . .
> Western notions of homosexuality and gay identity are also being
> accommodated within the Thai cultural framework, in the process
> becoming as much Thai as Western, if not more so.[47]

The unsettled nature of these issues impels me to ask some
metacritical questions about the parameters, assumptions, and
methods employed here. As with any historical project, the initial step is the construction of an archive—by which I simply
mean the identification of a corpus of relevant texts. For scholars studying the Middle East, this process can be hindered by
politically motivated barriers to access to "sensitive" materials.
At the same time, the corpus of texts that comprise the archive
of sexuality studies must be construed in the broadest possible
of terms, including canonical and noncanonical texts, "high" literary genres and "low" obscenity, texts that explicitly name
body parts and sexual acts and texts that don't. The importance
of such archival research cannot be underestimated.[48] Before
Jeannette Foster published *Sex Variant Women in Literature: A
Historical and Quantitative Survey,* for instance,[49] no scholar
could have identified recurrent tropes in the figuring of female-
female desire in Western literature, analyze the relationship between emotional intimacy and genital sex, or track changes in
societal discourses. This commitment to constructing a site of
analysis, whether literary or legal, is exemplified in chapter 5 in
the present volume in Frédéric Lagrange's essay on medieval deployments of the insult, as well as Afsaneh Najmabadi's essay
(chapter 8) on the regulation of sexuality in Qajar Iran. No less
crucial is the ability to cast a queer eye on familiar texts, as in

Leyla Rouhi's reading of *Don Quixote* (chapter 2), which argues, on the basis of its fluid politics of identity, that this "masterpiece" of Spanish literature "be included in the vast canon of Islamicate studies." The essays included here demonstrate that the discursive domains of knowledge production about sex over the centuries are multiple, that they traverse the canonical/noncanonical divide, and that they include works of satire and insult, humor and bawdy entertainment, political and legal commentary, medical treatises, love poetry, drama, prose fiction, and epic romance. There is much that is historically specific to the ways in which sexuality is organized, regulated, and understood in the different cultures, geographies, and political and religious formations discussed here—which, after all, range temporally from the tenth to the early twentieth centuries and include secular and religious, traditional and modernizing states, each of which has its own complicated relationship to multiple Western powers.

Despite this millennial range, however, and despite the individual complexity of the texts, cultures, and traditions explored, much of the collection is focused on issues that are largely congruent with lesbian/gay/queer historiography as it has evolved in the West. The point of noting these corollaries in themes across cultures is not to claim them as more Western than Eastern nor to use the West as the gauge but to begin to differentiate between what is culturally specific and what is not. Central areas of analysis explored by the contributors include essentialism versus constructionism and acts versus identities; the role of gender taxonomies and typologies of gender and desire; the relation between friendship, love, and sexual practices; the embeddedness of sexuality in other social formations; patriarchal hierarchy and social discipline; fear of erotic excess; ideological subversion and containment; the enforcement of heteronormativity; the meanings of individual body parts; the function of rhetoric, speech, and silence; the effects of textual genre; the role of humor and insult in creating erotic typologies; the erotics of religiosity and mysticism; gender segregation and gender crossing; effeminacy and age hierarchy; and the beauty of androgynous boys. The individual essays included here locate these concerns within discrete social, historical, and literary contexts, and their deployments are shown to be contingent, not universal. Nonetheless, their ability to transmigrate beyond what is already, in the words of the editors, a "vast geocultural domain" provides part of their interest. Moreover, as familiar as these themes may be to Euro-American lesbian/gay/queer studies, they are crucially defamiliarized and redrawn by the essays in this volume.

The fact of this congruence, however, does lead me to wonder whether there exist certain questions that are *askable only* from within this new field of knowledge production. I suspect that there may be many. Let me elaborate on one.[50] As Al-Kassim notes, one point on which all the contributors agree is that Foucault's axiomatic division of East from West in his description of the *ars erotica* and the *scientia sexualis* is historically inaccurate. The contributors' attention to the historical and material specificities of their various archives pushes vigorously against this organizing assumption. Joining other scholars working on other geographies,[51] they argue that disciplinary apparatuses and taxonomic classifications regulated sexuality long before the nineteenth century—in the East as well as in the West (the most extensive European example may be the bureaucracy set up in Renaissance Florence to prosecute sodomy).[52] But what has gone unexplored heretofore is the extent to which Foucault's deployment of an East/West divide is motivated in part by his concern to establish a premodern/modern periodization. Starting to unpack this conflation, Najmabadi details the ways in which changes in sexual arrangements in Qajar Iran do not fit the Foucaultian model. In a more theoretical vein, Al-Kassim suggests (in the epilogue) that "[T]he premodern and the Eastern are . . . always defined by an opposition [between sodomy and homosexuality] that secures their uniqueness by saving them from modern disciplinary projections." As Epps contends, just as we must challenge Foucault's historical division between a repressive, juridical West and a permissive, erotic East, we need to resist inverting this binary by acquiescing to the shadow picture that "obtains in the West today: a permissive polysexual West and a repressive heteronormative Middle East." Both forms of binary construction, as Epps makes clear, are politically motivated fantasies. Needless to say, both the East and the West are currently in a state of political crisis about sexuality. Neither is entirely repressive or entirely permissive. The boundaries between the enforcement of normativity and tolerance reside at the place where gender ideologies, circulations of global capital, and discourses of civil/human rights both intersect and collide.

Pushing further the "welcome complication of the epistemic model" that Al-Kassim describes, I would suggest that a further problem with the concept of an Eastern *ars erotica* is the changelessness that it implicitly ascribes. Just as Foucault's *History of Sexuality* demonstrates the changes wrought on the confessional model, the meanings and practices of sexuality in the Middle East altered over the ten centuries covered in this volume, both of their own accord and due to their interaction with the West.

Finally, of the triple conflation of the East with the *ars erotica* and the premodern, we need to ask: What are the effects of this association from the standpoint of not only periodization and geography but of the relationship between modernity and traditionalism? As Najmabadi's essay urges us to ask: How does one identify and assess the advent of sexual modernity in the Middle East? What are the techniques of its emergence, and how does the uneven acquisition of different forms of modernity (political, technological, social) play out for different populations (urban/rural, literate/illiterate, secular/religious)? The simultaneous existence of temporalities and discourses of modernity and traditionalism in many Middle Eastern cultures and the contested role of sexuality in that tension complicate this issue, not only for the present and not only to provide a further gloss on (or refutation of) Foucault. Understanding its dynamics has the potential to affect not only what may be specific to the sexualities of Muslim and Middle Eastern cultures, but the ways we analyze *all* premodern, early modern, and modern sexualities—and thus what we mean by sexuality itself.

It is always difficult to think outside of the prevailing analytical box. One example of this difficulty arises in the course of Najmabadi's worry about the effects of Iranian modernists' understanding of men's sexual relations with other men as a temporary phase rather than a minority identity. Is this not, she asks, "a deferral of recognition of same-sex desire as an erotic preference? Is it not yet another way of denial and disavowal of homosexuality?" As she points out, such an attitude "marginalizes same-sex desire through temporal boxing rather than through minoritization." True enough—but to pose the issue in these terms and, more important, *to rest with them there* is to come perilously close to reimposing a concept of homosexual identity before, as her careful historical research shows, it was possible to have one.

The contributors also agree that the widespread distinction between acts and identities is not a sufficiently nuanced or flexible instrument for describing erotic meanings and relations, either in the premodern/early modern periods or today.[53] However, we need to be wary of too quickly scuttling the distinction simply because it seems to enforce a specious binary. During the Radcliffe seminar, one participant suggested that all identities imply acts and all acts imply identities. Likewise, Al-Kassim argues that the division of acts from identities is "incoherent because the performative character of identity cannot do without its acts. . . . to be defined by acts is to become a type." If the distinction between acts and identities seems analytically incoherent—or even a red herring—this does not mean that no distinction exists or that the distinction isn't important. To say that a modality of eroticism is not *only* an act is not necessarily to imply that it *is* an identity (in the sense of socially defined role, subjective desire, and specific acts all sutured together).[54]

The state of sexuality studies is such that we are now in a position to insist that what is meant by sexual identity be more precisely defined, taking care to differentiate between such concepts as sexual inclination, tendency, preference, predisposition, orientation, consciousness, subjectivity, self-perception, and subculture. Listed here according to a spectrum from "soft" to "hard" identity claims, the problems and questions that arise from their conflation include the following: Are identity, orientation, and subjectivity synonymous?[55] If they are, do they mean the same thing as inclination, predisposition, and tendency? Does an inclination, even if defined as innate, necessarily signify something causal, or is it merely probabilistic? Does a subcultural grouping necessarily constitute an identity or subjectivity? Does the *content* of a homoerotic subjectivity alter historically?

We also might consider bracketing the question of identity in favor of a more deliberately epistemological strategy and ask whether there are other ways of producing knowledge about sexuality in history than either the *ars erotica* or *scientia sexualis*. Introducing these concepts in the first volume of *The History of Sexuality*, Foucault claimed, "Historically, there have been two great procedures for producing the truth of sex."[56] But is the separation of art from science the only way of understanding the production of knowledge about sexual desires and sexual practices? A passage in the tale of *Don Quixote*'s Ana Félix (which follows the reference discussed by Rouhi to the "barbarous Turks") provides a paradigmatic case. This is *Don Quixote*'s quick mention of the risk to the beautiful stranger (the cross-dressed Don Gaspar) by the women of the king's seraglio, articulated in Ana's rendition of the king's words: "To avoid the risk she [the stranger] might run among the women of his seraglio, and distrustful of himself, he commanded her to be placed in the house of some Moorish ladies of rank who would protect and attend her." Despite its indirect allusion to what we might term an *ars erotica*—the risk of women initiating each other into erotic caresses within the harem—Cervantes's own narrative is not a discourse of initiation. Nor, despite the prohibition that is implied in the narrator's desire to protect the cross-dressed Don Gaspar, is his exposition a science, a taxonomy, or a confessional apparatus. This brief textual moment, embedded in a larger narrative structured by specific textual traditions, prompts me to suggest that there might be other procedures— not great, much less official, but nonetheless effective in producing erotic meaning and knowledge. The indirection and innuendo at work in the defamations analyzed by Lagrange provide further support for this hypothesis.[57]

This is but one way in which Islamicate sexuality studies—in conversation with but not determined by sexuality studies focused on the West—might challenge or nuance some of the central paradigms of Euro-American lesbian/gay/queer studies. At the same time, the paradigms of Western historiography and theory are still very much in process and have neither derived from nor have settled into a stable method, position, or orthodoxy. Queer theory, in particular, should be seen as "provisional and dynamic, strategic and mobilizing, rather than prescriptive or doctrinal."[58] The same is true for the history of sexuality. One need only consider the challenge that Alan Bray repeatedly issued to other historians to witness the fundamental dynamism of this field. This early modernist, who did more than anyone to create a history of premodern male homosexuality in the West, insisted that to begin with sexuality is to begin with the wrong question. The goal was to always view sexuality in a wider social and interpretive frame, whereas "the effect of a shaping concern with sexuality is precisely to obscure that wider frame."[59]

Given the point-counterpoint structure of this volume, it makes sense that there exist within it unresolved tensions, contradictions and conflicts, and different levels of willingness to scrutinize one or another key term of analysis. Certain contributors, for instance, see no problem in applying contemporary terms and concepts to the distant past. Although this is most explicitly addressed in Epps's critique (chapter 4) of Sahar Amer's treatment of the "medieval lesbian" (chapter 3), it was also a point of contention during the Radcliffe seminar, when Everett Rowson suggested that Lagrange was overstating the extent to which Arabic libertine discourses contribute, however "accidentally," to the construction of a "field of homosexuality" in premodern Islamic culture. One perspective on this question can be found in Halperin's critique of Bernadette Brooten's *Love between Women: Early Christian Responses to Female Homoeroticism.*[60] Halperin takes Brooten to task, not because the modern concept of lesbianism frames her account (he agrees that interest in the homoerotic past is likely to be motivated by investments in the present) but because she allows modern concepts of lesbianism to permeate the frame of her analysis in ways that go unacknowledged in her exposition. Lagrange's attempt to nuance social constructionism displays his awareness of this problem, although he veers more toward inflecting his historical account with present concerns than either Halperin or Rowson might allow. Yet his general point is a crucial one. Deploying the vocabularies of the medieval era, Lagrange argues that the genre of the insult links active and passive roles within male-male sexuality in a way that reveals the limitations of more explicitly taxonomic discourses that depend exclusively on the categorization of behaviors. In this respect and despite their disagreement, both his and Rowson's essays are in synch with the edict that Epps proffers: "Any reading of classical, medieval, or early modern texts that involves gays, lesbians, straights, and so on is historically challenged; so too is any reading that perfunctorily discounts gays, lesbians, straights, and so on. The challenge, as I see it, is to negotiate, without perforce eliminating or codifying, doubts, gaps, silences, opacities, differences, inconsistencies, and uncertainties."

Another difference among the contributors, related to the issue of modern nomenclatures and taxonomies, is the degree to which they view stable social/ideological boundaries existing in the historical periods they examine (boundaries that are then available to be subverted or transgressed). Like identity categories, such boundaries are historical formations; they cannot be a priori assumed. For instance, if there is no such identity as "lesbian" available to medieval women, as Epps and I would contend, then how can the representation of a woman's erotic caresses of another woman "interrogate" or "subvert" a system of sexuality *that has yet to come into being?* To insist on this question is not to diminish the importance of representations of female same-sex desire but rather to place them within the social frame in which they would have been intelligible—in this case, not a codified system of sexuality per se but a pervasive medieval structure in support of patriarchal marriage.

Even among contributors who would eschew the labels *gay* and *lesbian* to describe premodern sexualities, there is a tendency to use the term *heteronormativity* to describe earlier systems of sexuality and gender. This is the case more generally in the scholarship, first, because very little effort has gone toward historicizing *hetero*sexuality and, second, because of the pervasive influence of Judith Butler's theoretical work on modern systems of gender and erotic intelligibility.[61] The unfortunate result is that many scholars employ the terms *heteronorm* and *heteronormative* with little reflection on just what they mean for their historical period. Heterosexuality and heteronormativity then function as ahistorical categories and forces, as if the particular configurations of desire, subjectivity, emotional affect, and marital structure were not various and culturally contingent. What, one might ask, is normative about heterosexuality across Islamic, Christian, and Judaic early modern cultures if the term can include polygamy and monogamy, dynastic marriage and companionate marriage, arranged marriage and romantic love, denigration of female erotic pleasure and celebration of it, elaborately organized households inhabited by husband, wives, concubines, servants, slaves, and extended kin and single-family households composed of husband, wife, and children? It is not so much "heterosexuality" that is common here as it is religiously sanctioned marriage, the patriarchal household, reproductive imperatives, and women's enclosure within domestic space.

A related question is whether "norms" operate in the same way as concepts of the licit and the illicit, sin and penance, criminality and punishment. The advent of norms, normality, normativity, and normalization in the West may be yet another distinctive feature of its modernity. This, at least, is the case made by Foucault, inspired by the work of Georges Canguilhem.[62] If this is so, then we need to ask more systematically: How and when are sexual norms produced in the Middle East? Did the Islamic moral code function differently than concepts of Christian sin? And which specific methods of normalization and "heterosocialization" pertain? Najmabadi's brief discussion of an emerging discourse of the "unnatural and abnormal" in twentieth-century Iran is an important beginning to this effort.[63] So too is the attempt, represented most fully by Rouhi's essay, to define sexuality studies via more ample and flexible rubrics whereby same-sex and cross-sex desires, as well as the forces that regulate them, are shown to be constitutively interrelated.

That the discourses of Islamicate sexuality are permeated throughout by gender asymmetries is undeniable. Arab-Islamic texts, for instance, speak volubly about the androgynous beauty of beardless boys and are explicit too about anal intercourse and fellatio, but they are relatively quiet about female-female desire and sexual acts (although more explicit than Western texts). In the representation of male homoerotic desire, wives generally are not mentioned. In contrast, in tales of female homoeroticism, the reader usually is not allowed to forget the hapless, distraught, or revengeful husband. Because of the patriarchal structure of marriage and the household, men seem to have had the opportunity to lead a sexual double life, combining marriage, reproduction, and family with same-sex sex. On the other hand, whereas the Islamic patriarchal household confined women's sexuality in multiple ways, it is also possible to discover, as Kathryn Babayan's essay (chapter 7) on an Isfahani widow's travelogue shows, glimpses of female-female love and desire existing just beyond or outside of male control. In such textual and social interstices, we gain access to possibilities beyond the notorious figure of the tribade (the woman who uses her enlarged clitoris to pleasure other women), which is a recurrent motif in

Arabic texts, from erotic manuals and medicine to humorous literature and satirical poetry.[64] Amer argues that the more developed Arabic vocabulary for describing female same-sex activity may have been adopted and revised by medieval French writers. It certainly appears that it was by reference to alleged Islamic customs and sources that, after a long hiatus, the tribade (re)entered early modern Western travel and medical discourses.[65] Questions for future inquiry include: How do representations of the tribade and the lustful women of the harem circulate discursively in Middle Eastern cultures and in which genres and geographies? To what ends are these figures mobilized? Is it possible to discern how these representations relate to actual sexual practices? Are such figures of excess merely the product of Orientalism, or are they fantasies, as well, born of the anxieties of Islamic patriarchy?

For fantasy, as Epps astutely suggests, can cut both ways. Both he and Al-Kassim imply that a method attuned to the psychic investments of texts, cultures, and critics might generate different sets of questions—and different answers—than the ones represented in the resolutely historicist work represented here. A historicist orientation is not in itself a problem, except insofar as its tacit privileging precludes other modes of insight. Yet I suspect that there is more at stake within Islamicate studies in the avoidance of psychoanalytic methods than simply a preference for historical questions, procedures, and narratives. It seems more than coincidental (1) that only once during the Radcliffe seminar did forceful disagreement arise, (2) that this was the only moment when "the real"—represented by an insistence on philology and cultural specificity—was deployed to bolster a textual interpretation and to stabilize textual heteroglossia, and (3) that this was also the sole moment when a psychoanalytic interpretation was proffered—only to encounter vehement objection.

Meditating on the dynamics of this conflict, I want to repeat the psychoanalytic provocation in a more general guise by returning to that moment of disagreement. Al-Kassim suggested that it might be pertinent to analyze the concept of "eating sorrow" in Babayan's essay by means of the psychoanalytic theory of incorporation.[66] Insofar as the widow's narrative of mourning was structured through repetition, it seemed to Al-Kassim to be coterminous with a psychoanalytic understanding of (a historically specific) unresolved mourning or melancholy. For this reason, she suggested that incorporation, as a failed introjection, was salient to the widow's psychic state and to the overall meaning of her travelogue.

The opposition to this interpretation by several participants largely took the form of insisting on the philological meaning and cultural specificity of the verb *to eat* in early modern Persian. Was this resistance to interpretation primarily due to the misuse of a verb, or was it symptomatic of resistance to psychoanalysis itself? Given queer theory's complicated dependence on various forms of psychoanalysis,[67] and especially because, as Al-Kassim makes clear, psychoanalysis in North Africa has developed since Franz Fanon as an indigenous method of interpreting and confronting modernity, this question has implications for the ways in which Islamicate sexuality studies might develop (or not) in the future. I am not suggesting that studies of sexuality need draw from psychoanalytic paradigms or that those paradigms are impervious to critique. I am suggesting that this might be one place where the dominant disciplinary common sense of Middle Eastern studies—a dependence on philological, linguistic, and historical methods—is being imported, without sufficient self-reflection, into this new field.

To what extent should the project outlined by *Islamicate Sexualities* move in a more comparativist direction? Clearly, the impulse is already present. Najmabadi, for instance, pursues her interpretation of the anus and the role of sexual ownership in Iranian discourses of prohibition by drawing comparisons to Talmudic understandings of bimorphic genders. Rowson frames his discussion of the Mamluk elite with reference to the scandal of England's homoerotic king, Edward II. And in the essays by

Rouhi and Amer, comparativism becomes a crucial lens for examining cross-cultural interaction and textual negotiation, East and West. Comparative scholarship that cuts across both space and time and that puts into contact the asymmetrical temporalities and divergent periodizations of the East and the West (including those of contemporary societies and past ones) is one way to do justice to the forms of sexuality that are not congruent with identitarian epistemologies (including those that have their own elaborate taxonomies), while also inviting us to reconsider the terms by which we have constructed our histories of the West. Indeed, as a way to examine simultaneously similarity and difference, resemblance and divergence, comparativism would seem to be an intrinsically appealing approach for the cross-cultural project enacted here. Yet as Epps argues, it also poses dangers, particularly a "competitive cultural ethos" whose attachment to cultural specificity results in special pleading: "cultural specificity is often . . . purchased by way of excisions, exclusions, and omissions and by way of a denial or disavowal of convoluted histories of translations and transmissions." Comparativism often seems to depend on the gesture of evacuating complexity from one side of the comparative axis. Even as meticulous a historian as Rowson avoids the difficulties of medieval English discourses of masculine friendship, sodomy, patronage, and favoritism by choosing *not* to investigate the particular nature of the scandal that Edward II's attachment to Piers Gaveston posed—that is, by taking at face value the assumption of social unacceptability whose suitability as a critical axis he queries in his investigation of attitudes among the Mamluks.[68] Rather than assume that comparativism is innocent, we need to ask: What does a comparativist approach accomplish, and what are its pitfalls? How does one do justice to the complexity of each culture examined? What questions—about cultural transmission, about cultural uniqueness, about the specificity of genre, religion, and social practices, about ways to interpret temporal change—can a comparative approach prompt that a focus on a single culture may not? How cross-cultural of a

conversation does the field of Islamicate sexuality studies want
or need to have? And with which cultures, literatures, and
histories—East, West, and "betwixt-and-between," as Epps puts
it—is it most important for this field to engage?

The question of this field's comparativism will no doubt impact its institutional locations. One of the motives for calling
this particular group of scholars together was to offset the isolation faced by those working on Islamicate sexuality, many of
whom have encountered a lack of support for their work within
their own institutions or have found their work hampered by
area studies' institutional formations and disciplinary practices.
Variously located in departments and programs of language and
literature, international area studies (Asian, Arab, Near Eastern,
Middle Eastern), and women's and gender studies and trained in
disciplines as varied as linguistics, history, and literary criticism,
they are determined to make connections not only across temporal and historical divides but also across radically different
Islamic (and Judaic and Christian) cultures. It may be that the
disciplinary model of discrete area studies will need to be dis-
mantled before the transnational emphasis that motivates this
project, much less an unapologetic focus on sexuality, can be
fostered by the structures within which they work. It thus makes
sense to ask whether other institutional locations—comparative
literature, women's, gender, and sexuality studies, cultural studies, and postcolonial studies—have a better track record than
others for providing a welcoming home. What are the structural
conditions of knowledge production that would foster future
work?

In his examination of the political modernity of India,
Chakrabarty argues that Western European historicism is simultaneously inadequate *and indispensable.* His book "both begins
and ends by acknowledging the indispensability of European
political thought to representations of non-European political
modernity, and yet struggles with the problems of representations that this indispensability invariably creates."[69] To adopt
Chakrabarty's terms, it may not be possible to create Islamicate

sexuality studies without recourse to the analytical categories of European and Anglo-American gay/lesbian/queer historicism, even while struggling with and against them. Beyond the questions of terminology, concepts, and historical narratives, a further case in point may be the fundamental importance of the analytical paradigms provided by the Greco-Roman classical period to the history of homosexuality. Yet given the way that this cultural inheritance often slides into an assumption of an unbroken continuity between the Greco-Roman past and the present, as well as the way that this formation is used to cordon off the Middle East (thereby enabling the appropriation of Greece and Rome to the West as well),[70] it provides an occasion to insist on both sides of Chakrabarty's historicist dynamic— indispensability and struggle. The questions then become how, concretely, the struggle against Western analytical priority might be effected and how those scholars of sexuality who work outside of Islamicate cultures could serve as effective allies. What kinds of interventions would be welcome? What are the new terms of engagement with Euro-American lesbian/gay/queer studies to be?

The metaphor of "crossing paths" of sexuality studies and Middle Eastern studies under which the Radcliffe seminar initially convened inaugurated one set of terms. Deploying the spatial trope of intersecting axes, it conveyed respect for a divergence of intellectual and disciplinary directions while encouraging travel and cross-cultural contact: the lines of crossing could seem multiple, the horizons of possibility infinite. Nonetheless, the trope of crossing paths is an irreducibly spatial figure that carries its own historical baggage along with it—namely, a redeployment of a geopolitical formation of the Middle East that is also conflated with an ethnoreligious formation, "Islamic," both of which are conceived as *separate* from the history of sexuality. From my perspective, the work of this volume *is* gay/lesbian and, to some extent, queer historiography. It *is* the history of sexuality, and if it doesn't break much new theoretical or methodological ground, that also is true of most current work in the history of sexuality, period. At the same time, assimilating it to lesbian/gay/queer studies is every bit as tendentious as is queering the Middle East. How can we avoid repeating, on a theoretical level, the worst tendencies of "contact history"?

Resisting the imperative of assimilation, the editors have chosen to put an additional metaphor in play—translation. The deployment of translation serves as an apt figure for describing the pleasures and perils involved in the production and reception of this new field of knowledge. Acts of translation require recognition of linguistic, cultural, and temporal difference, while also demanding awareness of multiple fields of reception. Those on the receiving end might be resistant or eager, and they might possess the requisite linguistic skills or might not. Translation simultaneously involves contradictory methods and imperatives: fueled by the utopian desire for transparency of signification across incommensurate linguistic entities, it nonetheless confronts lapses in the seamless conveyance of meaning. It is necessarily a betrayal of the origin for, as Al-Kassim notes, translation manages its act of transfer and transmission only by also leaving something behind—meanings "lost in translation," nuance falling by the wayside. Such textual remainders signify not the end of the project of translation, however, but the necessity of a recursive attempt toward new acts of approximation and meaning making. One danger is that, in the words of Rosello, a site of translation can also be "a site of production of meaning that remains invisible to itself, a point of crossing that no one wants to police because it goes unnoticed, perceived as banal conversation. . . . as though two people talked to each other from within two different ideological closets without realizing how much difference lies between them."[71] The extent to which this volume queries the presuppositions that create cross-cultural "banality" and instead invites further self-reflective acts of dialogue, comparativism, and translation will be the measure of its success.

What is at stake is no less than the terms by which sexualities of the past and the present will be understood, both within and without the academy, in the Middle East and beyond. But there is also something more. In the present political climate, the cultures and traditions of the Middle East and the West are positioned—by governments, religious leaders, CEOs, the media, and ordinary people—as dangerously antithetical. Many of those who are reading this volume would no doubt challenge the conceptual adequacy of the terms of that opposition. To do this, we require conceptual paradigms adequate to our divergent yet interrelated histories. The messy, contingent, often unrealized, but necessarily hopeful figure of translation offers one rubric under which we can approach the histories of mutual incomprehension that are part of our common legacy—and in so doing, learn something of what motivates each other's interest in and appreciation of the cultures we study and the communities within which we live and work.

My perceptions of the worth of and the questions raised by *Islamicate Sexualities* are influenced by my own scholarly training, field of expertise, ongoing research interests, and implication in the "national sexual" of the United States. In responding to the invitation to engage with the essays included in this volume, I am conscious of the risks that the editors take in appearing to authorize a Western, white, queer perspective. Authorization in this case, however, does not convey priority, and I have approached this task with an acute sense of my own limitations as an interlocutor. Necessarily so, the real work—and worth—of this volume inheres in the patient archival excavation, nuanced hermeneutical activity, and deep cultural and philological knowledge that has been brought to bear on the texts examined by the contributors, as well as the ways their scholarship pressures Western lesbian/gay/queer studies. If my comments demonstrate the partial nature of my own perspective (even, as Epps might have it, my own "wishful thinking"), it just may be that a strategy appropriate to the spaces and times of Islamicate sexuality studies is the kind of wishful thinking that, motivated by curiosity and sustained by others' knowledge, seeks to enable—and find oneself challenged by—difficult acts of dialogue, translation, and comparativism.

NOTES

I would like to thank Chad Thomas and Katie Will for their valuable research assistance, Carol Bardenstein for her responses to an early draft, and Kathryn Babayan and Afsaneh Najmabadi for their generous invitation to participate in their Radcliffe seminar.

1. Catherine Brown, "In the Middle," *Journal of Medieval and Early Modern Studies* 30, no. 3 (2000): 547n.

2. Ibid., 550.

3. Ibid., 563.

4. Edward Said, *Orientalism* (New York: Vintage, 1979).

5. Dipesh Chakrabarty, *Provincializing Europe: Postcolonial Thought and Historical Difference* (Princeton: Princeton University Press, 2000), 8.

6. The way in which Joseph Massad punctuates his critique with reference to the nationality and location of scholars would seem to disallow the legitimacy of non-Arab scholars producing work on Muslims on the basis of their necessary Orientalism. Massad denies this charge in "The Intransigence of Orientalist Desires: A Reply to Arno Schmitt," *Public Culture* 15, no. 3 (2003): 594: "I welcome anyone, Arab or not, who has done his or her homework in language and history to write about these important topics." Anyone as attuned to the effects of discourse as Massad presents himself should not be surprised by the charge of territorialism.

7. See Bruce Dunne, "Homosexuality in the Middle East: An Agenda for Historical Research," *Arab Studies Quarterly* 12, nos. 3–4 (1990): 55–82; J. W. Wright and Everett Rowson, eds., *Homoeroticism in Classical Arabic Literature* (New York: Columbia University Press, 1997); Everett K. Rowson, "The Effeminates of Early Medina," *Journal of the American Oriental Society* 111, no. 4 (1991): 671–93; Everett K. Rowson, "The Categorization of Gender and Sexual Irregularity in Medieval Arabic Vice Lists," in *Body Guards: The Cultural Politics of Gender Ambiguity,* ed. Julia Epstein and Kristina Straub (New York: Routledge, 1991), 50–79; Kathryn Babayan, "The 'Aqa'id al-nisa': A Glimpse of Safavi Women in Local Isfahani Culture," in *Women in the Medieval Islamic World: Power, Patronage, Piety,* ed. Gavin R. G. Hambly (New York: St. Martin's Press, 1998), 349–81; Sahar Amer, "Lesbian Sex and the Military: From the Medieval Arabic Tradition

to French Literature," and Fedwa Malti-Douglas, "Tribadism/ Lesbianism and the Sexualized Body in Medieval Arabo-Islamic Narratives," both in *Same Sex Love and Desire among Women in the Middle Ages,* ed. Francesca Canadé Sautman and Pamela Sheingorn (New York: Palgrave, 2001), 179–98 and 123–41; Dror Ze'evi, "Changes in Legal-Sexual Discourses: Sex Crimes in the Ottoman Empire," *Continuity and Change* 16, no. 2 (2001): 219–42; Khaled El-Rouayheb, *Before Homosexuality in the Arab-Islamic World, 1500–1800* (Chicago: University of Chicago Press, 2005); Frédéric Lagrange, "Sexualities and Queer Studies," in *Encyclopedia of Women and Islamic Cultures,* ed. Suad Joseph (Leiden: Brill, 2003), 1:419–22; Martin F. Manalansan IV, "In the Shadows of Stonewall: Examining Gay Transnational Politics and the Diasporic Dilemma," *GLQ: A Journal of Lesbian and Gay Studies* 2, no. 4 (1995): 425–38; and Jarrod Hayes, "Queer Roots in Africa," in *Topographies of Race and Gender: Mapping Cultural Representations,* ed. Patricia Penn Hilden and Shari Huhndorf (Trenton, NJ: Africa World Press, forthcoming).

8. Rosello defines the national-sexual as "a code, a set of linguistic and cultural reflexes, a collection of myths, images, metaphors, and clichés by which each national entity defines the realm of the sexual." In Mireille Rosello, "The National-Sexual: From the Fear of Ghettos to the Banalization of Queer Practices," in *Articulations of Difference: Gender Studies and Writing in French,* ed. Dominique D. Fisher and Lawrence R. Schehr (Stanford: Stanford University Press, 1997), 246.

9. Jonathan Goldberg, ed., *Queering the Renaissance* (Durham: Duke University Press, 1994).

10. Joseph Massad, "Re-Orienting Desire: The Gay International and the Arab World," *Public Culture* 14, no. 2 (2002): 361–85, 363–64n.

11. Ibid., 362.

12. It is perhaps worth pointing out that the lack of historical understanding and political sensitivity of Westerners fighting on behalf of gay/lesbian rights is hardly limited to those who make uninformed comments about the Middle East. Nor does the identity of "gay" sit uncomfortably only on Muslim men who have sex with men, as attested by the global HIV/AIDs discourse of prevention for MSMs (men who have sex with men).

13. Massad, "Re-Orienting Desire," 364–65.

14. Ibid., 369. Given the charge of identarian essentialism, it is also ironic that in support of a notion of compulsory heterosexuality, Massad cites Adrienne Rich's largely superseded, because transhistorical and essentialist, essay, "Compulsory Heterosexuality and Lesbian Existence," *Signs* 5, no. 4 (1980): 631–60.

15. Massad, "Re-Orienting Desire," 362.

16. Arno Schmitt and Jehoeda Sofer, eds., *Sexuality and Eroticism among Males in Moslem Societies* (New York: Haworth Press, 1992).

17. Arno Schmitt, "Different Approaches to Male-Male Sexuality/ Eroticism from Morocco to Uzbekistan," in Schmitt and Sofer, *Sexuality and Eroticism among Males in Moslem Societies*, 1–24. One comment, drawn from Schmitt's overview, suffices to give a flavor of much of the collection: "It is easy to impress boys—in this respect they are similar to women, who have less experience in and less knowledge of the world than men," 5–6.

18. Massad, "Re-Orienting Desire," 367.

19. Ibid.

20. Ibid., 369.

21. Ibid., 368.

22. Scholars seeking to describe something as large as "an epistemology" need to account for differences as well as similarities and recognize that, although academic and mainstream discourses may be related, they are just as often at odds. Mainstream gay/lesbian discourse is, at best, an imperfect political strategy, bolstered by its success in gaining certain (limited) legal rights within neoliberal states, as well as by the ascendance of the medical discourse of genetics and the susceptibility of the media to circulating stereotypes (even as it contests them). Many Western queers have articulated a critique of the mainstream LGBT movement for some time, most recently Michael Warner, *The Trouble with Normal: Sex, Politics, and the Ethics of Queer Life* (New York: Free Press, 1999).

23. On the distinctive aspects of modern sexual identity categories, see David M. Halperin, *How to Do the History of Homosexuality* (Chicago: University of Chicago Press, 2002).

24. Eve Kosofsky Sedgwick, *Epistemology of the Closet* (Berkeley: University of California Press, 1990).

25. On the transnational flow of bodies and capital, see M. Jacqui Al-

exander, *Pedagogies of Crossing: Meditations on Feminism, Sexual Politics, Memory, and the Sacred* (Durham: Duke University Press, 2005).

26. Stephen O. Murray and Will Roscoe, eds., Introduction, *Islamic Homosexualities: Culture, History, and Literature* (New York: New York University Press, 1997), 5.

27. Murray and Roscoe, *Islamic Homosexualities*, 6.

28. For my analysis of the problem of teleology in lesbian/gay/queer history, see Valerie Traub, "The Present Future of Lesbian Historiography," in *Companion to Lesbian, Gay, Bisexual, Transgender, and Queer Studies*, ed. George Haggerty and Molly McGarry (London: Blackwell, 2007), pp. 124–45.

29. This is not to imply that there is any consensus about the chronological date of this emergence, which is variously taken to occur anytime after the sixteenth century.

30. See, for instance, Roderick A. Ferguson, *Aberrations in Black: Toward a Queer of Color Critique* (Minneapolis: University of Minnesota Press, 2004); *Black Queer Studies: A Critical Anthology*, ed. E. Patrick Johnson and Mae G. Henderson (Durham: Duke University Press, 2005); David L. Eng, *Racial Castration: Managing Masculinity in Asian America* (Durham: Duke University Press, 2001); and José Esteban Muñoz, *Disidentifications: Queers of Color and the Performance of Politics* (Minneapolis: University of Minnesota Press, 1999).

31. "Queer Transexions of Race, Nation, and Gender," ed. Phillip Brian Harper, Anne McClintock, José Esteban Muñoz, and Trish Rosen, special issue, *Social Text* nos. 52–53 (1997).

32. See Joseph Boone, "Vacation Cruises; or, The Homoerotics of Orientalism," *PMLA* 110, no. 1 (1995): 89–107; Carolyn Dinshaw, "The History of *GLQ*, Volume 1: LGBTQ Studies, Censorship, and Other Transnational Problems," *GLQ: A Journal of Lesbian and Gay Studies* 12, no. 1 (2006): 5–26; "Thinking Sex Transnationally," ed. Elizabeth A. Povinelli and George Chauncey, special issue, *GLQ: A Journal of Lesbian and Gay Studies* 5, no. 4 (1999); Jasbir Kauer Puar, "Circuits of Queer Mobility: Tourism, Travel, and Globalization," *GLQ: A Journal of Lesbian and Gay Studies* 8, nos. 1–2 (2002): 101–37; *Postcolonial, Queer: Theoretical Intersections*, ed. John C. Hawley (Albany: State University of New York Press, 2001); and *Comparatively Queer: Crossing Time,*

Crossing Cultures, ed. Jarrod Hayes, William Spurlin, and Margaret Higonnet (forthcoming).

33. Gayatri Gopinath, *Impossible Desires: Queer Diasporas and South Asian Public Cultures* (Durham: Duke University Press, 2005), 11.

34. Ibid., 11.

35. Lee Patterson, "On the Margin: Postmodernism, Ironic History, and Medieval Studies," *Speculum* 65, no. 1 (1990): 87–108; Carolyn Dinshaw, *Getting Medieval: Sexualities and Communities, Pre- and Postmodern* (Durham: Duke University Press, 1999).

36. Brown, "In the Middle," 549. Brown hastens to add that it is not her intent to "appropriate or apply" postcolonial theory because "the knowledge/power activities of the two disciplines in the world of the living are incommensurable in ethically crucial ways" (550).

37. No doubt because of the epistemic privilege of the Renaissance over the "Middle Ages," early modernists generally have been more enamored of the radical alterity of the past than have medievalists.

38. "Preposterous historicism" is a term coined by Glenn Burger and Steven F. Kruger in their introduction to *Queering the Middle Ages* (Minneapolis: University of Minnesota Press, 2001). See also Carla Freccero and Louise Fradenberg, eds., *Premodern Sexualities* (New York: Routledge, 1996), as well as Freccero's recent book, *Queer/Early/Modern* (Durham: Duke University Press, 2006).

39. Halperin, *How to Do the History of Homosexuality*, 16.

40. Rosello, "The National-Sexual," 247n.

41. As Chakrabarty notes, it is the peculiar privilege of Western scholars not to have to take into account scholarship produced in the rest of the world.

42. Annamarie Jagose, *Inconsequence: Lesbian Representation and the Logic of Sexual Sequence* (Ithaca: Cornell University Press, 2002).

43. Murray and Roscoe, *Islamic Homosexualities*, 5.

44. Ruth Vanita, ed., *Queering India: Same-Sex Love and Eroticism in Indian Culture and Society* (New York: Routledge, 2002), 5.

45. Ibid., 6.

46. Peter A. Jackson, "The Persistence of Gender: From Ancient Indian *Pandakas* to Modern Thai *Gay-Quings*," in "Australia

Queer," ed. Chris Berry and Annamarie Jagose, special issue, *Meanjin* 55, no. 1 (1996): 118. For a challenge to Jackson's research, see Rosalind C. Morris, "Educating Desire: Thailand, Transnationalism, and Transgression," in Harper et al., "Queer Transexions of Race, Nation, and Gender," 53–79.

47. Jackson, "The Persistence of Gender," 118–19.

48. See Gayle Rubin, "Geologies of Queer Studies: It's Déjà Vu All Over Again," *CLAGS News* 14, no. 2 (2004): 6–10.

49. Jeannette Foster, *Sex Variant Women in Literature: A Historical and Quantitative Survey* (New York: Vantage Press, 1956).

50. I suspect that the occasions afforded to female homoerotic desire by the marital structure of polygamy is another—although Sahar Amer suggests in an endnote to her essay included in this volume (chapter 3) that "the Western-held association [of] lesbianism-harem culture . . . has still not been established definitively, and may reflect Western Orientalist fantasies rather than an Oriental reality."

51. In addition to Jackson and Rowson, see Michael Sweet and Leonard Zwilling, "The First Medicalization: The Taxonomy and Etiology of Queers in Classical Indian Medicine," *Journal of the History of Sexuality* 3, no. 4 (1993): 590–607; and Charlotte Furth, "Androgynous Males and Deficient Females: Biology and Gender Boundaries in Sixteenth- and Seventeenth-Century China," in *The Lesbian and Gay Studies Reader,* ed. Henry Abelove, Michèle Aina Barale, and David M. Halperin (New York: Routledge, 1993), 479–97.

52. Michael Rocke, *Forbidden Friendships: Homosexuality and Male Culture in Renaissance Florence* (New York: Oxford University Press, 1996).

53. This remains the case whether the distinction is attributable to Foucault or, as Halperin has argued in *How to Do the History of Homosexuality,* to misreadings of Foucault.

54. In early modern English and French representations, for instance, the tribade—despite the proper name and a distinct bodily morphology (her allegedly enlarged clitoris)—did not inhabit a social identity or subjectivity defined by her erotic desires. See Valerie Traub, *The Renaissance of Lesbianism in Early Modern England* (Cambridge: Cambridge University Press, 2002), 220–23, 356–60.

55. Sautman and Sheinghorn remark, "[I]t is possible to be visible, and

perhaps even to find power in visibility, without being named."
They describe their project as "to render visible without insisting
upon categorizing or naming" and "do not assume that medieval
women expressed a clearly defined and public 'identity.' But that is
something quite different from assuming that they had no consciousness or self-perception at all." "Introduction: Charting the
Field," *Same Sex Love and Desire among Women in the Middle
Ages,* 1–47; citations pp. 2, 12.

56. Michel Foucault, *The History of Sexuality* (New York: Random
House, 1990), 1:57.

57. My research on the representation of sexual knowledge in seventeenth-century English culture reveals that for early modern
women, in particular, sexual knowledge may have operated outside of established procedures of producing truth. See Valerie
Traub, "The Joys of Martha Joyless: Queer Pedagogy and the
(Early Modern) Production of Sexual Knowledge," in *Renaissance
Culture and the New Millenium,* ed. Leonard Barkan, Bradin
Cormack, and Sean Keilen (New York: Palgrave Macmillan, forthcoming 2008).

58. Harper et al., "Queer Transexions of Race, Nation, and Gender,"
2.

59. Alan Bray, *The Friend* (Chicago: University of Chicago Press,
2003), 6; Alan Bray, *Homosexuality in Renaissance England* (New
York: Columbia University Press, 1982). See the special memorial
issue devoted to Bray in *GLQ: A Journal of Lesbian and Gay
Studies* 10, no. 3 (2004).

60. Halperin, *How to Do the History of Homosexuality,* 48–79.

61. Judith Butler, *Gender Trouble: Feminism and the Subversion of
Identity* (New York: Routledge, 1990); Judith Butler, *Bodies that
Matter: On the Discursive Limits of "Sex"* (New York: Routledge,
1993).

62. Michael Foucault, *Discipline and Punish: The Birth of the Prison,*
trans. Alan Sheridan (New York: Vintage Press, 1979), 182–84;
Georges Canguilhem, *The Normal and the Pathological,* trans.
Carolyn R. Fawcett (New York: Urzone, 1989).

63. A small group of scholars focusing on pre- and early modern England has begun to historicize the concepts of both heterosexuality
and normativity to discern the processes of their mutual entangle-

ment: Amy Hollywood, "The Normal, the Queer, and the Middle Ages," *Journal of the History of Sexuality* 10, no. 2 (2001): 173–79; Traub, *The Renaissance of Lesbianism in Early Modern England;* Valerie Traub, "Mapping the Global Body," in *Early Modern Visual Culture: Representation, Race, and Empire in Renaissance England,* ed. Peter Erickson and Clark Hulse (Philadelphia: University of Pennsylvania Press, 2000), 44–97; Karma Lochrie, *Heterosyncrasies: Female Sexuality When Normal Wasn't* (Minneapolis: University of Minnesota Press, 2005); Rebecca Ann Bach, *Shakespeare and Renaissance Literature before Heterosexuality* (New York: Palgrave Macmillan, 2007). Theresa Braunschneider's University of Michigan dissertation, *Maidenly Amusements: Narrating Female Sexuality in Eighteenth-Century England* (2002), and Jonathan Katz, *The Invention of Heterosexuality* (New York: Dutton, 1995), bring this question to bear on later periods.

64. So argues Fedwa Malti-Douglas, who focuses on the medieval anecdotal genre of *adab* in "Tribadism/Lesbianism and the Sexualized Body in Medieval Arabo-Islamic Narratives," in Sautman and Sheingorn, *Same-Sex Love and Desire among Women in the Middle Ages,* 123–41.

65. See Valerie Traub, "The Psychomorphology of the Clitoris; Or, the Reemergence of the Tribade in English Culture," in Traub, *The Renaissance of Lesbianism in Early Modern England,* 188–228.

66. The psychoanalytic concept of incorporation (and its counterpart, introjection) is part of the distinction between mourning and melancholy described by Sigmund Freud in "Mourning and Melancholia," in *The Standard Edition of the Complete Psychological Works of Sigmund Freud,* ed. and trans. James Strachey (London: Hogarth Press, 1953), 14:239–58. It was further developed by Nicolas Abraham and Maria Torok in *The Shell and the Kernel: Renewals of Psychoanalysis,* vol. 1, ed., trans., and intro. Nicholas T. Rand (Chicago: University of Chicago Press, 1994). Incorporation names the process when the melancholic refuses to mourn, wherein the ego incorporates not only the lost object but the prohibitions surrounding it.

67. The influence of psychoanalysis can be found in such queer theoretical work as Lauren Berlant, Leo Bersani, Judith Butler, Jonathan Dollimore, Lee Edelman, Diana Fuss, Judith Roof, Eve Sedg-

wick, and Alan Sinfield. In addition, see the work collected in Tim Dean and Chris Lane, eds., *Homosexuality and Psychoanalysis* (Chicago: University of Chicago Press, 2001).

68. On the scandal of Edward II and a brilliant contextualization of it within a tradition of sworn brotherhood, see Bray, *The Friend.*

69. Chakrabarty, *Provincializing Europe,* 22. He also notes the "Everyday paradox of third-world social science is that *we* find these [Western] theories, in spite of their inherent ignorance of 'us,' eminently useful in understanding our societies," 29.

70. This point was made forcefully by Lagrange during the course of our seminar.

71. Rosello, "The National-Sexual," 259.

TWO

A Handsome Boy among Those Barbarous Turks: Cervantes's Muslims and the Art and Science of Desire

Leyla Rouhi

[He] spoke to me in the language used between captives and Moors through-out Barbary, and even in Constantinople; it is not Moorish or Castilian, not the language of any nation, but a mixture of all tongues and with it we can understand one another.[1]

—Miguel de Cervantes, *Don Quixote (1605–1615)*

The current state of research on sexuality and gender in early modern Iberia sets up a compelling point of reference for inquiries on the same topics in Islamicate studies. For several decades, medievalists and scholars of the Middle Ages and the Renaissance who have been working on questions related to sexuality and gender in the Iberian Peninsula have grappled with issues that are raised in the field of Islamicate studies as well. Many of these questions are cogently articulated in the proposal that brought us together for the 2003 Radcliffe Institute for Advanced Study seminar on "Crossing Paths of Middle Eastern and Sexuality Studies: Challenges of Theory, History, and Comparative Methods." The "dynamic interplay between cultural constructions of gender and sexuality" to which the proposal refers is at the crux of epistemological inquiry for Peninsular Hispanists, largely because of Spain's peculiar, hybrid, and unquestionably multicultural history, which involves Islam more intimately than any other Western European country.

The research on sexuality in the work of Miguel de Cervantes Saavedra (1547–1616) might seem and indeed is deeply rooted in Western methodologies and perceptions. Cervantes is a European novelist—the first, by most accounts. There is no school of Western literary theory—Foucauldian, psychoanalytic, Marxist, feminist, formalist, poststructural—that has not found a comfortable home in Cervantine studies. As a subfield, the author's complex representation of sexuality accommodates a vast range of European and North American theories of gender.[2]

At the same time, Hispanists today are—or should be—aware that any study of the Spanish literature of the medieval and early modern periods must deal with Spain's multicultural history. In this context, Islam is in direct contact with Catholicism in numerous ways, even if by Cervantes's time this relationship is defined in terms of conquest and reconquest (of Christian by Muslim and vice versa). In the late sixteenth and early seventeenth centuries, when *Don Quixote* was being written, Spain was increasingly subject to monumental efforts at rewriting its own history. The result is the head-on collision of an historical reality (the complicated coexistence of three religions) with a new world order that wished to deny the complexities of that reality. In this new order, Ottoman (Muslim) was defined against Christian as enemy, a distinction that perhaps worked fine for England or France. But for Spain, whose own being was intertwined on the deepest levels with Muslim coexistence, the issue was tangled.

This is not to imply that a unified Spanish spirit stood up in the sixteenth century to defend its hybrid past against the new order or that Spaniards did not perceive Ottomans as the enemy. Turks, after all, are different from Moors. Still, it is important to acknowledge that different regions of the country, depending on the degree of their involvement with their Muslim past, came face to face at this point with the need for a redefinition of this engagement. At the same time and at a furious pace, the Catholic leadership began to affect an erasure of this history.

Not until the relatively recent past did some Hispanists began to consider the role of medieval and early modern literature in preserving, problematizing, and critiquing the convoluted coexistence of the three religions in Spain. Spearheaded by scholars such as Américo Castro and Stephen Gilman, a new critical inquiry was launched in the 1950s and 1960s to recover Spain's "secret" history against the impression of comfortably Western, Catholic, and monolithic identity projected by mainstream thinking. This inquiry, in the words of Gregory Hutcheson and Josiah Blackmore had all the markers of an outing:

> Castro and his school effected in essence a "queering" of Iberian history by exposing the Semitic roots of modern Spanish identity and by "outing" as the descendants of Jews or Muslims such icons as Fernando "el Católico," Teresa of Ávila, and Cervantes. His was not a campaign of cultural iconoclasm, as some of his detractors have implied, but rather an embracing of difference that obliterated the need to read Spain always as an appendage to greater Europe. It was Castro who brought Spain out of the closet and forced it to face—ultimately to celebrate—the complexities of its cultural and even its racial identities. It is in this sense that we might understand queerness, as that which normativity—in this case a cultural normativity—must reject or conceal in order to exist. Its presence is always palpable in the incongruities, excesses, or anxieties of normative discourse, but it is only exceptionally given expression, and this only at the margins.[3]

This citation is from the introduction to a 1999 volume put together by Hutcheson and Blackmore titled *Queer Iberia,* in which the contributors address a wide range of issues related to gender and homosexuality in medieval and Renaissance Spain. Hutcheson, in a follow-up to discussions on this volume called "Return to *Queer Iberia,*" notes that the terms of his exploration in such a project are informed more by Castro than by Foucault.[4] Castro was no queer theorist by any stretch of the imagination. The field did not even exist in his time, and many of his immediate followers are not in any shape or form invested in queer theory. If anything, they identify themselves as philologists interested in bringing texts back to context and giving Islam and Judaism credit for their impact on Spain in the process. In terms of methodology, language, and discourse, in many ways Castro and his immediate school could not be further away from Foucault, postmodern theory, or anything poststructural, while the editors of *Queer Iberia* are of a different generation and well-versed in postmodern theory. Still, Hutcheson is right to add that the move toward Castro and therefore away from Foucault "cost us credibility in some quarters" (though he points out that it earned accolades in others—for example, in the person of none other than Juan Goytisolo, considered one of contemporary Spain's most prominent writers).

Queer Iberia generated many deserving positive reactions and has become an indispensable reference in the bibliography concerning the ongoing exploration of a "hidden" Spain.[5] But the volume also led to some disapproval and criticism, primarily in Spain. The types of reproach recall some of the questions that face scholars of the Islamicate world in an investigation such as ours today. One Spanish publication took exception to the "colonization of Iberian materials by American interlopers" and worried about a monolithic Anglo-Saxon attitude to these. Hutcheson recalls a meeting in which the Argentine activist Alejandra Sardi warned against "American gay cultural imperialism" and the "presumption of a common sociopolitical agenda." He notes the implication: even when informed by Castro (as opposed to Foucault), any strain of queer theory is ultimately an Anglo-American innovation: "Castro may have founded a school of historicism, but it was the Americans and the Spanish ex-patriots living in the U.S. who were his most zealous disciples[.]"[6]

Taking stock of the Spanish and Latin American reactions to queer theory, the editor's conclusions are thoughtful and pertinent:

I suppose we shouldn't underestimate the extent to which our selection of the title *"Queer" Iberia* smacks precisely of this sort of imperialism, the extent to which the term "queer" is shorthand in some circles for Anglo-American gay activism at its most self-serving and myopic. What we didn't bank on when devising the title was its absolute resistance to translation. I had occasion to ponder possible Spanish titles with Goytisolo when he was in Chicago: *Iberia mariconil* (hopelessly reductionist); *Iberia torcida* (taking off on the term coined by Ricardo Llamas in his landmark *Teoría torcida: Prejuicios y discursos en torno a "la homosexualidad"*); and finally, a translation suggested by Goytisolo himself, *Iberia loca,* which, to my mind, is as problematic as *mariconil* in that it imposes a female-identified male homosexuality as the default. Ultimately, "queer" is a term so entrenched in both its etymology and the history of its deliberate appropriation by the Anglo-American gay community that it cannot be rendered by any single term in the Spanish. By using "queer" in our title, we unwittingly created an entity that resists a priori a quick-and-easy translation of the whole, that appears to impose English as the default when speaking about the Iberian subjects we study, that perpetuates Anglo-American models of writing queer history.[7]

The history of this one volume within the context of medieval and early modern Iberian studies provides an excellent frame of reference for my essay. Just as with *Queer Iberia,* my debt to Américo Castro and his school is unquestionable in what follows. Basically, any work on medieval and early modern Spanish literature that seeks to foreground the role of Islam therein is, ultimately, obliged to Castro and his intellectual brood. In fact, today, largely thanks to the work initiated by that generation, medievalists no longer have to exert themselves to prove that Spain's history and literature are profoundly marked by a multireligious past. What was in Castro's time a struggle is now a given for many and considered a prominent point of departure for most scholars in the field.

At the same time, if this foregrounding of Islam in Spain is done to broaden "the landscape of sexualities studies," then the question of "translation" as expressed by Hutcheson becomes an important emblem for the epistemological questions raised when bringing together Islam, Iberia, and the early modern period.

Islam and the Muslim are not unfamiliar entities in the European literature of the early seventeenth century.[8] This is an era of war with the Ottoman empire and of seas "infested" with North African, Turkish, and Arab pirates as well as renegades who take Christians hostage. Captivity is a topic itself and is exploited by many writers. Of the Spanish playwrights and authors who depict Moors and Turks in their works, Cervantes stands out as one who problematizes the issues of identity (among them gender) as they relate to the Christian perception of the Muslim and vice versa.[9] For Cervantes, captivity in the hands of the Muslim set against the Ottoman threat is also a topic, but he factors the past and the hybrid present into this: the reality of coexistence in the not-too-distant past is always implicit on his horizon. As the critic Barbara Fuchs shows, a playwright such as Lope de Vega prefers to keep the definitions rigid and separate when treating Islam: the Moor/Turk is the enemy, and there is no question about it. But

> the stagings of opaque selves in Cervantes' texts suggest the difficulty of distinguishing the true Spaniard from the pirated, or piratical, copy. Identity remains surprisingly fluid in these representations, despite, or perhaps because of, the Counter Reformation context in which they were written. Whether they exist within Spain or menace it from North Africa, renegadoes, Christian Moors, and false captives complicate the consolidation of Spanish identity around notions of timeless Christianity and pure blood. In many of these tales, it is not clear what constitutes an authentic commitment to Christianity, or where Spanish identity begins or ends—the individual cases challenge the usefulness of any blanket definitions.[10]

Fuchs, who has also researched cross-dressing in Cervantes's work, enables us to see how ambiguous and difficult identity construction is for seventeenth-century Spain. As many scholars who are working today on early modern Spain claim, she convincingly argues that fiction reveals the "permeable" nature of Spain in relation to its Moor, Morisco, and Turkish environment. In other words, she highlights the tensions inherent in an empire as it attempts to separate authentic and valuable identity from fake and worthless. What goes on in Cervantes's representation of cross-dressing is a challenge to "the prevailing patriarchal modes of racialized homogeneity and masculinity[.]"[11] Fuchs's work is emblematic of the kind of research and reflection that contributes to a deeper understanding of Spain's particular position.[12] For example, noting that the Catholic agenda for the construction of Spanish identity was fraudulent, E. C. Graf asserts that Cervantes seeks to replace this fake division of identity with "the hybridized truth of said history—that is, with more historically accurate, less ideal, identities."[13]

The use of the Morisco—the descendant of Spanish Muslims now converted, often forcefully, to Catholicism—advances this project along the complex terms that it deserves. It expands the "Christian foundation myth so as to include the Arab Other in the definition of the Christian self. Such is Cervantes' final appeal for a new Catholicism that returns to the essence of the Christian myth by shunning hostility, displaying compassion, and seeking dialogue."[14]

Even if all critics may not agree that the ultimate project is a return to an ideal Christianity, there can be no doubt that many prominent Cervantes scholars today concur on the following point. In a time of rigid definitions and clear battle lines, Cervantes uses fiction to debunk illusions of a solid, certain truth, as well as the supremacy of one race over another. He draws attention instead to the paradoxical nature of human interaction, whether in terms of gender, race, power, class, or nationality.

We have established, then, the crucial contribution of Cervantes to a modern poetics that favors paradox, hybridity, and ambivalence over certainty and dogmatism. The influence of this on

subsequent European letters and thought cannot be overesti-
mated. Cervantes's fiction, with visionary narrative and aesthetic strategies, seemingly playful yet totally serious blurring of
definitions, continues to this day to stress the value of ambiguity
and complexity in Western poetics. A word of caution is at the
same time needed here. Acknowledging Cervantes's work as a
masterpiece can be an ideological move toward affirming a certain supremacy about a pure Spain. This indeed has been done,
as pointed out astutely by Brad Epps in this collection. I am
aware of the potentially imperialist connotations of labeling a
work of literature a masterpiece. At the same time, I am convinced that the work *is* a masterpiece, even if this word can unfortunately lend itself to ideologically motivated appropriations
of Cervantes to mark a xenophobic boundary. The novel, I
hope, is far too generous and subtle to be erased by such politically motivated gestures.

Cervantes's fiction presents a busy but always well-propor-
tioned tapestry of sixteenth- and early seventeenth-century
Spain, with an eye for the sexual identity, appetite, and habits of
Muslim subjects. This look is essentially different from, say, a
contemporary French or English glance at the Turk or the Moor.
The Spanish gaze on the Muslim works from without but also
from within because Spain was for centuries an insider within
Islam. Cervantes takes on this issue with self-awareness as a
Spaniard and as an artist. That is precisely why his fiction ought
to be included in the vast canon of Islamicate studies and why
his work will indeed broaden the scope of Islamicate sexuality
studies.

In examining the extent to which Cervantes perceived an or-
ganic link between Muslim identity and the definition of identity
in general, one important element within the broader context is
Cervantes's sensitivity to the question of language and translation in *Don Quixote*. This takes me back to the notion that
translation is the most vital emblem of my inquiry. Whereas for

many European authors, "Sarracen," without elaboration, suffices to denote a generally foreign language and whereas the medieval epic *La chanson de Roland* speaks of Muslims speaking *"en lor Latin"* (their kind of Latin)—a trend that continues into the sixteenth and seventeenth centuries—Cervantes takes note of the frustrations, difficulties, and ease of communication in another language. Critics have pointed out that in so doing, Cervantes looks ahead to what literary theory was to call "levels of discourse" and "heteroglossia." More immediately, this also shows his sensitivity to the multilingualism of his own country. Another general observation of importance, also noted by scholars, is Cervantes's ability to discern Turk from Moor. Note that in the passage that is discuss below, Ana displays her anxiety over the Turk's predilection for sodomy.

These types of general awareness, which permeate Cervantes's work at different stages of evolution, act as a fundamental backdrop to his representation of the Muslim's sexual otherness, inviting the reader to transcend the mere picturesque, grotesque, or marginal character of this and to consider instead an innate connection to the whole work.

Inside the novel's very design, a number of elements that otherwise have nothing to do with sexuality help foreground and sustain the narrative's subsequent projection of sexual otherness. The fact that much of the novel is supposedly produced by one Cid Hamete Benengeli, an Arab whose manuscript is translated into Spanish at the Christian author's insistence, is one such element. In chapter 8 of the first part of the novel—before this Arab enters the picture and while the reader is under the impression that the tale is relatively unmediated and is following the madman Quixote's adventures—the action suddenly freezes. This leaves the author to move on to chapter 9 frustrated, wondering where the rest of the story might be. The passage deserves full citation to show the extent to which Arabic as a language and descendants of Muslims (Moriscos) as a nation are at once alien and familiar to late sixteenth-century Spanish society. It also highlights the active role of translation in Cervantes' poetics. The author-in-search-of-his-novel tells us that he could not find the rest of the tale, until one day,

> When I was in the Alcana market in Toledo, a boy came by to sell some notebooks and old papers to a silk merchant; as I am very fond of reading, even torn papers in the streets, I was moved by my natural inclinations to pick up one of the volumes the boy was selling, and I saw that it was written in characters I knew to be Arabic. And since I recognized but could not read it, I looked around to see if some Morisco who knew Castilian, and could read it for me, was in the vicinity, and it was not very difficult to find this kind of interpreter, for even if I had sought a speaker in a better and older language, I would have found him. In short, fortune provided me with one, and when I told him what I wanted and placed the book in his hands, he opened it in the middle, read for a short while, and began to laugh.[15]

The laughter turns out to be in reaction to a comment on one Dulcinea del Toboso, which arouses the author's curiosity, for he realizes that he might have stumbled on the original manuscript of *Don Quixote*. Indeed, this turns out to be the case, for the beginning of the volume says in Arabic "History of Don Quixote of La Mancha. Written by Cide Hamete Benengeli, an Arab Historian."[16] This fictional Arab narrator to whom the rest of the tale is attributed goes on to become one of the novel's most slippery yet suggestive figures. At critical junctures, he is characterized by the Christian author (and at times, by the Morisco translator) in diverse and sometimes contradictory ways, making impossible the arrival at any set definition of his role. But of specific importance is an early judgment on his character as an Arab, which looms over the narrative. The Christian author informs us that

> . . . no history is bad if it is true.
> If any objection can be raised regarding the truth of this one, it can only be that its author was Arabic, since the people of that nation are very prone to telling falsehoods, but because they are such great enemies of ours, it can be assumed that he has given us too

little rather than too much. So it appears to me, for when he could and should have wielded his pen to praise the virtues of so good a knight, it seems he intentionally passes over them in silence; this is something badly done and poorly thought out, since historians must and ought to be exact, truthful, and absolutely free of passions[.][17]

The passage is replete with irony, given that this "good knight" is an insane, bizarre-looking man and that the entire literary project of this novel centers on the debunking of rigid certainties.[18] So the Arab is a liar, as all Arabs are, but not for the reasons you might think. Cervantes has deftly set the scene: he has begun with a tired stereotype that is a staple of mundane Christian thinking (all Arabs are liars: they invent things), and he then has turned the accusation on its head by showing that the subject and object of lies are not at all what we assumed them to be. If this one Arab is guilty of anything, it is silence.

Cervantes's gesture is deliberate. The powerful critique of any pretense to total access to the total truth, sustained through the figure of an Arab narrator, is filtered in Cervantes's work through a type of irony that offers categorical and overly exaggerated statements that beg the reader to consider their opposite implications. One other element that strengthens this rhetorical strategy involves physical beauty in men and women. The apparently unwavering and hyperbolic discourse on the truth commands Cervantes's presentation of certain beautiful characters. Such hyperbolic projection of beauty will become an important axis of interpretation for the Ana Félix episode.

To contextualize this, one must recall a previous episode from the novel that has been much discussed by scholars and illuminated in helpful ways.[19] At one point, Don Quixote's squire Sancho comes across an apparently German pilgrim who turns out to be an old friend named Ricote, now in disguise.[20] Ricote is from Sancho's village but has been deported from Spain due to his status as Morisco. He has now returned in secret, disguised as a German pilgrim, and is risking his life to recover a treasure he claims to have buried in the village. The two men part company fast after a meal in the open air. Later, in chapter 53 of part 2, Quixote and Sancho witness a remarkable scene in Barcelona. A dazzlingly handsome young man, captain to a ship of Turks and Moors, has just been taken prisoner in Barcelona harbor by Christian authorities and is about to be hanged. This beautiful young man turns out to be neither Turk, Moor, nor Spanish renegade but, in his own words, a "Christian woman," Ana Félix, who is the daughter of Ricote to boot.

A principal force from which the entire narrative derives its momentum is the notion of physical beauty. The thirty-six Turkish musketeers are all described as "gallardos," rendered "valiant" by the skilled translator Edith Grossman but also translatable as "good-looking." Ana, as boy, is one "the handsomest and the most gallant boys that one could imagine."[21] The Catholic viceroy, gazing on this youth, "saw him so handsome and so gallant and so humble that the boy's good looks provided him with an immediate letter of recommendation, and the viceroy felt a desire to pardon his death[.]"[22] Ana recalls her own adolescence in terms of her increasing beauty. Her boyfriend Don Gaspar Gregorio is one of the "most gallant and handsome men imaginable," a young man whose "beauty far surpasses any other."[23] Beauty is a constant and not open to doubt, while ethnic, religious, and gender identities are fluid and continually usurped. Ana is a new Christian dressed as a young man who might be Turkish, Arab, or renegade. Don Gaspar Gregorio is an old Christian dressed as a Moorish woman. The Turk to whom he is being sent, by Ana's account (and exactly how does she know this?), prefers boys to women. But by the same token, the Catholic viceroy in Barcelona is moved so deeply by Ana (as boy)'s beauty that he wishes to spare his (her) life. One is intrigued by the absence of any moral anxiety regarding the Christian viceroy's attraction to the boy, while there is ample moral anxiety around the idea that "among those barbarous Turks a handsome boy or youth is more highly esteemed than a woman, no matter how beautiful she may be."[24]

The disguises taken on by Ana and Gaspar Gregorio suggest

alienation. They distance the two young people from their supposedly true gender and racial identity, leading to the question of exactly what true gender and identity might be in their cases. The central characters of this drama display a curious measure of familiarity with the fake identity assumed. Don Gaspar Gregorio joins the Moriscos who are leaving the village after the expulsion edict "for he knew the language very well."[25] Ricote, Ana's father, has been living as German pilgrim since the expulsion and knows their language. Ana, Ricote, and Don Gaspar Gregorio are at least bilingual and well traveled, especially compared to Don Quixote and Sancho. The latter pair have never seen the sea, are confused by the urban clutter and size of Barcelona, and take part as bystanders in Ana Félix's narrative.

And finally, Ana is categorical in her assertion that male Turks prefer boys to women, which was what led her to disguise her boyfriend as a girl. What experiences have led her to know this fact about Turks, we are not told. They might have occurred in Algiers, where she settled with her mother after the expulsion and to which she refers as "Hell." But her assertion might also be an instance of Freud's uncanny, a concept used by the critic Mary Gossy in the above-mentioned dialogue on *Queer Iberia*. Gossy reminds us that for Freud, "the uncanny is that class of the frightening which leads back to what is known of old and long familiar"—"known and embodied," she continues, "but repressed."[26] Gossy applies this concept to Spain's discomfort with its non-Christian past, suggesting that any reluctance to acknowledge that past within the Spanish academy is precisely a result of the uncanny. Likewise, with Ana Félix, one is tempted to ask: Is the young and new Christian's fear of the Muslim as sodomite not a manifestation of the uncanny? How does this knowledge come to a young woman of her hybrid heritage, and why does she pick it as the focus of her anxiety?

I return to this later, but for now I wish to continue with the presence of Ana and her brood in contrast to Quixote and Sancho. She and her father are seasoned travelers and at ease with disguise, dissimulation, and fluid shifts of identity. Yet they appear to have a firm sense of who they are, even though they are both initially presented to the reader as what—apparently—they are not. Ricote appears to Sancho as a German pilgrim, and Ana to her audience as a Muslim boy. Both must shed their disguises to go back to what they were, an identity about which they seem certain.[27]

To know oneself is a prominent and overarching concern in Cervantes's literary project. Much earlier in the novel, in chapter 5 of part 1, when Don Quixote has barely ventured out for the first time, he falls off his thin horse and a peasant helps him up. Don Quixote begins to wax eloquent on mythical and fictional figures in romances, addressing the peasant as two characters in chivalric fiction. The man answers that he is not any of those fancy fictional people but just the simple "Pedro Alonso your neighbor" and that "your grace isn't Valdovinos or Abindarraez, but an honorable gentleman Señor Quijana."[28] (Quijana is one of the two or three possible names given at the beginning of the novel to the man who later dubs himself Don Quixote.) To this identification made by the peasant, the mad knight answers: "I know who I am." Does he, really? Charles Presberg, in his essay on paradox in _Don Quixote,_ notes: "It seems fitting that a text which playfully takes the measure of its own identity and ontological status should include a cast of parodic characters who are wrestling with the delphic and Socratic dictum: 'Know thyself.'"[29]

Presberg chooses an encounter in part 1 of the novel between Quixote and a man called Don Diego de Miranda, who by all appearances seems to be the knight's exact opposite, though he is also similar in age and social class. The scholar reads this encounter as a tribute to paradox and its role in unfolding human identity:

[A]s thematized and dramatized in Cervantes' narrative, an openness to paradox engenders a sense of communion between self and other in a common quest for truth. But that quest pursues a necessarily elusive and unfolding truth—perhaps "infinitely" approachable and knowable in itself, yet clearly surpassing the limits of time and history, and those of our consoling fictions. Especially in these chapters, Cervantes' fictional paradox depicts seemingly ordinary encounters between self and other, and between reader, text and life, as *potential* encounters with the marvelous ("est Deus in nobis"). Hence, such encounters are not an occasion for final certainty. Instead, they call for *contemplation* in the face of unfolding mystery, and for the attendant *action* of *mutual* self-creation and self-renewal.[30]

"Self-creation," "self-renewal," and the fight against "absolute certainty": Presberg is correct to highlight these as Cervantes's major concerns. The whole work centers on primary and secondary characters who are watching their identity unfold before their eyes, lose its contours, and build itself again into an always flexible entity. Ana Félix is an example of this "self-creation" and "self-renewal," for she is transformed both by an external edict (the expulsion of her people from Spain in 1609) and by a will of her own that carves a path of disguise and adventure for her. Barbara Fuchs suggests pertinently that had Ana not been preoccupied with Don Gaspar Gregrio, she might well have continued as a cross-dressed pirate for quite a while.[31] She does it well, after all: she is made captain of her vessel.

So what is one to make of two categorical statements of "absolute certainty" (about the Turk's appetites and about her own self) that are uttered by such a fluid, flowing, almost amorphous figure—Ana, the paradox; Ana, almost always in disguise, displaying a masculine beauty that confuses Christians and moves them to pity and a feminine beauty that causes an upper-class boy to risk all for her; Ana, whose religion, identity, language, cannot be determined in terms of "absolute certainty." Such a nebulous, imprecise figure issues two precise statements: "I am a Christian woman," and "I was troubled when I considered the danger to him, because among those barbarous Turks a handsome boy or youth is more highly esteemed than a woman no matter how beautiful she may be."[32]

Barbara Fuchs offers a compelling interpretation for the refer-

ence to the Turk's "perversity." It "shifts the focus of the narrative away from the transgressive nature of Ana's strategies."[33]
Further, it complicates Don Gaspar Gregorio's beauty and his
increasing effeminacy, given his stint as a Moorish woman in a
harem: "Thus, 'sodomy' abroad is brought home, so to speak, in
Gregorio's enduring femininity[.]" A "chain of transvestism"
has begun "in which the return to normalcy becomes impossible
without a new act of cross-dressing somewhere."[34] Fuchs continues:

> [I]t is one thing when Ana cross-dresses her lover to save him from
> the supposed sodomy of the vicious Turk and another when both
> she and he fail to shed their androgyny, once back within Spain's
> borders . . . . The "Moorish" perversity exists within Spain, not
> only because, in the absence of an ending, Ana and her father
> Ricote seem to stay on, but because sanctioned Spanish virtues,
> such as the beauty of Don Gregorio or Ana's sober chastity, al-
> ready have the potential to destabilize gender roles and ethnic cat-
> egories regardless of the actual presence of Islam.[35]

I believe that the actual presence of Islam has much to do with
this scene, but it is also clear that Fuchs's reading illuminates the
broad preoccupation of Cervantes who, as a Spaniard, seems
adamant about rewriting Muslims into the history of his country. Such a rewriting will necessarily destabilize any firm ideas
on identity, on knowing oneself, and on clear ethnic contours.
But the wrinkle, brought up a little earlier, still remains: how is
one to explain the rigid definition of the vicious Turk as pervert
within a novel whose greatest aversion seems to be to rigid, unfaltering definitions? The answer that first comes to mind is that
the Turks were the enemy after all. Cervantes himself fought
against them, was injured, and was held captive for five years in
Algiers under what seem to have been less than pleasant conditions. Can one resort here to biography and history and claim
that it makes perfect sense for Cervantes to provide inflexible,
cut-and-dry definitions for Turks, given his own vital context?
    That would solve the problem except that Ana says this about

Turks and nothing else in Cervantes's poetic vision substantiates the validity of any definition (especially one as loaded as this, which propels a whole narrative of disguise, desire, and cross-dressing) as literal and absolute. In Cervantes's work, irony is so forceful that moral and physical descriptions can never remain on the literal level, especially if they occur at crucial junctures (as this one does), however small the space they appear to occupy. Throughout *Don Quixote,* stunningly beautiful women, crazed madmen, simple country bumpkins, distinguished gentlemen, and ardent lovers invariably open out their own stories to problematize the epithets that characterize them. At the risk of entering the murky and highly ineffectual waters of authorial intention, this is not to say that the real Cervantes rejected the idea of the Turk as pervert. It may well be that he did think such a thing, as did many Europeans of his time. Our main concern here is the fact that the utterance is placed in Ana's discourse.

Ana tries to represent the Western *scientia sexualis* that imagines its opposite, which is an Eastern *ars erotica.* But she is also the producer of an Islamicate discourse on the practices of same-sex desire because she is the daughter of two Moriscos. She literally speaks two languages—Arabic and Spanish. In young man's clothing, which she dons gracefully, she speaks a fluent Castilian (and Cervantes deliberately highlights this to remind us that it is Castilian as opposed to the language of the Moriscos) to report on a certain practice common in a Muslim country. Her report is filtered through two levels of disguise, at least one of which—Muslim—is not unfamiliar to her.

The crux of the matter is that by virtue of her time period and her fate, Ana cannot exist in any form other than that of a translator.[36] If some people speak Spanish and some speak Arabic, Ana speaks Translation. No language is her native language. So when she reports on this Eastern practice, she does so as Spaniard and Christian and female (in her view). But in spite of her genuine will to the contrary, she also does so from the exact opposite point. She is too far removed from the centered and rooted Western *locus* (read, established Catholic and nontainted

Spaniard) to declare the Turk's sodomite tendencies and to have
this be understood as a product of Catholic discourse. To project sodomy as an Eastern vice was a common tactic in Cervantes's time, but Ana as speaker complicates this because she does
not occupy the subject position to utter the statement with the
comfort of an old Christian. She is, from one angle, a Muslim
declaring a horrific fact about Muslims.

Thus, Ana—the essential translator—claims to have observed
something about Turks. She then draws on a Western terminology of sexual deviance to describe it and translates her observation back into Spanish. In the process, she conflates Western
taxonomy and Eastern "art of love." And the entire passage en-
crypts same-sex desire as though to problematize her position.
The Turks who sail with her are "good-looking," the Christian
viceroy who sees her (as boy) is moved a little too much by his
beauty, and Don Gaspar Gregorio is recalled as so beautiful he
could pass for a girl. The central question of our proposal is
turned on its head for a moment. We had asked, "What is at
stake in appropriating and attributing homosexualities as Western?" This passage responds in two stages. First, "What is at
stake in appropriating and attributing homosexualities as *Eastern*?" It then moves forward and asks, "What is at stake in appropriating and attributing homosexualities as *translations*?"

If Cervantes broadens the landscape of sexualities for the
Islamicate canon, then here is his major contribution to the discourses made available on the topic. With his Arab narrator
Cide Hamete in the background, he foregrounds Ana (another
unreliable "Arab?") as quintessential translator and chooses a
common adage—Turks are sodomites—as the structural crux of
her tale. This sentence undergoes a compelling transformation
in Ana's mouth because she puts it to surprising use.

As one who speaks a language foreign to all, she is miles
ahead of Cide Hamete the narrator, who literally needed a physical translator to make himself comprehensible, but she is also
miles behind established Christians who apparently make their
meanings known without any mediation. In this space, when she

as interpreter refers to the Turk's love of boys, she continues to include the statement as an element in an *ars erotica* of her own. It leads her to the cross-dressing of her pretty boyfriend and her own dashing drag as the pirate who will save him: the utterance on the Turk begins her process of self-creation.

In their preface to *Hispanism and Homosexualities,* Sylvia Molloy and Robert McKee Irwin reflect on the notion of Hispanism, which has a broad and complex reach, and suggest a bringing out of "submerged meanings." They note that "[i]ndeed, strangely unfriendly to bricolage, Hispanism has traditionally conceived itself in monolithic terms, as an oddly defensive family whose members supposedly share basic cultural values." There has been an aversion to "re-readings," "reformulation," and "the unsettling impact of critical inquiry."[37] When Ana Félix brings sodomy home, to use Fuchs's term, she compels us to reread her episode precisely to reveal a submerged meaning. But Ana also manages to texture, revise, and unsettle a certain Islamicate discourse on sodomy. Her initially rigid categorization of the Turk as sodomite, followed by the colorful, adventurous, and dashing story that follows it, recalls a structure dear to classical Arabic manuals of erotology. In these (Sheikh Nafzawi's *The Perfumed Garden,* al-Tifachi's *Delight of Hearts,* al-Baghdadi's *The Blooming Flowers,* to name a well-known few), vast ranges of sexual behavior are neatly categorized, in anthology form, and the headings then lead to amusing stories that show the definition put into practice. Entertainment often ends up overshadowing moral concern. In the same uncanny frame evoked above by Mary Gossy, Ana culls this Islamicate way of seeing. She offers an unwavering definition of sexual deviance and uses it to segue into a vivid anecdote filled with adventure. The end result is much like the one seen in the erotological manuals of Arabic: a certain behavior has been condemned, but a really good story has come out of it. Examples of this abound in the profane belle-lettriste genres of classical Arabic.

Making her way in from the West, Ana is to be inscribed into the list of mostly male Muslim storytellers who contributed to the creation of a rich and entertaining corpus of stories built around perversions *(inhirafat)*. But she also subverts the tradition (which means enriching it) by being a Christian girl from a Catholic country—uncomfortably close to an apostate, in fact. This is the worst departure from orthodox Islam. The effect is the same as the one charted by those working on the margins of Iberian literature: Molloy and McKee invite the reader to remobilize a canon that might be deadened by its "sheer canonicity."[38] Ana invites us to reconsider the canon of erotological material produced mostly by male Muslim and to see what happens to it when she joins their ranks.

Translations are critiques of the original. A translation is successful only if it comes out of a process in which the meaning of the original is understood and interpreted. What Ana does is the very enactment of translation, and in her case her interpretation rests on a profoundly private reason. She uses structures and materials familiar to both sides of the Mediterranean to ensure the survival of her own fragile identity formation. This is no longer a playful anthology written by a well-educated Muslim belle-letterist or a dogmatic pronouncement made by a Catholic official on Turks. Ana needs this information to find her bearings in an otherwise hopelessly confused topography. She takes the threat of Turkish sodomy, a well-known Western attribution, to give a point of origin to her adventures as boy and to Gaspar Gregorio's life as girl, a strategy that recalls Arabic erotology. She translates herself into boy pirate and her fiancé into harem girl. Who is to say that she and Gregorio do not on some level enjoy this, even if she schemed it above all to save his honor? In any event, the end result is unique. *Scientia sexualis* and *ars erotica* have met, in translation, to aid the process of becoming a young Christian girl who has understood what it is to be a young Muslim boy. In the process, she expands the limits of the Islamicate discourse by giving it a new use altogether—to shape the contours of her own unique self, hailing from the lost and last periphery of the Islamic empire, yet desperate to sever that link.[39]

I am not interested in proving beyond a shadow of a doubt that Cervantes read Arab erotological manuals. What matters most is that Iberian milieux were substantially infused with non-Christian presence. The more insightful Spanish authors of the medieval and early modern periods show some familiarity with some of the major discourses of the Islamic world. The links are not difficult to establish. From physical proximity to the transmission of erudition, this vital context certainly allowed for plenty of exposure, however indirect or difficult, for those who had the curiosity for it. More important, what is distilled from Iberian texts themselves is more compelling proof of sensitivity to Muslim coexistence and the inevitable inclusion of some aspect of it inside the fabric of fiction.

In just such an instance in the novel, *Don Quixote* provides a foreshadowing to the concept of *ars erotica* as it relates to the notion of honor and translation. The concept of honor is at the root of Ana's anxiety for Gregorio and intertwined with her projection of the Turk as deviant. Ana is both a producer and an interpreter of an Islamicate discourse on sexual perversion, expanding the semiotic field available to discuss sexualities across cultures and for a meaningful reason. But her episode is not the only one in *Don Quixote* in which Muslim identity and sexuality are foregrounded to encourage the reader to think about definitions of normal and abnormal within the politics of identity formation. In fact, her episode relates closely to chapters 38 to 42 of part 1, often referred to as "The Captive's Tale." This episode has inspired numerous observations and commentaries by critics and is one of the most multifaceted narratives in the whole novel. It is used it here in relation to the Ana Félix narrative, which appears long after it.[40]

Don Quixote and Sancho are at an inn in Castile with a group of other Spaniards when an older man appears accompanied by a younger Moorish woman who does not speak Castilian. The older man, originally a native of León (a region known for its old Christians and its generally conservative attitudes), tells his story. He has been away from Spain for years, having fought in battles against the Ottomans, taken captive, and subsequently imprisoned in Algiers. There, enslaved as many other Christians were, he is one day approached in secret by Zoraida, a beautiful and wealthy Moorish girl who communicates to him (via translations of her naïve notes) that she wishes to help him escape and go back to Spain, as long as he takes her with him so that she can convert to Christianity. He learns that she had a nanny who told her about the Virgin Mary (Lela Marién, in her adapted language) and that Zoraida as a child vowed to become a Christian to be able to worship Lela Marién.

The Captive and Zoraida go through adventures on land and sea in their escape, and they are attacked by pirates and pursued by Zoraida's father until they finally reach Spain dressed in Moorish garb. Throughout the Captive's narrative, there is an absence of any overt reference to eroticism. Though he is sensitive to her beauty and the attraction of Zoraida's exotic appearance, as the critic Luis Andrés Murillo has observed, the Captive appears to occupy the role of a benign paternal figure and not of an impassioned husband-to-be.[41] I would like to draw attention to one event during their escape.

They are on board a ship headed for Spain when French corsairs sail close to them and ask them in French who they are. The renegade who is the Captive's and Zoraida's main aid and who has designed the escape advises against answering. Armed with muskets, the French board their ship. The Captive recalls what happened to Zoraida's trunk, which contained much money and gold: "Our renegade picked up the chest of Zoraida's treasure and threw it into the sea without anyone noticing what he was doing."[42] He continues the narrative:

> In short, when we were all on board the French ship, and they had learned everything they wanted to know about us, as if they were our mortal enemies they stole everything we had and stripped Zoraida even of the anklets she wore on her feet. But I was not as perturbed by Zoraida's distress as I was by my own fear that after they had taken her rich and precious jewels they would take her

most valuable jewel, the one she prized most highly. But the desires of these people do not go beyond money, for which their lust is never satisfied, and on this occasion it was so inflamed that they would have taken even our captives' attire if it had been of any use to them. . . . But their captain, the man who had robbed my dear Zoraida, said that he was satisfied with the booty he already had[.][43]

And so the French captain gives them their skiff and lets them go.

It is easy to consider that the Captive is rewriting the story, erasing what really did happen. When he says, "But the desires of these people do not go beyond money" (to reassure his listeners that Zoraida was not raped), his claim sounds feeble set against an avalanche of images to the contrary: the Frenchmen's lust is "inflamed," they "strip" and "rob" his beloved Zoraida, the captain is "satisfied." Zoraida is a defenseless beautiful woman, and pirates are vicious men. Rhetorically, the loss of her most precious jewel is enacted in the image of her trunk, forever gone though not noticed by anyone except the Captive. The loss is also compounded by the Captive's sensitivity to her ankle jewelry. Earlier, when he first catches a glimpse of her in Algiers, in an uncharacteristic moment of sensual awareness he remembers her beauty and the fact that "Around her ankles, which were bare, in accordance with Moorish custom, she wore two *carcajes* (the Moorish names for bracelets and bangles for the feet) of purest gold[.]"[44] If all this were not sufficient to raise doubts regarding the Captive's reconstruction of the story, we are also told by him that "as the beautiful Zoraida was getting into the skiff, the Captain, moved by some sort of mercy, gave her forty gold *escudos* and would not allow his men to take the very clothing she is wearing now."[45] How far-fetched is it to assume that the French corsair is paying Zoraida for what he has taken away from her?

This scene has preoccupied me for some time because I wonder if Zoraida's most valuable jewel *is* taken from her at this moment and the Captive is doing his best to hide that fact, hoping that this will go unnoticed as much as Zoraida's trunk, which has not gone unnoticed at all ("Our renegade picked up the chest of Zoraida's treasure and threw it into the sea without anyone noticing what he was doing": who exactly did the "not noticing"?). The initial explanation for the Captive's revisionist narrative is that for his audience at the inn, honor is so closely tied with female chastity that he will effectively dishonor Zoraida if he reveals that she was raped. But why, in that case, does he present the narrative in a way that leaves room for inferring that fact anyway?

The Captive, like Ana Félix many chapters later, is a traveler and a translator. For years, he has closely observed other cultures and customs (most of them Muslim) without the luxury of liberty or distance. He recalls the language spoken in Algiers, remembering a conversation with Zoraida's father: "[he] spoke to me in the language used between captives and Moors throughout Barbary, and even in Constantinople; it is not Moorish or Castilian, not the language of any nation, but a mixture of all tongues and with it we can understand one another."[46] He has cohabited under duress with people whose core identifying features seem to undergo change according to the events around them. Algiers is a place of temporary people—renegades, converts, former soldiers, and ultimately prisoners. By definition, a prisoner is someone whose identity is temporary; he must have been something before, and he will usually become something after. Everyone around the Captive is, to use Julia Kristeva's term, a subject-in-process. They are all becoming something else—pirates who become rich, Muslims who convert, former Christian soldiers who are now slaves. Fittingly, they speak a language that belongs to no nation.

Once again, translation commands the vision and discourse of those who are immersed in this world and whose identities are subject to radical fluctuation. When the Captive reports on the (non)incident on the ship, he articulates an element of a new *ars amatoria* that can exist only in translation and not in the specific language of any nation. In his world vision, a wife who has lost her most valuable jewel ceases to figure prominently in his narrative. If it did, either he would say it and face the consequences of her dishonor or not say it and leave no room for speculation. His construction of this aspect of the narrative is a major step in his painful efforts to build himself an identity now that he has passed through so many guises. His years of exile and transformation have distanced him from his conservative, conformist native León, where the point of honor is forever tied to chastity. He cannot say that Zoraida was robbed of her jewel but that this is not a prominent part of his narrative because his credibility would be destroyed, given that he speaks at the inn to a group of Spaniards who highly esteem chastity and honor. And so he translates his acquired vision of chastity, sex, and honor: he presents the narrative in terms that neither allow nor refute the thesis that she has been dishonored. This is ultimately an inward-looking process: a husband—probably the only one in all of Spain—for whom the wife's virginity is not important.[47]

The incident begins with a known and traditional Spanish posture: "But I was not as perturbed by Zoraida's distress as I was by my own fear that . . . ." A "real" Spaniard would say and think just this. Then the captive begins to reassure the reader with "But the desires of these people do not go beyond money, for which their lust is never satisfied . . . ," setting up the expectation that he will elaborate and explain the "But." He does not, and instead leaves the sentence hovering. Starting with "On this occasion," he leads the reader further into thinking that an explanation is to come, and yet he continues to a totally different matter: "on this occasion it was so inflamed that they would have taken even our captives' attire if it had been of any use to them." In short, we never are told what did (not) happen to Zoraida.

The Captive's distress that French pirates will rob his Muslim beloved of her jewel mirrors the distress of Ana Félix that the Turk will sodomize her Christian beloved. In both cases, the speakers start the tale of their sexual anxiety by reproducing information that is *scientia sexualis:* Turks are deviants, pirates are rapists, and honor is at stake. This recalls Cervantes's own declaration about Cide Hamete: our narrator is an Arab, all Arabs are liars. But like Cervantes with Cide Hamete, Ana and the Captive surprise us by not sustaining the cliché along familiar lines. Ana, as a new Christian who is intent on looking like a genuine (old) Christian,[48] describes instead an in-between Muslim/Christian sexual landscape in which the sodomy of the Turk becomes subject to critical scrutiny because it appears in translation and serves as a starting point for the formation of her difficult identity. The Captive is an old Christian dressed in Moorish garb. His decision to encrypt the probable rape while showing no anguish about it is also a translation, aimed eventually at helping him figure out who he is. Here, in the language that is "neither Moorish nor Castilian," he presents a possibility that is neither Moorish nor Castilian. In one move, he holds up for critique the *scientia sexualis* of the West and that of the East, both of which are obsessed with female honor. His complicated multilingual existence, set against his lost conservative background, has taught him to stop foregrounding his wife's chastity as the ultimate test of honor and the futility of believing in unwavering sexual codes. He cannot come out and say it, but he can imply it. And what safer object for this experiment with nonbelief than a Muslim woman, who, in the eyes of those listening at the inn, is hopelessly foreign and therefore open to complete objectification?[49]

The Captive's Tale is not about same-sex desire. But to the extent that it is a reversal of Ana Félix's tale, it illuminates her translation project by looking at it from an opposite angle. It shows and foreshadows how the process of turning the *ars* and *scientia* of sex on their heads is needed for identity formation for those who belong in both the Islamic and the Christian canon. All the roles are reversed: the predator is French, the victim is Muslim, the protector is male and old Christian. Once again, sexual honor is at stake. The Captive is able to invent a new way of telling this because he has access to the language of no nation, neither Moorish nor Castilian. In other words, he transforms a burdensome and essentially Western understanding of sexual misdemeanor into a possibility for redemption that transcends both Zoraida's orthodox Islamic upbringing and his conservative Leonese past. In this way, his narration becomes the foundation for Ana Félix's discourse, which is also built on translation.

Even if Ana speaks after 1609, when Spain has proved itself unwilling to accept coexistence with its minorities, she manages to go beyond the grand narrative of the privileged positions within the Western *scientia sexualis* and to draw attention, albeit hesitantly, to secondary (half-Islamicate, half-Christian) ways of seeing the Turk's sodomy. Given that the Turk's appetite functions in the context of the one who tells the story, Cervantes—ever true to his love of paradox—now invites his readers to contemplate sexual deviance through translation, above and beyond pure Castilian and distant Arabic. He allows us in this way to observe, step by step, how a new self is formed.

NOTES

1. Miguel de Cervantes, *Don Quixote,* trans. Edith Grossman (New York: HarperCollins, 2003), 353 (part 1, chapter 41, the episode referred to as "The Captive's Tale"). Part 1 was originally published in 1605; part 2, in 1615.
2. See, for example, *Cervantes and His Postmodern Constituencies,* ed. Anne J. Cruz and Carroll B. Johnson (New York: Garland, 1998); *Quixotic Desire: Psychoanalytic Perspectives on Cervantes,* ed. Ruth Anthony El Saffar and Diana de Armas Wilson (Ithaca: Cornell University Press, 1993); *Gender, Identity, and Representation in Spain's Golden Age,* ed. Anita K. Stoll and Dawn L. Smith (Lewisburg: Bucknell University Press, 2000); Barbara Fuchs, *Passing for Spain: Cervantes and the Fictions of Identity* (Urbana: University of Illinois, 2003); Anne J. Cruz, "Psyche and Gender in Cervantes," in *The Cambridge Companion to Cervantes,* ed. Anthony J. Cascardi (Cambridge: Cambridge University Press, 2002), 186–205.
3. *Queer Iberia,* ed. Gregory Hutcheson and Josiah Blackmore (Durham: Duke University Press, 1999), 3.
4. Forum on "Return to Queer Iberia," eds. Sidney Donnell and

Gregory Hutcheson, *La Corónica* 30.1 (Fall 2001) 215–265. This forum is available at http://www.wm.edu/msll/lacoronica/qi/qi-main. html, with indices and guidelines. My citations from Gregory Hutcheson's "Return to *Queer Iberia*" are from this site.

5. Other valuable studies are *Hispanisms and Homosexualities,* ed. Sylvia Molloy and Robert McKee Irwins (Durham: Duke University Press, 1998); *¿Entiendes?,* ed. Paul Julian Smith and Emilie Bergman (Durham: Duke University Press, 1995); *Lesbianism and Homosexuality in Early Modern Spain: Literature and Theater in Context,* ed. María José Delgado and Alain Saint-Saëns (New Orleans: University Press of the South, 2000).

6. Hutcheson, "Return to *Queer Iberia.*"

7. Ibid.

8. See Barbara Fuchs, *Mimesis and Empire: The New World, Islam, and European Identities* (Cambridge: Cambridge University Press, 2001). In addition to its own important content, the bibliography provided in this study is valuable for further reading on the matter of Renaissance Europe's representation of Islam. See also Israel Burshatin, "The Moor in the Text: Metaphor, Emblem, and Silence," *Critical Inquiry* 12, no. 1 (Autumn 1985): 98–118.

9. In the study of Cervantes's *Don Quixote,* the bibliography is vast to the point of being overwhelming. For a start, see Jaime Fernández, *Bibliografía del Quijote por unidades narrativas y materials de la novela* (Alcalá de Henares: Centro de estudios cervantinos, 1995); also *Cervantes' Don Quixote: A Casebook,* ed. Roberto González Echevarría (Oxford: Oxford University Press, 2005); *The Cambridge Companion to Cervantes,* ed. Anthony J. Cascardi (Cambridge: Cambridge University Press, 2002).

10. Fuchs, *Mimesis and Empire,* 162–63.

11. Fuchs, *Passing for Spain,* 44.

12. The bibliography on Cervantes and his attitudes to Islam is also growing and by no means gives the impression of unanimous agreement among scholars. See *Las dos grandes minorías étnico-religiosas en la literature española del Siglo de Oro: los judeo-conversos y los moriscos,* ed. Irene Andres-Suárez (Paris: Annales littéraires de l'Université de Besançon, 1995); Darío Fernández-Morera, "Cervantes and Islam: A Contemporary Analogy," in *Cervantes y su mundo,* ed. Robert Lauer and Kurt Reichenberger (Kassel: Reichenberger, 2005): 123–66; Luce López-Baralt, "The

Supreme Pen (Al-Qalam Al-A'Ala)of Cide Hamete Benengeli in *Don Quixote*," trans. Marikay McCabe, *Journal of Medieval and Early Modern Studies* 30, no. 3 (Fall 2000): 505–18; Roberto A. Véguez, "*Don Quijote* and 9-11: The Clash of Civilizations and the Birth of the Modern Novel," *Hispania* 88, no. 1 (2005): 101–13.

13. E. C. Graf, "When an Arab Laughs in Toledo," *Diacritics* 29, no. 2 (1999): 68–85, 80.

14. Ibid., 80–81.

15. *Don Quixote*, 67.

16. Ibid.,

17. Ibid., 68.

18. Don Quixote's insanity is the subject of much valid debate. Whether he is truly insane has been asked frequently and will continue to be asked. He has been understood as an idealist, an outsider, and a dreamer. All these interpretations apply to him, but they do not annul the fact that the novel itself projects him as insane in no uncertain terms, subsequently inviting the reader to define the concept against key frames of reference such as clinical, aesthetic, narrative, sexual, social. The concept transforms and grows with Quixote himself.

19. See Christina H. Lee, "Don Antonio Moreno y el 'discreto' negocio de los moriscos Ricote y Ana Félix," *Hispania* 88, no. 1 (2005): 32–40. Lee begins her study by asserting correctly that most critics today base their analysis of this famous episode on the groundbreaking work of Francisco Márquez Villanueva, who, in *Personajes y temas del Quixote* (Madrid: Taurus, 1975), came to a number of significant conclusions about the nature and function of the episode. Lee suggests that one of Márquez Villanueva's most important contributions to the study of this episode lies in the following conjecture. By marrying Ana Félix (of Muslim descent) to Don Gaspar Gregorio (a "true" Christian), Cervantes causes a "biological fusion of blood" that could solve the problem of Morisco existence in Spain (Lee, "Don Antonio Moreno," 32). See also Joseph V. Ricapito, "Cervantes y la conciencia: 'Yo sé quién soy,' el caballero de los leones y Ricote el Moro," in Lauer and Reichenberger, *Cervantes y su mundo III*, 505–17; Richard Hitchcock, "Cervantes, Ricote, and the Expulsion of the Moriscos," *Bulletin of Spanish Studies* 81, no. 2 (2004): 175–85.

20. In 1609, after years of increasingly difficult coexistence, descendants of Spanish Muslims (called Moriscos) were deported from Spain under the reign of Felipe IV. This was the culmination of several decades of legislation against this community, many of whose members had been baptized and whose genuine Christianity continued to be questioned even in cases where no proof could be found to the contrary. Starting in 1492, when the last Muslim kingdom fell, the Catholic monarchs began to impose harsher restrictions on the everyday lives of Muslims who remained in Spain (many of whom converted). See Mercedes García Arenal, *Los moriscos* (Granada: Universidad de Granada, 1995); Anwar Chejne, *Islam and the West: The Moriscos, a Cultural and Social History* (Albany: SUNY Press, 1983).

21. *Don Quixote,* 878. Richard Hitchcock, in the article cited above, considers several related meanings for *gallardo.* Hitchcock, "Cervantes, Ricote, and the Expulsion of the Moriscos," 180–81.

22. *Don Quixote,* 879.

23. Ibid., 881.

24. Ibid.

25. Ibid., 880.

26. Mary Gossy, in Hutcheson, "Return to *Queer Iberia.*"

27. See Fuch's analysis of this chapter in *Passing for Spain.*

28. *Don Quixote,* 43.

29. Charles Presberg, "'Yo sé quién soy': Don Quixote, Don Diego de Miranda and the Paradox of Self-Knowledge," *Bulletin of the Cervantes Society of America* 14, no. 2 (1994): 41–69.

30. Ibid., 69.

31. Fuchs, *Passing for Spain,* 42.

32. *Don Quixote,* 881.

33. Fuchs, *Passing for Spain,* 42.

34. Ibid., 43.

35. Ibid., 44.

36. Brought up a "new" Catholic in a household of Moriscos—where the father Ricote all but declares his lack of strong faith—she is deported to a place that supposedly is her origin but obviously is not. Her life is marked by a general confusion about when she is "inside" and when she is "outside." In an increasingly hostile Spain, she fast becomes an outsider and is finally deported. In her wandering life in Algiers and the East, she still needs to don a disguise

to look native. In all cases, one can infer that any language that she speaks might be construed as not being her own. Note that when her father Ricote runs into Sancho earlier, Cervantes offers the information that Ricote speaks "fluent Castilian," even though the man was born and brought up in Sancho's village.

37. Molloy and Irvins, *Hispanisms and Homosexualities,* x–xi.
38. Ibid., xi.
39. This use works hand in hand with Fuchs's idea of her challenge to the monolithic shape of Spain and also highlights the fact that actual Islam is very much present in the process.
40. For this episode, often referred to as "The Captive's Tale," see, in particular, Diane E. Sieber, "Mapping Identity in the Captive's Tale: Cervantes and Ethnographic Narrative," *Cervantes: Bulletin of the Cervantes Society of America* 18, no. 1 (1998): 115–33; Maria Antonia Garces, *Cervantes in Algiers: A Captive's Tale* (Nashville: University of Vanderbilt Press, 2002).
41. Luis Andrés Murillo, "El Ur-*Quijote*: nueva hipótesis," *Cervantes: Bulletin of the Cervantes Society of America* 1, nos. 1–2 (1981): 43–50.
42. *Don Quixote,* 364.
43. Ibid., 365.
44. Ibid., 354.
45. Ibid., 365.
46. Ibid., 353.
47. On an equally important issue that might underlie the Captive's attitude, see William Childers, "The Captive's Tale and Circumcision," in *Annals of Scholarship: Don Quixote and Race,* ed. Baltasar Fra Molinero (Philadelphia: Temple University Press, forthcoming). Childers argues convincingly that this episode is "haunted by circumcision" and that the Captive himself is fraught with inconsistencies and gaps in his self-representation, aware that suspicions—such as that of having been circumcised—surround those who return to Spain after long captivity.
48. Old versus new Christian refers to the genealogy of Spaniards as either long-standing Christians or recent converts (or the offspring of one or the other).
49. The objectification of Zoraida is aptly noted by María Antonio Garcés in *Cervantes in Algiers*. The scholar shows this objectification to be a strategy for the Captive's recovery from trauma.

THREE

Cross-Dressing and Female Same-Sex Marriage in Medieval French and Arabic Literatures

Sahar Amer

The presuppositions we make about sexed bodies . . . are suddenly and significantly upset by those examples that fail to comply with the categories that naturalize and stabilize that field of bodies for us within the terms of cultural conventions. Hence, the strange, the incoherent, that which falls "outside," gives us a way of understanding the taken-for-granted world of sexual categorization as a constructed one, indeed, as one that might be constructed differently.

—*Judith Butler, Gender Trouble*[1]

The title of Jacqueline Murray's essay ("Twice Marginal and Twice Invisible") in Bullough and Brundage's *Handbook of Medieval Sexuality* is revealing of the status of the medieval lesbian in contemporary scholarship.[2] In this essay, Murray decries the fact that the medieval Western lesbian has been regularly elided in most literary criticism under the rubric "homosexual" in mainstream woman history and under the rubric "woman" in studies of medieval homosexuality, which both focus almost exclusively on male homosexuality. She observes: "Of all groups within medieval society lesbians are the most marginalized and least visible."[3]

One reason that medieval French lesbians as a category of

analysis or as evidence of a certain textual (or social) reality have been occulted is that many medieval French literary writings continue to be read in isolation from the cultural context of interaction, seduction, and anxiety between the Arab Islamicate world and Western Christian Europe.[4] Steven F. Kruger has tellingly pointed out that "medieval thinking about the sexuality of Christians is crucially different from, and yet intimately intertwined with medieval constructions of the sexuality of . . . Muslims."[5] It is this idea of sexual, textual, and cultural interconnections that I explore here by reading several Old French texts through the lens of medieval Arabic literature to uncover a discourse on female same-sex desire in French that has remained thus far unnoticed. I explore the ways in which the Arabic homoerotic tradition was adapted and rewritten by medieval French Christian writers and the extent to which much of medieval French literary writings can be read in terms of hybridization and cross-fertilization. Just as the Middle Ages can no longer be viewed as a monocultural, monolithic historical era, Western sexuality (contrary to the beliefs of many) is not reducible to heterosexuality or heterosexism. The question that I pose here is therefore not only "Where is the lesbian?" but also "Can the literary expression of lesbian desire and lesbian love in medieval French literature claim an Arabic literary genealogy?"

Before examining specific medieval French and Arabic texts describing lesbian practices, a few words must be said of the challenges posed by cross-cultural research, especially when dealing with representations of sexuality (homosexuality, lesbianism) in the East and the West. One of these challenges has to do with the audience's contemporary presuppositions of the relations between France and the Arab Islamicate world in the Middle Ages. Even today, these presuppositions continue to be shaped and informed by implicit (and explicit) Orientalist fantasies. In addition, the contemporary Western audience's own understanding of sexuality (homosexuality and lesbianism) still affects the ways that medieval cross-cultural sexuality studies are apprehended. Much research has recently been conducted on the vast differences in the ways in which sexuality studies (and thus also homosexuality and lesbianism) are understood by French and U.S. scholars. These differences have important implications for gay and lesbian studies as a field of scholarship. While they have by now become part of U.S. universities and scholarly publications, gay and lesbian studies still remain greatly marginalized in the French academic system, as Dominique Fisher and Lawrence Schehr argue in their *Articulations of Difference: Gender Studies and Writing in French*.[6] There is still no tenure track or established chair in this field or in sexuality studies in French universities, and there is still no equivalent to "queer studies" in French academe. The U.S. and French understanding of sexuality is determined by national affiliation, a situation that has been coined as the "national-sexual" by Mireille Rosello.[7]

The "national-sexual" affects not only the ways that each culture perceives the other (the way the French perceive the United States and vice versa) but also the ways that each of them perceives Middle Eastern and Islamicate sexualities. France, much more than the United States, has had a long history of interactions with the Middle East and Islamicate world. This Franco/Christian-Arab/Islamicate history extends beyond the medieval encounters I am interested in. It was sustained (under very different political and ideological configurations) in the history of France's imperialist interests in North Africa throughout the nineteenth century and manifests itself today through the tense relations with its Maghrebian immigrant population since the 1970s. France's long and complex history of interaction with the Muslim and Arab world renders the cross-cultural investigation into France's past and particularly into the recovery of its possible Arabic literary lineage an especially sensitive topic for some Western audiences.

France (and the West generally) thus has a great deal at stake in cross-cultural research, particularly research that compares French textual culture with the literary production of the Arab world. One possible outcome of such an investigation is the destabilization of current power and intellectual relations. The crux of the problem lies in the West's (both the United States and France) contemporary discursive self-presentation as secular, sexually liberated, and firmly positioned in the first world. This perspective is opposed to the contemporary assumption of Muslim and Arab women as an always already constituted coherent, stable category of sexually oppressed, sociopolitically subordinated objects, victims of an all-powerful patriarchal, legal, and religious system regardless of class or of marginal and resistant modes of experiences. Such a definition of the West and of Muslim Arab women locks all analysis into binary structures: Muslim women versus Muslim men and the Arab Islamicate world versus the West. It also ends up "colonizing" once more Arab Muslim women and freezes them into a structurally unequal first-world and third-world relation.[8] Ultimately, the plurality of their (literary) experiences, their historical agency, and their resistant literary modes of sexual expression are effaced and replaced by cultural (and homophobia-induced) amnesia both in the West and in the Arab Islamicate world today. Cross-cultural gender and sexuality research is not a neutral field of inquiry. Like many disciplines, it does not produce objective knowledge but raises fundamental political and ethical questions.[9]

I have shown elsewhere that compared to the explicitness and detailed descriptions of lesbian sexual practices in the Arabic tradition, few French medieval literary texts discuss lesbianism or lesbian sexuality *explicitly*.[10] Much more frequently, the medieval French literary tradition addresses the question of homosexuality and of lesbianism via cross-dressing, a phenomenon that Michèle Perret has dubbed second-degree homosexuality.[11]

Instances of cross-dressing are abundant in both the French and Arabic traditions. Joan of Arc may be the most famous Western historical female cross-dresser, and the French tradition of miracle plays and the hagiographic literature are replete with female-to-male cross-dressers.[12] In addition, the hero(ine) of several thirteenth- and fourteenth-century French romances is a woman disguised as a knight (examples include *Le Roman de Silence,* the story of Blanchandine in *Tristan de Nanteuil,* and the story of Grisandole in *L'Estoire de Merlin*).[13] Similarly, the Arabic epic tradition offers countless examples of women warriors and amazons (Princess 'Ain al-Hayat in *Qissat Firuz Shah,* the characters of Queen al-Rabab, al-Gayda', Gamra and Nitra in the *Romance of 'Antar,* Al-Samta' and Aluf in *Dhat al-Himma,* Princess Turban in *Hamza al-Bahlawan,* and the female community in the *Romance of Sayf*).[14] Furthermore, the eighth-century poetry by Abu Nuwas (763–814) develops an entire genre *(ghulamiyyat)* in which the beloved is a woman dressed as a man. All these texts (French and Arabic) certainly invite an exploration and an interrogation of gender relations and hierarchy through the proliferation of the ambiguous situations they describe. In most of them, however, homosexuality may indeed be considered to function "in the second degree" in the sense that it is always suggested and never actualized or addressed directly.

CROSS-DRESSING AND SAME-SEX MARRIAGE

What is of greater interest to me here is a special category of French and Arabic texts that combine female cross-dressing with same-sex marriage, texts in which the cross-dressed woman ends up marrying another woman. This particular combination (cross-dressing and female same-sex marriage) occurs in a small corpus of Old French texts, most notably in the story of *Yde et Olive,* which is one of the mid-thirteenth-century continuations of the epic poem *Huon de Bordeaux,*[15] its late fourteenth-century dramatic adaptation known as the *Miracle de la fille d'un roy;*[16] and its fifteenth-century French prose version written for three nobles at the court of Charles VII in 1454 (in the midst of Joan of Arc's rehabilitation) and printed in the early sixteenth century as part of *Les prouesses et faictz du trespreux noble et vaillant Huon de Bordeaulx* (fols. 166v–178r).[17] Because of space limitations, I address here the Yde and Olive stories only in their verse epic and dramatic renditions and compare them to what I consider to be their main Arabic literary and cultural model, one of the tales from *The Thousand and One Nights* known as the story of Qamar al-Zaman and the Princess Budur. A close reading of the lesbian interlude in the French and Arabic traditions demonstrate the extent to which the French story is heir to the Arabic framed tale, taking as its source of inspiration the names of the main characters, the general story line, and the combination of cross-dressing and same-sex marriage. While borrowing multiple thematic features from the Arabic version of the story, French narrators have endeavored to transform it, censor parts of it, and replace them with other elements that reveal the vast differences in attitudes toward female same-sex unions in these two cultural traditions.

It must be emphasized from the outset that the changes that the lesbian story undergoes from the Arabic to the French tradition cannot be explained away as generic differences between *The Thousand and One Nights* and *Yde et Olive* or the requirements of the framed oral (popular) narrative tradition as opposed to the (written) epic. Recent scholarship has indeed pointed to the fact that texts such as the *Huon de Bordeaux* cycle are interdisciplinary productions (a crossing between the epic and romance genres), that they were equally enjoyed by men and women, and that they circulated freely in popular and courtly contexts. Similarly, *The Thousand and One Nights* enjoyed a much wider circulation than has been traditionally admitted and was the basis for multiple rewritings in divergent genres both in the Arab Islamicate world and the West since the Middle Ages. This interdisciplinary, intergeneric reconsideration of medieval Arabic and European writings is especially fruitful for the type of cross-cultural work proposed here since it allows a more productive discussion of texts that are often thought to be generic opposites. The differences uncovered between the Arabic and French traditions on lesbianism that are discussed below therefore go beyond genre and extend to deeper cultural thinking about sexuality, gender, and normative behavioral expectations.

THE YDE AND OLIVE STORIES

I begin by briefly summarizing the two French texts, which, despite some key differences to which I return later, tell a similar story. The king and queen of Aragon, after many prayers to God and the Virgin Mary, finally conceive a daughter named Yde in the epic (Ysabel in the miracle play). Yde's mother dies in childbirth, and the father, grieving still some fifteen years later, decides to marry his own daughter since she alone among all women resembles her mother perfectly. Yde, horrified at this incestuous plan,[18] runs away dressed as a man and adopts the name of Ydé to avoid being recognized. The text then recounts the various adventures and challenges that the cross-dressed Yde/Ysabel faces and overcomes, the details of which differ somewhat in the epic and the play. The cross-dressed heroine finally arrives in Rome where she successfully leads the king's army against the Spaniards who attacked his lands (in the play, Ysabel arrives in Greece where she fights the Turks and the Saracens on behalf of the emperor of Constantinople). After one year, King Oton of Rome decides to compensate Yde by making her/him his heir and marrying Yde to his daughter (Olive), who, we are told, loves the cross-dressed knight. Yde/Ysabel laments her fate but seeing no alternative puts herself in God's hands. The wedding is celebrated. In the play, Ysabel confesses her true sex to her wife on their wedding night, and in the epic Yde feigns an illness and fifteen days later, not finding any other pretext, confides her true identity to Olive, who promises to keep the secret. Their conversation is overheard (it is witnessed by a monk placed there as an observer of their wedding night by the emperor of Constantinople in the miracle play), and both women are denounced to the king. To ascertain the truth of this revelation and before rushing to burn his daughter and Yde both at the stake (as his advisers recommend), the king sends for the two women and orders a ritual bath in which Yde must bathe naked. At this point in the epic, an angel descends from heaven and announces that God has transformed Yde into a man. The angel also predicts the king's imminent death and the birth of Croissant, the son of Yde and Olive.

In the play, the ending is a bit more convoluted: God himself (who had already personally intervened on various occasions earlier in the text on behalf of Ysabel) sends Saint Michael, disguised as a white stag, to divert the witnesses of the bath. The angel reassures Ysabel about disrobing for the bath, revealing to her that God will reward her faith in him with a penis. The king, seeing that Ysabel indeed had the requisite male sexual organs, blesses the union of the couple and would have rushed to punish the monk who revealed to him the same-sex marriage had it not been for the timely and combined intervention of God and the Virgin Mary. Ysabel's sexual transformation is not permanent in the miracle play, however, since the story ends with Ysabel's return to her former biological sex and with the double wedding of Ysabel to the emperor of Constantinople and of the emperor's daughter to Ysabel's father.

Several critics have noted the obvious interrogation of gender roles and of sexual identities that these texts invite.[19] Evidently, the Yde and Olive stories destabilize the foundation of heteronormativity and challenge the notion of a stable binary sexuality. This goal is achieved not through cross-dressing alone but by adding one transgression to another—cross-dressing, same-sex marriage, and transsexual (transgender) transformation. The impact of each of these disruptive elements is greatly intensified by their simultaneous presence in the text and is a manifestation of what Marjorie Garber, in her *Vested Interests: Cross-Dressing and Cultural Anxiety,* has dubbed "the third term," which is not a term or a "sex" but rather "a mode of articulation, a way of describing a space of possibility. Three puts into question the idea of one: of identity, self-sufficiency, self-knowledge."[20]

This text also disrupts social norms and class hierarchy, both of which are closely regulated by medieval sumptuary laws.[21] In *Yde et Olive,* each gender or sexual transgression allows a space for subversion to open and allows an interrogation of social class, heteronormativity, and stable definitional social, sexual, and gender categories. When Yde (Ysabel) decides to cross-dress to escape her father's incestuous desires and plans, she introduces a "category crisis," thus exposing "a failure of definitional distinction."[22] By cross-dressing and leaving, Yde must put aside both her gender and her social standing as daughter of the king. Henceforth, she is often described as hungry. She associates with lower socioeconomic classes (thieves, in particular) and works as a servant for a German soldier. Cross-dressing is evidently located at the juncture of class and gender. As Yde transgresses against one set of boundaries (by adopting male garb), she transgresses against her socioeconomic class as well and thus "calls into question the inviolability of both."[23] She hence reconfigures social and sexual identities previously conceived of as stable and unchallengeable.

Yet these spaces that invite an interrogation of gender roles and of sociosexual identities end up being only a temporary interlude within the economy of the text, as the cross-dressed woman remains ultimately subordinated to traditional gender hierarchy and the upholding of heteronormativity (and social relations, as we will see).[24] Even though the Yde and Olive epic describes a same-sex union that is a disruption of the "normalcy" of heterosexual marriage[25] and despite the mental transgressive "residue" that the text may leave in the mind of the audience,[26] binary heterosexual relations are upheld and validated in the end.

The interpretation of the French text that I am proposing here is a result of a cross-cultural approach and a comparative intertextual analysis of the Arabic and French renditions of the same story. While it is indeed true that the French Yde and Olive story describes a subversive (homo)sexual relation and undermines the notion that heterosexuality is the only form of permissible textual sexual encounter, a cross-cultural reading further demonstrates the limitations of such a reading. For once juxtaposed to its Arabic model (which is examined in detail below), the French story appears under a much more normative light. By allowing us to ask new questions or to ask old questions in new ways, cross-cultural scholarship thus inevitably forces us to adjust our analysis of one cultural discourse taken singly. This is not to say that the French Yde and Olive is not a subversive text *within its own* literary and historical context or that cross-cultural research is equivalent to competitive cultural evaluation. Rather, cross-cultural research reveals the historical and ideological power structures that construct discursive representations of sexualities. It allows us to see the extent to which the French narrators had to modify their source text to make it suitable for their audience. It also gives us a glimpse of what else could have been there in the French text and how else sexuality and homosexuality could have been described. Ultimately, such an investigation is valuable for the insight it affords us into the medieval creative (and censoring) process more generally.

Returning to the French text and to its ultimately normative stance toward alternative sexuality (or more precisely, its *more* normative stance compared to the Arabic version of the story, as we see below), the greater normativity of the French Yde and Olive seems to be achieved through the heavy emphasis on religious concerns. Not surprisingly, religious sentiment is prevalent in the miracle play, but it is also already ubiquitous in the epic (which in itself may explain why the *Yde et Olive* epic would have been rewritten a century later as a miracle play; it already contained many of the miracle play's elements). Yde and Ysabel's most prominent characteristic is undoubtedly their steadfastness in the face of adversity and their firm religious attitude. Each time the female character faces an evil situation (the father's incestuous desires, the thieves, the war, even a marriage with another woman), mention is regularly made of her reli-

gious determination against all adversities. In the epic, we are
told how Yde behaves when she sees that she cannot escape the
same-sex marriage imposed on her:

Nostre Seignour a sovent reclamé:	She called often unto our Lord:
"Glorious Dix, qui mains en Trinité,	"Glorious God, who lives in Trinity,
De ceste lasse cor vous prengne pités,	Take pity on this weary heart [or body],
Cui il convient par force marïer."	Who has to marry by force."

(ll. 7105–8)[27]

At first reading, the adverb "par force" in line 7108 appears
to highlight the overall heterosexual paradigm that underlies the
entire epic: Yde is forced into this marriage, she is forced into an
alternative sexual relation, she is forced into actions she herself
decries. The narrator seems to insist on the fact that were she allowed to choose, Yde would *not* intentionally engage in the relationship that is about to be described. The epic maintains nevertheless an overall ambiguity over the status of lesbianism. In line
7107 above, the term "cor," meaning both heart *and* body, leads
the reader to question Yde's emotional stance. Is Yde really
forced into marriage with Olive as the adverb "par force" suggests? Or is she having erotic feelings towards her soon-to-be-
wedded wife and is seeking God's succor because she knows that
her body ("cor") might well follow her heart ("cor") and yield
to the erotic attraction?[28] The recourse to the religious motif in
the epic might therefore be interpreted as a means to highlight
rather than eliminate the subversive sexual element.[29] Let us not
forget that in medieval literature (both in the West and in Islam),
erotic expression occurs in the most spiritually charged discursive moments. Nevertheless, despite the ambiguity of the religious, the epic reverts to the normative. Yde's prayers always
lead her to the same conclusion—complete submission to God
and blind acceptance of his mysterious plans:

| J'espouserai la fille au couronné, | I will marry the daughter of the king. |
| Si face Dix de moi sa volenté | Let God accomplish his will with me |

(ll. 7128–29)

The faith placed in God by Yde and Ysabel seems to lead directly to direct divine intervention in their affairs and justifies their continuous appeal to him and thanksgiving. The final miracle, at the moment of the transsexual transformation, comes to be perceived as merely another divine intervention, expected by now in the narrative economy of the text (albeit more significant since it involves the actual crossing from one sex to the other). The concluding divine reward in both texts, in the form of the penis, annihilates any remaining thoughts about homoeroticism from the narrative, removes all possible gender ambiguity, and firmly establishes the definitive victory of heteronormativity.

But the upholding of heteronormativity in the French tradition in comparison to the Arabic version, which is discussed below,[30] is most evident in the details given (or rather withheld) at two key moments in the text—in the relation between the two women on their wedding night and at the moment of the sexual transformation at the end. I speak about these in turn.

In *Miracle de la fille d'un roy*, the interlacing of the erotic and the religious abruptly comes to an end on the wedding night, which resolutely splits both discourses and subordinates the sexual to the religious. After praying with Anne and after being reassured by St. Michael about the preservation of her honor (ll. 2472–85), Ysabel is only temporarily comforted. Distressed a few moments later, she turns to the Virgin Mary seeking guidance: "Doulce mére Dieu, que feray?" (Sweet mother of Jesus, what shall I do?) (l. 2562). In addition, as though to preclude any sexually jeopardizing encounter with her newly wedded wife and to avoid any potentially ambiguous and theologically compromising situation, Ysabel does not wait for fifteen days, as her homologue in the epic does, to reveal the truth of her sex but opts rather for immediate disclosure:

Dame, en vostre mercy
me met.

Lady, I place myself in your mercy.

Pour le confort que m'avez
fait,

For the comfort you showed me,

Vous vueil descouvrir tout
mon fait

I want to reveal you my entire story

Et ce pour quoy j'ay tel
annuy.

And the reason why I feel such trouble.

Sachiez conme vous femme
suy,

Know that I am a woman like you,

Fille de roy et de royne.

Daughter of a king and a queen.

. . .

. . .

Et pour moy garder de diffame

And in order to protect myself from dishonor

Ne me sui point monstrée fame,

I did not show myself as a woman,

Mais conme homme m'ay
maintenu,

But have dressed [acted, appeared] as a man,

Et Dieu m'a si bien soustenu

And God has helped me so much

Et donné de sa grace tant

And given me so much of his grace

Qu'en lieu n'ay esté combatant

That in no place have I fought

Don't je n'aye eu la victoire,

Where I was not successful.

Dont je ly rens loenge et gloire.

For this I give him thanks and glory.

Or savez conment il m'est,
dame,

Now you know what it is with me, lady,

Puis que je sui conme vous
femme

That I am a woman like you

Et que j'ai mamelles: tastez.

And that I have breasts: Feel them.

Pour Dieu mercy.

Have mercy on me, for God's sake.

(ll. 2581–609)

Here, again, gender and social class are linked, though they are now in an inverse relation to what we saw earlier. Ysabel's confession of her biological sex is intimately associated with the revelation of her high social status ("Sachiez conme vous femme suy / Fille de roy et de royne"). This double exposure eliminates all suspense from the play, as the heroine is shielded henceforth from any possible sexual or carnal temptation. At this moment and despite the preceding textual spaces devoted to cross-dressing, the text chooses the promotion of heteronormativity. Ysabel punctuates her entire confession with references to her infinite faith in God, her submission to his will, and her undeviating preoccupation with honor and reputation. Her proposition to her wife to touch her breasts ("mamelles") to ascertain the truth of the fact that her husband is in fact a woman (l. 2607) shifts the reader/viewer's attention from the visual to the tactile and highlights the deceptive nature of sight.[31] Gender as established by sight is revealed to be no longer *historia* but *fabula*, a lie, a discursive construction.

The move from seeing to touching in an attempt to reach some measure of "truth" and of gender stability is not taken up by the emperor's daughter. The proposition to touch the "mamelles" thus remains at the level of philosophical, intellectual subversion of gender construction. It is not permitted to become a potentially intimate moment between the spouses. The emperor's daughter's response is interesting in this respect:

De ce ne convient plus parler.	There is no need to speak further of this.
Or vous mettez hors de soussi,	Now put yourself at ease,
Car tout ce que m'avez dit cy	Because everything you have told me here
Je vous promet bien celeray,	I promise you to conceal,
Et tel honneur vous porteray	And I will show you such honor
Con doit faire a son mari femme.	As a woman must show her husband.

| En touz cas, ce vous jur par m'ame, | In all matters, I swear this upon my soul, |
| Ne ne vous aray ja mains chier. | Nor will I ever hold you less dear.[32] |

(ll. 2612–19)

Robert Clark has interpreted these lines as an endorsement of severely condemned forms of sexuality:[33] The emperor's daughter indicates that biological sex does not matter and that she is ready to uphold the sacrament of marriage despite the new information provided. I would argue instead that the emperor's daughter's response maintains the ideology of phallocentrism and heterosexuality.[34] The promise to continue to "honor" Ysabel as she would have, had Ysabel indeed been a man, maintains the emperor's daughter in a subordinate position not only in relation to biological masculinity but to any socially constructed or outward manifestation of masculinity.

In the Yde and Olive epic, however, one senses the narrator's struggle between conformity to religious and social norms and the titillating temptation to describe the sexual proximity (if not promiscuity) of two women in bed.[35] In the epic, the same-sex union is not devoid of sexual content. First, and despite her understandable distress, we are told that Yde begins by securely locking the door ("la cambre a bien veroullié et fermee," l. 7164). She then pretends to be ill and thus incapable of consummating their marriage that night. As Yde tells Olive of her sickness, she accompanies her words with hugs: "A ices mos fu Olive accolee" (With these words, Olive was hugged, l. 7171). The verb "accolee" (to hug) is repeated twice in that same scene; the next time, by Olive. It is Olive and not Yde who pleads to have their wedding consummation put off for fifteen days after all the guests have left, saying that she is looking forward to "doing more" later. For now, she will be satisfied with kisses and with being "accolee":

| Fors du basier bien voel estre accolee, | Besides kissing, I don't mind hugs, |

Mais de l'amour c'on dist qui est privee	But as to the love that is said to be intimate
Vous requier jou que soie deportee.	I request to be exempt from it.

(ll. 7185–88)

Yde happily agrees, and the narrator adds that the two women kiss and hug: "Dont ont l'un l'autre baisie et accolee" (They kissed and hugged each other, l. 7190). Although nothing in the epic specifies the kind of kiss or hug exchanged between the two women (sisterly, compassionate, respectful), the acts of "baisier" and "accoler" that are evoked nevertheless invite erotic and sexual readings that are entirely absent from the miracle play.[36] Diane Watt has gone so far as to suggest that these verbs may well denote sexual intercourse between the two characters.[37] Without going as far, it remains important to recognize the sexual connotations of these signifiers for, though limited and probably euphemistic, they appear to have disturbed some (medieval) scribes or readers. The next two lines of the epic are partly (purposely?) effaced and are supplied by other manuscript readings:

En cele nuit n'i [ot] cri ne mellee.	That night, there were no screams or fights.
La nu[i]s passa, si revint la journee.	The night ended, and the day shone.

(ll. 7191–92)

The silence that the text maintains over the details of the wedding night of the female couple speaks eloquently of the efforts made to keep the sexual and the titillating representation of lesbianism bracketed. The homoerotic is not entirely silenced, however, as seen with the repetition of "accolee."[38] The homoerotic is evident also in the demonstrative "*That* night" in the preceding quote, as though the narrator was pointing to the lack of violence of the lesbian wedding night in which there were no screams or fights, in contrast to the heterosexual wedding night in which there may have been screams and fights. The (possibly) (un)consummated lovemaking of Yde and Olive is highlighted finally in the use of battle metaphors ("cri ne mellee"). These metaphors are further evidence of the implicit sexual (military) language used to portray lesbian relations in the Middle Ages, as I have demonstrated elsewhere.[39] Moreover, when King Oton asks his daughter about her wedding night, Olive's answer is conveniently ambiguous:

"Fille," fait il, "comment iés marïee?"	"Daughter," he said, "How was your wedding night?"
"Sire," dist ele, "ensi com moi agree."	"Sire," she said, "the way it pleases me."

(ll. 7198–99)

Ultimately, Yde (just like Ysabel a century later) reveals her biological sex to Olive with apologies and prayers for mercy.[40] The affective transgressive dimension that had been present, however timidly, is henceforth banned altogether from the text. The text appropriates the cross-dresser as female and erases completely the "third term" that had been introduced earlier in the epic. This recuperative gesture is present in Olive's initial re-action to the revelation:

Olive l'ot, s'en fu espoëntee.	Olive listened, she was horrified.

(l. 7216)

Olive's distress has been greatly deemphasized by critics.[41] Yet it echoes the Deuteronomic injunction against transvestism (Deut. 22:5) and reveals social anxiety about the dissolution of boundaries. Yde's cross-dressing, which was threatening be-cause it blurred or obliterated legible gender distinctions, is henceforth annihilated by Olive's reaction. Olive's normative voice utterly silences the transgressive preceding section and sig-nals the return to sanctioned sexual and grammatical catego-ries.[42] As Jacqueline de Weever has noted, the grammatical gen-der instability that had been prevalent thus far in the text ceases at this point.[43] The restoration of the normative is heralded in the epic by the threat of capital punishment (ll. 7251–52), which under the *lex foedissimam* (edict of Roman law) of 1400 was indeed the classic penalty for lesbians.[44] It is accompanied by the appearance of an angel who reveals God's personal intervention in Yde's affairs and her timely sexual transformation into a man (ll. 7261–72) and (perhaps even more important) by the angel's announcement that Yde and Olive successfully conceive a son named Croissant on that very night: "Et en cel jour fu Croissans engenrés" (On this day, Croissant was conceived, l. 7283).

Yde receives a penis to reward her for her unswerving belief in God and her submission to his will, and it is a well functioning one too, we are reassured, as evident in the efficiency with which the conception of the child occurs. The angel's statement is not simply a premonition; it is a speech act. Revealing the miracle is accompanied by its accomplishment. Croissant's conception is all the more significant since it takes narrative precedence over any information the audience may have hoped for over Yde's successful sexual transformation. The transsexual miracle is far less amazing than it may appear at first sight, however, for according to Western Galenic medical theories, it was believed that women's sexual organs were identical to men's, except they were inverted (the vagina was thought to be an inverted penis).[45] However, from the perspective of the audience of the epic or drama, most of whom were probably *not* familiar with premodern theories of medicine, it can be argued that an explicit depiction of the transsexual transformation was expected.

Such a description, in contrast to its Ovidian textual precursor,[46] is absent from all the stories that have preserved the Yde and Olive tale. We do not see the growth of the penis on Yde's body, and this is unexpected in the narrative economy of the epic, where the narrator had not shied away from elaborately describing Yde's female body (ll. 6503–21). We do not hear Yde's reaction to the unexpected "gift" of the penis. Is she shocked? Relieved? Surprised at least? Did she even want to be a man? The question of gender identity is subsumed under that of sex. It is unproblematized as though it did not matter or as if it was expected that Yde would have wanted to be a man if given a choice. After all, according to the theological and scientific teachings of the time, if given a choice, any woman would have wanted to be a man. In *Yde et Olive,* perhaps precisely because it is an epic and thus concerned primarily with the question of lineage and foregrounding issues of marriage and procreation, there is a lingering presumption that male is better, that to wish to be a man (however inexplicitly or unconsciously since Yde never verbalizes such a longing) is perfectly "normal" and, culturally speaking, perfectly logical. These assumptions undermine whatever disruption of and challenge to easy notions of binarism that transvestism may have invited at first reading. Underlying this assumption of male supremacy, women are made into scapegoats.

The challenge or threat posed by cross-dressing is henceforth contained, as the epic moves unproblematically to the continuation of the Huon de Bordeaux family line. Diane Watt points out the advantages of such a narrative resolution in the context of an epic and for the male characters. In effect, such a resolution "provides not just Oton but also Florent [Yde's father] with a direct male descendant and thus enables the transmission of their property according to the rules of patrilineage."[47] For the female characters, however, gender construction and the possibility of alternative sexualities are stigmatized. The symbolic function of "transvestism *as* a powerful agent of destabilization and change, the sign of the *un*groundedness of identities on which social structures and hierarchies depend," is conveniently set aside and subordinated to genealogy and social heteronormativity.[48]

Finally, the narrative construction of the epic embeds the story of Croissant within two stories dealing with *Yde et Olive* (known as *Yde et Olive I* and *Yde et Olive II*). This choice of ending the first part of *Yde et Olive* precisely at the moment of the sexual transformation and returning to that story only about 400 hundred lines later is significant because it points to the narrator's effort to divert the audience's attention from sexuality to social normativity and sexual legitimacy. Just as narrative moves swiftly over the momentarily erotic behavior of the newlyweds, immediately following Yde's successful and rewarding sexual transformation the reader's attention is displaced from this sexual transformation to lineage and the successful continuation of the Huon de Bordeaux family line. The very space that could have been used by the audience to imagine the specifics of the sexual transformation (the erotic encounter between Olive and the now officially transsexual Yde) is replaced by a story that emphasizes family lineage and thus heteronormativity. And yet one could have easily imagined a narrative that binds the two sections of the Yde and Olive stories before turning to their son. This order would have probably been more expected in the context of an epic cycle where narrative development is typically chronological and historically linear. During the Croissant episode, the transsexual Yde disappears from the text and to some extent perhaps also from the reader's mind, and she remains invisible until her lineage has been firmly established. In fact, when Yde returns in *Yde et Olive II*, she has now fathered four sons and three daughters.[49] The displacement from the axis of sex and gender to that of lineage and social continuity reflects an anxiety over genealogy, fatherhood, and patriarchy. At the end of the epic, one fully measures the extent to which transvestism has been only a temporary interlude within the economy of the text and the extent to which questions about gender ambiguity have been displaced onto a sociopolitical axis.

In the miracle play, the reestablishment of the heterosexual status quo is manifested in the final double marriage that ends the play: Ysabel marries the emperor of Constantinople, while the emperor's daughter marries Ysabel's father. More than ever, it becomes evident that the erasure of gender and sociocultural distinctions that initiated the play was temporary. At the end, the audience returns to the safety of the religiously sanctioned happy heterosexual union.[50] The end of the miracle play supports Michelle Szkilnik's theory that by the end of the fourteenth century, transsexual transformation is no longer allowed to remain permanent. All possible gender ambiguity is effaced both from the textual remains and the audience's imagination.

YDE AND OLIVE AND THE MATTER OF ARABY

The extent of heteronormativity in the medieval French texts can be fully apprehended in comparison to the Arabic literary tradition on cross-dressing and female same-sex marriage. The comparative cross-cultural approach allows us to grasp nuances in each text that remain hidden when one cultural discourse is examined alone or is divorced from its multicultural context. While it has been impossible to date to trace the precise Arabic literary genealogy of *Yde et Olive*,[51] it appears undeniable that the "author" of the French epic was familiar with the Arabic tradition on homosexuality, as well as with a great number of the stories contained in *The Thousand and One Nights* (also known as *Arabian Nights*). The entire *Huon de Bordeaux* cycle seems heavily indebted to the Arabic storytelling tradition of *The Thousand and One Nights,* which was known in the West at least as early as the first quarter of the twelfth century with Petrus Alfonsi's *Disciplina Clericalis* (1120s). Francesca Canadé Sautman has observed that the place and people names and the geographic location of the epic all point to a southern (therefore Arabic or Islamicate) influence. She writes that "many clusters around the same-sex change are centered in Spain and Italy, which is consonant with the mention of Aragon, Castille, and Barcelona in *Yde and Olive* and the use of the Southern name Olive."[52]

The names of the main characters in the French Yde and Olive weave an intertext with the tales of *Arabian Nights,* and the presence of this intertext suggests a narrative and geographical proximity and invites a comparative reading of these two textual traditions.[53] Let us begin by examining the name of Yde and Olive's first son, Croissant, whose story had interrupted the epic at the moment of the sexual transformation as we saw earlier.

The first name Croissant (meaning "moon crescent") is unusual in French[54] but is quite common in Arabic and can be found with great regularity throughout the Arabic literary tradition. In *The Thousand and One Nights*, "Moon" (with its multiple synonyms and variations) is an androgynous name and is given with equal frequency to male and female characters. In the famous story that begins on the 170th night, "Story of Qamar al-Zaman and the Princess Budur"[55] (which is the story best known for its depiction of lesbianism and which I discuss in detail below), both heroes' names evoke the moon: Qamar al-Zaman means "the moon of the century," and Budur means "the moon of moons." This androgynous semantic field associated with the moon is again present in the tenth-century *Encyclopedia of Pleasure* written by Ibn Nasr al-Katib, which is one of the earliest erotic treatises in Arabic. This text goes one step further and compares the vulva to a full moon.[56] It may thus be possible to argue that in Arabic literature, the name Moon was used at times as a symbolic code word for (homo)eroticism or at least for androgyny. The choice in the French epic of naming Yde and Olive's son Croissant becomes significant.[57]

A second important intertext between the French and Arabic tales is the name of the female character Olive. Once again, the name Olive is unusual in French literary history. In the Arabic tale, even though we do not encounter the name of Olive per se, the title characters are reunited at the end through a scene that involves the sale of olives. The reference to olives/Olive in these texts may not be coincidental and may be associated with cross-dressing and androgyny more generally.

A third and final example of intertextual resonances between the two traditions is that of the name Yde, which is also highly unusual in the French medieval literary tradition. It is evocative of the name of the first lesbian known to the Arabs, according to Ibn Nasr al-Katib's *Encyclopedia of Pleasure*—Hind Bint al-Khuss al-Iyyadiyya.[58] The name Iyyadiyya (the final two syllables "iyya" represent a diminutive suffix in Arabic) could have become Yde in French. Taken separately, each of these three

name parallels discussed here (Croissant, Olive, and Yde) cannot be considered conclusive evidence of direct links between
Yde and Olive and the tale of Qamar al-Zaman and Princess
Budur. However, taken together, the selection of these Arabic
names by the French narrators point to an Arabic literary or cultural model and justify our comparative reading of the stories
and of the representation of gender fluidity therein.

The story of Qamar al-Zaman and the Princess Budur constitutes one of the main heretofore unacknowledged models of the
French Yde and Olive tales. Rather than examining the textual
parallels, I focus on the great differences in attitudes toward homosexuality, cross-dressing, and female same-sex marriage that
separate the medieval French and Arabic literary traditions. I begin by summarizing the second part of the Arabic tale—that is,
the section that deals directly with the topics of interest here,
cross-dressing and same-sex marriage. After a great resistance to
marriage, Qamar al-Zaman and Budur eventually do marry
through the intervention of magic and the active participation of
jinns. But once married, they are separated again. To find her
husband and to protect herself, Budur cross-dresses as a man
and because of her great resemblance to her lost husband, takes
on his name, Qamar al-Zaman. She arrives at the Isle of Ebony,
where King Armanos abdicates in her favor and forces her to
marry his daughter, "the most virgin of the island," named
Hayat al-Nufus or the Life of Souls. Qamar al-Zaman is finally
discovered through a scene that involves olives. Budur reveals
the truth to King Armanos, and all ends seemingly in the most
heteronormative and polygamous way: Budur is reunited with
Qamar al-Zaman, abdicates in his favor, and in addition gives
him Hayat al-Nufus as a second wife. And the three of them live
happily ever after.

In contrast to the function of cross-dressing in the French narratives of Yde and Olive, cross-dressing in *Alf layla wa layla*
(The Thousand and One Nights) does not introduce a "category
crisis." In fact, even after she adopts male clothing and her husband's name, Budur continues to occupy the same social posi-

tion as she did earlier in the tale—that of the offspring of a king. The stability in Budur's social identity means that this character will not need to prove herself to be a worthy knight or accomplish extraordinary military deeds to recover a social standing lost to cross-dressing, as Yde does. It also means that cross-dressing in *The Story of Qamar al-Zaman and the Princess Budur* is not a transgressive social act, as it will become in the process of translation into French. Rather, in the Arabic text, cross-dressing functions as a key narrative strategy that permits the storyteller to focus directly and explicitly on the erotic, if not sexual, ambiguities that encounters with a cross-dressed heroine necessarily elicit.

THE WEDDING NIGHT IN *THE STORY OF QAMAR AL-ZAMAN AND THE PRINCESS BUDUR*

In contrast to the French miracle play (in which Ysabel reveals her true sex to her wife immediately to avoid any sexually jeopardizing encounter) and to the French verse epic (where the wedding night is spent feigning illness to avoid lesbian sex between Yde and Olive), the Arabic tale focuses from the outset on the two young women's sexual relation. This is how their wedding night is depicted:

> They [the servants] made Hayat al-Nufus enter into the room where Budur, daughter of king Ghouyour, was [sitting], and they closed the door on them. They lit candles and lights for them and spread their bed with silk [sheets]. Budur entered into Hayat al-Nufus.[59]

The explicitness of the sexual encounter between the two girls is not evident in the English translation, for it rests on the use of the Arabic verb "dakhala" (to enter) twice in the above quote, first with the preposition "'ala" ("they made Hayat al-Nufus enter into the room where Budur was") and then with the preposition "ila" ("Budur entered into Hayat al-Nufus"). What must first be noted is the fact that the verb "dakhala" (to enter, to penetrate) does not require the use of any preposition. The fact that the redactor chose to add not one but two different prepositions for this verb must make us pause.[60] In its first occurrence with the preposition "'ala," the audience is led to understand that Budur is already present in the room into which Hayat al-Nufus enters. The second use of the verb "dakhala" with "ila" comes therefore as a surprise since such a combination can only mean (1) to penetrate into a physical space or (2) to penetrate sexually (to have intercourse). In the context of this scene, only the second meaning of "dakhala ila" is possible, leading us to conclude that Budur and Hayat al-Nufus's initial encounter is utterly sexual.

While the redactor of the fourteenth-century Syrian manuscript of _Alf layla wa layla_ does not further depict the lesbian wedding night, the power of such nondescription ought not be overlooked. For it is indeed in its very "indescribability" that the impact of lesbian sexuality and "its availability for cultural inscription and appropriation" resides.[61] In the oral performance of the tale of _Qamar al-Zaman and the Princess Budur,_ the sexual encounter between Hayat al-Nufus and Budur is likely to have been one of those key moments that would have invited further elaboration by the storyteller or, at the very least, stirred the imagination of the audience.[62] In contrast to the destiny of Yde and Olive's sexuality in the French thirteenth-century epic (which will be effaced by scribes or readers, as we saw earlier), Budur and Hayat al-Nufus's sexual relation will be expanded and amplified throughout the following centuries, leading to the detailed portrayal of lesbianism in Burton's English (1885–1888) and Mardrus's French (1899–1904) translations.[63]

After their initial overt sexual encounter, Budur and Hayat al-Nufus spend the next two nights "kissing" and "caressing." This is how the redactor of the fourteenth-century Syrian manuscript depicts their intimacy: "Budur sat down next to Hayat al-Nufus and kissed her."[64] On the following night, the redactor writes: "When [Budur] saw Hayat al-Nufus sitting, she sat beside her, caressed her and kissed her between the eyes."[65]

The words "hugging" and "kissing" used in the Arabic tale certainly evoke the way Yde and Olive's encounter had been depicted by the Old French narrator of the verse epic as discussed earlier. The meaning of these terms differs from their French counterparts, however, in that, in the Arabic erotic tradition, "kissing" and "hugging" have a specific and overtly sexual connotation. This is how "kissing" is defined in the *Encyclopedia of Pleasure:*

> Kissing is a means by which sexual desire is aroused. . . . Kissing becomes more effective when it is accompanied by biting, pinching, sucking, sighing, and hugging. It is then that both the man and the woman burn with sexual desire simultaneously. . . . Kissing is the penis's messenger to the vulva. It is also said that kissing is an essential part of sexual union. . . . [K]issing, like lubrication, facilitates sexual union. . . . Coition without kissing is imperfect.[66]

Not only is kissing a metaphor for sexual union, but the placement of the kiss is also important to consider. Though uncommon in the Western tradition, the placement of the kiss on or between the eyes is recommended specifically in the Arabic erotic tradition as a strategy to speed up a woman's orgasm.[67] Budur's kiss between Hayat al-Nufus's eyes should thus be interpreted as an unambiguous reference to their foreplay, sexual relation, perhaps even orgasm. We are hence permitted to conclude that while the Arabic and French texts under consideration use the same semantic field and linguistic terms (kissing, hugging) to portray female same-sex relations, the Arabic text is anchored in a sociocultural context where such conduct holds a precise sexual connotation. In this light, Budur and Hayat al-Nufus's kisses, much more clearly than those between Yde and Olive, are to be interpreted as foreplay or sexual intimacy, if not intercourse.

On the third night, Budur reveals her biological sex to her wedded wife. This scene is important because it represents the moment at which the French Yde and Olive narratives differ markedly from the Arabic tale. An investigation of the key differences between the two traditions reveals the extent to which medieval French narrators silenced some of the most daring homosexual features of the Arabic tale. It also exhibits the divergent attitudes held by each of these traditions toward female homosexuality.

An apologetic or repenting cross-dresser does not make Budur's revelation, as was the case with Yde/Ide in the French epic. It takes place instead in the midst of an erotic and sexually charged scene. This is how the scene is depicted in Mahdi's edition:

> [Budur] spoke [to Hayat al-Nufus] in a soft, feminine voice, and this was her true, natural voice, and she unveiled the truth about her situation. . . . She told her what had happened to her and her beloved husband Qamar al-Zaman, and she showed her vulva and said to her [I am] a woman who has vulva and breasts.[68]

While in the *Miracle de la fille d'un roy* Ysabel suggests that her wife touch her "mamelles" ("breasts") as proof that she is indeed a woman, the Arabic text goes further in the proofs that Budur is willing to give. Budur does not simply *offer* to show her female sexual characteristics; she actually *shows* them. She does not just show her breasts; she also uncovers her vulva. In fact, she exhibits that first. The unveiling of Budur's private parts is repeated twice in this scene, as though the redactor wished to highlight the sexual moment, as well as to encourage the audience's imagination concerning the implications of such a sexual exposition. As the text remains silent over Hayat al-Nufus's response to Budur's stripping, the reader is permitted to conclude that she may not have been displeased by what she saw. Staging a female character that willingly (and in titillation) uncovers her vulva and breasts thus becomes another step in the process of deepening the intimate contact between the two female spouses.

While in *Yde et Olive,* the revelation was overheard and rapidly divulged to the king, in the Arabic tale, Budur's secret remains for the greater part of the tale known only to Hayat al-

Nufus. The limited disclosure of Budur's biological sex allows the sexual transgression by the two women to continue undisturbed. In fact, the greater permissiveness of the Arabic text (in comparison to the French narratives) toward lesbianism becomes even more pronounced in the scenes that *follow,* rather than precede, Budur's revelation of her biological sex. Whereas in the Yde and Olive epics, the confession became the space of panic and the beginning of the return to heteronormativity, in the Arabic story, it is not accompanied by any anxiety about cross-dressing or about the lesbian sexuality that had taken place. There is no anxiety either about the necessity of maintaining visible, legible gender distinctions or enforcing social hierarchy. There is no divinely ordained injunction against lesbianism to worry about, no impending capital punishment, and (as we will see) no divine intervention to reestablish order in what must have appeared as sociocultural and moral chaos to the medieval West.

In fact, in the Arabic tale, Budur's revelation gives rise to an alternative female space in which both women become equal and hence enjoy mutual support and reciprocal intimacy. Budur's revelation is met with mere surprise on the part of Hayat al-Nufus, not with "panic" or "pain": Hayat al-Nufus is "surprised at her story," writes the redactor of the tale.[69] More important, perhaps, the revelation of Budur's womanhood is also met with pleasure: Hayat al-Nufus "was pleased with the news" (595). The fact that Budur is a woman and not a man puts Hayat al-Nufus more at ease. The presence of the cross-dresser in the Arabic text does not heighten anxiety, as it did in the French tradition, but opens up a space for dialogue between the two girls and ultimately increases their intimacy and pleasure. Immediately following the news about Budur's biological sex, the redactor writes that both women "spoke together, played together, laughed together, and slept [together?]" (595). We must note here the grammatical construction of the Arabic verbs used in this description. For the first time in the homoerotic interlude of this tale, the redactor uses the reflexive form to express Budur and Hayat al-Nufus's sexual play, laughter, conversation, and overall pleasure in each other's company. It is as though while Budur performed a male role, the redactor was compelled to depict her in the conventionally male active position of kissing and caressing Hayat al-Nufus. After Budur's revelation, however, Hayat al-Nufus becomes an equal partner in the relationship, both active giver and passive recipient of the same-sex intimacy. Some might argue that the fact that Budur's biological sex must remain a secret to everyone but Hayat al-Nufus and the reader indicates that medieval Arab Islamicate society, just like French culture, did not condone lesbianism. If this is true at a social and legal level, it is not necessarily so at a narrative and literary level. To the reader or listener, especially to the medieval lesbian in the audience, this tale must have provided a validation (albeit an imaginative one) for a way of life that differed radically from socially sanctioned sexual encounters.

Not only is Budur and Hayat al-Nufus's intimacy highlighted *after* Budur's revelation of her biological sex, but their marriage is finally consummated. Of course, it is not consummated in a heterosexual mode but rather by destabilizing the association of heterosexual marriage with virginal blood. As a matter of fact, Hayat al-Nufus, to assuage her father's mounting concern over her prolonged virginity, stages her own defloration. She kills a chicken and spreads its blood over her own thighs and handkerchief. She also screams, repeating thereby the expected association of heterosexuality with violence and pain:

> Hayat al-Nufus woke up before the morning call to prayer. She took a chicken, took off her pants, screamed after killing it and spreading its blood over herself and her handkerchief. She then hid the chicken, put her pants back on and called. So her family entered the room. (596)

As Hayat al-Nufus expected, the stained handkerchief is taken by King Armanos and his wife (and society at large) to be definitive proof of the consummation of their daughter's marriage. The proud parents rush to exhibit the bloody cloth, without worrying about the provenance of the blood. Ironically, the very moment that the two lovers are portrayed as maintaining heteronormativity is also the very space where binary sexual relations are exposed and where the very notion of stable identities is challenged. Judith Butler's analysis of homosexual marriage is particularly pertinent to this discussion:

> The replication of this heterosexual tradition in a non-heterosexual context brings into relief the utterly constructed status of the so-called heterosexual original. Thus, gay is to straight *not* as copy is to original, but rather, as copy is to copy. The parodic repetition of "the original," . . . reveals the original to be nothing other than a parody of the *idea* of the natural and the original.[70]

In the Arabic tale, the exhibition of the bloody cloth in the context of a homosexual marriage reveals that heterosexuality is critiqued, denaturalized, animalized. After all, marriage is legitimized here not by the virginal blood of a bride but by that of a lowly farm animal, the chicken. Meanwhile, Budur and Hayat al-Nufus are allowed to continue their intimate life together, inadvertently blessed this time by the entire social system.

THE END OF THE STORY: HOMOSEXUALITY WITHIN HETEROSEXUALITY

In fact, nothing disturbs the lesbian relation—neither Hayat al-Nufus's sexual maturity nor Budur's revelation of her biological sex to her partner and to the reader. Whereas in the French epic, the revelation of Yde's sex is closely followed by the threat of capital punishment and by the divine miracle (the transsexual transformation), in the Arabic tale, the revelation contributes to the development of the intimate relationship between the two women. Each night thereafter, Budur and Hayat al-Nufus live in the same bliss, tending to their emotional, intimate relationship, while awaiting the eventual return of Qamar al-Zaman:

> At night, [Budur] penetrated into Hayat al-Nufus. They spoke to each other and she told her about her worry and her love for Qamar al-Zaman.[71]

In this quote, the verb "dakhala" (to enter, to penetrate) is used again with the preposition "ila" that was discussed earlier, hence emphasizing the endurance of the sexual encounter between the two women, even after the revelation of Budur's biological sex. Even though the lesbian relationship is presented here as an ersatz for heterosexual relations (the two women's intimacy occurs seemingly only *because* they are waiting for Qamar al-Zaman's return), it seems clear nevertheless that a space is opened up for alternative emotional, if not sexual, satisfaction. In the Arabic tale, lesbianism is allowed to exist—is fostered, even—within a frame of heterosexuality, whereas in the French texts examined earlier lesbianism is placed at the other extreme of heterosexuality.

Only when Budur recognizes Qamar al-Zaman as the vendor of olives does the lesbian sexual relation come to a halt. At first reading, the end of the Arabic tale may be seen as a return not only to the androcentric model of marriage (Qamar al-Zaman and Budur are reunited) but also, and in keeping with the cultural background of *The Thousand and One Nights,* to polygamy: Hayat al-Nufus is given as second wife to Qamar al-Zaman. Moreover, the end of the text seems to herald the triumph of patriarchy since, once reunited with her husband, Budur abdicates in favor of the "true" man of the story, Qamar al-Zaman. The ultimate triumph of patriarchy is further manifested in the fact that Hayat al-Nufus is never consulted about becoming a second wife. However, once again, heterosexuality in the Arabic text is only a temporary interlude as lesbianism is never conveniently bracketed or completely and utterly contained and silenced. When King Armanos asks Qamar al-Zaman to marry his daughter, Hayat al-Nufus, Budur is the one who answers, and this is what she says:

> So Budur replied: By God, for me like for her; a night for me and a night for her. And I will live together with her in one house because I have gotten used to her [literally, I have returned to her repeatedly].[72]

On the surface, these lines suggest that Budur generously accepts the sharing of her husband with Hayat al-Nufus, but they also hint that the women's relationship is far from coming to a halt at the end of the tale. Even as she adheres to the basic legal principles of polygamy ("one night for me and one night for her"), Budur introduces an important departure from its conventions when she states her desire to live in the same house as Hayat al-Nufus. Her use of the verb "ta'awwadtu" (which means both "to get used to" and "to return repeatedly to") reveals that the main reason for refusing the common practice of the separation of households may well be her desire to continue "returning repeatedly to Hayat al-Nufus." Budur's desire to continue sharing Hayat al-Nufus's house thus has significant implications for their same-sex relations. Not surprisingly, the survival of the lesbian relationship beyond the polygamous ending is the way Mardrus (the celebrated nineteenth-century French translator of *Alf layla wa layla*) will render the end of *The Story of Qamar al-Zaman and the Princess Budur*:

> Qamar al-Zaman governed his kingdom as perfectly as he contented his two wives, with whom he passed alternate evenings. Budur and Hayat lived together in harmony, allowing the nights to their husband, but reserving the days for each other.[73]

Mardrus here explicitly restates what was depicted implicitly in the fourteenth-century Syrian manuscript that Mahdi edited. We must not disregard his translation out of hand, claiming that it merely constitutes nineteenth-century Orientalist presuppositions and in no way reflects medieval possibilities.[74] Such an end is consistent with the double meaning of "ta'awwadtu" in the

Syrian manuscript and resonates strongly with medieval Arabic erotic treatises that consider lesbianism as one of many sexual practices. The Arabic *Story of Qamar al-Zaman and the Princess Budur,* in contrast to the French narratives of Yde and Olive, thus permits the survival of Budur and Hayat al-Nufus's relationship, even as it places it within the parameters of heterosexuality and polygamy.[75] Whereas the French epic recuperates the cross-dressed Yde and silences the transgressive voice of the "third term," the Arabic tale does not interrupt the workings of this "third term" and allows a move toward a new structure where heterosexuality is viewed as only one possibility in a larger chain. The Arabic text thus, until the very end, permits border crossings and reveals a complete and utter failure of definitional distinctions. One may say that while her French sister, because of her transsexual transformation, is forced ultimately to embrace heterosexuality, the Arabic lesbian, despite her heterosexual and polygamous marriage, is allowed to maintain her commitment and faithfulness to her female partner.

NOTES

1. Judith Butler, *Gender Trouble: Feminism and the Subversion of Identity* (New York: Routledge, 1990), 110.
2. Jacqueline Murray, "Twice Marginal and Twice Invisible," in *The Handbook of Medieval Sexuality,* ed. Vern L. Bullough and James Brundage (New York: Garland, 1996), 191–222. For premodern Europe, my use of the word *lesbian* is not the same as what is often implied by it today but is an emotional and sexual attachment between two women. It does not include the dimensions of political activism or engagement with which the modern notions of lesbianism and homosexuality are often connected, nor is it associated with the politics of gender identity.
3. Ibid., 191.
4. The term *Islamicate,* which I use throughout this article, was coined by Marshall G. S. Hodgson, who defines it thus: "'Islamicate' would refer not directly to the religion, Islam, itself, but to the social and cultural complex historically associated with Islam

and the Muslims, both among Muslims themselves and even when found among non-Muslims." See Marshall G. S. Hodgson, *The Venture of Islam: Conscience and History in a World Civilization* (Chicago: University of Chicago Press, 1974), 1:59. The advantage of this term is that it highlights social and cultural dimensions over religious dimensions. For reasons of variety, I also use other terms *(Arab, East, Orient, Middle East),* even though I recognize the anachronism, limitations, and problems associated with each of these words. The same limitations apply to my use of the terms *West, medieval France,* or *medieval Europe.*

5. Steven F. Kruger, "Conversion and Medieval Sexual, Religious, and Racial Categories," in Karma Lochrie, Peggy McCracken, and James A. Schultz, eds., *Constructing Medieval Sexuality* (Minneapolis: Minnesota University Press, 1997), 159.

6. Dominique Fisher and Lawrence Schehr, eds., *Articulations of Difference: Gender Studies and Writing in French* (Stanford: Stanford University Press, 1997). See also Martine Antle and Dominique Fisher, eds., *The Rhetoric of the Other: Lesbian and Gay Strategies of Resistance in French and Francophone Contexts* (New Orleans: University Press of the South, 2002).

7. Mireille Rosello, "The National-Sexual: From the Fear of Ghettos to the Banalization of Queer Practices," in Fisher and Schehr, *Articulations of Difference,* 246–47.

8. This colonialist move has been aptly analyzed by Chandra Mohanty, in the context of Western feminists' "colonization" of third-world women. See her "Under Western Eyes: Feminist Scholarship and Colonial Discourses," *Feminist Review* 30 (Autumn 1988): 61–88. This paper extends many of Mohanty's conclusions on Western feminist and hegemonic discourses on "third-world women" to the particular case of medieval Arabic lesbianism and its reception by Western scholars.

9. The interconnections between knowledge and power and the political implications of the construction of truth and of disciplines have been analyzed by critics such as Michel Foucault, Edward Said, and Anouar Abdel Malek.

10. On the explicitness of the Arabic tradition, see my "Lesbian Sex and the Military: From the Arabic Tradition to French Literature," in *Same Sex Love and Desire among Women in the Middle Ages,* ed. Francesca Canadé Sautman and Pamela Sheingorn (New York:

Palgrave, 2001), 179–98. Similarly, in this chapter, I am interested only in explicit descriptions of lesbian sexual behavior, as opposed to what Judith Bennett has dubbed "lesbian-like"—that is, the proposition to study the social history of the lesbian in the Middle Ages by considering the lesbian as a larger category that would include all single women. See Judith M. Bennett, "'Lesbian-Like' and the Social History of Lesbianisms," *Journal of the History of Sexuality* 9, nos. 1–2 (2000): 1–24.

11. Michèle Perret, "Travesties et transsexuelles: Yde, Silence, Grisandole, Blanchandine," *Romance Notes* 25, no. 3 (1985): 328.

12. In Christianity, female cross-dressers (saints, real-life or fictional characters) were viewed more positively than one might assume because such women thus demonstrated their desire to become men and attain a higher level of being. For a useful overview of cross-dressing, see Vern L. Bullough's chapter, "Cross Dressing and Gender Role Change in the Middle Ages," in *Handbook of Medieval Sexuality,* ed. Vern L. Bullough and James A. Brundage (New York: Garland, 1996), 223–42. For cross-dressing in hagiography, see John Anson, "The Female Transvestite in Early Monasticism," *Viator* 5, no. 1 (1974): 1–32.

13. On cross-dressing in medieval French literature, see Michelle Szkilnik's "The Grammar of the Sexes in Medieval French Romance," in *Gender Transgressions: Crossing the Normative Barrier in Old French Literature,* ed. Karen J. Taylor (New York: Garland, 1998), 61–88. See also Valerie Hotchkiss, *Clothes Make the Man: Female Cross-Dressing in Medieval France* (New York: Garland, 1996), and Simon Gaunt, *Gender and Genre in Medieval French Literature* (Cambridge: Cambridge University Press, 1995).

14. Cf. M. C. Lyons, *The Arabic Epic: Heroic and Oral Story-Telling,* 3 vols. (Cambridge: Cambridge University Press, 1995). For an overview of women warriors in the Arabic tradition, see Driss Cherkaoui, *Le Roman de 'Antar: Perspective littéraire et historique* (Paris: Présence Africaine, 2000).

15. This romance is found in one single Turin manuscript and includes the five *chansons* that make up the cycle: *La Chanson d'Esclarmonde, La Chanson de Clariet et Florent, La Chanson d'Yde et Olive, La Chanson de Croissant,* and *La Chanson de Godin.*

16. *Les Miracles de Nostre Dame par personnages* is a collection of

forty plays that were performed on a yearly basis in Paris from 1339 to 1382 (except in the years of the urban insurrections of 1350s) by the Parisian goldsmiths' guild. They are preserved in only one luxury manuscript (Paris, BN, fr. 819–820) and have been edited by Gaston Paris and Ulysse Robert (Paris: Firmin et Didot, 1876). *Miracle de la fille d'un roy* is in volume 7, pp. 2–117.

17. The French prose text of *Yde et Olive* was translated into English prose in the first half of the sixteenth century by Sir John Bourchier (Lord Berners) and entitled *The Boke of Duke Huon of Burdeux.* This text was reprinted in 1570 and again in 1601. It was edited by S. L. Lee in 1882 to 1884 (London: N. Trübner) and reissued (New York: Kraus Reprint) in 1975 and 1981. Two additional French texts associate cross-dressing with female same-sex marriage—the mid-fourteenth-century story of Blanchandine developed in the epic of *Tristan de Nanteuil* and the story of Iphis in the fifteenth-century adaptation of Ovid (namely, the *Ovide Moralisé*).

18. On the relation between the incest motif and later lesbian episode, see Diane Watt, "Read My Lips: Clippying and Kyssyng in the Early Sixteenth Century," in *Queerly Phrased: Language, Gender and Sexuality,* ed. Anna Livia and Kira Hall (New York: Oxford University Press, 1997), 167–77. On incest in the Middle Ages, see Elizabeth Archibald, *Incest and the Medieval Imagination* (London: Oxford University Press, 2001).

19. Diane Watt, "Behaving Like a Man? Incest, Lesbian Desire, and Gender Play in *Yde et Olive,*" *Comparative Literature* 50, no. 4 (1998): 265–85; Watt, "Read My Lips"; Jacqueline de Weever, "The Lady, the Knight, and the Lover: Androgyny and Integration in *La Chanson d'Yde et Olive,*" *Romantic Review* 81, no. 4 (1991): 371–91; Nancy Vine Durling, "Rewriting Gender: *Yde et Olive* and Ovidian Myth," *Romance Languages Annual* 1 (1989): 256–62; Robert L. A. Clark, "A Heroine's Sexual Itinerary: Incest, Transvestism, and Same-Sex Marriage in *Yde et Olive,*" in *Gender Transgressions: Crossing the Normative Barrier in Old French Literature,* ed. Karen J. Taylor (New York: Garland, 1998), 889–905.

20. Marjorie Garber, *Vested Interests: Cross-Dressing and Cultural Anxiety* (New York: Routledge, 1992), 11.

21. This is the main point of Watt's important article "Behaving Like a Man?" My approach differs from hers.

22. Garber, *Vested Interests,* 16.

23. Ibid., 32.

24. This is Perret's conclusion as well.

25. Judith Butler writes, "The replication of heterosexual constructs in non-heterosexual frames brings into relief the utterly constructed status of the so-called heterosexual original," in *Gender Trouble: Feminism and the Subversion of Identity* (New York: Routledge, 1990), 31.

26. This is Robert L. A. Clark and Claire Sponsler's conclusion in "Queer Play: The Cultural Work of Crossdressing in Medieval Drama," *New Literary History* 28, no. 2 (1997), 341. It is also Watt's overall conclusion in both articles cited above.

27. All citations of the verse epic *Yde and Olive* are from the latest edition of the text, Barbara Anne Brewska's "*Esclarmonde, Clarisse et Florent, Yde et Olive I, Croissant, Yde et Olive II, Huon et les Geants*, Sequels to *Huon de* Bordeaux," PhD dissertation, Vanderbilt, 1977. All translations are mine. An earlier edition of this text is that of Max Schweigel, *Esclarmonde, Clarisse et Florent, Yde et Olive: Dreifortsetsungen der Chansun von Huon de Bordeaux, nach der einzigen Turiner Handschrift* (Marburg: Elwert, 1889).

28. Watt's reading is more resolutely on the side of reciprocal erotic feelings between Yde and Olive. While I agree with the fact that this text develops female homoeroticism, my reading of the French story, informed by the comparative reading that is presented below, strongly "curtails the subversive possibilities of the story" (Watt, "Read My Lips," 173).

29. None of the critics who have analyzed the Yde and Olive stories address the religious emphasis in the texts.

30. Again, I am not arguing for the absence of gender transgression in the French texts. Rather, I seek to qualify the *extent* of the transgressive element through cross-cultural research.

31. The deceptive nature of sight has by the thirteenth century become a *topos* in medieval literature. This *topos* was a logical development from the famous opposition between *historia* (sight, truth) and *fabula* (language, lie) developed by Cicero and popularized by Macrobius, Isidore of Seville, William of Conches, Bernardus Silvestris, Peter Abelard, and Alan of Lille, among many others.

32. Clark and Sponsler, "Queer Play," 325 (translation by Clark).

33. Clark and Sponsler, "Queer Play," 326.

34. The normativity of the French miracle play becomes more evident when compared both to the French epic and to the Arabic tradition, as I show below.

35. This observation supports Skzilnik's assertion that earlier medieval texts are more at ease with gender ambiguity and fluidity than later ones.

36. The verbs *baisier* and *accolee* in Old French literature can occur in nonsexual contexts as well.

37. Watt, "Read My Lips," 169.

38. The fifteenth-century prose version of the Yde and Olive story is even more explicit about this eroticism, as Watt demonstrates with her comments on the use of the verb *taster* (to touch) in her "Behaving Like a Man?," 280.

39. See my "Lesbian Sex and the Military."

40. Contrary to Ysabel, Yde does not reveal her social class, however.

41. See Watt, "Behaving Like a Man?," 266, 273.

42. From the church fathers' point of view, transvestism was tolerated only as long as the woman remained cross-dressed and no one knew about the cross-dressing. On this subject, see Bullough's chapter on "Cross Dressing" in *Handbook of Medieval Sexuality,* 227–31, in particular.

43. De Weever, "Lady," 388.

44. Louis Crompton, "The Myth of Lesbian Impunity: Capital Laws from 1270 to 1791," *Journal of Homosexuality* 6, nos. 1–2 (1980–1981): 11–25.

45. This has been particularly well articulated in Thomas Laqueur's *Making Sex: Body and Gender from the Greeks to Freud* (Boston: Harvard University Press, 1990).

46. Ovid's tale of Iphis and Ianthe spends a great deal of time describing the growth of the penis on Iphis's body. Ovid, *Iphis and Ianthe,* in *Metamorphoses,* trans. Rolfe Humphries (Bloomington: Indiana University Press, 1955), 9. 786–90, pp. 229–33. According to Watt, such a description is superfluous in the French epic since Yde's transformation (psychological and grammatical) had been anticipated earlier in the text (Watt, "Behaving Like a Man?," 281).

47. Watt, "Behaving Like a Man?," 274.

48. Garber, *Vested Interests,* 223 (emphasis in original).

49. Despite the effective transsexual transformation and the official

triumph of heteronormativity, the name of the hero(ine) remains in the feminine form Yde, and not Ydé, as one might have expected.

50. The double marriage at the end of the play could theoretically be considered incestuous. On the relation between incest and female homoeroticism, see Watt, "Behaving Like a Man?"

51. The Arabic sources of *Yde and Olive* have to date never been pointed out. On the classical sources of the text and its relation to Ovid's tale of Iphis and Ianthe, see Durling, "Rewriting Gender."

52. Francesca Canadé Sautman, "What Can They Possibly Do Together? Queer Epic Performances in *Tristan de Nanteuil,*" in Sautman and Sheingorn, *Same Sex Love and Desire,* 209.

53. Although *Yde and Olive* is written in a Picard dialect (with some East Frankish and Walloon forms) (and is thus associated with the north) and the *Arabian Nights* would have entered France through the south (Spain or Italy), one can still speak of cultural encounters. There is a growing body of evidence that documents commercial and religious links between northern France and the Mediterranean since at least 1087. Michel Rouche, "L'Age des pirates et des saints (Ve–Xie siècles)," in *Histoire de Boulogne-sur-mer,* ed. Alain Lottin (Lille: Presses Universitaires de Lille, 1983), 48.

54. Sautman points out that the name Croissant appears "under another guise" in the contemporary *Baudoin de Sebourc.* Unfortunately, she does not specify how (Sautman and Sheingorn, *Same Sex Love and Desire,* 226 n.43).

55. This tale is one of the longest in the entire *Arabian Nights* cycle, covering sixty-six nights (from 170th to 236th) and is also one of the eleven stories that made up the original nucleus of the tales. My research suggests that it would have circulated in medieval France either as an oral tradition or in a written version that is lost today. See also the important parallels between this tale and Jean Renart's *Escoufle,* which I discuss in my forthcoming *Crossing Borders: Love between Women in Medieval French and Arabic Literatures.*

56. Abul Hasan Ali Ibn Nasr al-Katib, *Encyclopedia of Pleasure,* ed. Salah Addin Khawwam, trans. Adnan Jarkas and Salah Addin Khawwam (Toronto: Aleppo, 1977), 192. A modern Arabic edition of this text has been done by Khaled Atiyya in a series entitled "Arabic Literary History of Sexuality," with the publisher's name

and date of publication (purposely?) blackened out. The entire text is printed on paper overlaid with prints of large red trees, making the reading challenging, possibly to evade easy recognition of the subject matter and censorship. The chapter on lesbianism is absent from the Arabic edition.

57. The choice of using an Arabic name in the context of the Christian West that we find in the epic *Yde et Olive* has a real-life parallel. Let us not forget that Abelard and Heloise's son was named Astrolabe.

58. This character was nicknamed al-Zarqa' and would have lived in the pre-Islamicate era Ibn Nasr al-Katib, *Encyclopedia of Pleasure*, 86 n.100).

59. References to *The Story of Qamar al-Zaman and the Princess Budur* come from Muhsin Mahdi's Arabic edition entitled *Alf layla wa layla* [*The Thousand and One Nights*] (Leiden: Brill, 1984), 1:592. Mahdi's edition has been translated by Husain Haddawy, *The Arabian Nights*, 2 vols. (New York: Norton, 1995). However, Haddawy did not translate *The Story of Qamar al-Zaman and the Princess Budur* as it appeared in Mahdi but combined it with material from two key nineteenth-century printed editions, Calcutta II (1839–1842) and Bulaq (1835). For this reason, I am providing my own translations of Mahdi's Arabic text.

60. I am using the term *redactor* when speaking about the authorship of the *Arabian Nights* for reasons of convenience, as outlined by Andras Hamori, "A Comic Romance from the *Thousand and One Nights*: The Tale of Two Viziers," *Arabica* 30, no. 1 (1983): 38 n.1. The term *redactor* has been further developed by David Pinault, who writes that "each redactor will doubtless have benefited from the creativity of oral reciters who transmitted and embellished the given tale before it was committed to writing. . . . The term *redactor* indicates that person who stands at the end of this chain of oral and textual transmission, that person responsible for the shape in which the story reaches us in its final written form in a given manuscript or printed text." See his *Story-Telling Techniques in the Arabian Nights* (Leiden: Brill, 1992), 16.

61. Marjorie Garber, "The Chic of Araby: Transvestism, Transsexualism and the Erotics of Cultural Appropriation," in *Body*

Guards: The Cultural Politics of Gender Ambiguity, ed. Julia Epstein and Kristina Straub (New York: Routledge, 1991), 229.

62. On oral performance as a privileged moment of creation, see Albert B. Lord, *The Singer of Tales* (Cambridge: Harvard University Press, 2000). While Lord focuses on Homer, his theoretical framework is helpful in understanding the complexity of the *Arabian Nights,* its oral and written existence in the Middle Ages, about which we have limited knowledge.

63. Although Mardrus claims to have translated the Bulaq (1835) and Calcutta II (1839–1842) editions of *Alf layla wa layla,* a close reading of his text and a comparison of his translation with both the Bulaq and the Calcutta II editions reveals that he added many details and scenes absent from these earlier renditions.

64. Mahdi, *Alf layla wa layla,* 592.

65. Ibid., 593.

66. Ibn Nasr al-Katib, *Encyclopedia of Pleasure,* 261–62.

67. Ibid., 235–36.

68. Mahdi, *Alf layla wa layla,* 595.

69. Ibid., 595.

70. Butler, *Gender Trouble,* 31.

71. Mahdi, *Alf layla wa layla,* 596.

72. Ibid., 609.

73. *One Thousand and One Nights,* ed. and trans. into French by Joseph Charles Mardrus (Paris: Laffont, 1999), trans. into English by Pomys Mathers (N.p., Yugoslovia: Dorset Press, 1964), 2:67.

74. There is a tendency in contemporary scholarship (both in the East and the West) to consider Mahdi's Arabic edition of *Alf layla wa layla* as the definitive, most "authentic" version. However, the manuscript that he used is simply the sole surviving one in the Middle Ages, and other renditions of *Alf layla wa layla* most certainly existed, though they left no trace. We must also keep in mind the oral nature of this work, which prohibits us from considering any of the surviving texts of the Arabian Nights as "definitive." On the relation between oral performance and the written text, see Lord, *Singer of Tales,* esp. chap. 6.

75. Commenting on my paper during the Radcliffe Institute for Advanced Study Conference as well as in this anthology, Brad Epps has perceptively suggested that lesbianism is permitted in the

Arabic tale precisely because of the cultural practice of the harem. Until today, however, the Western-held association of lesbianism-harem culture, though certainly possible and likely because the harem is an all-female community, has still not been established definitively and may reflect Western Orientalist fantasies rather than an Oriental reality.

FOUR

Comparison, Competition, and Cross-Dressing: Cross-Cultural Analysis in a Contested World

Brad Epps

COMPARATIVE COMPETITIONS IN A TALE OF *THE THOUSAND AND ONE NIGHTS*

On the hundred-eightieth night of her storytelling captivity, Shahrazad, central figure of *The Thousand and One Nights*, recounts that Maimunah does not take lightly Dahnash's claim that a girl that he has seen is as beautiful as a boy that she has seen.[1] Both Maimunah and Dahnash are *jinns*, winged and powerful supernatural creatures, though the female Maimunah clearly has ascendancy over the male Dahnash and smites him when he, after seeing the boy whose beauty she so admires, dares to compare him to the girl whose beauty he so admires: "I have never seen so many perfections in a boy, and I think I may claim to know something about them; and yet I tell you this, the mould which made him was not broken until it had cast a female copy also."[2] The mold may not be broken, but one of Dahnash's horns promptly is, for Maimunah strikes out against her weaker, male counterpart for refusing to place the boy's beauty above the girl's. The blow proves to be somewhat precipitous because once the two *jinns* place the boy, Qamar al-Zaman, the son of a sultan, and the girl, Princess Budur (or Boudour), side by side for a comparative examination, Maimunah is "forced to admit that the two upon the couch might be twins save in the matter of their middle parts."[3] Beauty may be beauty, but the "middle parts" are such that Maimunah, after a moment's hesitation, buttresses the quick and dubious justice of her blow to Dahnash by resorting to slow and sure convention: "you must be a fool or blind not to know," she says to him, "that, if there is equality between a male and a female, the male bears off the prize."[4] Undeterred by both Maimunah's physical force and by the force of convention, Dahnash answers that he knows what he knows and sees what he sees, but that he is willing to lie "if that would please" Maimunah.[5] Maimunah, however, will not be pleased with a lie or, it appears, with any "simple examination" and proposes instead that they settle their dispute "by putting the matter to the arbitrament of [their] inspiration"—that is, by recasting their visual comparison as a verbal competition.[6] In what amounts to a poetic joust of *jinns,* words will be among the weapons of a competitive, comparative exchange.

The dispute between Maimunah and Dahnash, in which rhetorical feints are interspersed with physical blows, has beauty at its core, but beauty, though in principle beyond gender in the classical Islamic tradition, is here so libidinally charged, so discreetly provocative in its focus on virginity and physical perfection, that it leaves the disputants striving to control their desire for more fleshly forms of contact. Controlled as they are toward the humans (and we will see how important the concept and practice of control is), they are less controlled with each other, particularly Maimunah, who continues to punch, prod, and poke Dahnash, even after she recognizes, by way of his appreciative recognition of beauty, that he has "a delicate soul under [his] strange exterior."[7] Dahnash's ugliness is partially compensated, that is, by his ability to see and value beauty and to give it secondary, verbal form. Thus, even though the power imbalance with Maimunah endures, Dahnash proves himself to be a worthy interlocutor or rival. The partial elevation of Dahnash by way of his appreciation of beauty and his command of rhetoric is crucial to the maintenance of the dispute and, what is more, to its conversion into a competition, one in which the conventions of gender and sexuality loom large.

Put all too simply, the tale presents a powerful female *jinn* who extols the qualities of a male mortal and a less powerful male *jinn* who extols the qualities of a female mortal. The competition would thus seem to be consistent with what some now call a heterosexual economy, or heteronormativity, in which desire is constructed as running between "opposites"—men and women—of uneven power. Indeed, amid all of the (a)symmetrical plays, it is as if Maimunah's admiration for the boy were a function of her impressive power and as if Dahnash's admiration for the girl were a function of his relatively less impressive power. In general terms, the two supernatural beings, in whom a supposedly natural gender hierarchy of physical strength is inverted (perhaps as a sign of the supernatural) and by whom it is reaffirmed (as a sign of the natural), are *impressed* by their objects of admiration and desire: the female *jinn* seems to be fortified by admiring and desiring the boy, and the male *jinn* seems to be weakened by admiring and desiring the girl. However much Dahnash's appreciation of beauty may compensate for his relative lack of physical strength and allow him to rise to the rank of respectable rival in Maimunah's eyes, the outcome of the competition, in keeping with the circular force of convention, is to all intents and purposes already decided, for the human male does indeed "bear off the prize."

And yet the plays of power, desire, admiration, and convention across natural and supernatural planes of gender and sexuality render the competition far from straightforward and complicate what might otherwise pass for a heteronormatively structured comparison. Among other things, the apparently heteronormative framing of the young man's "stronger" beauty can be read not just as making male beauty legible by at once likening it to and differentiating it from female beauty, but also as at once inciting and defending desire among readers or listeners of the tale—the majority of whom, historically speaking, were men—for the beautiful boy or *young* man.[8] Same-sex desire, in which age makes a critical difference, imbues, that is, the competitive comparison, rendering it more reticular. For starters, the weaker though wily Dahnash is by no means unwaveringly committed to the "other" or "opposite" sex. Claiming to know something about the perfections of boys, Dahnash jerks his head in a fit of stupefied fascination on first seeing the sleeping youth that Maimunah champions. His frenetic actions seem to confirm Maimunah's previous declaration that she "would not even trust [him] to stand guard over the bottom of a holy man," but they also indicate that Dahnash is more "ambivalent," more susceptible to a change of mind, than Maimunah.[9]

Although differences in ontological status (natural or supernatural), not unlike differences in age, render male same-sex desire here something of a misnomer and perhaps indeed a red herring, it nonetheless remains the case that in the tale of the *jinns* that frames the tale of the humans there is no mention of anything like female same-sex desire.[10] Although female same-sex desire marks the tale of the humans, the superhuman Maimunah experiences no fit of fascination on seeing the girl, nor is the reader made party to rumors about any other sexual proclivities of Maimunah. The imbalance in the *jinns'* power, partly compensated by Dahnash's ability to appreciate beauty and to speak eloquently, is accompanied by an imbalance in their commitment to the object of their admiration. Already designated as the weaker of the two, Dahnash is less inclined to control himself before the charms of the humans and, it appears, to control rumors about him. Control or rather self-control is here critical, for in a tale so rife with externally imposed constraints, not the least of which is Shahrazad's tell-or-die predicament, self-control functions, as we shall see, as the very act, or nonact, on which a conventional and supposedly "natural" sex-gender divide rises and falls.

As compensatory as Dahnash's appreciation of beauty and command of language may be, the imbalance between the two *jinns* contrasts with the balance between the two humans, who are both so beautiful as to be twinlike, equal except for their "middle parts." As already noted, the stronger, superhuman Maimunah, loath to resort to brute force alone, invokes convention in order to crack the ostensible balance between the two humans and to reassert a genitally fixated imbalance in which the "parts" effectively determine the whole. Yet convention, whose logic is relentlessly circular, is here not enough, and Maimunah, with Dahnash's consent, summons a "third party" to arbitrate the dispute.[11] The third party is Kashkash, another supernatural creature or Ifrit, likewise deferential to Maimunah but asymmetrical, ugly, and so gargantuan that his "zabb, which was forty times larger than that of an elephant, ran between his legs and rose triumphantly behind him."[12] The phallic excess of this third party or arbiter might give a measure of the outcome of the competition, for Kashkash declares Qamar al-Zaman, whose own hefty endowment had been noted previously ("his waist sometimes complained of the weight that went below it"), to be the victor but not on the size of his "middle parts" alone.[13] The decisive factor proves to be less one of objective measure than of subjective action—subjective *human* action. Rather than simply taking the "middle parts" as a palpable sign of value and declaring one of the two humans more beautiful, Kashkash arbitrates by shifting the burden of proof from himself and his fellow *jinns,* and hence from their physical force and rhetorical prowess, to the humans themselves—not to the materiality of their bodies alone but to their will as well.

After declaring that Qamar and Budur "are equal in beauty and [that] their difference is one of sex alone," Kashkash proposes that the two humans be confronted with the same sight that so moves the *jinns*—that is, that the two humans be confronted with the sight of each other's naked body.[14] The winner, he declares, will be whoever is *not* moved to translate the perception of physical beauty into a sexual act, whoever is *not* moved, that is, to translate seeing into touching, contemplation into consummation. In language that at once recalls and elides the classical Western distinction between *eros* and *agape* (which is itself not always clear), the grotesquely phallic Kashkash declares that "the one who shows greater love and hotter passion for the other will prove himself or herself vanquished in the test, by confessing that the charms of the other are more powerful."[15] In the competitive comparison of beauties that are equal except for their "middle parts," the putting into practice of these very parts entails a depletion of the value of whoever does so—and perhaps an increase in the prurient delight of the *jinns* who witness it all. After all, even as Kashkash brings to the fore the moral charge of aesthetic judgment by shifting from a principle of passive objectivity to one of active subjectivity, he proves himself to be decidedly less dispassionate than cunning: "seized with emotion," he grasps "his thing" on seeing the two naked youths and waits to declare the victor to be whoever does not do as he does.

The victor, as already amply intimated, is Qamar and hence by extension Maimunah. The victory itself is not so much a matter of conventionally coded parts as of performances, which, not surprisingly, also prove to be conventionally code. Given the mirror-like play of beauty in this tale of significant symmetries and asymmetries, the performances are twofold and reinforce the aforementioned sex-gender divide: *the boy is able to control himself* from copulating with the girl (he thinks of the displeasure that his illicit pleasure would cause his father), *and the girl is unable to control herself* from taking possession of the boy's "thing" (she thinks not of her father but only of herself and her newly found object of desire, it seems).[16] Inasmuch as both Qamar and Budur had already professed to reject not only marriage but also any interest in the opposite sex, Qamar's self-control may be as consistent with his previously expressed penchant as Budur's lack of self-control is inconsistent with hers.[17] In fact, the repulsion that Qamar had previously expressed toward women and Budur toward men, while not necessarily indicative of homosexual desire (rejection of the "opposite" sex does *not* perforce indicate desire for the "same" sex), does make the passion that they experience before each other more notable—that is to say, more passionate—and, by extension, their struggles for self-control more "noble," (Budur may "lose" the competition for Dahnash, but she is not stigmatized or deprived of her beauty. Quite the contrary: in her weakness and lack of control, she is reaffirmed, conventionally, as feminine). In Budur's case, desire is laced with phallic curiosity, for as she later explains to her nurse, the boy "had something below his navel which [she has] not," some "thing" that apparently makes the boy a boy and that "changed form every moment beneath the examination of her hand."[18] The mysteriously transformative power of this thing—and it should be remembered that one of the signs of the *jinns'* power is their ability to change form—is such that Budur cannot keep her hands off of it, off of him, and "while her lips sucked his, that happened which happened."[19]

What happens is sex, but sex within the context of a pledge to marry: Qamar al-Zaman had left a ring on Budur's finger, and Budur had corresponded with a ring of her own, but, as noted, she did not leave matters there. Unable to control herself, she mounts Qamar al-Zaman and, in the process, supposedly proves that his beauty is greater, for more irresistible, than hers. Then again, the narrator had already announced that, "even as desire is greater in women, so is their intelligence quicker to seize the correspondence between certain charming organs."[20] Men may have more "down there," but women have more "upstairs" (especially about things "down there") and know, it appears, what goes where. Budur's lack of self-control, part and parcel of her intuitive knowledge of matters sexual, breaks the balance with Qamar al-Zaman and proves the stronger, female *jinn* right for having championed the stronger, more self-controlled male human, who does not "succumb" to Budur's charms when he sees them and yet is stiff putty in her hands when asleep. Maimunah's victory is also, not incidentally, a victory for convention, which prescribes a sweeping, supplementary control in the form of male authority to "make good" the female lack of control and, just possibly, Budur's usurpation of the conventional male prerogative to mount the female sexually. The comparative contest, after having slighted convention as insufficient, returns to convention, reiterating and reaffirming it, and thus functions as a virtual redundancy for what is—or "should be"—known already.

Two things, at least, bear noting at this point. The first is the anxiously reiterative performance of a gender hierarchy, a performance that Judith Butler has taken, quite generally, as a sign of the instability and insufficiency of a heteronormative order that purports to be natural, self-evident, and beyond dispute.[21] The second is the presentation, crucial to the aforementioned hierarchy, of women as lacking "the thing" that men have and, perhaps on the basis of that "lack," as being less capable of self-control and thus in need of control by others, by men. The fetishized notion of honor—which runs through both Islamic and Christian societies, especially in the Middle Ages, and which entails, as a means to its reiterative preservation, an array of sartorial, architectonic, and legal barriers—would therefore be at once the residue and the supplement of this *comparatively* greater desire and lack of control. Determined by men (but also by women in what seems to be a process of social interiorization) to be lacking in self-control, "woman" becomes the legitimizing figure of an order whose measure is her control and constraint. Shahrazad, after all, spins her yarn to avoid the fate of the other wives of King Shahriyar, all of whom he has beheaded, after "deflowering" them, because of the infidelity of his first wife. Within all the twists and turns of *The Thousand and One Nights*, the master frame (which frames the tale of the *jinn*'s comparative competition, which in turn frames the tale of Budur and Qamar al-Zaman) is one of a violently uneven sex-gender system in which all women are forced to pay a terrible price for one woman's transgression.

In many respects, the picture is all too familiar and runs from one culture to another, one time to another, corresponding, by and large, to Gayle Rubin's claim that, "at the most general level, the social organization of sex rests upon gender, obligatory heterosexuality, and the constraint of female sexuality."[22] Men must strive, within the parameters of marriage and the law, to satisfy or control the desires of women and to keep them in check and out of the public eye, where the potential for havoc is incomparably greater—hence the veil, the harem, the closed and concealed domestic space, and the relative "freedom" for women to be with women. According to Fatna A. Sabbah, whose specific references to Islam may be as ahistorical as Rubin's general references to a cross-cultural sex-gender system, "for legal Islam, pleasure is the generating force of subversion, and Muslim civilization is defined as an attempt to control pleasure."[23] The contrast with the Orientalist notion of Islam as more sexually permissive and more appreciate of pleasure than the Christian West is extreme. And yet, as significant as such cultural markers as harems and veils are, such a state of affairs is hardly foreign to the West, where chastity belts, domestic confinement, the code of honor, and all sorts of sartorial binding, verbal censorship, and corporal punishment are among the trappings of a highly hierarchized sex-gender system as well.

The problem with the previously adduced theories is not merely their sweeping or passing attention to history but also their questionable pertinence to readings of fictional works that, whatever their basis in social reality, are likewise fraught with fantastic, ahistorical significance. Any reading of *The Thousand and One Nights*—indeed, of any imaginative work—must contend, for example, with an array of presuppositions that configure the past in terms that are intelligible to the present, here prominently among them such terms as *heterosexuality*, *heteronormativity, same-sex desire, sex-gender system,* but very much also *East* and *West.* The comparative competition between male and female *jinns* involving male and female human beings is centered on beauty, corporeality, sexual difference, desire, and self-control, but it has, not surprisingly, geopolitical, religious, and cultural ramifications as well. A principal tension hinges on another old binary—civilization and barbarism or, if you will, "us" and "them," commonly recast as East and West, West and East. Once the competition among the *jinns* is settled in favor of Qamar al-Zaman, his and Budur's story comes to the fore—in Mathers's translation of Mardrus's edition, at least— amid references to "western invaders" and to "an evil world, soiled by the barbarity of the West."[24] The issues of translation and cross-cultural transmission are critical because the West is here the West of the Islamic domains, *not* Europe. In fact, the notion of Europe as "the West" was not operant, as Afsaneh Najmabadi has reminded me, at the time the tales were composed (though the time of composition is vexed as well). Beauty, desire, love, sex, separation, the specter of madness, acts of cross-dressing, protracted journeys, and long-awaited and frustratingly interrupted reunions may be some of the hallmarks of this tale, but the division of the world into civilized beings and barbarians, believers and infidels, serves as its backdrop. This division further complicates already notoriously complex divisions and differences in sex, gender, age, rank, and ontological status (*jinn* versus human).

So deep are these geopolitical divisions that modern readers of the medieval tale of Qamar al-Zaman and Budur, and for that matter of *The Thousand and One Nights* in general, can find themselves hard-pressed to winnow out fantasy from reality and creative freedom from constraint. Robert Irwin, author of a highly successful reader's companion to the *Nights,* styles the work as a "product of a medieval culture that was confident, tolerant and pluralist" but adds that "[a] character in a *Nights* story is more likely to die as a martyr to love than to sacrifice him or herself in some ideologically motivated suicide attack."[25]

Irwin thus notes that the often effusive and rambunctious tenor of *The Thousand and One Nights,* a hybrid and heterogeneous work of multiple, uncertain sources, stands in contrast to the fanaticism, fear, and one-dimensional thinking that mark the present. But he also signals, perhaps in spite of himself how images of fanaticism and fear haunt even the most informed and best intended of critical endeavors and how the problems of the present bear on the past and those of the past on the present in ways that cause the act and idea of comparison, however bound to praise (you are a fair citadel topped by a dome, a pearl, a rose, as Qamar says on first seeing Budur), to bleed over and again into competition. The terms by which division, comparison, and competition acquire intelligible form are themselves caught in uneven and far-reaching power plays. It is to a few of these terms that I now turn before returning to the problem of competitive comparisons in a terribly divided world.

TERMS OF KNOWLEDGE AND MARKS OF IDENTITY

The preceding excursus centers on one of the tales of the *Nights* and is motivated by two comparative essays—Leyla Rouhi's "A Handsome Boy among Those Barbarous Turks: Cervantes's Muslims and the Art and Science of Desire" (chapter 2 in this book) and, much more directly, Sahar Amer's "Cross-Dressing and Female Same-Sex Marriage in Medieval French and Arabic Literatures" (chapter 3). Amer's chapter includes an engaging analysis of the tale of Qamar al-Zaman and Budur (though it refers only in passing to the dispute between the *jinns* Maimunah and Dahnash that frames the tale), which the author claims to be a principal model for a cluster of medieval French texts that involve cross-dressing and same-sex marriage. Rouhi, for her part, makes no mention of *The Thousand and One Nights* and concentrates instead on Miguel de Cervantes's *Don Quixote,* but she does address questions about appearance, reality, secrecy, and disclosure that are central to both Cervantes's novel and the Arabian tale. Both essays thus move between Western and Eastern—or perhaps more precisely, Christian and Islamic—texts and contexts, and both focus on cross-dressing and, though less in Rouhi's case, on same-sex desire. Both, furthermore, grapple with issues of tolerance, permissiveness, freedom, and their opposites, including barbarism, with Rouhi extolling *Don Quixote* for its generosity and subtlety and Amer extolling *The Thousand and One Nights* for its "fluid and complex oral" suppleness and for its portrayal of a variety of erotic possibilities. Amer is not, however, primarily interested in the Arabic text because her points of departure and arrival are in French medieval literature—a mid-thirteenth-century epic, *Yde et Olive,* and its late fourteenth-century dramatic adaptation, or miracle play, *Miracle de la fille d'un roy*—and because her basic claim, to which I return, is that "the French story is heir to the Arabic framed tale." Although both invoke cross-cultural movement, mostly by way of travel, translation, and transmission of source materials, Amer examines some of the ties and tensions between texts from different linguistic and cultural traditions, while Rouhi focuses on *Don Quixote,* a text that incorporates into its narrative a variety of cross-cultural moves.

That said, it is cross-dressing *as a sign of sexuality* that captures the attention of both Amer and Rouhi. In the tale of Qamar al-Zaman and Budur proper, Budur's "milk brother," Marzawan, who is also a young sorcerer, is the first to cross-dress, disguising himself as a woman to have access to his sister, who in her confinement appears to have become flushed with madness. For after being separated from Qamar al-Zaman and returned to her home by the *jinns* (who had brought the two together for their contest), Budur expresses a longing for her unknown beloved that others take as madness. The tale that Marzawan hears when he is before Budur leads him, however, to declare that "Budur was in love and nothing more."[26] Already, shortly after the genies exit, cross-dressing proves to be instrumental in the access to knowledge—here of love and "love sickness." Marzawan's transvestitic exploits momentarily allow him to trespass the heavily controlled border between men and women (the lovers, separated from each other, are confined and under surveillance by their own parents) and to see the truth to which everyone else has remained blind. Marzawan's performance thus serves as a prelude to subsequent performances, most important Budur's own reliance on the clothes and attributes of the "opposite" sex to travel in search of the man she loves—the same Qamar al-Zaman whose identity she assumes. What Budur finds by traveling as a man (and as her own husband, to boot) is not merely hospitality, greater wealth, and a new kingdom but also a young woman who is promptly made her wife, whom she appears to love, and whose virginity she feigns to take (with the willing complicity of her bride) in an elaborately deceptive game of show-and-tell replete with bloody sheets. The reality is that Budur, taken for a man, saves her bride's virginity for her husband—that is, for the man who will be *their* husband, Qamar al-Zaman. The story is clearly convoluted, and Budur, within it, is a most variegated being—wife to her husband (Budur with Qamar al-Zaman), husband to her wife (a cross-dressed Budur with Hayyat al-Nufus), husband to herself (a cross-dressed Budur as Qamar al-Zaman), procuress of her husband's second wife (Budur *vis-à-vis* Hayyat), and perhaps even wife to her wife (Budur with Hayyat al-Nufus).

For Amer, the marriage of a cross-dressed Budur to Hayyat al-Nufus, daughter of King Armanus, constitutes a "lesbian interlude," a story within a story within a story in which desire is as insistent as it is involute. Amer is admittedly working against the grain, for although the encounter is replete with kisses on the mouth, caresses, and the possibility of penetrating fingers, it appears to have received relatively short shrift from critics.[27] Irwin, for instance, acknowledges Budur's cross-dressing but ascribes it exclusively to her desire "to travel in security and to advance [her] fortunes."[28] In fact, he claims that, "[a]lthough cross-dressing features in a number of stories, this is as a literary device and not as a statement of sexual preference."[29] Budur's foster brother Marzawan might serve as a case in point inasmuch as his cross-dressing does not carry any additional sexual charge—other than perhaps a slightly incestuous one: "for he loved the princess with *a love which is unusual* between brothers and sisters."[30] All the same, the certainty with which Irwin discounts "sexual preference" should not be taken as symptomatic of disinterest, for he does refer briefly to lesbianism, which he describes as "'rubbing'" *(musahaqa)*" and which he claims, in turn, was linked to "witchcraft in the popular mind."[31] Still, Irwin's presentation is incongruous and not just because he asserts both that "[l]esbians do not seem to have been persecuted in medieval Islamic societies" *and* that "[t]he anonymous storytellers of the *Nights* went along with popular prejudice, and the presentation of lesbianism in the stories is consistently hostile."[32] (True, hostility is not necessarily the same as persecution, but it is one of its conditions of possibility.) Irwin's presentation is also incongruous because even as he decouples cross-dressing from sexuality, he deploys lesbianism and homosexuality more generally as if they were operant, *as such,* in medieval Islamic societies. The upshot of at once deploying such modern sexual categories and of refusing their applicability to acts of cross-dressing merits reflection. Though cross-dressing here in a literary text is a literary device, it is nonetheless shot through with extraliterary gendered and sexual meanings that are not, and certainly not necessarily, understandable in terms of heterosexuality or homosexuality, including lesbianism. The same holds for Amer's notion of the "lesbian interlude," which implicates not only literature and its devices, but history and its devices too.

Any reading of classic, medieval, or early modern texts—indeed of any text before the late nineteenth-century—that involves gays, lesbians, straights, and so on is historically challenged; so too is any reading that perfunctorily discounts gays, lesbians, straights, and so on. The challenge, as I see it, is to negotiate, without merely eliminating or codifying, doubts, gaps, silences, opacities, differences, inconsistencies, and uncertainties. Amer is on the whole more consistent than Irwin, deploying lesbianism quite matter-of-factly and reading Budur's cross-dressing almost entirely in relation to it. The certainty with which Irwin discounts cross-dressing as a sign of sexuality stands in contrast with the certainty with which Amer takes Budur's cross-dressing, presumably laid bare in her affection toward Hayyat, as a sign of lesbianism. To the degree that "lesbianism" designates a more or less coherent category by which human beings identify and are identified and by which individuals are collocated as some sort of community, the term can be misleading. But Amer not only presents the characters as being involved in a lesbian interlude. She also invokes "the medieval lesbian in the audience," thereby implying that there was a discernible group that took its place alongside other discernible groups and, for that matter, that the audience was as mixed as it might be in many places of the world today. Even though the group might not have been a group in the strict sense of the term and consisted instead of otherwise scattered individuals whose desire for a person of the same sex was sufficient to create some unspoken or unacknowledged tie or network, and even though Amer attempts to delimit the meaning of *lesbian* to an "emotional and sexual attachment between two women" devoid of "political activism" and "the politics of gender identity," the problem persists. The modern implications of modern terms, however old their etymologies, are not easily shaken.[33]

The problem is most directly one of nomination, of terminology, but it is also one of identification and classification, of historically marked understanding. In certain parts of the West, critical discourse on gender and sexuality operates, to greater or lesser degrees, in accordance with something like an evaluative temporal line in which one term, category, or concept is presented as more cutting-edge, more *au courant,* than another.[34] A particularly insistent if abbreviated version of the trajectory runs something as follows: sodomite, tribade, pederast, invert, homosexual, gay and lesbian, queer. The pejorative import of *sodomite* (whose topographical provenance is not maintained in the Arabic *liwat,* which means "crime of Lot's people"),[35] *pederast,* and *invert* (which invariably evokes *pervert*) is such that none of these terms is prevalent in current critical discourse. *Homosexual,* which is still prevalent internationally, is, as is well known, a late nineteenth-century neologism—a "bastard term compounded of Greek and Latin elements," as Havelock Ellis put it[36]—laden with clinical, even pathological, meaning and bound in intricate ways to *invert. Gay* and *lesbian* are older terms, recuperated from times and places past (the isle of Lesbos, home of Sappho, and the *gai savoir* of Provençal troubadours) but recharged with a more self-affirmative identitarian significance that has parallels with the civil rights movement and the women's movement. *Queer* is likewise an old term (as Eve Sedgwick notes, it derives from the Indo-European "*twerkw,* which also yields the German *quer* [transverse], Latin *torquere* [to twist], English *athwart*"), but one that is invested with transvaluative power, with some people taking it, often quite tendentiously, as the nonidentity to end all identities.[37] In many respects, *gay* and *lesbian* are, as already noted, identity categories and do not dispense with notions of being and essence, even when they are styled as constructions. *Queer,* on the other hand, is presumably more "available," less connected to any particular body, pleasure, or practice, and more a matter of positioning and becoming than of being. Old as all three terms are, they are all reinvested—*queer* most defiantly—with postmodern significance.

Leyla Rouhi tackles just such problems of terminology in her theoretical overview of the vicissitudes of the term *queer,* centering her comments on the first collection of studies on early modern Spain to give it a place of privilege: Gregory Hutcheson and Josiah Blackmore's *Queer Iberia,* published in 1999.[38] Along with the predictable criticisms of such a line of inquiry, some of them brimming with homophobic suppositions, there have been other criticisms, articulated from within progressive gay and lesbian sectors, of the word *queer* itself, which is all but untranslatable to other languages (here, Spanish, French, and Arabic). For many, myself included,[39] *queer* cannot entirely shake a sense of Anglo-American cultural imperialism that would dissemble its ethnonational provenance and affiliations under the banner of a would-be gay international. Hutcheson and Blackmore do not seem to have seriously fretted about the translatability, and hence applicability, of the word *queer* to other cultures until *after* their book appeared, but to their credit, Hutcheson offers an admirably self-critical review in a follow-up online article:

> Ultimately "queer" is a term so entrenched in both its etymology and the history of its deliberate appropriation by the Anglo-American gay community that it cannot be rendered by any single term in Spanish. By using "queer" in our title, we unwittingly created an entity that resists a priori a quick-and-easy translation of the whole, that appears to impose English as the default when speaking about the Iberian subjects we study, that perpetuates Anglo-American models of writing queer history.[40]

Despite the reference to "queer history" that ironically redoubles the problem here being addressed, Hutcheson and, by extension, Rouhi clearly understand that terminology bears on understanding—that words have their times and places too, multiple as they may be.

Amer understands something similar, but nonetheless insists on the interpretative value and, perhaps more important, the liberational potential of the term and concept *lesbian* throughout history and across cultures.[41] She opens her study with a reference to an essay by Jacqueline Murray titled "Twice Marginal and Twice Invisible," according to which, "[o]f all the groups within medieval society lesbians are the most marginalized and the least visible."[42] Rightfully noting that *lesbian* has typically been subsumed and erased under *homosexual* and *woman,* Amer claims that "[o]ne reason that medieval French lesbians as a category of analysis or as evidence of a certain textual (or social) reality have been occulted is that many medieval French literary writings continue to be read in isolation from the cultural context of interaction, seduction, and anxiety between the Arab Islamicate world and Western Christian Europe." What Amer asserts and attempts to demonstrate is that cross-cultural analysis, here by way of the tale of Qamar al-Zaman and Budur, can retrieve, reveal, or rescue heretofore hidden lesbians in medieval French literature (and society). The gesture is a venerable one, much practiced during the 1970s and 1980s. Whatever its ultimate legitimacy, the idea of a medieval lesbian, let alone of a medieval lesbian in the audience or of medieval lesbians across cultures (Amer writes of French and Arabic "sisters," of which more later), is vexed, for if the category is not operant in all societies today and certainly not evenly and equally, it is certainly not operant in all societies at all times. David Halperin's and John Boswell's skirmishes over terminology, history, and identity may help shed some light on what continues to constitute one of the major methodological problems of scholars who study gender and sexuality in ancient, medieval, and early modern periods, but there is little doubt that nomination has profound consequences for understanding and that it is particularly thorny when cross-dressing is at issue, implicating, among other things, the adequacy of male, female, or neutral parts of speech to designate the subjects in question.[43]

DIVIDES, DIFFERENCES, AUTHORITY, AND WISHFUL THINKING

The aforementioned questions of terminology, identity, and acts bear on the locations of the critic and, by extension, on the critic's authority. Neither Amer, Rouhi, nor I are scholars, at least not primarily, of Arabic, Turkish, Persian, or other languages and literatures of the Islamic sphere, though Rouhi and Amer are clearly familiar with one or more of these traditions. My expertise is in modern Spanish, Latin American, and Catalan literatures and in the forever incomplete cross-cultural study of gender and sexuality. I do not purport to offer a "corrective" to Rouhi's compelling, if idealistically tinged, presentation of the formation of "a new self" in Cervantes's text (of which more, shortly) or to Amer's compelling, if debatable, presentation of medieval lesbians and, no less important, of medieval Arabic *sources* and *realities* that she deploys in explicit opposition to modern "Orientalist fantasies." I submit, however, that "Orientalist fantasies" of some sort may be ineluctable when dealing with a text as full of fantasy as *The Thousand and One Nights* and, more pointedly, that Amer's presentation, inasmuch as it is articulated within the discourse of the Western academy, is not exempt from Orientalist fantasies of its own. These fantasies take the fairly well-trodden path of a nostalgic celebration of the *relative* permissiveness and freedom of Arabic sexuality—relative, needless to say, to Western sexuality. Sir Richard Burton, famed translator of *The Book of the Thousand Nights and a Night,* wrote of a "Sotadic Zone," a sort of torrid terrestrial swathe that embraced the Mediterranean, the Middle East, Asia Minor, Mesopotamia, Afghanistan, Kashmir, Indo-China, China, Japan, the South Sea Islands, and other parts of the globe and that was supposedly a natural space of relative permissiveness and feminine and masculine blendings.[44] The difference is that the permissiveness that Burton found so prurient and that functioned as the "savage" underside of repressive Victorian morality is now duly criticized and, in being criticized, tellingly recast as a badge of progressive academic honor in the West. According to this story, the Orient really *was* at one time more permissive and progressive than the West.

The truth value of such assessments is far from simple, for there and then, here and now, in the "East" and the "West," sexuality and its signs are ideologically charged. To begin with, the idea that there "is" an Eastern sexuality and a Western sexuality—and that there "was" one in antiquity, the Middle Ages, or early modernity—is far from self-evident. The historical and geographic *relativity* of such ideologically spatial divisions bears on gender and sexual divisions. Here, too, Rouhi and Amer follow different tracks, with the former teasing out differences between and among Spaniards and the French as well as between and among Moors, Arabs, and Turks and the latter essentially endorsing an overarching binary structure. Amer, to be sure, claims to work against binary structures and acknowledges that "the Middle Ages can no longer be viewed as a monocultural, monolithic historical era" and that "Western sexuality, contrary to the beliefs of many, is not reducible to heterosexuality or heterosexism," but she nonetheless relies on an East/West divide by which the French texts, for all their real and presumed ties to Eastern texts, are read as the relatively puritanical, censorial "heirs" (Amer's term) to the tale of Qamar al-Zaman and Princess Budur. The binary is thus not so much undone as done anew, only in inverse temporal form. Although Amer professes to destabilize the divide by which "the West's (both the United States and France) *contemporary* discursive self-presentation [is] secular, sexually liberated, and firmly positioned in the first world" (emphasis mine), she actually reinvigorates the divide by advancing a presentation of the Arabic world as, if not exactly secular, at least sexually liberated *in the past*. Invoking vague yet "*vast differences* in attitudes toward female same-sex unions in these two cultural traditions" (emphasis mine), Amer sidesteps the problems involved in taking *The Thousand and One Nights* as evidence of only one of the two cultural traditions here adduced (problems that are also problems of translation and transmission) in order to maintain the divide on which her argument hinges.[45] The divide, after all, allows not only for comparisons but also for ethically and politically colored competitions across and between cultures.

Even when she comes closest to complicating the East/West divide, as when she addresses the differences between French and American inquiries in gender and sexuality, Amer reaffirms an oppositional structure that appears to be all but iron-clad: "[t]he U.S. and French understanding of sexuality is determined by national affiliation." The complication of the West—which is here dependent on a more delimited binary between French and American—is not accompanied by the complication of the East, which remains, *by comparison,* silent and opaque in Amer's presentation of scholarship on sexuality. The result is an all too neat picture in which the differences between scholarship in the United States and France are overstated (which is not, I repeat,

to say that there are *no* differences) and the differences between
scholarship in the West and the East are also overstated, but,
paradoxically, by way of a partial omission. Amer thus indicates
that American and French scholars understand sexuality only by
misunderstanding the determinative force of their nationality;
that their understandings, furthermore, have few if any significant overlaps, coincidences, or points of agreement other
than those of a generalized West; and that there is little if any
contemporary scholarship on sexuality by, say, Moroccans,
Turks, or Egyptians. She also leaves her own location almost entirely out of the equation. Turning Amer's argument back on itself, one might say that the focus on the French in tension with
the Anglo-American as representative of the West conditions
(even here, I cannot bring myself to say "determines") her understanding of the divide. By putting Amer's argument into play
alongside Rouhi's, by comparing *them,* one might say that the
history of what now stands as the West and the East reveals differences that are not *determined* by national affiliation and that
trouble the *vastness* of the differences between the two. Herein
lies one of the many potential benefits of reading Rouhi and
Amer together—although the specter of a critically induced
competition arises as well.

In keeping with the theories of the Spanish philologist and historian Américo Castro, who advanced a vision of medieval
Spain that was marked by relatively peaceful Christian, Islamic,
and Judaic coexistence, Rouhi contends that "the head-on collision of an historical reality (the complicated coexistence of three
religions) with a new world order that wished to deny the complexities of that reality" is such that the aforementioned divide
"perhaps worked fine for England or France" but not for Spain,
"whose own being was intertwined at the deepest level with
Muslim coexistence." Amer does not refer to Spain, but she does
remark that, "France, much more than the United States, has
had a long history of interactions with the Middle East and the
Islamicate world" that "renders the cross-cultural investigation
into [its] past and particularly into the recovery of its possible

Arabic literary lineage an especially sensitive topic for some Western audiences." Even as Amer points to the history of a specifically French interaction with the Islamic world, she invokes a general Western audience that subsumes the specificity of the French. Rouhi, though likewise interested in Arabic sources, proceeds differently. For her, as for other Hispanists who follow Américo Castro, *Don Quijote de la Mancha*, one of the indisputable masterpieces of Western literature, "ought to be included in the vast canon of Islamic studies." If such a proposition has validity, as I believe it does (after all, *Don Quixote* is presented, within itself, as a work written by one Cide Hamete Benengeli and translated from the Arabic), then surely the other masterpiece here in play, *The Thousand and One Nights*, ought to be included in a vast Western canon—as indeed it has been. Amer, however, reads *The Thousand and One Nights* and the tale of Qamar and Budur within it as if it were a cloudless window on Arabic reality, free of Orientalist fantasies and the indisputable source of the French texts.

But clouded, and scintillatingly so, the window is. In fact, Irwin says that the Mardrus translation, which is the one on which Amer relies (along with Muhsin Mahdi's "far less detailed" edition of the fourteenth-century Syrian manuscript), is so rife with exaggeration and invention that "the stories appear at times to have been written by Oscar Wilde or Stéphane Mallarmé."[46] Irwin's assessment, backed by a welter of details, contrasts with Amer's, according to which the Mardrus translation is "highly regarded by *Nights* scholars" because it is "believed to include the least amount of anachronistic additions and to preserve best the style of the 'original.'" Not only is Amer's claim that the Mardrus's translation is accurate, faithful, and highly regarded debatable, but her assertion that "nineteenth-century versions of the *Arabian Nights* (Mardrus) are likely to have circulated in the medieval West and East with equal frequency as the fourteenth-century Syrian manuscript (Mahdi)" is clearly untenable—even if we grant that she means that some of the early versions or sources of the nineteenth-century versions so circulated.[47] At any rate, it is the reliance on "originals" and "sources" that is most dubious. If *Don Quixote* plays with translation and transmission in the very body of the narrative in a manner that indicates that originals and copies are deliciously intermixed, *The Thousand and One Nights* is arguably even more intermixed—a "book without authors," as Irwin styles it, that is also a book with a plethora of authors (translators included) who are Arabic, perhaps Persian, even Indian, but certainly Western as well. Spain and its greatest literary icon may occupy a space betwixt-and-between, but so too does the text that Amer takes as providing the key to a hidden lesbian truth and a benighted Western debt.[48]

Differences and divisions *do* exist, and they have mighty, even terribly violent, effects. But differences and divisions are shot though with other, "internal" differences and divisions and in such a fashion that the very integrity of the internal and the external is questionable.[49] Yet there is more. A competitive cultural ethos runs through Amer's comparative textual inquiry, snaking back on the aforementioned question of expertise or specialized knowledge. The question is hardly unique to Amer and may be inevitable to the degree that cultural specificity is often, as here, purchased by way of excisions, exclusions, and omissions and by way of a denial or disavowal of convoluted histories of translations and transmissions. In many respects, Amer's interest in cross-cultural analysis proceeds from a "Western" position that has become sufficiently mixed to recognize and criticize its own hegemony, part of an undeniable imbalance in cultural power today. Said imbalance implicates us all differently. The questions of cross-cultural transmission, influence, indebtedness, and competitive comparison that Amer addresses and enacts are not historically discrete and throw into renewed relief the contested and contestable status of any collectivity, any cultural grouping, any enunciation of the third-person plural. Rouhi's quite different take on cross-cultural analysis—in which a single work provides a space where "paradox, hybridity, and ambivalence" triumph "over certainty and dogmatism" and in which the East-

West divide is "always already" complicated—also throws into renewed relief the contested and contestable status of any collectivity. It does so, however, by expanding on the demythifying moves of poststructuralist analysis, including the destabilizing deployment of identity categories that bear on the past in ways that render philological, etymological, and genealogical analysis tricky, to say the least.

The status of genealogical analysis is important because Amer ends her second paragraph by asking—rhetorically, it appears—whether "the literary expression of lesbian desire and lesbian love in medieval French literature [can] claim an Arabic literary genealogy." An Arabic literary genealogy is here only implicitly intertwined with the "anxiety over genealogy, fatherhood, and patriarchy" that marks the French texts, *Yde et Olive* and *Miracle de la fille d'un roy,* which are at the core of Amer's reflections. Although Amer does not confront the twists of genealogy, whether literary, sexual, or both, it is worth pondering to what degree, if any, an "anxiety over genealogy" inflects Amer's interpretation as a whole. After all, what Amer presents as "the challenges posed by cross-cultural research" in large part derive from and remit to the *fragmented* state of the texts, both Arabic and French. Amer goes on to indicate that the challenges posed by source materials and transmission, if somehow overcome (a very big "if" indeed), would allow for a more seamless and secure genealogical line. Given the recalcitrant nature of such problems (texts are lost, destroyed, misplaced, translated, mistranslated, reworked, revised, glossed, "corrected," and so on), the anxiety that such fractured, incomplete, and occluded genealogies produce for the critic interested in issues of homosexuality or lesbianism has ironic implications, inasmuch as same-sex relations have long been denigrated and penalized—or, alternatively, tolerated and even sporadically celebrated—precisely because they do not maintain the generative ethos that characterizes genealogy in general. In earlier articulations of her essay, Amer invoked a space in which a lesbian relationship was "nourished," but in so doing she underestimated, in my opinion, the thrust of a repressive tolerance (the term is Herbert Marcuse's)[50] whose measure, in such a genealogically structured world view, is the *impossibility* of generating an heir that is not of the (male) husband's making. In a note, Amer rejects what she presents as "the Western-held association of lesbianism-harem" and dodges the price placed, then as now, on virginity and the spatial constraint of women—as if Shahrazad were not telling the tales she tells to eschew the death that the king has dictated for every virgin with whom he lies.

Amer is quick to assign any criticism of her argument to a general reservoir of Western fantasies and myths, which she invariably presents as *other* than her own. Her final sentence is, on this score, significant: "One may say that while her French sister, because of her transsexual transformation, is forced ultimately to embrace heterosexuality, the Arabic lesbian, despite her heterosexual and polygamous marriage, is allowed to maintain her commitment and faithfulness to her female partner." The implicit valorization of faithful coupling (a sort of monogamy within polygamy) and the assumption of cross-cultural sisterhood merit further attention, but so too does the previously remarked persistence, albeit in inversion, of a long-standing binary: a repressive heteronormative West and a relatively permissive homoerotic Middle East that "allows" one woman to maintain her faithful commitment to another. Shadowed forth and against such a picture is one that obtains in the West today: a permissive polysexual West and a repressive heteronormative Middle East. Amer does not tarry with this other, more recent image and does not consider how it may wind itself into her deployment of binary logic. Yet inasmuch as Amer deploys modern, even postmodern, categories, the more recent repressive image imposes itself nonetheless.

Rouhi likewise waxes wishful and does so, by no small coincidence, in a reading of virginity and its possible loss. The tale on which she focuses in *Don Quixote* is that of the Captive and Zoraida, which, as Rouhi rightly observes, is "one of the most multifaceted narratives in the whole novel." Rouhi, in good Cervantine fashion, is interested in the plays of appearance and the multifarious ways in which subjects can represent themselves by ostensibly, even ostentatiously, misrepresent themselves—girls as boys and boys as girls, Christians as Muslims and Muslims as Christians or would-be Christians, natives as foreigners and foreigners as natives—all against an elaborate backdrop of war, piracy, exile, travel, and translation. What strikes her most in the Captive's tale is the Captive's reference to his female companion's "most valuable jewel, the one she valued most highly." The jewel appears to be all the more valuable because endangered by French corsairs, who strip the couple of everything they have—except, the Captive stresses, Zoraida's "most valuable jewel." The danger seems to be overstated, however, because, as the Captive declares, "the desires of these people do not go beyond money." Rouhi is not convinced and asks if it is not "easy to consider that the Captive is rewriting the story, erasing what really did happen." Easy or not, it is an intriguing question, born of the doubt that runs through a work in which appearances are so often deceiving. Stating that the scene has "preoccupied [her] for some time," she suggests that "Zoraida's most valuable jewel *is* taken from her at this moment and that the Captive is doing his best to hide that fact" (emphasis in the original). Remaining suspicious of the Captive's claim, Rouhi keeps open the possibility of a nonliteral reading that is not just speculative but also paradoxical because it makes the loss of the jewel of virginity the condition for nothing less than a "new subject."

The new subject is a man, "a husband—probably the only one in all of Spain—for whom the wife's virginity is not important." Never mind that if his future's wife's virginity were *not* important, the Captive would not call it her "most valuable jewel" and would not go to narrative pains to ensure that his interlocutors understand that the encounter with the pirates was traumatic but not *that* traumatic. According to Rouhi, the Captive "articulates an element of a new *ars amatoria* that can exist only in translation and not in the specific language of any nation. In his world vision," she goes on to say, a wife who "has lost her most valuable jewel ceases to figure prominently in his narrative." Indifferent as the Captive might be to the loss of his future wife's virginity, the loss is here not attributable to a previous love, ignorance, curiosity, accident, or even desire, but rather to rape, an act of violence that still today does not leave even the newest of subjects indifferent, however accepting, loving, and supportive they might be of the person raped. The full force of Rouhi's speculative proposition comes into light if we substitute the rather euphemistic "loss of virginity" for "rape": the fact that his future wife "has been raped ceases to figure prominently in his narrative." Whatever the case, it is one thing to say that the Captive so loves Zoraida that he will love her no matter what happens and that she is "worth" more to him than her "most valuable" part, and another to say that her most valuable part does not figure prominently for him and that, in not figuring prominently, a new subject is formed. To shift the metaphorical register ever so slightly, a rose may be a rose may be a rose, but its "loss" can take a variety of strongly divergent forms.

Then again, the hyperbolic tenor of the assertion—the Captive is "probably the only one in all of Spain" who cares not—is indicative of the tenuousness of the assertion, which Rouhi herself recognizes and which dovetails, I might add, her celebratory vision of *Don Quixote* as a whole. Like the vast majority of Cervantine scholars, Rouhi presents Cervantes as an exceptionally open and tolerant man given to "debunk[ing] illusions of a solid, certain truth, and the supremacy of one race over another" and hence eminently suited to a "modern poetics that favors paradox, hybridity, and ambivalence over certainty and dogmatism." While I am in basic agreement with this assessment, I cannot but notice its idealist gestures and its presentation of Cervantes as a man of his time who is also, as luck would have it, a man for our time, exemplary in every way. Little wonder, then, that one might be inclined to take a minor character in a novel as nothing less than a new subject—kinder, gentler, and ever so tolerant, indifferent not only to the fetish of virginity but to rape as well. As Rouhi recognizes, however, it is impossible to know, *really know,* Cervantes and his text. But we do know that he is considered great and that his greatness, in turn, has been taken—regardless of what Cervantes's own views might have been on the matter—as standing for the greatness of Spain. Today, the greatness of Spain is increasingly measured by way of official and unofficial reencounters with its "hybrid" past, a hybridity that has long been instrumentalized to present Spain as a bridge to Africa and Latin America and hence as exceptionally poised to resume a place of power in a united Europe. Amer's attention to contemporary political manipulations of texts from the distant past might be productively brought to bear on Rouhi's more textually discrete analysis in a manner that would throw the very status of the masterpiece (here, *Don Quixote*) into a more demanding and perhaps unsettling historical light.[51] The text, characters, and author of *Quixote* (no less than the text, characters, and authors of *The Thousand and One Nights*) are not beyond contemporary political forces whose insistence is such that it is not enough to declare a work a masterpiece and, in the same sweep, to suggest that such a declaration is *not* political. After all, it is not by accident that the project of Spanish cultural reaffirmation is most visibly performed by way of the governmentally supported Instituto Cervantes.

But I grow somber and suspicious, and *Don Quixote* is a fun and funny book, serious in its comic take on serious things such as honor, virginity, fidelity, propriety, property, love, friendship, and freedom. Fun too is *The Thousand and One Nights,* which Amer takes as a lamp that casts the French texts she studies into a relatively benighted position—which is, all things considered, quite true. It is not that Amer and Rouhi do not acknowledge the fun of these texts but rather that they underscore their plays of freedom, tolerance, and permissiveness as if constraints were not operant in them too or as if the constraints operant in them were somehow lessened by comparative analysis and by the sheer creativity of the writings themselves. This is especially the case with Amer, who signals the forces of constraint in the French and the forces of freedom in the Arabic, but it is also the case with Rouhi, who takes Cervantes's work as "too generous and subtle to be erased by . . . politically motivated gestures." Rouhi's and Amer's own politically motivated gestures, different and well intentioned as they are, conjure up a history of relative tolerance and intolerance. What strikes me, however, is not that there are degrees of tolerance and intolerance (for there are), but that tolerance and intolerance, freedom and constraint, lesbian interludes and new subject formations, hinge on the notoriously slippery subject of cross-dressing, to which I finally turn.

HEIRS TO FREEDOM CONSTRAINED

Cross-dressing is crucial to all of the tales here examined, from that of Qamar and Budur to that of Yde and Olive, from that of the Captive and Zoraida to another Cervantine episode centered on Ana Félix—(once) cross-dressed daughter of the (once) disguised Ricote—and don Gaspar Gregorio, Ana's "very pretty boyfriend," as Rouhi puts it, who is cross-dressed as a very pretty girl. Differences abound, however, because while cross-dressing in the tales that Amer studies is mainly of women to men and enables female same-sex contact, in the tales that Rouhi studies it is of women to men and men to women but also of Christians to Moors, Arabs, or Turks; Moriscos to Christians; Spaniards to Germans—but all within contexts in which same-sex relations are avoided rather than enabled. The complexity of cross-dressing in Cervantes's work is such that gender takes its place alongside ethnicity, nationality, and religion as only one of many performances of identity. Same-sex desire does not fare so well in Cervantes's text and is consistently presented, by way of anxiety-ridden allusions to sodomy, as abject. That in and of itself might be enough to put the brakes on otherwise well-founded claims by such critics as Barbara Fuchs, for whom, "Cervantes's representation of cross-dressing is a challenge to 'the prevailing patriarchal modes of racialized homogeneity and masculinity'" (quoted in Rouhi).[52] Just how Ana's fear that the "barbarous Turks" might take a different "jewel" from don Gaspar challenges rather than bolsters prevailing modes of racialized masculinity remains unclear, but what is clear is that Rouhi takes cross-dressing as evidence that "ethnic and religious and gender identity are fluid and continually usurped."

But what if cross-dressing were not *also,* maybe even primarily, evidence that ethnic and religious and gender identity is still, *underneath it all,* quite static and secure? After all, dressing up to flout conventions within a relatively "liberal" political regime and playing at passing as the other sex before an audience that knows the "real" or "biological" sex of the one so playing (of which more later) are not the same as dressing up to hoodwink, overcome, or avoid conventions and constraints, even rape and death. Zoraida's and Ana's flights and the disguises that they assume are not dissociable from the worries that they and others have about sodomy and rape—and sodomitic rape. Rouhi certainly does not suggest the contrary and provides a concise and fascinating reading that links transvestism (a play of bodies and dress) and translation (a play of words) as strategies of survival. "Translations," Rouhi writes, "are critiques of the original. A translation is successful only if it comes out of a process in which the meaning of the original is understood and interpreted. What Ana does is the very enactment of translation, and in her case her interpretation rests on a profoundly private reason. She uses structures and materials familiar to both sides of the Mediterranean to ensure the survival of her own fragile identity formation." Although I would nuance Rouhi's assertion by adding that a successful translation is perhaps more a question of *not appearing* to be a translation and of *passing* as the original rather than of understanding and interpreting the meaning of the original, I think that the interlocking plays of translation and transvestism here, in the context of Cervantes's text, bear more on survival *tout court* than on "the survival of [Ana's] own fragile identity formation." That said, perhaps one of the many lessons of Cervantes's text is the following: identity formation is never entirely free and is never simply a matter of choice (as when Amer says that *Miracle de la fille d'un roy* "chooses the promotion of heteronormativity"), even when it is played in a realm of relative freedom. Instead, identity formation is shot through with constraints and is thus intrinsically fragile, "always already" in danger of potentially deadly deployments.

Deadly as it can be, constraint is crucial to the practice and play of cross-dressing. Amer is particularly attentive to such deadly, constraining forces, but she tends to mobilize the competitive turns of comparative inquiry to argue that in the French text "binary heterosexual relations are upheld and validated in the end," while in the Arabic text, even though "all ends seemingly in the most heteronormative and polygamous way," constraint is somehow gainsaid or depleted by virtue of the very female same-sex contact that a polygamous patriarchal structure enables or, at least, does not entirely disable. Amer offers some fascinating readings of the mid-thirteenth-century French epic and the late fourteenth-century miracle play centered on the story of Yde and Olive (Ysabel and Olive in the miracle play), in which a woman, cross-dressed as a man, marries or is *forced* to marry a woman. *Force* is the operant term here, at odds with agency and choice (though, given the religious framework of the text, it might be more accurate to speak of "will") and impinges decisively on Amer's readings of other readings. She does not, for instance, seem particularly patient with "transgressive" readings of the French texts. For instance, while "Robert Clark has interpreted [the emperor's daughter's vow never to hold 'less dear' her female husband] as an endorsement of severely condemned forms of sexuality," Amer argues that "the emperor's daughter's response maintains the ideology of phallocentrism and heterosexuality." While Amer's reading, or counterreading, is certainly viable, I would suggest that the emperor's daughter maintains more precisely the sanctity of marriage and the law of the father. What Amer calls Yde's "true sex" does *not* trump a sanctified bond, a vow taken before God. It would be interesting to have more information about ecclesiastical law and biblical hermeneutics, especially as they bear on marriage in the early modern period, for Amer's reference to "same-sex marriage" ring here, without such historical information, in an uncannily modern way.[53]

Paul's reference to the "spiritual body" (1 Corinthians 15:44) as well as other formulations of the interrelations of corporeality and spirituality might creatively complicate Amer's reading of Yde's or Ysabel's call to her wife to feel her breasts: "j'ai memelles: tastez." Among other things, the text moves from the visual to the tactile and suggests that sight may be deceptive, appearances may be deceiving, and the visible may be a play of light and shadows without "true" substance. Amer seems to agree, but I would add that the play of sight and touch bears in complex ways on the status of the gendered and sexual body. Within my own limited expertise, I cannot but think of the doubt of Thomas, in which seeing is at once supplemented and confirmed by touching (John 20:25). Islamic texts might be deployed to similar—or dissimilar—effect, though for such an openly Christian work as *Yde et Olive*, Christian sources, which Amer does not engage, are also significant. At any rate, a comparative reading (especially one that has competitive ethicopolitical ramifications that are densely suffused with religious import) might do well to consider a wider array of texts, religious and otherwise, that are prior to and contemporaneous with those under examination. It is not that modern works should not be deployed, but that they should be complemented and queried by earlier ones, and vice versa, in a manner that queries, in turn, the teleological thrust of many critical arguments.

Amid so much emphasis on the body, sexual desire, and "same-sex marriage," the status of the spiritual and the sacred is also at stake. But it is precisely the spiritual and the sacred that contemporary writers such as Judith Butler and Marjorie Garber, the two writers who provide the lion's share of Amer's theoretical support, have trouble engaging as anything other than a function of myth, delusion, fantasy, performance, parody, and so on.[54] I admit to having a similar bias, a profoundly secular-materialist one and one that necessarily troubles any contemporary conception of sexuality and gender, or gender trouble, that purports to account for the past. Among the aforementioned concepts, there is one that, for Amer at least, breaks, destabilizes, or undoes the rigid binary force that supposedly distinguishes Western and non-Western *myths* of gender, sexuality, marriage, relationality, and desire from their *realities*. I am referring to the concept of "three"—the "third term" that Amer draws from Garber's engaging study of cross-dressing and transvestism. According to Garber, "three puts into question the idea of one: of identity, self-sufficiency, self-knowledge."[55] Amer concurs and in an earlier version of her essay argued that the putting into question of the idea of one by way of the three secured what she called the "queering possibilities of the medieval text." These "queering possibilities" were here, I contended, largely of the critic's making (which is perhaps why they do not figure explicitly in subsequent versions of the essay), and made little of the possibility that three can also subtend and support the one: most famously, in the West at least, in and as the doctrine of the Christian trinity. But three as a number and term of resolution, of stability and stabilization, and of *the end of questioning* obtains elsewhere as well. Three mediates and resolves, as when Maimunah tells Dahnash in *The Thousand and One Nights,* "'there is only one way to end our dispute, and that is to refer it to a third party'."[56] Long associated with harmony and balance, three is, for instance, traditionally the minimum number of legs needed for a chair or a table to stand upright and be stable. To say that three always and everywhere puts into question the idea of one—just as to say that transvestism or cross-dressing always and everywhere puts into question normative gender and sexual identity (which is *not* what Butler says)—is not only historically untenable; it also ironically closes down the very questioning that it would open up.

Three is also, significantly enough, a number or, more accurately, a concept that inflects different matrimonial orders differently and that is critical to any comparison of medieval French and Arabic, or Christian and Muslim, accounts of *sanctified* forms of relationality, including "same-sex marriage." For it is the unevenly triangular configuration (unevenly triangular because one position, the male one, remains determinative) that is possible in polygamy but not in monogamy that allows for the "Arabic lesbian" in the texts here examined to "proclaim her commitment and unfaltering faithfulness to her female partner." She too is constrained, as Amer knows, but the force of the "Arabic lesbian's" constraint is part of a different matrimonial and spiritual economy that may indeed allow for different and differently loving relationships from those that hold in the Christian West. Indeed, one, two, three, and so on—part and parcel of a mathematical regime that is supposedly as universal as the aesthetic regime of beauty—pertain to and shape varying normative systems. Put more simply, one, two, and three, universal as they may be, are also historically and culturally specific. The point is important, especially for cross-cultural comparisons and competitions. For if, as Amer maintains, the French texts are "more normative" than the Arabic texts, that is itself an assessment that can *only* be made by appealing to a higher standard of measurement, a universal norm that, in its apparently mathematical purity, *transcends* its historical and cultural conditions. Studies on mathematical systems in the West and the East and on the varying place and impact of zero might complicate some of the more confidently straightforward assertions regarding more fleshly matters such as the love between a man and a woman, a woman and a woman, a man and two or more women, a woman dressed as a man and a woman dressed as a woman, and so on. Whatever the case, the French texts might be *less* normative than Amer indicates (or normative in ways that are not measured in contemporary terms of phallocentrism and heterosexuality) and the Arabic texts might be *more* normative, more constrained and "forced," than she indicates. The semblance of relativism that may arise from such an assessment has, however, its own curiously cross-cultural turns—*to wit,* those of force, constraint, and male-dominated power.

Put somewhat bluntly, I am not convinced that force is enacted on the women represented in the French texts but not, or not significantly, on the women in the Arabic texts. This is not to say that force, including the force of what we now call normativity, is enacted everywhere in the *same* way. According to Amer, the revelation of the "biological" or "true sex" in the Arabic text of *The Thousand and One Nights* (with Budur as protagonist) is not made by an apologetic or repenting crossdresser . . . as was the case with Yde/Ide in the French epic, but takes place instead in the midst of an erotic and sexually charged scene." The difference seems clear and divisively so. The upshot, however, is not innocuous: critical evaluation, contemporary as it is, is shadowed by ethicopolitical evaluation—and I do not mean to evaluate this, in turn, as "wrong" or "bad," but as a *problem* of the relations between critique, ethics, and politics. What is also shadowed forth is an *ars erotica,* or as Rouhi prefers, an *ars amatoria,* that Michel Foucault (among many others) ascribes to the East and by which he (among many others) claims that the West imagines itself as scientific, juridical, and, more critically, as at once constrained by and prone to force. Yet the play of occultation and revelation, force and freedom, is more complex than some geopolitical and cultural *divorce* of eroticism and science suggests. The fact that Budur's secret is revealed only to Hayyat and the reader—in contradistinction to the public exposure in *Yde et Olive*—is not necessarily a guarantee that there is no anxiety over cross-dressing or lesbian sexuality in the Arabic story, as Amer had first contended. Quite the contrary, secrecy and partially private revelation and exposure may *also* be functions of force. They may be symptomatic, that is, of prohibition and constraint. Anxiety over cross-dressing may actually feed on and into secrecy, and secrecy may feed on and into coercive prohibition. Freedom, in short, is *nowhere* secure.

But I have been reading Amer's reading of cross-dressing,

same-sex marriage, revelation, and exposure (but also Rouhi's reading of cross-dressing, heterosexual marriage, revelation, and exposure) as if I accepted, without a hitch, the notion that the parties involved are of the same sex and that the measure of said sex is the "true," "biological" sex. I do and yet do not accept such a notion. In the tale with which I opened my reflections, Budur reveals herself as a woman to her wife, but she does not renounce her husbandly privileges and does not immediately "come out" to her "real" husband, Qamar al-Zaman, when she finally reencounters him. In fact, she plays the part not only of a man but also of a man who enjoys the sexual company of men. In a complicated game of who-is-who, a cross-dressed Budur claims that Qamar is a "wicked cook" who "fled one day, for fear that [Budur] should punish him for having split a kitchen boy while trying hard and disproportionate embraces on his form."[57] When Qamar is brought before Budur (that is to say, the king), Qamar thinks that the king (Budur cross-dressed as Qamar, that is to say, as "himself," though he does not yet know it) "must think that [he, Qamar] is a lover of boys and has treated [him] thus splendidly on that account."[58] Budur has explained to Hayyat that she has gone to such convoluted extremes to preserve her disguise in order to keep Qamar from "betraying" them "in the sight of any who see one day's gardener made king the next"—or, I might add, of any who see one day's king made queen the next. But Budur's "explanation" does not explain the pains she takes to make Qamar accept the receptive role in male same-sex intercourse. Reciting poetry that extols the pleasures of "the age of Lot" and of "little boys and paint-and-perfume minions," of "new fashioned" or "modern" acts that do *not* "fill the suffering earth / With ranks and ranks and ranks / Of useless brats," Budur, dressed as king, pushes Qamar to accept that she, as he, penetrate him.[59] If there is a "lesbian interlude" here, it is punctured in turn by a "gay male interlude," in which a woman dressed as a man seems ready to take a man as if he were a woman and yet still very much a man.

The flip-flopping of gender and sexual positions throws into

relief the imbalances of power that are themselves indicative of
other well-entrenched balances. "Oh glorious King, you have
many young women and beautiful virgins in your palace,"
Qamar says to Budur as king. "Why then would you neglect all
these for me? Do you not know that it is lawful to use women in
any way which desire, curiosity, or experiment may suggest to
you?"[60] Budur, playing the part of the king to the hilt, responds
that it is precisely when "our senses become refined and our hu-
mours alter their direction" that one can do nothing but what
one must do.[61] Qamar, worn down by so much poetry and soph-
istry, so much power and fashion, but also "a little tempted to
experience for himself this new fashion of which the poets
spoke," submits, giving himself to the man who is, and it seems
still would be, his wife.[62] Tempted or not, Qamar is also under
the impression that the king is the king and that "it would be
useless to resist [him] any further." When the two finally set
about their sexual business, Qamar finds himself, "in the twin-
kling of an eye, up-ended by the king on the mattress."[63] Up-
ended, Qamar is not overturned, for as he rubs about Budur's,
or rather the king's, thighs, he "could not find a minaret" and
professes the king to be "neither man nor woman but a white
eunuch," which, he adds, he found "much less interesting."[64]
The third term that Amer adduces as destabilizing and that she
nonetheless ascribes to one of the two conventional sexes is
here, it seems, the eunuch, a man *partly* undone but who is here
actually a woman in drag, playing a man's *part*. The turns of the
text are myriad, and they throw into question—which is what
Amer purports to champion—nothing less than the consistency
of the male/female divide. What Amer presents, albeit in passing, as a "lesbian interlude" is troublesome not only because of
the relative modernity of the term *lesbian* but also because it is
simply not enough to assume that Budur's "real" or "biological" sex erases the performative and symbolic effects—endorsed
by Hayyat's parents and her society as a whole—of Budur's role
as a man.

In other words, the moment of revelation—the moment when

Budur strips naked in front of Hayyat—is *not* decisive because Budur still retains the social trappings of a man and the privileges of a husband. She is not "herself," or not entirely, but is other or more than a woman—a woman who is, for everyone else, a king. Amer reads gender as if it were merely a function of biology, as if it were only a matter of "middle parts" and their laying bare and not also a matter of social perception, veiled as it is by prejudice, fantasy, fictions, and wishes. If Budur keeps her "secret" from everyone but Hayyat, she also keeps her masculinity, her *pronominal status* as *he* (at least in the English translation), but she does not, even before Hayyat, entirely lose her status or power as *he* either. Hayyat's willingness to have Budur "take" her virginity is not, therefore, perforce a manifestation of her "lesbian" desire, but rather a manifestation of her continued commitment to the sacred bond performed before her mother and father, a bond in which Budur remains a man who is also her husband. As Sherry Velasco notes in her study of Catalina de Erauso, the "lieutenant nun" whose cross-dressing exploits in the first half of the seventeenth century Spain have garnered increasing critical attention, it is not enough to assume that clothes do *not* make the man—or the woman:

> Undoubtedly informed by late twentieth-century theories on transgenderism, current studies on Erauso reveal a growing division among scholars regarding the gender markers and how female-to-male individuals "should" be represented in texts. While most references to Erauso use feminine adjectives and subject pronouns, scholars and students have recently begun to question what seems to be a privileging of sex-at-birth over gender adoption. . . . Chloe Rutter prefers "he" in reference to Erauso since "his actions make him a man, his actions under the guise of a woman would have been impossible."[65]

Erauso's case is undoubtedly "different" (she, or he, was a real person), but it bears some important similarities to the cross-dressed matrimonial narratives that Amer examines. Amer, however, does not acknowledge the complexities that Velasco signals, and maintains instead the "privileging of sex-at-birth over gender adoption" by which cross-dressing is taken, in essence, to be a mere mask. Qamar, however, *is* at first "fooled," and even when he finds no "minaret" in the person to whom he has upturned his end, he thinks not that she is a he but that he is *other* than he *and* she—a eunuch, a "man-unmade" being, a third term, or perhaps a third gender that neither simply destabilizes or stabilizes but that conjures forth a different sexual economy than one that rises and falls on a modern hetero/homo, male/female divide.

Enjoyable and entertaining as these comedies of sexual confusion and cross-dressing may be, violent death, as the ultimate measure of constraint and force, haunts all of the texts and contexts here under consideration. It is the potentiality for violent death, here and there, now and then, that impels me to question what I have earlier signaled, in passing, as the wishful thinking of Amer and Rouhi. Wishful thinking is, I realize, a profoundly subjective experience in which good and bad, better and worse, can vary as widely as the subjects who wish. It is also a creative act that nourishes, in many ways, art itself. *Don Quixote, The Thousand and One Nights,* and even *Yde et Olive* are rife with wishful thinking—with created subjects creatively refiguring themselves, often, though not always, under duress. In referring to wishful thinking—whether in Amer's notions of a "lesbian interlude," "unfaltering faithfulness," or a cross-cultural sisterhood or whether in Rouhi's notions of a new self indifferent to virginity or of a literary masterpiece of unwavering generosity beyond political manipulations—I do not mean to suggest that I am free from wishful thinking (or from what I have earlier called ideology) or that I am not also constrained into imagining something different, something better. My own dreams, hopes, and desires for a better world—more just, permissive, promiscuous, peaceful, and loving—may or may not be of interest to anyone else, but they do not understand the current struggle for the vindication of queerness, lesbianism, or same-sex desire as a *resurrection* of queerness, lesbianism, or same-sex desire in times long past or as a competitive comparison in which one culture *then* becomes the nostalgic reserve of another culture *now*. Force, constraint, and the lack of freedom can stimulate, that is, other forms of wishful thinking that fold in and out of other forms of critical thinking that do not rely on masterpieces, interludes, and other beautiful things.

NOTES

Editors' note: as indicated in the Preface, our authors have revised their original papers in response to discussants' critiques and seminar conversations. Since we decided to include these discussants' remarks as integral and rich contributions to this volume, our discussants revised their critiques as well, prompting even further revisions on the part of both discussants and original authors. In this case, some of Brad Epps' theoretical interventions in Sahar Amer's chapter may seem, at first, no longer relevant, as they have been incorporated into Amer's final version, published in the volume. Nevertheless, we have decided to publish these sections of Epps' critique because they hold important ramifications for the field of Islamicate Sexuality Studies and give a sense of the productive back-and-forth of collaborative criticism.

1. I follow standard practice and use the title *The Thousand and One Nights* although all citations are from *The Book of the Thousand Nights and One Night,* vol. 2., trans. Powys Mathers from the French translation by J. C. Mardrus (London: Routledge, 1996). The tale of Qamar al-Zaman and Princess Budur begins on the hundred-and-seventieth night with a presentation of a sultan named Shahriman, who is distressed at having no heir. After taking his wazir's advice to follow the sacred rituals and to pray fervently to Allah, the sultan engenders a child, Qamar al-Zaman, "moon of the time." The narrative then jumps to Qamar as a young man and to the sultan's renewed worries that his bloodline might not continue: "Fearing that [Qamar] might dissipate his strength and beauty in excess, [the sultan] wished to marry him during his lifetime and to rejoice in his posterity" (2). Yet Qamar is not interested in marriage or in women and is eventually confined to a tower to force him to comply with his father's wishes. In the tower,

Maimunah first sees Qamar, whose beauty she fears might lead Dahnash to "perpetrate some nameless thing" (7).

2. *Thousand Nights and One Night,* 11.

3. *Thousand Nights and One Night,* 12. According to Amer (chapter 3 in this book), "Qamar al-Zaman means 'the moon of the century,' while Boudour [or Budur] means 'the moon of moons.' This androgynous semantic field associated with the moon is again present in the tenth-century *Encyclopedia of Pleasure* written by Ibn Nasr al-Katib, which is one of the earliest erotic treatises in Arabic."

4. *Thousand Nights and One Night,* 12.

5. Ibid.

6. Ibid.

7. Ibid., 13.

8. I want to thank my friend and colleague Afsaneh Najmabadi for her help on this and other points.

9. *Thousand Nights and One Night,* 11.

10. The presence and play of such markers of difference as age, knowledge, social rank, and, here, ontological status make any reading of "same-sex desire" in this or other premodern texts—indeed, perhaps any text—slippery at best and reductive at worst. This is not to deny that genitally similar subjects desired each other and had sex with each other, but it is to sound a note of caution about deploying essentially modern categories such as "heterosexuality" and "homosexuality" as the *key* to understanding intersubjective relations and furthermore about deploying the essentially modern notion of same-sex desire as a way out of the terminological impasse. Indeed, when considered alongside many differences, same-sex desire—in which sex would appear to rely in the first and last instance on some raw, presymbolic anatomy—may well be a logical impossibility. The upshot of such a claim would not be to secure heterosexuality or "opposite-sex desire," by which difference is reduced and constrained as running only between anatomically determined men and women (indeed opposite-sex desire would likewise be a logical impossibility), but rather to recognize the structural necessity of difference to *any* relation, however designated. Then again, that same-sex desire and opposite-sex desire may be logical impossibilities does not mean that they do not exist as social-symbolic concepts and practices.

11. *Thousand Nights and One Night,* 13
12. Ibid., 14.
13. Ibid., 2.
14. Ibid., 14.
15. Ibid., 15.
16. Ibid., 18.
17. Ibid. Qamar and Budur are clearly presented, at first, as disinterested in, even repelled by, the opposite sex. Qamar says, "I have no inclination towards marriage and my heart feels no delight in women. Apart from the distaste I have for them, I have read so much in the books of the wise concerning the wickedness and perfidy of that sex that I would rather die than allow a woman to approach me." Ibid., 3. And Budur says, "I am queen and mistress of myself. How shall my body, which can hardly bear the touch of silks, tolerate the rough approaches of a man?" Ibid., 9.
18. *Thousand Nights and One Night,* 26, 18. That Budur has something below her navel that Qamar does not have does not seem to signify here—just as it does not seem to signify, or signifies only negatively, for instance, for Freud.
19. Ibid., 18.
20. Ibid.
21. See Judith Butler, "Imitation and Gender Insubordination," in *Inside/Out: Lesbian Theories, Gay Theories,* ed. Diana Fuss, 157–210 (New York: Routledge, 1991).
22. Gayle Rubin, "The Traffic in Women: Notes on the 'Political Economy' of Sex," in *Toward an Anthropology of Women,* ed. Rayna R. Reiter (New York: Monthly Review, 1975), 179. Rubin also examines the problems with rigorous differentiation and categorization. As she observes, "men and women are, of course, different. But they are not as different as day and night, earth and sky, yin and yang, life and death. In fact, from the standpoint of nature, men and women are closer to each other than either is to anything else—for instance, mountains, kangaroos, or coconut palms. . . . But the idea that men and women are two mutually exclusive categories must arise out of something other than a nonexistent 'natural' opposition. Far from being an expression of natural differences, exclusive gender identity is the suppression of natural similarities. It requires repression: in men, of whatever is the local

version of 'feminine' traits; in women, of the local definition of 'masculine' traits" (179–80).

23. Fatna A. Sabbah, *Woman in the Muslim Unconscious,* trans. Mary Jo Lakeland (New York: Pergamon, 1984), 4.

24. *Thousand Nights and One Night,* 67, 53.

25. Robert Irwin, *The Arabian Nights: A Companion* (London: Tauris Parke, 2004), ix.

26. *Thousand Nights and One Night,* 29.

27. Ibid. There may be no allusions to female same-sex desire before the story of Budur and Hayyat proper, but after the story ends, Dunyazad, Shahrazad's sister, blushes with delight while Shahrazad looks at her "out of the corners of her eyes" (68). King Shahryar, for his part, is "incited . . . to find out more about that new fashion which Budur described in prose and verse" (68).

28. Irwin, *Arabian Nights,* 172.

29. Ibid., 171–72.

30. *Thousand Nights and One Night,* 28 (emphasis mine).

31. Irwin, *Arabian Nights,* 171. We might remember that Budur's brother is presented as a sorcerer, but Budur herself is not.

32. Ibid.

33. I do not mean to suggest that Amer blithely shakes off such modern implications. As she says, "the contemporary Western audience's own understanding of sexuality (homosexuality and lesbianism) still affects the ways that medieval cross-cultural sexuality studies are apprehended."

34. The tension gets cast in evaluative-temporal terms. The trajectory affects, as Biddy Martin argues, feminism itself, which is cast, via the queer, into a benighted, old-fashioned, puritanical position. See, for example, Biddy Martin, "Extraordinary Homosexuals and the Fear of Being Ordinary," in *Feminism Meets Queer Theory,* ed. Naomi Schor and Elizabeth Weed, 109–35 (Bloomington: Indiana UP, 1997).

35. Irwin, *Arabian Nights,* 169.

36. Quoted in David Halperin, "Sex before Sexuality: Pederasty, Politics, and Power in Classical Athens," in *Hidden from History: Reclaiming the Gay and Lesbian Past,* ed. Martin Duberman, Martha Vicinus, and George Chauncey, Jr. (New York: Meridian, 1989), 485 n.11.

37. Eve Kosofsky Sedgwick, *Tendencies* (Durham: Duke University

Press, 1993), xii. Sedgwick deploys etymology to make a "counter-claim against [the] obsolescence" of the "queer," a "claim that something about *queer* is inextinguishable" (xii, original emphasis). The cross-cultural, transhistorical sweep of Sedgwick's rehearsal of etymology (typical of etymologies, by the way) is nonetheless quite bounded. From the Indo-European to Latin, German, English, and, in Sedgwick's own gloss, French (she says that *queer* is *"troublant,"* not just "troubling"), a peculiarly Western term is bodied forth. If I hold on to the term *queer* and deploy it, it is in a provisional, indeed strategic way. Contrary to what Sedgwick so anxiously asserts, *queer* is *not* inextinguishable, nor is it always and everywhere the term, category, or concept that is necessarily the most effective, compelling, significant, or "liberating."

38. See Gregory Hutcheson and Josiah Blackmore, eds., *Queer Iberia* (Durham: Duke University Press, 1999).

39. I refer the reader to my "The Fetish of Fluidity," in *Homosexuality and Psychoanalysis,* ed. Tim Dean and Christopher Lane, 412–31 (Chicago: University of Chicago Press, 2001), and, more pointedly, the significantly different Spanish version, "El peso de la lengua y el fetiche de la fluidez," *Revista de Crítica Cultural* 25 (2002): 66–70.

40. Gregory Hutcheson, "Return to *Queer Iberia,*" http://www.wm.edu/msll/lacoronica/qi/qi-main.html.

41. True, *lesbian, lesbienne, lesbiana,* and so on is a more venerable and international word than *queer,* but it is not without snares of its own, even when identity is figured negatively, as in Monique Wittig's famous "lesbians are not women." Monique Wittig, "The Straight Mind," *Feminist Issues* 1, no. 1 (1980): 111.

42. Jacqueline Murray, "Twice Marginal and Twice Invisible," in *The Handbook of Medieval Sexuality,* ed. Vern L. Bullough and James Brundage (New York: Garland, 1996), 191 (quoted in Amer, "Lesbian Sex and the Military").

43. See Halperin, "Sex before Sexuality"; and John Boswell, "Revolutions, Universals, and Sexual Categories," in *Hidden from History: Reclaiming the Gay and Lesbian Past,* ed. Martin Duberman, Martha Vicinus, and George Chauncey, Jr. (New York: Meridian, 1989), 17–36, 478–81. Halperin in contrast to Boswell disputes the validity of such monikers as *gay* and *lesbian* before the modern period.

44. Sir Richard Francis Burton, tr., *The Book of the Thousand Nights and a Night, with Introduction Explanatory Notes on the Manners and Customs of Moslem Men and a Terminal Essay upon the History of The Nights,* 10 vols (Privately printed by the Burton Club, c. 1900), 10:206–7. Burton's "etiology" of *pederasty* is too delicious to not quote: "The only physical cause for the practice which suggests itself to me and that must be owned to be purely conjectural, is that within the Sotadic Zone there is a blending of the masculine and feminine temperaments, a crasis which elsewhere occurs only sporadically. Hence the male *féminisme* whereby the man becomes patiens as well as agens, and the woman a tribade, a votary of mascula Sappho, Queen of Fricatrices or Rubbers" (10:208).

45. After asking, "What is at stake in appropriating and attributing homosexualities as Western?," Rouhi, as if recognizing the aforementioned historical problems with "West" and "East," goes on to ask, "What is at stake in appropriating and attributing homosexualities as *Eastern*?" and then, more intriguingly, "What is at stake in appropriating and attributing homosexualities as *translations*?" Translation, as an inevitable feature of cross-cultural analysis, as a cross-dressing of a more figurative sort, harbors for Rouhi the promise of "a new self" that rises with modernity. But the time, or timing, of this "*new* self" is not the only concern. The scholar's location—his or her formations and deformations, affiliations, affinities, and fantasies, "native" and "non-native" languages—is also implicated.

46. Irwin, *Arabian Nights,* 37.

47. In an earlier version of her essay, Amer remarked that it was difficult to know what aspects of the relationship between Budur and Hayat al-Nufus had circulated orally or in writing in the medieval East and West and what aspects were later seventeenth- to nineteenth-century additions by scribes. And yet, it is not just a matter of knowing *what* aspects of the tale circulated, and when, but indeed whether the tale circulated at all in the early modern period. As Irwin notes, "The very existence of the *Nights* was unknown in western Europe until Galland began to publish his translation in 1704," though "individual stories from the *Nights* had been included in medieval and Renaissance story collections." Irwin, *Arabian Nights,* 42. It is not, in other words, that the tale

that Amer studies did not circulate, but that its circulation, let alone its impact, remains uncertain.

48. "Neglected until modern times in the Near East," Irwin writes, "the *Arabian Nights* has been so widely and frequently translated into western languages that, despite the Arab antecedents of the tales, it is a little tempting to consider the *Nights* as primarily a work of European literature. Yet there is no remotely satisfactory translation of the great bulk of the *Nights* into either English or French." Irwin, *Arabian Nights*, 9. Irwin's assessment, which includes a detailed account of the various sources, translations, and transmissions of the text(s), could not be more different from Amer's deployment of the *Nights,* or more precisely the tale of Qamar and Budur, as if it circulated as such in medieval France. I find Irwin much more persuasive.

49. Amer does say that "much of medieval French literary writings can be read in terms of hybridization and cross-fertilization" (Western and Eastern), but she does not make a similar claim for *The Thousand and One Nights.*

50. Herbert Marcuse, "Repressive Tolerance," in *A Critique of Pure Tolerance* (Boston: Beacon Press, 1965), 81–117.

51. I am not the only one to hesitate before celebrating Cervantes or the *Quixote*—or *any* author or text. Fernando Savater, a polemical Basque thinker (polemical for his support of the unity of Spain against Basque separatism), takes on the greatness that is mobilized in the postmodernized name of Cervantes and his masterpiece. In his *Instructions to Forget* El Quijote *and Other General Essays* from 1984, Savater notes that "it is evident that Don Quijote de la Mancha is not only a character of literary fiction but also many more and many graver things—a national myth, an ironic ideal, the silhouette of a conception of the world, the origin of a pejorative or praiseful adjective, the last hero, and the first antihero. . . . It is not [Cervantes's] fault; indeed, I suspect that it is not even his merit. There is something in *Don Quijote* that begs to be transcendentalized, something that relates it to the *religious* world." Fernando Savater, *Instrucciones para olvidar el* Quijote *y otros ensayos generales* (Madrid: Taurus, 1995), 17 (translation and emphasis mine). What Savater signals is the national and religious appropriation of Cervantes and the *Quixote*. I do not say that Rouhi merely follows suit (she is far too sophisticated a critic

for that), but she does present Cervantes and the *Quixote* as if messages of nondogmatic noncertainty were certain and as if those messages and lessons could *not* be used for less ethically laudable ends—say, the symbolic self-fashioning of Spain as an *exceptionally* pluralistic country that is perfectly suited to a mode of hegemony in which culturalism masks commercialism and in which racial, ethnic, and sexual differences are recast as so many signs that sell.

52. Barbara Fuchs, *Passing for Spain: Cervantes and the Fictions of Identity* (Urbana: University of Illinois Press, 2003).
53. I use the quotation marks to indicate that the marriage is not here openly sanctified and indeed must remain shielded in secrecy.
54. Marjorie Garber, *Vested Interests: Cross-Dressing and Cultural Anxiety* (New York: Routledge, 1992).
55. Ibid., 11.
56. *Thousand Nights and One Night*, 13.
57. Ibid., 57.
58. Ibid., 60.
59. Ibid., 61, 64, 63.
60. Ibid., 62.
61. Ibid.
62. Ibid., 64.
63. Ibid., 64, 65.
64. Ibid.
65. Sherry Velasco, *The Lieutenant Nun: Transgenderism, Lesbian Desire and Catalina de Erauso* (Austin: University of Texas Press, 2000), 6.

FIVE

The Obscenity of the Vizier[1]

Frédéric Lagrange

No, in the end all I could conclude was that the fault lay with categorization itself, that crude and elementary tool the inadequacy of which becomes more evident the deeper one probes. For homosexuality is a discipline the advanced study of which necessitates, as it were, its own transcendence, which is why all its serious students finally dispense with terminology altogether, and focus their attentions solely on the particulars of human lives.

—*David Leavitt,* Martin Bauman[2]

SITUATING THE INSULT

Eve Kosofsky Sedgwick, advocating the construction of queer significations, has it that "sexual desire is a powerful and unpredictable solvent of stable identities."[3] What if certain modes of speech, such as the insult, also revealed the limitations of our feeble taxonomies? What if, in those premodern and non-Western cultures in which the irrelevance of the concept of homosexuality is now universally agreed on, insult could *fortuitously* construct an identity for which those cultures had no formal terminology—an identity that would imply preference of gender over role and that would associate attitudes or appearances that are usually situated on different sides of constructed gender roles, such as effeminacy and the dominant role in male-male sexuality?

This chapter explores the following hypothesis: could insult, as a mode of speech, reveal conceptions about same-gender sexuality that are left unexplored or unthought of in other types of discourse? My interest in this topic developed as I started translating, from Arabic into French, a tenth-century libel written by one of the most prominent prose writers in medieval Islamic culture, Abu Hayyan al-Tawhidi (d. circa 1010). In this text, a historical character, the vizier Ibn 'Abbad, is described in terms that constitute a portrait of what a contemporary academic would call a paradigmatic homosexual. This was a surprise because although medieval Arabic literature frequently includes homoerotic narratives and mentions of homosexual intercourse, this literature does not conceive of homosexuality and homosexual characters in the modern sense of the term. Instead, the contemporary Western reader who has never perhaps questioned his holistic conception of homosexuality finds it "sliced up" into a multitude of role specializations, since medieval authors usually sees no "community of desire" between, for instance, the active and the passive partners of homosexual intercourse.

Much recently published research in Arabic literature has been undertaken from a "gender studies" or "gay and lesbian studies" angle[4] and analyzes poetry or literary prose (*adab*) to explore issues of social acceptability (as opposed to religious proscription) in classic and premodern Arab Islamic culture and questions of sexual and emotional relations between persons of the same sex. These studies show that the *majin* (the rake) who functions as a "ritual clown" (to use the expression coined by A. Hamori)[5]—whether as an *adib* (a cultivated upper-class man) or a poet or as a producer or an object of this discourse—is a figure tolerated within the limits of the "space of transgression" assumed within Arab Islamic culture, from the Abbasid period until the dawn of the colonial era. The studies even demonstrate that chaste homoeroticism does not constitute a transgression *per se*. A number of texts of *adab* (high literature) legitimize the *reference* to an attraction for the same sex at the emotional, spiritual, or physical level through the various but distinct figures of the *mukhannath* (effeminate, sometimes transvestite male), the *luti* (active sodomite), the *ma'bun or halaqi*[6] (passive sodomite), the *mu'ajar* (male prostitute playing the passive role), and the *amrad* (young beardless page courted by the *luti* or simply an admirer of beauty). However, if mere attraction goes uncondemned, sexual lust cannot be formally legitimized, at least outside *hazl* (banter), which establishes itself as a parody of the normative discourse of the *jidd* (serious).[7]

Within the highly ritualized framework of the *mujun* (libertine discourse), medieval texts sometimes flaunt a disrespect for sacred law. The right to transgress the natural order and the divine order is here asserted when the discourse, whether direct or reported speech, is that of a *majin* (libertine). In general, this transgression is narrated or collected with neutrality—or at the worst with an affected frown. For form's sake, the authors of anecdotic compilations express feigned outrage, this being essentially a way of expressing within their discourse illicit lust under the pretext of condemning it. The underlying principle is that a denunciation always remains an enunciation. One could then speak of a mode of transgression that could be termed "paraliptic."[8] Given the ritual nature of this transgression, it is not entirely possible to determine whether this literary acceptability of same-sex attraction refers to a true social acceptability (about which the limits remain to be defined) or whether it refers to simple poetic posturing or even provocation.[9] I would argue that *adab* prose literature and the poetry it contains is certainly not a reflection of that society but that it allows for the perception of concepts that the Arab Islamic elite formed about human complexity:

> The *adab,* by the very nature of its normative function and its search for uniqueness, and poetry, by its extreme codification, can, I believe, shed light on the practices and occurrences of a society or mentality such as have been perceived and represented by a specific social group, that called the *Khassa* by the sources—i.e., the milieu of the production and reception of this literature.[10]

The discourse expressing tolerance of transgression has on the whole been studied in greater depth by Arabists than scholars whose mother tongue is Arabic. This is due to obvious though perhaps subconscious ideological reasons: the "rehabilitation" of the damned figure of the homosexual in (former) Arab Islamic societies can be achieved only through the creation of an anthology of its recurring presence in love poetry and in the sexology of the Arabs.[11] Such an apparent appraisal, in premodern texts of anecdotal form, constitutes a "cultural legitimization through which homosexuality might have a right of entry to the order of discourse" *(légitimation culturelle à travers laquelle l'homosexualité pou[rrait] accéder à l'ordre du discours).*[12] In a move similar to the search by nineteenth- and early twentieth-century authors for a legitimization of homosexual desire in Spartan, Doric, or Athenian models (in the no doubt mythic foundations of Western culture),[13] scholars studying classical Arabic literature in Western universities react to the moralist tensions in modern Arab societies (and especially of their governments) by bringing up past permissiveness, long gone and presently out of reach. The vast majority of research on same-gender sexual practice in Arab Muslim societies is conducted and published outside the Arab world, regardless of the authors' origins, and it is rarely written in the Arabic language. In this respect, Ibrahim Mahmud's recent work *Al-Mut'a al-Mahzura* (The pleasure of the forbidden), despite its methodological limits, constitutes an exception as the author abstains from making any moral judgments.[14]

But if the image of "homoerotic" relationships seems to be (at least partially) a legitimate representation in the literature of the Abbasid, Ayyubid, and Mamluk periods, it would perhaps be wrong to limit our knowledge of the place of same-sex attraction in classical society[15] to simply positive or pseudo-pejorative descriptions. Outside religious discourse (a discourse of condemnation that should not be too rigorously distinguished from that of the *adab,* which itself aims at the establishment of behavioral norms through a reversal in parody's discourse) and the law, there is another negative discourse that is concerned with the attraction and relations between partners of the same sex. This other discourse is to be found in prose as well as in poetry. It is the discourse of satire, insult, libel, and epigram, in which sexuality plays a central role, particularly beginning with the Abbasid period.

The present chapter examines a particular example of this satiric discourse—the strategy of discredit adopted by the tenth-century writer Abu Hayyan al-Tawhidi in his famous libelous satire targeting the Buyid viziers al-Sahib b. 'Abbad (938–995) and Abu al-Fadl b. al-'Amid (d. 970)—the *Kitab Akhlaq al-Wazirayn* (The blame of the two viziers).[16] I show how Tawhidi constructs his argument against one of his two targets, Ibn 'Abbad, by encircling him with anecdotes that evoke *khinath* (effeminateness), *ubna* (passive sodomy), and *liwat* (active sodomy)—first concerning other characters and in a second sequence directly attacking him.

However, the interest in insult is not limited to establishing the obvious—the existence at the heart of *adab* of a pejorative discourse that disavows homoeroticism and counterbalances the fragile legitimization of sexual transgression in the *hazl* (jest) discourse or the tolerance of chaste homoeroticism in poetry. In the course of this study, I suggest that the problem of the insult indirectly questions the pertinence or inappropriateness of the modern concept of homosexuality for the study of a premodern society. The classic debate within the field of gender studies between constructionist or essentialist approaches is once again relevant. Does classic Arab Islamic culture consider only sexual acts, no matter what the propensity of the subject for the sex of his or her partner, and does it socially condemn only the man who takes on a role of voluntary sexual submission (passive penetration), as is in fact the case in a large number of premodern cultures?[17] Or rather does there exist within the interstices of discourse, beyond this division between roles, a link between *ubna* (passive sodomy) and *liwat* (active sodomy) that would place these two practices on the same side of a divide?

Are effeminateness and passivity the only attitudes or acts that are condemned by satire, or might one detect within this discourse the first crystallization of a line of demarcation between the partners' sex (in opposition to the distinction between roles)?

Al-Tawhidi's tenth-century text invites us to explore the importance of the insult in the construction of heteronormalization. The insult, in its colloquial usage, stigmatizes the passive partner by its very vocabulary. Insult seems to be, in our contemporary cultures, a vestige of older definitions of sexual normalcy.[18] But the question that should then be asked is how new norms of normalcy could be so quickly adopted. Could they have been in gestation? These observations lead to an investigation into the role of the insult in the "preconstruction" of a homosexual "character" (to avoid mentioning identity), following earlier work by Didier Eribon.[19]

IBN 'ABBAD: VIZIER OR DEGENERATE?
A SETTLING OF SCORES

The *Kitab Akhlaq al-Wazirayn* is presented by Abu Hayyan al-Tawhidi as a work commissioned by the Baghdadi vizier Ibn Sa'dan, servant to Samsam al-Dawla, son of 'Adud al-Dawla.[20] It is the portrait of two viziers under Buyid emirs, two former secretaries who had reached the highest post to which a man of letters could aspire. These two people knew Tawhidi personally, and Tawhidi, who considers himself wronged, is out to settle the score. Of the 550 pages of the Tanji edition, the first 79 are a theoretical introduction to the reasons that led Tawhidi to compose a work of "denunciation of shortcomings" *(mathalib)* of such uncommon scale. The portrait of Sahib b. 'Abbad then takes up pages 80 to 320, and the rest are theoretically dedicated to Ibn al-'Amid, though the author actually frequently returns to the case of Ibn 'Abbad, his principle object of resentment. The imbalance is patent, and the author paints a fascinating portrait of vizier Ibn 'Abbad as a degenerate, half-crazy, ridiculous, and arrogant prince, through which the characteristics of the ideal leader may be read "in negative."

A whole book of insult is unprecedented in the field of medieval Arabic prose. Insult in Arabic belles-lettres, although common, is to be found mainly in poetry as the main topic of a *qasida* (ode). It can be aimed at a tribe, an ethnic group, or an individual. It can be put in measured words or in the coarsest language, but it generally revolves around the exact opposite of the qualities appraised in the laudatory ode: miserliness (instead of generosity), lack of virility (instead of courage), unethical behavior. Other literary expressions of insult (such as the short rhymed epigram or the prosaic libel epistle) are to be found in this extraordinary book, which incidentally offers a short anthology of insult literature in its avant-propos. Extreme vulgarity of language seems to be common in this highly codified genre, in which one often suspects that the attack is not sincere and simply fits in the wider genre of *mujun* (ribaldry) literature, as *exercices de style* that were undoubtedly appreciated as forbidden pleasures in the caliphal or vizieral courts of the ninth and tenth centuries. The pervasiveness of insults related to sexual matters helps establish the boundaries of normality in this field. But Tawhidi's work goes far beyond those limited genres.

In classic Arab Islamic civilization, certain forms of behavior break with divine law and the domain of good morality *(husn al-akhlaq)*. Nevertheless, if one is to believe *adab* literature, these forms of behavior were common, accepted customs of the princely courts, though without being recognized as legitimate. The consumption of intoxicating beverages and sexual relations with young (beardless) prepubescent or barely pubescent page boys are examples of such behavior. The cardinal sin lies not as much in the transgression of a religious norm as in the affirmation—indeed, the assertion—of the right to this transgression or even worse in the negation of the sinful nature of this action. To announce and to brag about an offense limits the range, denies the very nature, and denies the generosity of God, who covers the offense with his protective veil *(sitr)*. Poets were the first to affirm transgression in literature, and the poetry of the Abbasid *muhdathin* (modernists) is filled with "rights advocates." Abu Nuwas (d. circa 815) is the most flagrant example of those who were to transgress and subvert these codes to take pleasure in their transgression or to ridicule the codes.

This avowed transgression has room for expression within the framework of the classic *adab*. Sure of its values, this dominant society has nothing to fear from maintaining a margin of tolerance at its heart. But if the prince's fools can take advantage of this margin, the prince cannot do the same, since it is his duty to be a model Muslim, worthy of imitation. It is necessary to keep this in mind in the charges brought by Tawhidi against Ibn 'Abbad. It is a question not of condemning the *mujun* (ribaldry) or the *sukhf* (obscenity) in all of their manifestations but only of when they emanate from the one whose responsibility it is to censure them, although he might possibly and secretly be a consumer but not producer or advocate of those transgressions. Ibn 'Abbad is depicted as ceaselessly humoring *sukhf, khala'a,* and *mujun*.[21] Because the boundary is overstepped, the author considers it his duty to denounce his personal enemy. The text[22] includes a revealing question. While Ibn 'Abbad delights in recounting inappropriate anecdotes and making misplaced remarks, such as the sacrilegious comparison between the flatulence of a table guest and the second caliph 'Umar b. al-Khattab's pledge of allegiance to the first successor of Muhammad Abu Bakr, which would both have "escaped" them, Tawhidi asks, *"'a fa-hadha min al-mujun al-mustatab"* (is that the level of effrontery that is appreciated?), a formulation that implies therefore that, on the contrary, there does exist a fully permissible type of effrontery and obscenity.

The accusations against Ibn 'Abbad by Tawhidi, who it seems was wronged by 'Abbad, cannot be taken at face value, even if Tawhidi were to dispense with a long introduction that tries to convince us of the contrary (all the while recognizing the right to exaggeration).[23] Nevertheless, the reproaches formulated against Ibn 'Abbad and Ibn al-'Amid are slightly different. The former is reproached for his inconsistency, megalomania, avarice, inappropriate behavior, love of obscenity, mixing with the populace at the expense of the literati *(udaba')*, incompetence in debate, and ridiculously bombastic speech. The latter is under fire for his arrogance, lies, misery, and cruelty. As for the evocation of sexual habits, this concerns only Ibn 'Abbad and, in a particularly recurrent way, concentrates on two aspects that are generally understood as distinct in classic Arabic culture—his avowed love for boys as an active partner and the secret reality of his character, which is passively effeminate and obsessed by obscenity.

IBN 'ABBAD ACCORDING TO HISTORY VERSUS IBN 'ABBAD ACCORDING TO TAWHIDI

The historic truth about Tawhidi's accusation is of no importance. One should simply note that the portrait of Ibn 'Abbad as vizier is contrary to the hyperbolic praise that one finds in the notice dedicated to the Sahib by al-Tha'alibi in his *Tatimmat al-Yatima,* the most famous anthology of tenth-century authors:

> No words are strong enough that come to my mind to express the height of his rank in matters of knowledge and of education, the splendor of his munificence and of his generosity, his unique position at the peak of all virtues and of all glories . . . . I will therefore content myself to say that he is the Summit of the Orient, the Memory of Glories, the Star of Times, Source of Justice and Benevolence, he whom one can praise more than any of God's creatures, he without whom virtue in our times could only be forsaken merchandise[.][24]

No source other than al-Tawhidi denounces either the *luti* or the *ma'bun* sides of Ibn 'Abbad. It is nonetheless clear that the Sahib composed, within the framework of his verse collection,[25] numerous works of *ghazal* (love poetry) or poems containing *ghazal* verses evoking the charms of beautiful young men[26] and that no clearly feminine figure is present in this collection. But this *qawl fi l-murdan* (poetry on adolescent boys), which found its place in the literary canon between the end of the eighth and the ninth centuries, had become a literary cliché by the tenth century. It should also be stressed that the canons of adolescent beauty in the classical imaginary were not clearly gendered. The terms used to describe young, fifteen-year-old heroes in *The Thousand and One Nights* and the standards of beauty that are applied to them are identical for boys and girls. However, one particular trait, the appearance of a beard, transforms the boy into an adult male. A *ghazal* poem describes the charms of a very young man who does not yet have a beard or whose first beard *('idhar)* has just appeared, marking a black line on his rosy cheek. It can be seen as an exercise in style or mere appreciation of beauty, not necessarily a revelation of the author's actual sexuality. On the other hand, the recurrence of this theme reveals the literary legitimacy of an adult man's expression of desire for a young man who has barely reached manhood and therefore reveals at least an aesthetic formula. One can grasp from this the degree to which the aesthetic formulas of homosexuality in the modern sense and the adulation of the beautiful adolescent boy in classic Arabic literature diverge. What is turned into an object of desire is not extreme virility but rather its timid blossoming under an androgynous surface. The Sahib is hardly different from his contemporaries. One should notice principally the loaded meaning of the topos of the first beard *('idhar)*, an allusion to that of the *'aqarib* (kiss curl). The following verses dedicated to a lisping effeminate young man seem to me exemplary:

> I asked a young fawn: What is your name?
> He answered simpering: 'Abbath [for Abbas, a common name].
> I started to lisp myself,
> I asked him: where are the cupth and the plateth?[27]

The modern reader is, however, struck by the recurring presence of homoerotic *ghazal* sections used as introduction of the *nasib* type[28] in the works praising the family of the Prophet *(Ahl al-Bayt),* in which the Sahib underscores his Shiite faith. This astonishing freedom culminates in four works where the Sahib praises the beauty of a young 'Ali whose name alone evokes charms, bringing together the image of an ephebe-type with that of 'Ali b. Abi Talib, mentioned indirectly yet nevertheless obviously present.[29] Is this simple literary convention or rather amusing provocation? The second hypothesis cannot be ignored, especially since the Sahib is said to have linked, in the same way, his Mu'tazilite faith to the love of boys. Yaqut's *Mu'jam al-Udaba'* thus shows the Sahib confronted by his master Fakhr al-Dawla with his provocations:

> I heard Ibn 'Abbad tell the following facts: "I never asked permission to be let into the court of Fakhr al-Dawla, when he was in pleasant company *(fi majlis al-uns)*, without him regaining his most prudish demeanor *(illa wa-ntaqala ila majlis al-hishma)* before allowing me to enter. I don't recall that he ever fell into vulgarity or that he ever joked with me, except for one particular occasion when he asked me, "They tell me that you recited this verse:
>
> > My ideological school is that of the Mu'tazilites
> > And my way of fucking is that of a sodomite."
>
> I pretended to be shocked by his frankness of tone and responded: "Between us, there is enough serious business to deal with for us to avoid trifles *(hazl)*." I then stood up, feigning anger. And he then had sent to me so many apology letters that I again took up his company. Afterward he never again told jokes or made offhand remarks.[30]

With respect to this verse, it is necessary to make the distinction between a provocation by a vizier who is assured of his master's protection and who knows himself to be indispensable and a veritable affirmation of his sexual tastes. This affirmation, if it is one, is primarily literary: it would be an affirmation of the right of a prince to grapple with the domain of the *mujun*. Ibn 'Abbad's angry reaction to Fakhr al-Dawla's ribbing on this subject (does he tease him about his habits or about the public display of his indecency?) is moreover eloquent: he gets carried away and demands an apology.

Beyond the complaints that Tawhidi brings against Ibn 'Abbad, it can be discerned that the underlying reason for this hostility and resentment is the competition that is brought about by power against knowledge on its own turf. Even though the intellectual should have a privileged position next to the prince, here is the prince who prides himself on his knowledge of *adab* and who compares himself to poets, letter writers, and savants, placing himself as judge and participant in all of these domains. Ibn 'Abbad is perhaps the most prolific of these enlightened princes of the tenth century. However, according to the notices dedicated to certain princes and viziers in al-Tha'alibi's *Yatimat al-Dahr*, every great leader of the Islamic world in the tenth century had to be a man of great sophistication. It would not have been possible to represent the Buyid princes as brutish. They all knew at the very least how to write verse of delicate composition. Romantic, including homoerotic, subject matter is thus widespread in works by princes of this period.

Earlier I remarked that it would be risky (and perhaps of little relevance) to speculate on whether the historical Ibn 'Abbad really pursued boys for love interest or whether he was an active or a passive sodomite. But Tawhidi's accusations need to be examined with texts other than Ibn 'Abbad's collection of poems (for example, with the written works of contemporaries in high office). Is the evocation of the androgynous beauty of young pages reserved for court poets, or is it common only among the rulers of this tenth-century Muslim Empire? The *Yatima* is yet again the best guide for answering this question. If no verse on boys is attributed to the celebrated master of Aleppo, Sayf al-Dawla, other Hamdanite princes take up this theme. Thus, Abu al-'Asha'ir al-Hamdani, who himself writes about the 'idhar (first beard) of a young man, and whose anthology features a short story with clearly homoerotic content:

An informer told us the following story: "Having just paid a visit to Abu al-'Asha'ir, who had fallen ill, I asked him: how is our Emir doing? He pointed to a young man standing in front of him, named Nastas, who was so handsome that one could have said that Ridwan, in a moment of carelessness, let him escape from paradise. Then he recited these lines to me:

> This young man made my body languid
> By the languor of his gaze.
>
> There is so much coquetry in the torpor of his eyes
> That the torpor has been transmitted to my bones.
>
> My soul mixes with his
> As water mixes with wine.[31]

While this is a rather banal story expressed in common verse, it proves that the allusion to the three slightly transgressive topoi (a languor attributable to the sight of a young ephebe *(al-nazar)*, a gaze charged with erotic torpor, and the habitual mixing of wine and water) can be expressed by the prince. The Buyids themselves are not to be outdone: 'Adud al-Dawla writes about *'idhar*:

> Your beauty spot in your first beard in the night
> Is blackness upon blackness upon blackness.[32]

Similarly, a story taken by al-Tha'alibi from Abu Ishaq al-Sabi's *Kitab al-Taji* shows Mu'izz al-Dawla at the mercy of a young Turk, to the point of provoking the mockery of vizier al-Muhallabi, apparently himself somewhat aroused by the young man:

Mu'izz al-Dawla Abu al-Husayn had a young Turkish page by the name of Takin al-Jamidar, beardless, with a striking face, who drank continuously without ever sobering up and would always give into pleasure. But Mu'izz al-Dawla became so infatuated with him and liked him so much that he placed him at the head of a cavalry regiment destined to fight the Hamdanites. Al-Muhallabi [the vizier] found him charming and of great beauty but saw in him a person made for love and not for war. And so he declaimed this verse about him:

A fawn of striking features and gracious figure
So like young virgins that one could almost see his breasts
    pointing out.

A sword and a belt were hung from his waist that weighed
    heavy upon him.
For having placed him at the head of the army, the troop was
    lost and the general with it.

It was not long before the [new] general was beaten in com-
    bat, and so it happened just as
the al-Muhallabi's verse had foreseen.[33]

The tone of this epigram, between *ghazal* and *hija'*, suggests that neither the prince nor his minister was immune to the charms of a young man whose seduction lied demonstrably in his androgynous appearance. While the Egyptian and Andalusian poetry attributed to leaders cited in al-Tha'alibi's anthology does not feature homoerotic themes and motifs, the preceding discussion shows that Ibn 'Abbad, in his exaltation of male adolescent charms, is no exception among the princes of the tenth-century Arab Orient. And if Ibn 'Abbad is not an exception, al-Tawhidi will also demonstrate that he too, in his condemnation of the vizier, follows and respects a double literary and moral canon.

OBSCENITY AND SEXUALITY IN SATIRE AND INSULT

Justifications in Favor of Satire in Prose and Poetry

Throughout his introduction, al-Tawhidi develops a discourse arguing the legitimacy of his composition of a *kitab* that is entirely dedicated to a satire on two people. What the author attempts to justify is not simply the denunciation of the vices of a prince whose true nature no one dares expose. Abu Hayyan's justification is in fact threefold. First, he sets out to define his project in relation to the classical poetic genre of the *hija'* (libel). Second, he seeks to elaborate a moral justification for writing a work based on insult. Finally, he wants to situate himself in a certain literary continuity, even though his work could be seen as the founding of a new genre. Every creation at the heart of the *adab* has to be camouflaged through its location in a preexisting literary movement, a tradition through which one could award oneself predecessors, thereby guaranteeing for oneself a sort of generic *isnad*. Abu Hayyan knows that his enterprise is risqué and reprehensible. Certainly, the rhetorical excesses of invective are tolerated for the same reason that the positive presentation of transgression is tolerated in poetry: in both cases, the excess is ritual. But the author ceaselessly tries to protect himself against the moral condemnation of his project (from which, however, he will not escape), on the one hand, by references to precedents in the field of *adab* prose and, on the other, by a religious defense making the denunciation of the crimes of the unjust prince appear to be a religious duty.

As used by Tawhidi in the *Akhlaq al-Wazirayn,* this line of approach—passing off satire as a pious act on the basis that covering up the Sahib's misdeeds would represent major wrong-doing—must be made convincing to his readers. The stakes are high, since the accusations of *ubna* (passive sodomy) scattered throughout his text are part of those morally dubious themes in the treatment of poetic *hija'* that tarnish the accuser's reputation as much as that of the accused. In no way does Tawhidi hold back from citing anecdotes and writings (which he may have forged) of unexpected obscenity. Certainly, citation and production are not of the same order. Nevertheless, the argumentation formerly developed by al-Jahiz and taken up again by Tawhidi in the *Imta'* to justify the presence of *hazl* (jest) and in addition *sukhf* (obscenity) in the domain of the *adab* no longer holds. It is not a question here of creating a breathing space within scholarly discourse but rather the central element of his textual pillo-rying of Ibn 'Abbad.

Sexual Insults, Passive Sodomy, Active Sodomy

G. J. Van Gelder notes that "Homosexuality is an extremely common topic of *hija'* since Abbasid times; but in some contexts being the active partner is a reason for boastful poetry."[34] This remark confuses different modes of discourse. Affirming the right to be a *luti* (active sodomite) is unthinkable in the framework of the serious *(jidd)* boastful poetry *(fakhr)*. This affirmation finds its place only in the various parodies of the *fakhr* authorized by the *mujun* mode, such as *ghazal majin, khamriyya,* where the assertion of transgressions becomes possible, or even in another mode, that of diatribe, that can easily be linked to the *mujun* and to the *sukhf.* The association of virility and the values that it disseminates *(muru'a)* with the penetrator's sexual role, no matter what the object of his penetration, is probably a universal image in patriarchal cultures. But the articulation of this conception does not have its place in the discourse of *'ilm* (science), which on the contrary limits natural desire's field of action to the religiously licit. Nor does this articulation have its place in the *adab* in the strictest sense, inasmuch as it is the avowed word of its author. It can break through only in the interstices of discourse. This association can be seen particularly in the insult, which stigmatizes the supposed loss of the manly role. One technique in *hija'*, recurrent since pre-Islamic times, consists in calling a man a woman, a predictable insult in a culture where a free man is at the top of the social pyramid. The representation through synecdoche of this comparison by the evocation of women's sexual roles is also quite predictable.

But while it makes sense in the literature of invectives, in poetry as well as in prose, to belittle the insulted's virility by mentioning his role as an invert, two remarks may be added. First, no one could seriously affirm the right to be a *ma'bun* (passive sodomite), even within the literary framework of *mujun.* If provocative remarks can be credited to certain characters who belong to the *mukhannathun* (effeminates caste, verses of the pseudo-*fakhr* genre that assert the practice of passive sodomy are few and are not taken seriously by anthologists, who prefer to see in them the pinnacle of *sukhf* rather than the expression of reality. One might counter that there exists at least one exception to the anonymity of the *adib-ma'bun*—the poet Jahshawayh (ninth century). Though an *adib,* a recognized poet, he flaunted his status as a catamite. Strikingly, however, the anthologists refuse to listen to his discourse. They deny the reality of his transgression and prefer to see in it a game. Take for example Ibn al-Mu'tazz:

> Jahshawayh was the most active sodomite that there could be [*min alwat al-nas*] and the furthest from what he accused himself of [*wa-ab'adihim mimma rama bihi nafsahu*]. He would say that he was passive [*yansibu nafsahu ila l-bigha'*] and would compose verse about this facetious topic that does not represent the truth.[35]

Note the terms used by Ibn al-Mu'tazz: to *qualify* oneself as a passive sodomite is expressed in terms of an *accusation (rama bihi nafsahu).*

Second, with respect to attacks on virility, in the *hija'* genre the word *luti* is not used as a term of abuse, as if the role of active sodomite were blameworthy only in the framework of religious rather than social norms. (This works in support of the constructionist argument.) From these remarks, the ambiguity of al-Tawhidi's charges can be seen clearly. The literature for which Sahib b. 'Abbad is reproached and his public excesses of *mujun* serve only to categorize him as a *luti,* blameworthy with respect to divine law and to the prince's duty to set an example but not with respect to the literary norms of *hija'* or perhaps to society's norms. Since this accusation alone does not make enough sense within the literature of diatribe, so clearly codified, it is therefore coupled by Tawhidi with that of effeminateness and passive sodomy. Are these the requirements of an accusatory rhetoric that would remain otherwise unsupported, or rather do they signify the perception of a natural link between *liwat* (active sodomy) and *ubna* (passive sodomy)? I return to this.

TAWHIDI'S STRATEGY

An Obscenity Disowned

The modern reader, probably just as the medieval one, is led to wonder what makes the difference between the overwhelming presence of *sukhf* in the *Akhlaq al-Wazirayn* and between the collections of anecdotes that sometimes contain entire sections of obscene material. See, for example, al-Abi's *Nathr al-Durr*, al-Shabushti's *Kitab al-Diyarat*, and al-Raghib al-Isfahani's *Muhadarat al-Udaba'*, among others. In the intentions of the author, the nuance is clear. The theme of *sukhf* is rendered here not as a collection of risqué anecdotes focusing on Ibn 'Abbad, as one would focus on ninth-century buffoons such as 'Abbada or Jahshawayh or other *ma'bun* amusers, but rather either as jokes or poetry or as epistles of libel.

Jokes or outrageous poetry, supposedly recited in public by an Ibn 'Abbad taking endless pleasure in *sukhf*, would not be appropriate to his rank of vizier. Ibn 'Abbad would have declaimed them to rail against courtesans or illustrious predecessors in control of the Vizierate and, according to witnesses solicited by Tawhidi, to avoid suspicions against himself. The connection established by Abu Hayyan between Ibn 'Abbad's enunciation of scabrous anecdotes stigmatizing homosexuals and his own corruption is reaffirmed in a later passage in the text.

> Ibn 'Abbad exhibited no shame in the presence of filthy remarks: it was this very fact that led him to be suspected and allowed him to be slandered. By mentioning his faults, no one feared committing a sin or exposing himself to blame. At any rate, his faults were innumerable, and no one could have gone through them all.[36]

Abu Hayyan is careful to cite (or to put in the Sahib's mouth) jokes that spread doubt and confusion. But they probably form a part of a stock of humorous replies known to the author, who decides in this case to adjust their meaning to make his case.

Supposedly famous epistles of libel, written by predecessors or contemporaneous litterati, by their very (alleged) existence are justifications that bring the project to a successful conclusion by virtue of the presence of a precedent. In general, any obscene citation in the *Akhlaq al-Wazirayn* is surrounded by a "safety device" distinguishing it and protecting it from the words *avowed* by Tawhidi, which takes its distance from any *sukhf* (condemnable obscenity). However, this denunciation-enunciation is an occasion to spice up the work with an ensemble of stories and of texts of utter and comic crudeness. The author cannot be unaware that these texts constitute for the reader the principle worth and incitement to read his work. Are the theoretical elaborations and all the reflections on the relations between the prince and the intellectual only a smokescreen to justify, under the dressing of a hypocritical posturing, a pleasure taken in scabrous enunciation?[37] This may be all the more the case since the author's duplicity is extraordinary. Collectors of anecdotes can always argue that their enunciation is denunciation, but Tawhidi carries this out in two stages. It is precisely enunciation under the cover of denunciation itself that he condemns—in the person of Ibn 'Abbad—but he ironically appears in the role of the denunciator-enunciator.

The inclusion of the *sukhf* in the form of citation, without ever assuming authorship, not only responds to a moral precaution but also allows for the denunciation of Ibn 'Abbad as being indirectly responsible for the moral transgression in his opponents' discourse.

The Three Phases of the Attack

Whatever the authenticity of his sources, Tawhidi's accusation consists of three successive stages. The author encircles Ibn 'Abbad with the two connected themes of effeminacy and passive sodomy,[38] adds them to those of *sukhf* (obscenity) and of *mujun* (profligacy), and therefore implicitly or explicitly to that of *liwat* (active sodomy).

First, the theoretical introduction is the opportunity to estab-

lish an oblique strategy. One of the stakes of the introduction is
the justification for the writing of a *kitab* entirely dedicated to
reproach, a work of *mathalib* consisting of a succession of dis-
crediting anecdotes. Abu Hayyan summons up (besides al-Jahiz
(d. 869), his model in the composition of epistles) all the eighth-
and ninth-century masters of *adab*: Ibn al-Muqaffa', a reference
in chancellery writing; Abu al-'Ayna', the sharp-tongued poet-
courtier; the secretary Sahl b. Harun; al-Suli. All these authors
have one characteristic in common: they were either secretaries
of the chancellery, *kuttab,* or councilors (even if indirectly) to
the prince. The people of his own caste are the ones called on to
justify his enterprise. But the texts he cites are extracts (or the
whole) of a collection of letters, which by their lesser length and
ambitious scope are not on the same scale as his own *Kitab
Akhlaq al-Wazirayn.* However, Tawhidi defines these fragments
as forming a genre *(hadha l-fann)*,[39] taking care nonetheless to
distinguish it from that of poets, who are known to dally in a
different genre. He thus allows himself, not without some bad
faith, to denounce the unjustified satires of poets and to authorize others only if they follow three conditions—*sidq* (sincerity),
haqq (truth), and *sawab* (accuracy). Tawhidi judges, moreover,
allusion to be more efficient than direct accusation, all the while
pretending to deplore its use by poets:

> They only earn their living in this fashion and live only by this
> choice. Their satire is blameworthy, their remarks shameful, they
> attack [the adversary] with filthy words and wounding words and
> allusions [*ta'rid*] that surpass even direct reference[.][40]

This, however, is a practice that Tawhidi himself will use in
the choice of excerpts from letters that he has selected for the
reader and that all aim to distinguish his observations from
those of his predecessors and to cast doubt on the Sahib. In fact,
the verse excerpts of *hija'* and the letters brought up to attest the
legitimacy of the project have in common, for the most part, attacks on the supposed passive homosexuality of the recipient. In

the four instances that he quotes, the recipient is accused of being not a *luti,* which would be a trifle and hardly a subject for libel, but rather a *ma'bun.* This is the case for the excerpts to be read in the annex.

If these various epigrams mention a supposed practice of passive sodomy on the part of the accused, it is not by chance. These texts prepare the reader to listen to a similar discourse about Ibn 'Abbad, one quite beyond a simple moralist libel against the inadequacies of a degenerate vizierate.

The second phase of the strategy emerges as the actual portrait of Ibn 'Abbad begins, starting with the astonishing scene of the *hadith al-istiqbal* (the speeches of welcoming).[41] From this episode on, Abu Hayyan pays particular attention to noting the obscenities recounted by the Sahib (many of which are of a specifically sexual character, consisting in accusing others of being either active or passive sodomites) and to stigmatizing the Sahib's physique, his gestures, his way of expressing himself and of reacting in conversation, all of which lie within the classic Arabic representation of *takhannuth* (effeminateness)— flexibility of the body, curves instead of straight lines, and softness instead of hardness. The first instance of this strategy in the *hadith al-istiqbal* (see excerpts in appendix 5D at the end of this chapter) culminates in the Sahib's last three dialogues illustrating, one by one, his "stupidity" *(raqa'a).* In the first dialogue, he jokingly blames his *muhtasib* (chief of police) for isolating himself with his darlings though he is in charge of the police. In the second, he takes pleasure in accusing a courtier of stealing the verse of others, which amounts to supporting himself on others' penises instead of his own, since poetic productivity is here linked to manly vigor. In the third, he reproaches one of his most charming servants for having attempted to seek him out, even though the boy is as delicate as a girl, hinting at the commerce that exists between them. Tawhidi, the narrator present during this scene, describes the vizier's gestures in detail, all the better to reveal his effeminacy. The same procedure is repeated subse-

quently. Thus, Abu Hayyan starts by "citing" the first person
who is responsible for Ibn 'Abbad's fortune:

> When Abu al-Fadl saw him—that is, Ibn al-'Amid—he exclaimed:
> "You would think that his eyes were made of quick-silver and
> that his neck were mounted on a spring!" He spoke the truth,
> since Ibn 'Abbad was comical to the point of making one want to
> wiggle and dance, always upsetting and dislocating, rippling and
> undulating—like the worst kind of whore or an aging invert.[42]

Al-Tawhidi takes it on himself to drive the point home, using
the cruel image of the *mukhannath ashmat* (the "old queen")
who has lost all the possible charm that sexual ambiguity contains, for its enthusiasts, in the prime of youth. The repeated allusion to the ridiculous movements of the Sahib reflect in negative the sovereign's necessary *hilm*—his self-control.

The third and final move in this strategy consists in letting intervening parties, explicitly solicited by Tawhidi, to elaborate
themselves on the vizier's habits. I cite only a few instances,
though they are constant throughout the work. For example,
take al-Khawarizmi:

> He preaches "Justice and Unity," feigns to profess "the divine
> Promise and Eternity" then goes away by himself to put many a
> penis in his ass, and practices the entire range of abominations
> and wickedness, goes to sleep every morning without his face hav-
> ing been touched by the light of the Creator.[43]

The contradiction should be noticed between the Zaidite,
Shi'ite, and Mu'tazilite *madhab* proclaimed by Ibn 'Abbad and
his actions, a contradiction ceaselessly put forward, the author
taking care not to condemn *madhab* as such but rather to condemn the Sahib as being the worst kind of example and a subject
of shame. And then there is Abu Tayyib al-Nasrani, a Christian
secretary, who is called to testify:

> He knew about the shameful secrets of Ibn 'Abbad the most prodi-
> gious facts, and I heard him say: "If I were to reveal everything

that I know about this invert, the mountains would crumble and
the rocks would burst."[44]

This remains a good example of paralipsis. But one of the
most powerful illustrations in the text of this strategy of "dele-
gation" adopted by Tawhidi is to be found in the very long denunciation of Ibn 'Abbad that is attributed to al-Khath'ami.[45] Al-
Khath'ami's long testimonial deals one by one with the whole
spectrum of sexual themes developed in the work. Led astray by
his talents, his luck, and his arrogance, the Sahib, we learn, is a
bad Mu'tazilite who goes off and preaches to the populace in
Persian while at the same time exciting some beardless darling
boy.[46] Next, his scatological penchants are brought up through
the mention of various stories about flatulence that Ibn 'Abbad
enjoyed telling. The mention of bottoms naturally leads the obscene prince to the evocation of a *ma'bun*, named Tays al-Jinn
(Djinns' Goat), who would be better nicknamed Na'jat al-Ins
(Men's Ewe). Ibn 'Abbad then cites some outrageous satirical
verse by the crude poet al-Hajjaj, which he judges superior to
that of Imru' al-Qays, pre-Islamic founder of Arabic poetry. He
then brings up another anecdote of the type that "princes do not
lower themselves to repeat" and that evokes a scene of voyeurism in which a Bedouin is offered a young girl by one of the al-
Muhallab aristocrats if he would agree to deflower her in front
of him.[47] The Sahib mentions in the course of the crude anecdote
that the Bedouin's "equipment" *(mata'ahu)* is as impressive as
the "column of a house," hardly an original comparison since
this is precisely one of the recurring images used by adorers of
the phallus in anecdotes or *sukhf* poetry attributed to them. Abu
Hayyan is thus able to include Ibn 'Abbad in their camp by his
mere choice of simile. The vizier finally quotes verses by the famous Abu Hukayma, the poet of the (in)famous *ayriyyat* in
which he always complains about the loss of vigor in his member,[48] the mention of which implicitly comes back at Ibn 'Abbad,
stigmatizing such a loss of virility. The groundwork being laid,
the Sahib boldly cites 'Abbada and Jahshawayh, famous ninth-

century court effeminates, while in Tawhidi's writing strategy,
the joke-trap is set. The passage closes with a last sexual allusion, a display of bragging by one of the prince's darlings:

> As for the other Ibn al-Munajjim, Abu Muhammad, he was a mis-
> erable being, an ignorant person and an idiot. He used to say:
> "When I introduced myself to our master the Sahib, I was as
> handsome as the rising of the full moon. He immediately adored
> me, he went crazy over my budding beard, he fell hopelessly in
> love with me, and in this way I made a fortune. I earned a place in
> his heart and in his favor, and what he loved about me is not ap-
> propriate to talk about."[49]

Abu Hayyan is quick to confirm that his informer al-
Khath'ami is telling the truth, especially since this final allusive
line (even though it leaves no doubt about the Vizier's intimate
relationship with his darling) leaves in doubt the roles played by
each of them. What the young poet cannot reveal could just as
easily be his talents as a passive prostitute as much as his abili-
ties as an active sodomite.

This long digression attributed to al-Khath'ami exposes the
"mirror" or autoreferential dimension of the work. Throughout
his texts, al-Tawhidi scatters motifs that he takes up again later
on, drawing attention to the first reference. Thus, vulgar war
metaphors used by Abu al-'Ayna' in his letter against Ibn al-
Mukarram[50] at the beginning of the work echo later on some
verse in which Ibn 'Abbad is compared to a "spear" that became
a "shield" (a former *luti* who moved to the passive camp):

> I asked al-Natif, the theologian, one day: "I see that Ibn 'Abbad
> seems to spend a lot of time with those young devils who have
> passed the age of adolescence. Isn't this a sign of some sort of un-
> speakable turpitude and of inversion [*fahsha' wa-tuhma*]?" He
> then answered: "Aren't you familiar with these lines by the poet:
>
> Oh, how many spears quiver and line up their points . . . .
> Let's not speak about it! There would be so much to say . . . .

When a noble lord showers favor on him whose beard begins
    to bristle
And shows his heart, the worst is to be feared![51]

Two remarks should be made about this verse. The comparison of Ibn 'Abbad to an invert is this time clearly sought by Abu Hayyan himself, who proceeds almost unmasked but only because he has almost reached the end of his work. In addition, it is interesting that the formulation of the pernicious question asked by al-Tawhidi recognizes the normalcy in the extensive frequenting of young men who have not passed this *hadd al-ghulumiyya* (the age when one becomes a bearded man), just like the poems cited, which make fun of those who fall in love with young men whose beard has grown. Yet again, the boundary between normalcy and vice, between *liwat* and *ubna*, is implicitly affirmed, just as it is stressed that the boundary is not to be crossed.

Similarly, the scene of voyeurism enjoyed by the Muhallabid aristocrat, supposedly brought up by Ibn 'Abbad, anticipates its own reflection in an analogous scene where Ibn 'Abbad himself is the voyeur. Al-Aqta', the man with one hand, a thug among Ibn 'Abbad's protégés, copulates with his wife in the vizier's own palace:

> [Ibn 'Abbad] did not authorize al-Aqta' to go home, with the result that he complained about being tormented with desire. . . .
> One day, when al-Aqta' found his antechamber empty, the torrid afternoon heat hardly motivated him to move. He told his wife of his desire, he lay her down right there, on the floor, mounted her, and started his business. He was then observed by one of the chamberlains, who ran to report the event to Ibn 'Abbad, describing the whole portrait in detail. Ibn 'Abbad got up at once from his nap in a cool and shady place, left the soft bed on which he rested, and went off hatless and barefoot, a scrap of shirt wrapped around his head, without any pants on. His feet not touching the ground, he arrived in front of al-Aqta' in the middle of coitus, putting in and taking out his device and moving like a madman.

Islamicate Sexualities

Ibn 'Abbad derided him: "Criminal! Damn you son of an adulterer! What's going on in my own home?" "Oh Sahib," answered the other. "Go away. This isn't a spectacle! This is my legitimate wife, married with witnesses, notarized, with a contract and a duplicate. Go away, go away!" And he raved on and hurled abuse until he finished, while our master, in front of him, laughed, applauded, and even danced. Then he took his hand, as the other was still tightening the cord of his breeches, helped him to get dressed, and invited him to follow him back to where he was napping, all the while reproaching him and asking him questions: "How did all this happen? How did he feel? Did he feel any pleasure? How did he ever get so excited?" Then he offered him a fancy robe and some money and offered clothes and perfume to the man's wife.[52]

The voyeur is implicitly linked to an impotent (and impotence is a common theme of *hija'*), since he can copulate only by proxy. By mentioning al-Aqta''s wife (very few legitimate wives are mentioned in *adab*), Abu Hayyan pretends to oppose Ibn 'Abbad's peculiarity (a bachelor who is taking a siesta alone) (the historical Sahib, of course, had wive(s), children, and grandchildren)[53] to al-Aqta''s normalcy (a married man who, during siesta time, has relations with his legitimate wife). The thug is then much more of an honest man that the usurper prince.

By his three-step course of action, Tawhidi succeeds in preparing his reader for the centrality of the homosexual theme, tying the public practice of a discourse on the form of the *mujun* and of the *sukhf* to the will to hide an immoral secret and establishing a connection between the frequenting of effeminate young men and the effeminateness and passivity of a client. Is this purely circumstantial evidence? Not necessarily so.

CONCLUSION: ON THE AMBIGUITIES OF INSULT

Tawhidi's accusation exploits the Sahib's presumptuousness, which, by means of flaunting his love for prepubescent boys and therefore what is called *liwat* ends up by laying himself open to the accusation of *ubna,* which is socially more damaging (even if the former is just as serious, according to the *fiqh*). One cannot be sure about what happens in secret under the covers: the Sahib is victim of his own intrigues.

Ibn 'Abbad is moreover always walking the tightrope, playing with fire. He defends himself too much and too often and thereby spreads more doubt. This can be observed in the witticism cited by the Sahib that denies (all the better to assert it) that the epitome of *liwat* is *ubna,* a comment obviously exploited by Abu Hayyan to suggest that this description is based on some truth. The slippery slope down which the *fa'il* (active partner) slides to become *maf'ul bihi* (passive partner) is presented implicitly as inescapable for the man who places attraction for boys at the center of his discourse.[54] The author's own discourse is of a vast ambiguity, and what is found in its interstices is paradoxical.

Such a feeling is reinforced all the more by the strategy adopted by al-Tawhidi, who is always present although hiding behind the more or less fictive speakers that he manipulates. Take, for example, the letter by Abu al-'Ayna' that denounces the al-Mukarram clan as men failing in their dominant role and who, "[are] probably relieved that [their] wives have gone to find [their] guests and that [their] servants play with [their] young men." How can one not conclude from such a statement that playing with beautiful young men is of the utmost normalcy and that the real symptom of male degeneracy is to let the servants play with them instead?

I suggest we could resolve this contradiction between the "normalcy" in attraction for young men and the relationship of necessary complementarity established between two distinct types of homoerotic relations (distinct in law as well as in social standing) by proposing that mere appreciation of *young* and *fresh out of androgynity* male beauty is commonplace, that occasional and discrete affairs with young men fit into or indeed reinforce masculinity, but that the affirmation of a right to this kind of relationship or even of its repeated evocation (implying a suspicious interest, a preference, or possibly even an exclusive preference) takes the author dangerously close to the limit. It should be remembered that Ibn al-Mu'tazz "defended" the catamite poet Jahshawayh by labeling him *"alwat al-nas"* (the most active sodomite among men). Was it the individual that he was defending, or was it *adab* itself that he was desperately attempting to rescue from such a shame? The result speaks for itself, for al-Tawhidi is no dupe and classifies Jahshawayh the *adib* in the same category as a king's dandy like 'Addaba. But Tawhidi's text points out that the revelation of the porosity of this boundary between the "pansexual" and the "homosexual" (understood here as preferring gender over role) happens, in classical Arabic culture, through insult.

What positive discourse cannot conceptualize or construct, denunciation provides. A man is characterized by his sexual acts as well as his desires, which are based on a preference for gender and not merely role. An effeminate in behavior is a man who seemingly combines at least three of the four premodern categories of homoerotic behaviors mentioned by David M. Halperin in his demonstration of the uniqueness of the modern category of the homosexual,[55] as if Tawhidi had accidentally happened on the concept without knowing it.

At least two objections can be raised here. The penchant for *amrad*s can be recognized as same-sex desire only in the measure that *amrad*s are constructed as male gendered. Let us answer that they are clearly so in the discourse of the law, the transgression of which plays no small part in the pleasure of their company. Their maleness could be described as just-attained, and it is clearly a source of attractiveness. If not, why the pervasive *topos* of the first beard, that utterly masculine first trace of body hair? The second objection is that this search for the "homosexual" in premodern literature might be read as the latest expression of an essentialist agenda to uncover hidden homosexuals in a prehomosexual past and thus acknowledge homosexuality as the ultimate end-of-history concept.

I do not feel that there should be any second thoughts concerning the relevance of the constructionist hypothesis, which is entirely justified considering that all homoerotic relations mentioned in classical Arabic literature cannot be described accurately by the term *homosexuality*. But it should be slightly altered on one point: what is not articulated is not necessarily what is inconceivable, if only in the case where the unarticulated finds its expression in the realm of insult, a paradoxical caviling over trifles with respect to the extreme obscenity of the charges. The *Akhlaq al-Wazirayn* does not *say* that Ibn 'Abbad was a homosexual, for such a labeled identity does not exist, but it certainly *calls* him one. The author probably has some good reasons to insult Ibn 'Abbad and not Ibn al-'Amid in this fashion, but the question is pointless. The crucial thing is that insult may accidentally construct what it denounces, building this field of "homosexuality," which in theory remains unthought.

In the light of the present analysis of the insult in Abu Hayyan al-Tawhidi's *Kitab Akhlaq al-Wazirayn*, it seems clear to me that men in a given premodern and non-Western society had perceived some sort of link between active and passive roles within male-male relationships, that they had perceived that perpetual boasting about acts had something to do with preferences of genre, and that effeminacy in manners sometimes could be associated with being the active partner of anal sex. Does it mean that they had perceived the uniqueness of a man who is drawn to individuals of his same constructed gender, whatever the nature of his practices within the framework of this relationship, and that there were idiosyncratic attitudes connected with this particular desire? The singular case of the insult may incline us to address this possibility. The study of other types of discourse, such as humor, might also reveal that our reading of the way that medieval cultures perceived same-sex relationships might need to be refined.

APPENDIX 5A. AN EXCHANGE OF INSULTS
BETWEEN IBN AL-MUKARRAM AND
ABU AL-'AYNA'[56]

Abu al-'Ayna' answered [in those terms to a letter of insults he received from Ibn al-Mukarram]:

"In the name of God the Forgiving, the Merciful,

You lash out, as God mentions,
Insults that would better suit yourself.

"We acknowledge receipt of your missive, of its invectives, and of its calumnies . . . . What is most astonishing is that neither you nor your brother screws women. It would be wondered therefore why you try to lead astray noble ladies and demand to be offered women with large dowries, even though you "swallow up what they wave around" and "God only knows what inhabits you."[57] Why therefore ask for the hand in marriage of these women, when your own [hand] is out for the taking? Why pay the elevated dowries when it's men that you need? Why pretend to love women when their very character runs through your veins?[58] How dare you, on the day of combat, pretend to inflict deadly blows to the enemy when you bend all the way down to your chin every day, when at every battle it's in your bed that the charge is sounded and where you are found chest to the ground, while spears plow your ass. . . . You are probably quite content that your wives have gone searching for your guests and the men of your clan are enjoying the company of your male servants. Should you call them adulterers, they would call you catamites. . . . On my life, you have your wedding nights announced, but you are later discovered as a female drum player! You stray in insults and derision, all the while pretending to exact revenge, but when your help is needed and you are asked to honor your engagements, *the company disperses and you turn your back.* . . .[59] And so scorn to you, clan of Mukarram—a persistent, permanent scorn and one that will remain stuck to your name:

Your wounds do not bleed from jousting,
But it is from your asses that the blood drips.

Poor young bride whose virginal veil was never deflowered and whose fork was not watered! Poor girl duped despite her bewitching gaze, who will go off to inquire her friends: Don't the Mukarram have virile members? . . .

"You said that you know of no road more rough nor more harsh than one that one is forced to take to serve us or to offer us a favor or of no fields less fertile and less destined to bear fruit than ours even though some good is sewn there. If it were so, you would have no reason at all to deplore the ingratitude shown to you, nor would you have heard thanks for your supposed favors. You refuse to give away your riches, and you try your best not to give anything away. Worse—may God forgive me!—had you any scraps left over to throw away, you would have given them to those who strove to satisfy it. I mean your insatiable derrière, which will lead to your final end.[60] And how then could you prove your generosity toward us or the benefits of your favors? Alas! To receive some sort of goods from you would still be a lesser evil, but the torrent [of your stinginess] has very well destroyed the last traces of generosity in you. Oh, Abu Ja'far—and how could Ja'far be a son of yours?[61]—Fornication knows of no other easier road nor one simpler to cross than the one that leads to you and no other territory better to penetrate than your being. All this doesn't even take into account the filth of your clothes, the repulsive dirtiness of your hands, or the stench you exhale.

"You maintain that the generosity shown to me is vainly offered to my vileness and to my impudence. Why don't you—curse you!—think about the history of your own rise to power and all those whom you cheated, exceeding all limits? Is there then some more glorious origin above that of God's Messenger—hail and prayer to Him? Can one wish for an affiliation that is more noble than that of the caliphs, vicars of God?[62] Were it not for the leniency of our sovereign and for our excessive indulgence (of course, the possession of power orders the gentleman to abstain from unnecessary triumphs), without even taking into consideration the fact that you are too unimportant to be bothered to be punished and are hardly worth quarreling with, I would have some firm resolutions to take on your account. . . . Be grateful, then, for your avarice and your paltriness (they save you) and for your adversary (since he will not lower himself and punish you). As for the impudence of my speech, I certainly don't have to look for excuses for having cursed a vile miser and exalted nobility!"

> If I didn't sincerely praise generosity
> And did not thrash the sordid miser,
> How would I tell good from evil
> And why would have God granted me hearing and speech?

APPENDIX 5B. A LETTER ATTRIBUTED TO AL-JAHIZ[63]

As for al-Jahiz, he wrote in one of his letters:[64]

"You questioned me—God grant you a long life—about *So-and-SO*. I answer by proving to you the sincerity of my information, in terms so clear that they will reveal the most obscure aspects of the person and will show in the light of day the shame of what is hidden. Consider this, May God accord you his mercy, and there is no power other than God's.

"It happened that I saw him among his guests as respected as a tossed-out rag dirtied by menses. Everyone reputed him to be a catamite.[65] He had at his service a very slim page, whose head was very handsome, his back straight, his thighs and hips of the nicest curves, ringlets resting on his temples, and hair falling down his neck. He was dressed in the finest fabrics, constantly perfumed, always attentive to go to the baths, adorned in jewels, and his nails were always filed.

However, despite appearances, he was the slave that took care of all business affairs, it was from him that all the beggars obtained intervention, and it was he who directed his master in all things, making himself more important than the sons, the clan, and the servants. He was able to make his master change his mind and adopt his opinion, imposing his whims. No one participated more than he in his master's literary circles, nor was anyone alone with his master long in private conversation. *So-and-so* had to spend every night with him, and it happened that he became angry, his anger saddened him, and he begged for forgiveness. As long as *So-and-so* was in charge, no close or distant relative had the least advantage over the page, and noble lords and commoners alike were treated in the same manner. Were he to mount his horse, the page would be by his side like the head of the caliph's guard. Were he to sit, the page would become his dear child or his virtuous wife. If some courtier had some business to resolve or request to register, it was once again the page who was found behind the solution, which was easier for him than taking off his shoes. They slept every night under the same cover."

APPENDIX 5C. EXCERPTS FROM A LETTER ATTRIBUTED TO ABU HIFFAN[66]

I have also found a letter by Abu Hiffan[67] addressed to Ibn al-Mukarram:

"Oh, Ibn al-Mukarram. This is a name that you do not deserve.[68] Product of the sin of your parents, you are only shameful insult on shameful insult and curse of Iblis on curse. I cannot imagine that you were conceived from a drop of semen or that your mother could ever have been a virgin. No doubt you came from some excrement fertilized by defecation. Your father and your mother joined themselves at the asshole for such a creation, and as the poet says:

> May God damn their two stenches,,
> Two pubic hairs which look to rub together.

"You were born in sin and have lived as a catamite! You are nothing but an accumulation of maledictions—lousy to the point of smashing vermin in one's teeth, sniveling to the point of swallowing snot, masturbator who only lets his liquor flow through his ten fingers, and catamite who only lets other people's liquor flow through his bottom. Your slaves slap you, your servants lead you by the stick, your dogs lick your ass as if it were dripping menstrual blood, and your friends whip you. Open your mouth and one would think that you farted, and what flows from your nose is only shit. Moreover, your spit is like excrement, and the gaps in your teeth are full of refuse. You allow yourself to deride decent men and to calumny generous souls, envious as you are of refined men of letters. You insult the wise, speak ill of your literary friends, and denigrate your benefactors—thereby exposing your lack of rectitude[69] and going beyond the boundary of your condition and your attitude. Your soul is vile, and you are an embarrassment for your species. You swear and promise without rhyme or reason and lie scandalously about the slightest as well as the most serious affairs. You seem to complain that you are denounced and that you are called a bastard! The poets have, moreover, already pinned down your like, the lowness of your actions, and the sordidness of your lineage:

> To deride you? Your honor is much too thin to be hit,
> And praise is a genre too noble for you. You know it well!
> Come on! Your lack of honor frees you of my derision!
> Were you proud of it? Now you are despised.

"Bastard, son of a jerk whose father prostituted his mother and who was nothing but a poor creature who was only slapped for pleasure.[70] You aren't even a slave whom one can free to please God but rather someone whom one gets rid of and wishes to the devil's ass. To rail at you is to be forced to put up with you away from your misdeeds, even though you derive all of your power from your miserliness. To know you is a dishonor. To break with you is a blessing. Your name is an insult, your execution an offering of worship. No one would be able to count all of your vices, and the angels at your side have given up remov-

ing your sins. You find equals to the only God, torment his creatures with a thousand evils, and force on others your faults, and
all blame your irreligion. You are attributed every stain, and you
are hated by all[.]"

APPENDIX 5D. EXCERPTS FROM THE HADITH
AL-ISTIQBAL[71]

Then he said to Ibn Abi Khurasan, the Shafi'ite jurist:

"Oh Sheikh, you have banished from your tongue our name,
as you were in such a hurry to be alone or to give yourself up to
some sort of frivolousness with your young rascals, while obsti-
nately ignoring us and forgetting your brothers and your companions. Were it not for a past that you left behind and that I
still honor and without the benevolence that I grant you and
that you refuse to me, we would have much to say to each other
once words of pleasure, now the expression of my ire. I ap-
pointed you *muhtasib*.[72] I found you now busy enriching yourself. You used to have as your mission to work for the good.
Now here, you are taking on all the worst vices.[73] One can be
wrong and let oneself be taken advantage of. Hopes are sometimes dashed. . . . And as the poet of old said:

How many good councilors do you hear that you take for cheats,
And how many men worthy of confidence are proven of little
  faith . . . ."

He then turned toward al-Shadiyashi and inquired: "Abu 'Ali!
how are you doing, and how were you doing?" The other answered: "Sire,

May I not exist if I remembered what I said.
And more still, may I not exist if I remember what I never was!"

The Sahib called to him then:

"Out of my sight, vile insolent, rake, who wipes his ass
against the wall after he shits! These lines were not chiseled by

your hand and are not born from your mind. They are by Muhammad b. ʿAbdallah b. Tahir. The beginning of it is

> You wrote to me asking how I was doing,
> What snubs and what concerns I underwent after you.
> May I not exist if I remember what I was,
> And more still, may I not exist if I remember what I was not!

"He recited this verse all the while veering his neck, rolling his eyes, dislocating his shoulders, liquefying himself while undulating, illustrating this line from the book of God: *"as whom the devil hath prostrated by his touch."*[74]

Then he continued:

"Oh, Abu ʿAli. Don't trust then another penis than the one that lies in your breeches. Nothing is worth the one that runs along your thighs! Were you to rely on another, he would only cheat you and discredit you, dishonor your private home, and rip your conscience."[75]

He turned finally toward a young page whose face was covered by its first down and with whom the Sahib was suspected of the worst turpitude. Moving around in every direction and twisting himself, he murmured to him: "Come over here, my sweet! How are you? And why have you given yourself such trouble? Your handsome face could not bear the least alteration. The sun, between its rise and its fall, would risk leaving a burn. A boy like you is destined for seclusion in beautiful adornments under a canopy and a screen to heal our deleterious states, to make our little gargoyle rise, and to quench with your charms our insatiable thirst."

NOTES

1. This article is a shorter and gender-studies-oriented version of my Arab-studies-oriented article in French, "L'obscénité du vizir," *Arabica* 53 (2006): 54–107.
2. David Leavitt, *Martin Bauman; or, A Sure Thing*. Boston: Houghton Mifflin, 2000.
3. Eve Kosofsky Sedgwick, "Construire des significations queer," *Les*

Etudes gay et lesbiennes, ed. D. Eribon (Paris: Centre George Pompidou, supplémentaires, 1998, 112.

4. See principally the studies published in the collection *Homoeroticism in Classical Arabic Literature,* ed. J. W. Wright and Everett Rowson (New York: Columbia University Press, 1997), and Khaled El-Rouayheb, *Before Homosexuality in the Arab-Islamic World, 1500–1800* (Chicago: Chicago University Press, 2005).

5. Andras Hamori, *On the Art of Medieval Arabic Literature* (Princeton: Princeton University Press, 1974). See chapter 2, "The Poet as Ritual Clown."

6. The term *halaqi* is more common in the Umayyad period, replaced by *baghgha'* in later periods, while *ma'bun* remains the standard term for passive sodomist.

7. Certain fundamental concepts, such as *jidd* and *hazl,* will be translated according to context throughout this article, particularly in the rendering of literary texts, for stylistic reasons. Despite the variation in translation, the Arabic term will be indicated in parentheses if it presents a justified conceptual interest.

8. In the sense of the pragmatic procedure that rhetoricians call paralipsis: *"figure macrostructurale selon laquelle le locuteur prétend qu'il ne dit pas ce qu'il dit"* (macrostructural figure of speech according to which the speaker maintains that what he says is not what he says), J. Mazaleyrat and G. Molinié, *Vocabulaire de la stylistique* (Paris: PUF, 1989), 273.

9. In ancient Greece, a debate rages between those who, like B. Sergent, see in the homosexuality evoked by classical texts a real fact of the Indo-European world and those who, like John Boswell, speak of a "cultural myth" that has been mistaken as real practice by historians. On this subject, see Didier Eribon, *Réflexions sur la question gay* (Paris: Fayard, 1999), 234.

10. A. Cheikh-Moussa, "L'Historien et la littérature Arabe médiévale" *Arabica* 43 (1996): 155.

11. The term *Arabs* is used here to mean speakers of Arabic and does not presuppose any ethnic group or any specific identity whatsoever.

12. Eribon, *Réflexions sur la question gay,* 225.

13. K. O. Müller in Germany at the beginning of the nineteenth century and J. Seymonds and W. Pater in England. See Eribon, *Réflexions sur la question gay.*

14. Ibrahim Mahmud, *Al-Mut'a al-Mahzura* (London: Riyad al-Rayyis, 2000). The principal methodological pitfall of the work lies in the naïveté of using a classical lexicon, which is never defined for the modern reader, thus leading to serious confusions. It should also be noted that the work was published in London. Riyad al-Rayyis, Dar al-Saqi (also London-based), and Manshurat al-Jamal/Al-Kamel Verlag (in Cologne) publish the majority of new works dealing with sexuality in the Arab Muslim domain. These publishers also bring out reprints of texts with patently homoerotic content. This is the extent of the parallel.

15. I do not imply that this society might be a monolithic object or that it is possible to talk about a sort of "monad" that would be typical of Arab Muslim society, unchanged in all places and in all times without any evolution in its representations. I refer the matter of the precautions and conclusions on the relevance of the constitution of these societies within the field of investigation of sexuality to Abdelwahab Boudhiba's introduction in *Sexuality in Islam,* trans. Alan Sherman (London: Routledge, 1985) (original work *La sexualité en Islam* published in Paris: PUF, 1975).

16. The original title of Muhammad b. Tawit al-Tanji's edition (1965, republished by Dar Sadir, Beirut, 1992), to which all citations in this article refer, is *Akhlaq al-Sahib wa-bn al-'Amid.* The title *Mathalib al-Wazirayn* is common and is the one used by the Ibrahim al-Kaylani, Damascus, edition.

17. This is hardly a phenomenon unique to Arab-Muslim societies. This is the case of ancient Greece (see K. J. Dover, *Greek Homosexuality* [London: Duckworth, 1978] and also of some less ancient or exotic cultures. G. Chauncey, in his *Gay New York* (New York: Basic Books, 1994), presents a study that "reconstructs the gay world that existed before the hetero-homosexual binarism was consolidated as an hegemonic sexual regime in American culture" (23): "Many men alternated between male and female partners without believing that interest in one precluded interest in the other, or that their occasional recourse to male sexual partners, in particular, indicated an abnormal, 'homosexual' or even 'bisexual' disposition, for they neither understood nor organized their sexual practices along a hetero-homosexual axis." Of particular interest is chapter 3, which shows that the line of demarcation between normalcy and abnormality was drawn at the level of the roles and

not of the sex of the partner. At most, the image of the Sicilian taken as "pansexual" in the New York of the 1930s might be reminiscent of a Mediterranean model. But the insult, as we will see, reveals an infinitely more common paradigm.

18. In French, one calls another *enculé* (literally, one who is sodomized) and not *enculeur* (one who sodomizes), just as in English one says *cocksucker* (though it would make no sense to say *cocksuckee*). The common insult *fuck you* actually means *I fuck you*. The humiliation of the one who is insulted can be passed onto the insulter without embarrassment by assuming a posture in which the insulter positions himself as the active sexual partner in a possibly homosexual intercourse. Even if the proposition remains purely rhetorical, it is not at all perceived as compromising. The threat or promise of penetration is understood solely as a bellicose metaphor when the receiver is of the same sex.

19. Eribon, *Réflexions sur la question gay*. Eribon entitles the first part of his work "Un monde d'injures" (A world of insults), underlining the powerful contribution of the insult in the establishment of limits of normalcy that are internalized by the subject from the time of childhood and that force homosexuals to define themselves as the object of insult. This chapter speculates in what measure the nature of the *hija'* in poetry and of the *thalb* in prose similarly contributes to the internalization of a norm.

20. The reign of Amir 'Adud al-Dawla (977–983) was followed by that of his son, Samsam al-Dawla, who reigned from 983 to 987, and it was under Samsam's reign that Ibn Sa'dan was vizier. The circumstances of this commission are related in the fourth night of the *al-Imta' wa-l-Mu'anasa* by Tawhidi.

21. al-Tanji, *Akhlaq*, 150.

22. Ibid., 228.

23. Ibid., 74.

24. al-Tha'alibi, *Tatimmat al-Yatima*, ed. Mufid Muhammad Qamiha (Beirut: Dar al-Kutub al-'Illmiyya, 1983), 3:225 (originally published in 1947).

25. Edition Muhammad Hasan al Yasin (Bagdad: Maktabat al-Nahda, 1965). The works of the *diwan* are designated here by their number; those of the *mustadrak al-diwan* by their number preceded by *m*.

26. Ibid., works 10, 29, 51, 52, 53, m21, m22, m36, m42, m43, m65,

m102, m103, m104, m110, m139, m140, m141, m159, m160, m182, m183, m242, m245.

27. Sahib, *Mustadrak al-diwan,* m36, 99.
28. Traditional erotic section placed at the beginning of long praise odes.
29. Sahib *Mustadrak al-diwan,* m180, m182, m183, m245.
30. Ibid.
31. al-Tha'alibi, *Yatima,* 1:116.
32. Ibid., 2:260.
33. Ibid., 2:267.
34. G. J. Van Gelder, *The Bad and the Ugly: Attitudes towards Invective Poetry (Hija') in Classical Arabic Literature* (Leiden: Brill, 1988), 11.
35. Ibn al-Mu'tazz, *Tabaqat al-shu'ara',* ed. Abd al-Sattar Ahmed Farraj (Cairo: Dar al-Ma'arif, 1968), 387. Ibn al-Mu'tazz also denies that Abu Nuwas was a *luti,* which does little for his credibility. But the main point is that the defense of Jahshawayh demands the transformation of *ubna* into *liwat.*
36. Ibid., 374.
37. G. J. Van Gelder poses this question when bringing up the *Akhlaq al-Wazirayn* in his chapter dedicated to "inconsistencies East and West": "His masterpiece of invective, *Mathalib* (or *Akhlaq*) *al-Wazirayn*—a book so intensely virulent that the very possession of a copy was thought to attract misfortune—is an inextricable mixture of literary and 'metaliterary' or critical discourse; its introduction is a long justification and apology for *hija'.* In the course of it, the grossest obscenities in poetry or prose are quoted: yet among the things that the two viziers are blamed for is their love of obscenities and vilification." Van Gelder, *The Bad and the Ugly,* 80.
38. Everett K. Rowson judges in "The Categorization of Gender and Sexual Irregularity in Medieval Arabic Vice Lists," in *Body Guards: The Cultural Politics of Gender Ambiguity,* ed. Julia Epstein and Kristina Straub (New York: Routledge, 1991), 71: "rarely is the term *ubna* applied to a *mukhannath* and it would appear that the gender inversion of the latter rationalized a sexual behavioral pattern that in conventionally gendered males (who were, we may be sure, usually married) was considered pathological." If this judgment can be defended for the seventh century, I am little convinced by its pertinence for the tenth century. If *ubna* (private

attitude) does not imply *takhannuth* (public attitude), the opposite is, on the contrary, evident for our author and the speakers he brings up.

39. Tawhidi, *Akhlaq,* 75.

40. Ibid.

41. This is the reception of Ibn ʿAbbad, returning from a voyage, by the notables of Rayy. It is a chance for him to crucify one of them by way of a personalized diatribe of extreme arrogance. Tawhidi, *Akhlaq,* 94–104.

42. Ibid.

43. Ibid., 110.

44. Ibid.

45. Ibid., 142–72.

46. Ibid., 144.

47. Ibid., 148.

48. m. 240/855. *Diwan,* ed. Muhammad Husayn al-Aʿraji (Köln: Manshurat al-Jamal, 1997).

49. Tawhidi, *Akhlaq,* 161.

50. Ibid., 58.

51. Ibid., 373–4.

52. Ibid.

53. One grandson named ʿAbbad is mentioned in a poem. See al-Aʿraji, *Diwan* m237, p. 294.

54. Rowson acknowledges this ambiguity but refuses to draw the conclusion in "The Categorization of Gender": "And according to one anecdote, a man known for *liwat* 'got the disease' when he became older, and explained, "We used to play with spears, but when they broke, we started playing with shields" (yet again the same military metaphor). Such statements seem to be the closest the tradition comes to any suggestion that choice of a male partner on the basis of his sex might transcend considerations of behavior role, although this is probably an overreading" (65). The same military metaphor can be observed in the verse already cited from the *Akhlaq.*

55. In David M. Halperin, *How to Do the History of Homosexuality* (Chicago: University of Chicago Press, 2002), 104–37, particularly 134–5.

56. Tawhidi, *Akhlaq,* 55–60.

57. A double deformation of Quranic verse (7,117) and (84,23), the

first alluding to Moses's stick "swallowing" and the *sticks* changed into magicians' *snakes* (see Tabari's *tafsir*).

58. There is a pun between *'irq al-nisa* (the vein of women) and *'irq al-nasa* (sciatic nerve). Ibn al-Mukarram is vilified as a catamite in the veins of whom female blood flows and who got sciatica out of his ill habit.

59. Perversion with obscene references to the Quranic verse (54,45).

60. The expression *umm al-fulk,* invented by Abu al-'Ayna', is not found in Arabic literature and doesn't seem to have been understood as a proper noun. We might choose to understand its obscene meaning—*fulk,* referring to any globular body, and the adjective *falk,* that of rounded buttocks.

61. Pun: *Ja'far* is both a proper name and a common one, meaning "brook" or "rivulet" (of generosity).

62. The grandfather of Abu al-'Ayna' was a protégé, the Abbasid caliph Abu Ja'far al-Mansur, and the letter asserts this noble parentage.

63. Tawhidi, *Akhlaq,* 61–62.

64. This fragment does not correspond to any other text published by al-Jahiz.

65. The receiver of anal penetration is a catamite, while the active partner is a sodomite.

66. Tawhidi, *Akhlaq,* 63–65.

67. Libertine poet (d. 869). It is quite probable that such outrageously insulting epistles are highly codified exercises in style.

68. Ibn al-Mukarram means literally "son of the honorable."

69. *Jawr* does not mean here "injustice" but "wandering off the straight path."

70. The figure of the *saf'an* is recurrent in classical literature. This is a category of court jesters whose job it was to receive humiliating blows to the neck. Ibn al-Nadim's *Fihrist* even points out the existence of a *Kitab al-Safa'ina* by al-Katanji.

71. Tawhidi, *Akhlaq,* 102–04.

72. Chief of police or provost of the Islamic city.

73. Play on words on the "the order of the good and the prohibition of the evil," a stereotypical formula describing the function of the *muhtasib.*

74. Quran (2,275), Pickthal translation. The verse designates the usurer who is thus treated on judgment day.

75. *"fadaha khanak wa-manak."* *Khan* is a *tawriya* (pun), meaning "house" or "female sex organ." *Manak* can be used for *ma'nak* (noun) or *ma'anak* (verb)—"to wound the stomach around the navel." One also finds the verb *mana* (to dig a ditch). The meaning is the same. . . .

SIX

Homoerotic Liaisons among the Mamluk Elite in Late Medieval Egypt and Syria

Everett K. Rowson

In the year 1307, Edward I of England died and was succeeded by his twenty-three-year-old son, Edward II, whose reign, a remarkably unhappy one, extended over the next twenty years. Contemporary chronicles attribute many of the disasters of his rule to his inordinate attachment to a French peer named Piers Gaveston who was a few years his senior. Originally, it appears, brought to the English court by Edward I to be a companion and indeed model for his son, Gaveston came to exercise a powerful hold over the young man. The young king lavished attention, gifts, and titles on Gaveston, ultimately neglecting affairs of state and incensing the nobles, who forced him twice to exile Gaveston and finally, in 1312, captured and beheaded the despised favorite. Relations between the king and his nobles did not improve, however, and soon Edward had adopted another pair of favorites, the Despensers, father and son, with the latter of whom he was rumored to be maintaining the same sort of intimate relationship widely assumed to have obtained earlier between him and Gaveston. Things came to a head when Edward's estranged wife, the sister of the king of France, took up with a Welsh earl and launched an invasion of England. Edward fled but was captured, and the Despensers were executed. Given an opportunity to abdicate, Edward did so but was nevertheless murdered in 1327—according to some later accounts, by having a red-hot poker rammed up his anus.[1]

Edward's attachment to his favorites was clearly a major scandal and one that somewhat muffles the force of the crusader tracts that were composed during his reign against the Saracens and attacked their sodomitical profligacy. Most famously, the French Dominican William of Adam, writing about 1318, explains, "In the Saracen sect any sexual act at all is not only not forbidden, but permitted and praised." He goes on to excoriate, among the Saracens, effeminate men who shave their beards, adorn themselves in women's finery, and sell themselves to other men with whom they proceed to cohabit as husband and wife, as well as eastern Christians who fatten up and adorn their sons to cater to the unnatural lusts of the Saracens, who race to buy them up.[2] However distorted his polemic may be, William was clearly aware not only of the phenomenon of the *mukhannath* (the effeminate cross-dresser to whom Muslim societies accorded a recognized, if not universally approved, role)[3] but also of the recruiting practices of the Mamluk regime in Egypt and Syria (1250–1517 CE), whereby boys from outside the realm of Islam—mostly Turks and some of them Christian—were purchased as slaves, imported, converted to Islam, trained as soldiers, and manumitted, thereby becoming part of the ruling elite (with the possibility of rising to the position of sultan).[4] Where sodomy actually fits into this picture is not an idle question, although it is a complicated one, and the world of the Mamluk sultans is not devoid of parallels to the case of Edward II, although the differences are as important as the similarities.[5]

Perhaps the closest parallel to the unfortunate Edward is Ahmad b. al-Nasir Muhammad, who ruled briefly (four months) in 742/1342 as sultan over Egypt and Syria some fifteen years after Edward's death.[6] Ahmad's father had enjoyed the longest reign of any of the Mamluks (albeit with two interruptions)—ascending the throne in 693/1293, reigning for forty-eight years, and dying in 741/1341.[7] Ahmad grew up largely apart from his family in Karak, an important fortress a few miles southeast of the Dead Sea, where al-Nasir Muhammad had spent his time away from the capital, Cairo, during the two temporarily successful revolts against his reign. When his father heard that the young man (then about twenty-one) had developed a friendship with someone "unsuitable" *(man la yaslah)* in Karak, he brought him to Cairo, married him off to the daughter of one of his own *mamluk*s (military slaves), and then sent him back to Karak. There Ahmad, we are told, "fell madly in love with a beautiful young man named al-Shuhayb"— but perhaps this was the unsuitable relationship he had already developed—"and disgraced himself over him, showering him with money." On being informed of this, the indignant al-Nasir Muhammad had the boy's favorite seized and got the money back, but the distraught Ahmad appealed to two of his father's most powerful *mamluk*s, declaring, "If this young man is punished, I will kill myself!" He proceeded to stop eating and drinking and took to his bed. At that, al-Nasir Muhammad relented and released al-Shuhayb but sought—in vain—to deflect his son's obsession by offering him one hundred of his own *mamluk*s in his place.[8]

The situation worsened when one of the eunuchs mistreated al-Shuhayb (a hint that the young man was in fact a soldier in training, subject to the customary eunuch supervision, although our sources do not say this explicitly), and Ahmad had the offending eunuch beaten almost to death.[9] In response, al-Nasir Muhammad threatened to banish Ahmad himself if he refused to banish his favorite. Ahmad's response was to declare to his father's envoys—the same two powerful *mamluk*s to whom he had initially appealed—that "Each of you has a hundred pretty young boys and girls, and you are merely my father's slaves [*mamalik*], while I, who am his son, have contented myself with regard to worldly pleasures with only this boy because he has shared my exile, having left his family. How can I expel him? If the sultan commands that I do so, then let him expel me too!"

And in fact, the disgruntled father did exactly that, for a brief period, until intercession from the boy's female relatives led him again to relent.[10]

He disinherited his son, however, choosing another son, Abu Bakr, to succeed him, which he did on al-Nasir's death shortly thereafter in 742/1342. At this point, the story becomes exceedingly—and typically, for the Mamluks—complicated. The late sultan's powerful *mamluks* promptly divided into factions, some supporting the new (and very young) sultan and others backing other sons, including Ahmad. Abu Bakr lasted on the throne only a few months and was succeeded by another and even younger brother, Kujuk. Meanwhile, Ahmad had garnered support from the *mamluks* in Syria, but in the midst of all these machinations, Ahmad's own *mamluks* murdered the unfortunate al-Shuhayb. Ahmad was devastated—he almost went mad, we are told—but persevered in his drive for the throne in Cairo and was duly installed shortly thereafter. Barely a month later, he decided to return to Karak and govern from there—or not to govern, as the sources report, but rather to immerse himself in private pleasures (including wine) and, fatally, to turn on his erstwhile supporters, whom he had murdered, one by one. To make matters worse, he imprisoned their female relatives and permitted the local Christians to commit all manner of abuses against them. Revulsion at his actions was universal, and back in Cairo yet another brother, al-Salih Isma'il, was raised to the throne. After a lengthy siege, Ahmad was captured and killed in Karak in 745/1345, and his head was delivered to his (temporarily) triumphant brother.[11]

The historian Ibn Hajar al-'Asqalani, to whom we owe the most detailed account of Ahmad's lamentable career, sums it up by saying that he was "a truly terrible administrator, a hedonist, and a drunkard."[12] He does not, however, focus on Ahmad's favoritism, and it would certainly be a mistake to attribute his problems to his "homosexuality"—rather than, perhaps, to his obsessiveness. Al-Shuhayb may have been an "unsuitable" object for Ahmad's obsession, but the material available to us for contextualizing this account does not suggest that his unsuitability was due to his sex; more likely, he was just inappropriately plebeian. It is the contextualizing material that is the focus of this chapter, and it shows the degree to which the world in which Ahmad lived was in fact saturated in homoeroticism. To that extent, perhaps, William of Adam was not so very wide of the mark. On the other hand, he could hardly be expected—at least, until he was posted to Iran *after* composing his anti-Saracen diatribe—to appreciate how homoeroticism actually fit into Middle Eastern societies.[13]

We may address two kinds of questions to our sources—one synchronic and the other diachronic. Synchronically, we may ask whether homoerotic attachments (whether they resulted in acts of sodomy or not—itself a significant question) were or were perceived to be particularly associated with one group within the larger society of the Mamluk realm. Was there something about the Mamluks themselves—that alien presence in Arab society, paradoxically both a slave class and a fairly stringently segregated ruling class—that was particularly conducive to homoeroticism? Or was homoeroticism an indulgence of the elite generally, also encompassing the native elite, the Arabs who made their mark in the world of high culture and in particular religious scholarship? Or, rather, were homoerotic relationships a commonplace throughout society, extending beyond the elite to the middle and lower classes as well?

Diachronically, can we detect a significant shift in the conceptualization of homoeroticism in the Arab (or Muslim) world under the Mamluk regime? It could be (and has been) argued that the intensely homosocial environment of the Mamluk barracks, in which the future leaders of society were trained in warfare, kept strictly separate from women, and presided over by attentive eunuchs, was every bit as likely to foster homoerotic attachments as was the nineteenth-century English public school. Or did the importation of *mamluk*s from radically different social environments—the Eurasian steppes—result in the importation as well of indulgent attitudes toward homoeroticism, as some medieval observers claimed? Altogether, did tolerance for homoeroticism increase during the Mamluk period? And given such stories as that of Ahmad b. al-Nasir Muhammad, can we posit a more "coeval" pattern than in earlier periods, in which, it seems, an age- and role-differentiated, "pederastic" pattern of adult/active-adolescent/passive homoerotic relationships seems to have prevailed?

But the first task is to show that Ahmad's story did not represent (like that of Edward II)[14] an unprecedented, abhorrent departure from societal norms. This is easily done, even if we focus exclusively on rulers. In Egypt itself, two hundred years previously, we may note the lurid end of the Fatimid caliph al-Zafir.[15] An exceptionally good-looking young man, al-Zafir had come to the throne in 544/1149 at the age of sixteen and quickly established a reputation for frivolity and self-indulgence, including both music and dalliance with slave girls. He also became very close to the young and equally handsome Nasr b. 'Abbas, whose father was a stepson and ally of the governor of Alexandria, Ibn al-Sallar, whom 'Abbas assisted in his successful plot to murder the caliph's vizier and take his place. Ibn al-Sallar took a dim view of Nasr's friendship with the caliph and urged the boy's father to intervene, "for two young men together can result in inappropriate things."[16] In an apparently unrelated development, 'Abbas then resolved himself to supplant his stepfather in the vizierate, and in the event it was his son Nasr who undertook, with the caliph's explicit approval, to surprise Ibn al-Sallar (who was cohabiting with the boy's grandmother) and behead him. Seriously implicated in this plot was the famous "Syrian gentleman," Usama b. Munqidh, who, fearing retribution from the late vizier's supporters, found a way to incite 'Abbas against the caliph himself.[17] Pointing to al-Zafir's ongoing extravagant generosity to Nasr and his habit of visiting him in his home on a regular basis, accompanied only by two of his trusted eunuchs, he asked the boy's father, "How can you put up with what people are saying to your son's discredit and their insinuations that the caliph does with him what is done with women?"[18] Some of our sources add that when Nasr boasted to his father that al-Zafir had granted him the revenues of the entire district of Qalyub, Usama wryly remarked, "Hardly an excessive bride-price for such as you!"[19] 'Abbas was more direct, telling his son, "You have destroyed your honor by consorting with al-Zafir, and people have begun to talk about the two of you. Kill him in order to free yourself from this accusation!"[20] Stung and carried away by youthful impetuousness, Nasr arranged for an ambush to meet and hack down the caliph on his next visit. At court the morning after this had been accomplished, when al-Zafir appeared to have gone missing, 'Abbas summoned his two younger brothers to inquire about his whereabouts, but they simply replied, "Ask your son! He knows more about his comings and goings than we!"[21] But 'Abbas promptly accused *them* of the murder and had them executed on the spot.

In this case, it was not concern for good government doomed a ruler with a favorite, and despite the appearance of remarks about "inappropriateness," we should not assume that the caliph's honor was irremediably tarnished by his relationship with Nasr. On the contrary, the plot turns, which have everything to do with real politics, depend only indirectly on sexual politics: it was *Nasr*, as the presumed passive partner, whose honor was at stake and who could thus be goaded into disposing of his (putative) lover.[22]

Nor is it a given that this sort of favoritism led inexorably to scandal and bloodshed. Unquestionably, the most famous male favorite in all of Islamic history was Ayaz, the beloved of the sultan Mahmud (d. 421/1030), who was the founder of the Ghaznavid dynasty in Afghanistan and eastern Iran. Ayaz was Mahmud's cupbearer and his acknowledged intimate for some years. While we can assume that he was younger than the sultan, he was presumably a mature (bearded) man or at least became one fairly early on in their relationship (although our meager historical sources do not permit precision on this point). In any case, we hear nothing of scandal in this instance. On the contrary, the love of Mahmud and Ayaz was quickly to take on legendary trappings, to the point that Persian romances extolling it—often in the form of Sufi mystical allegories for the love between the believer and God—took their place beside such established heteroerotic tales as those of the Arab lovers Majnun and Layla and the Persian lovers Khusraw and Shirin.[23]

It could be argued that Mahmud and Ayaz lived in and were celebrated by a cultural environment that was significantly different from that of Arab Egypt and Syria—that is, that the Iranian world exhibited a more tolerant attitude, either toward the phenomenon of the adult male beloved specifically or toward publicly acknowledged homoerotic relationships in general. Other instances of royal favoritism, both east and west, offer only ambiguous evidence on this point. We hear, for example, that the Seljuq ruler Tughril Beg (d. 455/1063, ruled over Iran and Iraq) was so entranced *(mashghuf)* by his commander Khumartakin al-Tughra'i that he not only honored him to the point of stirring up his vizier's jealousy but even had him castrated so that he could be present "at home" with the sultan in the presence of his wife; the erotic dimension of this relationship is not at all clear.[24] Further west and somewhat later, we are told that the ruler of northern Iraq and Syria, Zangi (d. 541/1146, ruled from Mosul) was infatuated with eunuchs, whether Turkish, Armenian, or Greek, and would castrate the sons of his enemies so as to perpetuate their beardlessness—although one of them eventually murdered him.[25] Zangi's son Nur al-Din (d. 569/1174, ruled from Damascus) seems to have been more impervious to the attractions of either eunuchs or intact young men. According to the historian Sibt Ibn al-Jawzi, he succumbed to lust for a beautiful boy only once, buying a beautiful *mamluk* for ten times the regular price, but God came to his aid and the *mamluk* died.[26] More clearly a case of favoritism but again involving a eunuch is that of the tragic Khwarazmshah Jalal al-Din (d. 628/1231), who late in his ultimately futile defense against the Mongols flagged at one point because of the death of

his beloved young eunuch Qilij, for whom he ordered elaborate
obsequies and spent some time in mourning when he should
have been fighting.[27]

Whatever the stance taken by those reporting on such rulers'
homoerotic interests, the latter were clearly often unconcerned
about their becoming public. The same could be said, presumably, for the Ayyubid ruler in Damascus, al-Malik al-Ashraf
Musa (d. 635/1237), who, we are informed in a single breath,
"restrained himself from seizing the wealth of the populace and
was devoted to his pleasures, famous for his love of young Turkish soldiers [al-ghilman al-Atrak] and his attraction to them, and
quite unrestrained with regard to them [mustahtir bihim]." He
composed a lot of bad poetry about them, such as the following
about a Turkish young man who was in charge of his treasury:

> May I be the ransom for a full moon whom description is at a loss
>   to encompass,
>   One who is liberal with my blood, despite being honest and
>   trustworthy.
> Should I marvel? He keeps my wealth safe,
>   But sees my soul destroyed by him and pays it no mind![28]

Such proclivities by no means prevented al-Malik al-Ashraf
from coming down hard on the Sufi shaykh Abu l-Hasan 'Ali al-
Hariri (d. 645/1247), who is said to have corrupted many young
aristocrats in Damascus through his sessions of "music, dance,
and beardless boys" and who was once found in the baths with
a group of boys without loincloths and when asked "What is
this?" simply replied, "Nothing but this!" and ordered one of
the boys to lie down prone (as a preliminary to being sexually
penetrated), which the boy did. Al-Malik al-Ashraf had him imprisoned and then exiled, to the intense satisfaction of various
conservative religious scholars, who had in fact issued *fatwas*
calling for his execution.[29]

That the public expression of homoerotic sentiments (especially in poetry) was fully sanctioned by Islamic societies both
before and during the Mamluk period while too-public, too-

sexual homosexual behavior was not can be abundantly documented, and in that sense, at least, rulers constitute no exceptional case. On the negative side, measures taken by Mamluk sultans against potential "scandal" that are roughly parallel to those by al-Malik al-Ashraf against al-Hariri are recorded throughout the eighth/fourteenth and ninth/fifteenth centuries, each case, however, having its own interesting specificities.

Under al-Ashraf Khalil (r. 689–693/1290–1293), for example, the notoriously harsh vizier Ibn Sal'us was looking for ways to attack 'Abd al-Rahman b. 'Abd al-Wahhab, the son of the preeminent jurist Ibn Bint al-A'azz. Besides enlisting various false witnesses to unspecified offenses on 'Abd al-Rahman's part, he also suborned a good-looking young man to claim that 'Abd al-Rahman had committed sodomy with him *(lata bihi)* and found someone else to allege that he had donned the *zunnar,* the girdle stipulated as Christian dress. 'Abd al-Rahman denied all the charges but admitted they were all *plausible,* except for that concerning the *zunnar,* since in fact even Christians donned the *zunnur* only under duress. Despite lack of proof, he was nevertheless discharged, publicly humiliated, and briefly imprisoned.[30]

There seems to have been more substance to another, long-running case against a prominent religious scholar that began under al-Ashraf Khalil's father Qalawun and concluded only under his brother and successor al-Nasir Muhammad. In 686/1287, the jurist, littérateur, and impressive debater Ibn al-Baqaqi was accused of committing immorality, mocking Islam, and, even more gravely, declaring illicit things licit *(istihlal al-muharramat),* a charge that was legally understood to imply apostasy and thus justify the death penalty. According to one source, he had gathered around himself a group of impious Turks and other ignorant people to whom he taught that both wine and sodomy *(liwat)* were permissible; it is not specified whether he (and they) practiced what he preached. Ibn al-Baqaqi was thrown into prison, where he appears to have languished for many years, engaged in defending himself and sparring with imminent jurisprudents. Finally, in 701/1302, he was beheaded in Bayn al-Qasrayn, the central square of Cairo.[31]

Although suspicions or accusations of sodomy could be a danger for some of the religious scholars *('ulama')*, specific love affairs seem to have been an Achilles' heel for both Mamluks and bureaucrats. A particularly complex case revolved, some thirty years later, around the decline and fall of al-Nasir Muhammad's chief financial officer, al-Nashw, whose attempts to impose fiscal responsibility earned him the general enmity of the sultan's *mamluks*. At one point, the sultan received an anonymous note attacking al-Nashw and his relatives, including the charge that al-Nashw's brother-in-law Wali al-Din had fallen in love with a young Turk named 'Umayr, was spending vast amounts on him, and, along with other relatives, carousing with him. (In an aside, our sources identify 'Umayr as the "boy from the Husayniyya quarter" over whom the extremely prominent *mamluk* Almas had earlier made a fool of himself—one of the factors that had led to Almas's execution.) Al-Nashw dismissed the charges as just a crude slander cooked up by the retinue of his enemy the *mamluk* Qawsun, but Qawsun insisted they were true and suggested that the sultan have the boy arrested and tortured to get him to reveal the names of those with whom he had been consorting. This was carried out, and the boy named Wali al-Din as one of a large number of the sultan's bureaucrats. Distrusting the boy's testimony but also fearful of scandal, al-Nasir Muhammad—who "hated immorality [*fahsh*]"—contented himself with sending the boy and his father into exile in Gaza.

This was not the end of the story, however. Sometimes later, the irrepressible Wali al-Din took up with another handsome young *mamluk,* this one the slave of his neighbor the prominent *mamluk* Taybugha al-Qasimi. Taybugha became aware of the situation, kept watch, and finally managed to catch Wali al-Din, again with other relatives, carousing with the boy in al-Nashw's house. Before he could complain to the sultan, al-Nashw anticipated him, reporting that Taybugha was involved in an affair with his *mamluk* and wasting his money on him and that he "invaded my home in a drunken fury, drew his sword, and screamed abuse at my family." Al-Nasir Muhammad—who "hated drunkenness"—promptly had Taybugha and his *mamluk* exiled to Syria. While our sources indicate these events as the first to instill doubts in the sultan about al-Nashw, it was several years before the Mamluks succeeded in having him deposed and executed, along with several of his (fun-loving) relatives.[32]

The persistent linkage between sodomy—or at least homoeroticism—and wine in these accounts is hardly surprising. One need think only of the celebrated tavern poems—with wine and cupbearer—of the ninth-century Abu Nuwas and indeed the torrent of similarly themed poetry throughout the intervening centuries.[33] More pertinently, perhaps, the entire Mamluk period was punctuated by a series of antivice campaigns by various sultans, of which the first and most famous was certainly that of Baybars in 665/1257, immortalized by Ibn Daniyal's (d. 710/1310) shadow play *Tayf al-khayal,* with its celebrated elegy on the devil (clearly dead in cleaned-up Cairo) as well as other poems in which winebibbers, hashish eaters, prostitutes, and sodomites all lament their fate.[34] Ibn Daniyal responded in a similar way to a later campaign by Lajin (r. 696–698/1296–1299), and Mamluk chronicles make it clear that there was a rhythm to these efforts, whose effects seem never to have been very long-lasting (in part, no doubt, because of the loss of income from taxes assessed on taverns and brothels when they were tolerated). In 831/1428, for example, sultan Barsbay abolished the taxes on wine and hashish in Cairo but directed special efforts to wiping out vice in Damietta. In this context, we are told about a complaint lodged by residents of the town against a Christian named Ibn al-Mallah, whose sodomitical goings-on were scandalously public. He made a practice of hiring beautiful boys as servants, entertaining them with gifts, wine, and music, and often brazenly retiring to another room to have sex with them and reemerging in a disheveled state. The sultan himself presided over his trial, at which he first denied the charges but when confronted with irrefutable testimony promptly converted to Islam. This obtained his forgiveness, although with a stern warning from the judge not to revert to his wicked ways—which, we are told, he managed not to do.[35]

Less fortunate was a Turk later in the ninth/fifteenth century, about whom the sultan Qaytbay was informed in 879/1496 that he was consorting with and had committed sodomy with several of his own *mamluks*. All we are told about this case is that the sultan had the offender castrated—apparently a then unprecedented punishment.[36] A few years after that, in 920/1514, we have an exceedingly unusual report of a man who raped and murdered a ten-year-old boy and was sentenced by the sultan Qansawh al-Ghawri to be hanged at the scene of his crime, according to some reports with his amputated genitals hung about his neck.[37]

William of Adam was wrong when he maintained that "any sexual act at all is not only not forbidden but permitted and praised"—even if our relatively meager sources perhaps suggest a somewhat more lenient attitude toward sodomy in his own day than 150 or 200 years later. On the other hand, the persistent references in those sources to young Mamluks (or Turks, which amounts to much, if not exactly, the same thing)[38] as the object of homoerotic interest offer some idea of where William may have got his ideas about sexual motives for the competitive purchase of them and raise the larger question of whether there was something about the Mamluk system altogether that encouraged homoeroticism and its public expression. Mamluk historians on occasion express their own opinions on this question as well, and although there is no consensus among them on the answer, these discussions serve to modify and balance the picture one might draw from an exclusive focus on scandals, prosecutions, and antivice campaigns.

Al-Maqrizi (d. 845/1441) has no doubt that homoeroticism and the concomitant sin of sodomy have increased in his own day, and he knows exactly where to lay the blame—on the founder of the second, "Circassian" Mamluk dynasty, the sultan Barquq (r. 784–801/1382–1399, with one brief interruption). Although it is only one of three lamentable developments for which he holds Barquq responsible—the other two are the practice of accepting bribes for appointments to major offices, for which the sultan served as a model, and the general deterioration of the economy, for which the sultan's personal parsimony is to blame—al-Maqrizi gives pride of place to (the prevalence of) "sodomy, due to his notorious practice of showing favor to handsome Mamluks [*ityan al-dhukran . . . li-shtiharihi bi-taqrib al-mamalik al-hisan*]."[39] He elaborates further on this theme in a different context in a description of one of the markets of Cairo, where various sorts of headgear were sold. Speaking of skull-caps *(tawaqi)*, formerly worn primarily by children (of both sexes), he notes that they were taken up as a fashion by the Mamluks and the military generally under the Circassians (meaning under Barquq) and quickly became subject to diversification in color and form, until under Barquq's successor Faraj (r. 801–815/1399–1412, with one brief interruption) there appeared the extravagant "Circassian cap." Al-Maqrizi finds this an appalling development that was made worse by the fact that women began to ape men in adopting the dreadful headgear, for two reasons. First, "love of males [*mahabbat al-dhukran*] had become prevalent among the ruling elite, so their wives decided to imitate males in an attempt to win over their husbands' hearts, and then the women of the city in general followed their lead in doing this," and second, the economic crisis forced women to cut back on their customary adornments and do their best in the more constrained area of their hats.[40]

Al-Maqrizi's implied contrast between the Circassian sultanate and happier earlier times might seem plausible, at least with regard to the sultans themselves, if we consider the early Mamluk period. Love of handsome young *mamluks* does not seem to have been characteristic of the first few Mamluk sultans and certainly not of the stern Baybars. We are told that Baybars's son Salamish, who reigned briefly in 678/1279 before being deposed and retired to private life, was extremely handsome (and wore his hair long), so that "many of the sodomites [*lutiyya*] who love beardless boys [*murdan*] were bewitched by him, and poets composed love lyrics about him,"[41] but nowhere are we informed of homoerotic interests on the part of Salamish himself. Nor do we hear of such regarding Qalawun (r. 678–689/1279–1290) (during whose reign occurred the arrest of the notorious shaykh al-Baqaqi). It was under Qalawun's son al-Ashraf Khalil that the vizier Ibn Sal'us attempted to frame the jurist Ibn Bint al-A'azz with a trumped-up charge of sodomy. For al-Ashraf himself, the only hint of any impropriety is a peculiar aside in an eyewitness account by an aide-de-camp of his assassination, which occurred during a hunting expedition near Alexandria. Before the appearance of the sultan's murderous *mamluks*, this man reports that al-Ashraf stopped to urinate, and while doing so "he began to show off his penis and tease me," but nothing more is made of this, and it is unclear why it was included in the account.[42]

With al-Ashraf's successor al-Nasir Muhammad, however, we do encounter a problem for al-Maqrizi's theory. In a recent account of al-Nasir Muhammad's (third) reign, Amalia Levanoni has stressed the dire consequences of his penchant for promoting his *mamluk* far more quickly than had heretofore been customary and for doing so on the basis of their good looks and his intense love for them.[43] Given what we are told about the sultan's "hatred of immorality" and his outraged response to reports of homoerotic infatuations and perhaps actual sodomy among his *mamluks* and bureaucrats, one might interpret this in terms of platonic admiration and more or less appropriate assessment of his slaves' qualities, discounting any truly homoerotic overtones. In fact, however, Levanoni's observations echo those of the historian Ibn Taghri Birdi (d. 874/1470), who is considerably more explicit and tackles al-Maqrizi straight on. Assessing the career of Barquq, Ibn Taghri Birdi first quotes al-Maqrizi's remarks on his three deplorable "innovations," and then proceeds to refute them one by one. His refutations of the second and third may be ignored here, as not germane to the present topic, but his response to the first is of considerable interest:

> As for sodomy [*ityan al-dhukran*], this scourge [*bala'*] is a very old one. Its appearance as a major phenomenon has been attributed to the advance of the Khurasanians on Iraq under the command of Abu Muslim al-Khurasani in the year 132 of the *hijra* [749–750 CE]. And as for acquiring handsome *mamluks*, what would the shaykh Taqi al-Din [al-Maqrizi] have to say about al-Malik al-Nasir Muhammad b. Qalawun's purchase of handsome *mamluks* at the highest prices, far beyond anything that al-Malik al-Zahir [Barquq] could match? Al-Malik al-Nasir Muhammad went so far as to promote an entire group of his *mamluks* with whom he was madly in love [*shughifa bi-mahabbatihim*] and wildly generous [*an'ama 'alayhim*] to the Command of a Thousand in Egypt before a single one's mustache had begun to sprout, including Baktamur al-Saqi, Yalbugha al-Yahyawi, Altunbugha al-Maridani, Qawsun, Maliktamur al-Hijazi, Tuquzdamur al-Hamawi, Bashtak, and Tughay the Elder, and married them to his daughters. The difference between [al-Nasir Muhammad and Barquq] in this respect is obvious![44]

Ibn Taghri Birdi's appeal to ancient history is commented on below. As for his detailed catalogue of al-Nasir Muhammad's favorite *mamluks*, other earlier sources by and large confirm his claims and supply a wealth of detail (including some important additions to the list), which cannot be canvassed here except for some brief remarks. Maliktamur seems to have won the prize both for looks and for the amount he cost al-Nasir Muhammad—in excess of 50,000 dirhams, despite the fact that he was technically free, not a slave.[45] But the dearest of all to the sultan was surely Baktamur, from whom he was inseparable, day or night, for several years, although in the end al-Nasir probably poisoned him (and his son) because of suspicion that he was plotting (with Almas) to assassinate him.[46] His place was quickly taken by the stunning Bashtak, despite the fact that the latter was a notorious womanizer. Bashtak had been given by al-

Nasir to Qawsun to raise, and the two became firm allies—they served as envoys to al-Nasir's besotted son Ahmad at Karak—until al-Nasir's death, at which point succession politics divided them, and Bashtak ended up being the first major casualty of the conflict.[47]

It could be argued, perhaps rather persuasively, that al-Nasir Muhammad collected beautiful boys but did not "do anything" with them; there is no way, of course, that we will ever know (although this seems to be a bit of a stretch with Baktamur, at least). In any case, that at least some of the Mamluk sultans, well before Barquq, had homoerotic interests in their *mamluks* seems to be incontrovertible. After Barquq, Ibn Taghri Birdi is inclined, in his assessment of each sultan, to continue to pick quarrels with al-Maqrizi and also, among other criteria, to note the sultan's position on homoeroticism. He defends al-Mu'ayyad Shaykh (r. 815–824/1412–1421), for example, against al-Maqrizi's criticisms, approving his passion for music, his appreciation of literature, and his sense of humor and illustrating the latter with two anecdotes, both of which turn on homoerotic topics. According to one of these, al-Mu'ayyad's stable superintendent Tughan offered Jani Bak, one of the sultan's bodyguards, 1,000 dinars to visit him; offended, the latter complained to the sultan, who was furious and summoned Tughan. Tughan defended himself, however, by pointing out that if the delectable Jani Bak were not al-Mu'ayyad's own *mamluk,* the sultan himself would have gladly offered him 10,000 dinars for a visit—a response that enormously amused al-Mu'ayyad and completely dissipated his anger.[48]

Ibn Taghri Birdi is equally positive about al-Mu'ayyad's short-lived successor Tatar (r. 824/1421), considering him the second of only two Circassian sultans (al-Mu'ayyad himself being the other one) who cared anything about high culture and absolving him of any interest in alcohol, while refusing to adjudge the truth of rumors about his "love of young men [*mahabbat al-shabab*]."[49] About the sultan Jaqmaq (r. 842–857/1438–1453), who seems to be his hero, the historian is considerably more emphatic. Not only was he uninterested in either wine or boys, but "we know of no ruler of Egypt, either Ayyubid[50] or Mamluk [*Turkiyya*], who can compare with him in this respect: neither in his adolescence nor in his adulthood was it ever reported that he had indulged in alcohol or any other prohibited thing; in fact, he is said never to have committed anything forbidden. With regard to love of young men, he might not even have believed that anyone could succumb to it, given his remoteness from even knowing about such things."[51] Jaqmaq's successor Inal (r. 857–865/1453–1461) fares rather less well. Aside from his effeminate voice and his near total illiteracy (he signed documents by tracing), "he was not sexually continent; indeed, he was accused in some quarters of loving pretty faces and beautiful young men—but God alone knows; on the other hand, he did abstain from forbidden intoxicants."[52]

With regard to the *longue durée* of homoeroticism in Islamic societies, Ibn Taghri Birdi clearly has a firmer grasp on reality than al-Maqrizi. It is in fact difficult not to accuse the latter of bad faith in his rush to attribute all of contemporary society's ills to the maleficent influence of Barquq. On the other hand, neither author seems to have any problem subscribing to an "importation" theory of homoeroticism: the idea that they "got" it from someone else seems to be well nigh universal. But while al-Maqrizi seems to be ignoring a sizable chunk of Islamic intellectual and literary history, Ibn Taghri Birdi is obliquely referring to one of the early icons of that history, al-Jahiz (d. 255/869). Al-Jahiz famously (if unbelievably) opined that the fashion for boy love in Iraq in his own day (illustrated most vividly by the poetry of Abu Nuwas) was the result of the commander Abu Muslim's decision, some decades earlier, to forbid the eastern Iranian soldiers of the 'Abbasid revolution to bring their wives along on campaign, resulting in their turning, *faute de mieux*, to their male pages for sexual satisfaction, a "habit" with which they subsequently infected the populace of the 'Abbasids' new capital of Baghdad.[53]

While Ibn Taghri Birdi seems to have denied that the Mamluk

regime represented any innovation in the societal role of homoeroticism, al-Maqrizi was not the only one to perceive some change in the situation in this period. The historian Ibn al-Dawadari preserves a precious record of an embassy from al-Nasir Muhammad to the Ilkhanid (Mongol) ruler of Persia, Ghazan, reported by the (terrified) ambassador, al-Mujiri, directly. Among the many tricky subjects broached by the Iranian monarch was that of homoeroticism. "How is it," asked Ghazan, "that your amirs abandon women and have recourse to [*yastakhdimun*] young men [*shabab*]?" Al-Mujiri replied, "Our amirs formerly knew nothing of this; it was an innovation introduced into our lands when Turghay came to us from you. He arrived with young men from the Tatars, and people were distracted by them from women." Ghazan was apparently not pleased by this reply but, distracted by the mention of women, quickly passed on to the next question, that of comparing the women in Iran with those in Egypt and Syria.⁵⁴ It is ironic that Ghazan should find the homoeroticism of the Mamluk realms surprising in the first place, considering that our sources leave little doubt that the public face of homoeroticism in Iran in this period well outshone that in the Arab lands: was Ghazan not paying attention, or was he being disingenuous?⁵⁵

But al-Mujiri was pointing to a significant phenomenon with his reference to Turghay. As the Mongols advanced across western Asia in the mid-seventh/thirteenth century, some of their numbers, for various reasons, defected from their military campaigns and took refuge in the Mamluk realm of Syria and Egypt. These were the *Wafidiyya*, among whom the largest contingent came from the Oirat Mongols. Among the first of the Oirats to arrive in Cairo was Kitbugha, who managed to ascend to the sultanate, briefly (r. 694–696/1294–1296), during one of the interruptions to the reign of al-Nasir Muhammad. While on the throne, he welcomed a large contingent of his fellow Oirats into Syria, where he settled most of the rank and file, and Egypt, to which he permitted the elite commanders to proceed, the latter being led by Turghay, the son-in-law of Hülegü, the Mongol conqueror of Baghdad. In Cairo, the Oirats (who were settled in the quarter of al-Husayniyya) were both a burden—they were non-Muslims and badly behaved—and a sensation: they were, both male and female, perceived as extraordinarily beautiful.[56]

It is al-Maqrizi, again, who best describes the resulting situation (despite his remarks elsewhere about the much later Barquq):

The amirs were entranced by them and competed (to obtain) their children, male and female. They took quite a number of them (from among the males) and added them to their troops and courted them. One of them would seek to obtain from another someone he had singled out and made the object of his desire. Then the amirs decided there were not enough of them in Egypt and sent to Syria summoning a large group of them. Thus their offspring became numerous in Cairo and everyone became desirous of their children, according to their tastes for females or males [*'ala khtilaf al-ara' fi l-inath wa-l-dhukur*], so that mutual envy and quarreling arose among the ruling elite, until finally, due to this and other reasons, the sultan al-Malik al-'Adil Kitbugha was deposed, in Safar 696 [December 1296]. His successor, al-Malik al-Mansur Husam l-Din Lajin, arrested Turghay, the Oirats' leader, and a number of their other important men and sent them to Alexandria, where he had them imprisoned and then executed. Then he distributed the rest of the Oirats among the amirs to serve them and join their troops. All this is why the people of al-Husayniyya are known for their extreme beauty—something that is still largely true even today. Some people were eager to marry their women, while others were bewitched by their sons. How well the shaykh Taqi al-Din al-Saruji has expressed himself in the following verses!

O messenger of desire, who setting out finds
    My tears running with him and serving as his aides:
Bring me a reply to my letter
    That I have addressed to al-Husayniyya!
For that is the place they call the Protected Valley,
    And its inhabitants are, in their beauty, its gazelles.
Walk a bit, and then turn left,

And you will find before you a lane bordered by tall build-
ings.
Go to the house at the top of that lane, belonging to one
Whose beauty makes all his neighbors beautiful too.
Greet him, and say, "*Yahşi misin? İyi misin?* [Are you fine? Are
you well?]
İşte [There you have] words that have long been hidden!"
Then ask him to come to me, and if he says "*Yok!* [No!]"
Say "*Evet!* [Yes!]"—for he has stayed away too long![57]

Unlike al-Mujiri, al-Maqrizi does not here imply that the
beauty of Oirat boys led to any *increase* in homoeroticism. Indeed, verses like al-Saruji's about the beauty of *Turkish* boys had
already long been a staple of Arabic poetry, even if his macaronic use of Turkish was something of an innovation. The available biographical information on al-Saruji himself (who died in
693/1294 and thus must have been rhapsodizing about some of
the earlier Oirat arrivals) tells us something more about attitudes in his day. According to Ibn Shakir al-Kutubi, he was "a
good man, chaste, a Qur'an reciter, well versed in grammar, lexi-
cography, and literature, and abstemious in his lifestyle. His
chief preoccupation was love of beauty but that accompanied by
complete chastity and respectability. He wrote quite a lot of
verse, which the musicians sang as lyrics." Furthermore, he
rarely socialized, and when he did, he had a personal rule that
his friends had to observe: he would not attend any gathering
where there were women present. And "when he died, the father
of his beloved said, 'I will bury him nowhere but in my son's
grave, for he loved him [*kana yahwahu*], and I will not part
them'—so convinced was he of al-Saruji's piety and chastity."[58]

Love of this sort—passionate but chaste—had a very long history in Arabic literature and presumably life and had been seen
as a homoerotic as well as heteroerotic ideal since at least the
time of Muhammad b. Dawud al-Zahiri (d. 297/901), author of
the first Arabic book of "love theory," the *Kitab al-Zahra* (The
book of the flower), and famous for dying of chaste love for a
pharmacist friend.[59] By no means all love poetry, addressed to ei-

ther sex, conformed to this particular ideal, but it certainly did offer one way—in both poetry and life—for expressing homo-erotic sentiments positively and publicly without incurring the opprobrium, or punishment, prescribed for homosexual behavior.

Al-Saruji's macaronic verse was imitated by others, notably by the high-level bureaucrat Ibn Katib Qarasunqur (d 744/1343), who addressed a poetic "letter" to a boy in Baha' al-Din Lane, just inside the city's Gate of Conquests (Bab al-Futuh) and thus adjoining the Husayniyya quarter, where, he tells the messenger,

> Look there and you will see one with an innocent gaze,
>   Ruby-lipped, gazing with an eye adorned by kohl,
> A son of the Turks, whose languid glances are arrows [*nibal*]
>   Shot from his eyelashes at every noble man [*nabil*].[60]

It was in fact the Turks' narrow eyes, above all, that were admired, and this shift in taste—from the wide-eyed Arab, as well as from the Bedouin (and heteroerotic) to the urban (and homo-erotic)—did not go unrecorded, as in these lines recorded by the famous littérateur al-Safadi (d. 764/1363) (himself the son of a Mamluk) in a richly documented discussion precisely of the change:

> O Arab maiden of the nomads, get you away,
>   For I have hitched my fate to a Turkish city boy!
> Go back to your family, you with the wide eyes,
>   For it is this narrow glance that has captivated me![61]

Further attestation to this cult of the Turkish ephebe is provided by a *maqama* of al-Safadi's composition, entitled *Law'at al-shaki wa-dam'at al-baki* (The plaint of the lovelorn and tears of the disconsolate), which in eighty pages of elaborate Arabic rhetorical prose describes the progression of the narrator's (apparently ultimately consummated) love affair with a beautiful young Turk, whom he first encounters riding with a group of his friends, all of them carrying bows. Although the text is not ex-

plicit, they are presumably all young Mamluks. (It may be noted
in passing that in 733/1333 al-Nasir Muhammad forbade ar-
chery contests because the amateurs of such contests were "cor-
rupting" the sons of the Mamluks, being themselves notorious
for "sodomy, immorality, and impiety.")[62] Equally eloquent but
in a very different register is Ibn Daniyal's shadow-play *al-
Mutayyam wa-l-da'i' al-yutayyim* (The man distracted by passion and the little vagabond orphan), a scabrous send-up of the
ideals represented by al-Safadi's *maqama*, in which getting the
boy into bed is the protagonist's only (and ultimately unfulfilled)
objective.[63]

The Mamluks themselves did not, on the whole, go in much
for Arabic literature. Some never even really learned the
language—Almas (another fan of Husayniyya boys, it will be remembered) being an example.[64] But there were exceptions.
Perhaps the best-known Mamluk scholar and littérateur from
the reign of al-Nasir Muhammad was Altunbugha al-Jawuli
(d. 744/1343), whose studies in the jurisprudence of the Shafi'i
legal school, as well as his admiration for the influential but con-
troversial religious conservative Ibn Taymiyya, did not prevent
him from writing love lyrics (about both sexes) and even incor-
porating into them quotations from the Qur'an, as in this two-
line poem:

> Your coming to me will be only when the Pleiades are in conjunc-
> tion [i.e., never],
> > While your standoffishness and cruelty are two steeds in a
> > close race.
> May I be your ransom! It is my bad luck that all you have man-
> aged
> > To memorize from the Qur'an is "You will not see me!"

The quoted words (Qur'an 7:143) are God's response to Moses's
request to show Himself to him.[65]

The high degree of homoerotic attention focused on young
Turks and young Mamluks in particular raises questions about
what went on in the homosocial world of the Mamluk barracks,

where recently arrived adolescent *mamluk*s were put through a rigorous training course and forged the intense ties of loyalty to their fellow recruits known as *khushdashiyya*. It is al-Maqrizi, again, who alerts us to the concerns we might expect. Looking back nostalgically to the good old days when discipline was enforced, he explains that when the eunuch officer in charge of the young *mamluks (muqaddam al-mamalik)* was informed by the supervisor of the barracks *(muqaddam al-tibaq)* that one of his charges was performing the major ablution, he would send someone to investigate the source of the pollution from which the boy was purifying himself. He would examine the boy's underwear, looking for evidence of a nocturnal emission, but if he did not find any, there would be hell to pay.[66] These remarks may be compared to what the Shafi'i jurist Taj al-Din al-Subki (d. 771/1370) has to say in his moral tract on the professions, the *Restorer of Blessings and Annihilator of Banes,* about the duties of the *muqaddam al-mamalik:* "Being charged with supervision of beardless boys, he is not permitted to engage in sexual immorality [*al-muwata'a 'ala l-fujur*] with them, nor should he allow two of them to sleep together in a single bed; but these officials have now become notorious for pimping their charges."[67] And al-Subki is equally distressed about the immoral possibilities presented to the valets *(jamdariyya),*

> most of whom are pretty beardless young boys, sought after by kings and amirs. They serve their masters in shifts, staying with them until bedtime. They are in extremely high demand because the desire for pretty beardless boys has captured the hearts of most of those who succumb to worldly desires [*ahl al-dunya*]. The *jamdariyya* have worked out new fashions in clothing designed to stimulate lust; they outdo women in adorning themselves and seduce people with their loveliness. But it is forbidden for any *jamdar* who believes in God and the Last Day to set himself up for such a purpose or to imitate women in what they were created for. He must not permit his master to commit sodomy with him [*yalut bihi*] nor even to kiss him. Let him fear God, his Lord, and have mercy on his own youth.[68]

Such strictures are echoed in numerous other texts, especially in the literature of moral exhortation that enjoyed a particular efflorescence in the Mamluk period—at the same time that a fashion in poetic anthologies devoted entirely to the attractions of boys can be documented.[69] But while condemnatory religious scholars and exuberant littérateurs each had their own reasons for devoting some particular attention to aspects of the Mamluk institution (opportunities for immorality) or to young Mamluks themselves (concentration of beauty), in neither sort of literature is it suggested that there was any real difference in *attitudes* toward homoeroticism between the Mamluks and everybody else.

The evidence brought to bear in this essay on those attitudes and on the place of homoeroticism generally in Mamluk society and among the Mamluk elite is far from comprehensive, given the vast quantity of relevant sources available.[70] It does, however, permit some tentative answers to the questions posed. First of all, the particular attractiveness of Turks was an aesthetic and erotic taste that predated the Mamluk period but was certainly reinforced by the Mamluk system, as well as by such events as the descent of the Oirats on Cairo. Mamluks themselves were *perhaps* particularly susceptible to such charms because of the segregation (in both gender and more broadly societal terms) built into their world, but the non-Mamluk elite and probably the populace understood and to a significant extent shared such tastes. Widespread homoerotic interest in adolescent males was in any case a given, although the sexual activities to which it naturally gave rise were widely deplored, not only by the professionally pious but (at least pro forma) by almost everyone. That members of the Mamluk elite would frequently have "favorites" or even that sultans would consider physical beauty a major criterion in choosing and promoting their *mamluk*s made perfect sense under such circumstances. If a young heir to the throne like Ahmad b. al-Nasir Muhammad lost his head over a young soldier, it was certainly unfortunate but neither insane nor hopelessly perverted.[71]

Questions about change over time are more difficult. Of the

two major red herrings offered to explain the presence of homoeroticism in a given society, the "importation" theory, while appealed to by al-Maqrizi (and much earlier by al-Jahiz), was clearly invalid. The "hydraulic" theory—that heterosexual impulses checked by sexual segregation were redirected in homosexual directions—was *not* appealed to by local observers, and while it perhaps retains some degree of plausibility with regard to medieval Muslim society in general, its particular applicability to the case of the Mamluks remains undocumentable.[72] A satisfactory answer to the question whether "tolerance" toward homoeroticism (or sodomy) increased, decreased, or stayed the same in the Mamluk period would depend on a much fuller assessment of the pre-Mamluk situation than has been attempted here, but contemporary perceptions would perhaps favor an increase—of which the fairly impressive log of prosecutions and persecutions for too-blatant sodomitical practices throughout the period may in fact be an index. Finally, the "pederastic" pattern of homoerotic relationships, with the "beloved" assumed to be adolescent or slightly out of adolescence, clearly remained dominant (in terms of expectations, at least) during this period, although the military Mamluk environment probably did encourage some increased elasticity in the understanding of what was acceptable.

None of this would William of Adam have understood, but his caricature of the situation (leaving aside the question of cross-dressers, which this essay has not attempted to address) is what one might expect from an observer from a different society with such different presuppositions. As for Edward II and Ahmad b. al-Nasir Muhammad, the parallels are clear enough—disgust and resentment at a ruler's or potential ruler's obsession with a private passion, rendered worse by its object being a male who was as such part of the public world of power. With regard to the differences, from a Middle East perspective it is tempting to point first of all to the fact that Ahmad was perceived to be the active partner (the "man") in his relationship, whereas Edward looks like the passive partner (judging from the age difference between him and Gaveston, as well as the reported nature of his execution). Whether or to what extent such considerations are in fact relevant in the case of Edward is a question for Europeanists (and one I have not seen addressed), but the general contours sketched here of how homoeroticism worked in Mamluk society should make it clear that Cairo was a long way from London.

NOTES

1. On Edward, see Caroline Bingham, *The Life and Times of Edward II* (London: Weidenfeld and Nicolson, 1973); on Gaveston, see J. S. Hamilton, *Piers Gaveston, Earl of Cornwall 1307–1312: Politics and Patronage in the Reign of Edward II* (Detroit: Wayne State University Press, 1988), and Pierre Chaplais, *Piers Gaveston: Edward II's Adoptive Brother* (Oxford: Oxford University Press, 1994). Bingham and Hamilton accept the sexual dimension of the relationship between the two men as obvious; Chaplais (not entirely convincingly) rejects it as unwarranted by contemporary evidence; Hamilton has responded to Chaplais with arguments for Edward and Piers being more than friends in "Ménage à Roi: Edward II and Piers Gaveston," *History Today* 49(6)(June 1999): 26–31.

2. Cited and translated by Michael Uebel, "Re-Orienting Desire: Writing on Gender Trouble in Fourteenth-Century Egypt," in *Gender and Difference in the Middle Ages,* ed. Sharon Farmer and Carol Braun Pasternack (Minneapolis: University of Minnesota Press, 2003), 244–45 and n. 63.

3. On the *mukhannath,* see my articles (dealing with earlier periods) "The Effeminates of Early Medina," *Journal of the American Oriental Society* 111(1991): 671–93, and "Gender Irregularity as Entertainment: Institutionalized Transvestism at the Caliphal Court in Medieval Baghdad," in Farmer and Pasternack, *Gender and Difference in the Middle Ages,* 45–72. Beard-shaving, cross-dressing, and passive homosexuality are all very well attested for the *mukhannath*s in this period; cohabitation is not.

4. The peculiar system of the Mamluk (literally, "slave") regime is most fully laid out by David Ayalon, *The Mamluk Military Society*

(London: Variorum Reprints, 1979). "Turk" here, following Arabic usage of the time, refers (rather imprecisely) to members of various ethnic groups speaking Turkic languages.

5. For useful, if brief, discussions of sexuality and homosexuality in Mamluk society (and literature), see Robert Irwin, "'Ali al-Baghdadi and the Joy of Mamluk Sex," in *The Historiography of Islamic Egypt (c. 950–1800)*, ed. Hugh Kennedy (Leiden: Brill, 2001), 45–57, and Louis Pouzet, *Damas au VIIe/XIIIe siècle: vie et structures religieuses dans une métropole islamique* (Beirut: Dar El-Machreq Sarl, 1991), 365–72. Stephen O. Murray, "Male Homosexuality, Inheritance Rules, and the Status of Women in Medieval Egypt: The Case of the Mamluks," in *Islamic Homosexualities*, ed. Stephen O. Murray and Will Roscoe (New York: New York University Press, 1997), 161–73, which is based entirely on secondary literature and a few translated sources, is less helpful.

6. Ahmad's biography is succinctly presented by Ibn Hajar al-'Asqalani, *al-Durar al-kamina fi a'yan al-mi'a al-thamina* (Hyderabad, 1348–1350), 1:294–96. See also al-Maqrizi, *Kitab al-Suluk li-ma'rifat duwal al-muluk*, vol. 2, ed. Muhammad Mustafa Ziyada (Cairo: Lajnat al-Ta'lif wa-l-Tarjama wa-l-Nashr, 1942), 461, 578, 593–619; Ibn Taghri Birdi, *al-Nujum al-zahira fi muluk Misr wa-l-Qahira* (Cairo: al-Mu'assasa al-Misriyya al-'Amma li-l-Ta'lif wa-l-Tiba'a wa-l-Nashr, 1963–1971), 10:23, 50, 69–72.

7. The bibliography on al-Nasir Muhammad is extensive; see *The Encyclopaedia of Islam*, 2nd ed. (Leiden: Brill, 1954–2002), s.v. al-Nasir; and Amalia Levanoni, *A Turning Point in Mamluk History: The Third Reign of al-Nasir Muhammad Ibn Qalawun 1310–1341* (Leiden: Brill, 1995).

8. Ibn Hajar al-'Asqalani, *al-Durar al-kamina*, 1:294.

9. On the role of eunuchs in the Mamluk military (and society), see David Ayalon, *Eunuchs, Caliphs and Sultans: A Study of Power Relationships* (Jerusalem: Magnes Press, 1999), and earlier scholarship cited therein.

10. Ibn Hajar al-'Asqalani, *al-Durar al-kamina*, 1:294–95.

11. Ibn Hajar al-'Asqalani, *al-Durar al-kamina*, 1:295–96. For the general political history and primary references, see Robert Irwin, *The Middle East in the Middle Ages: The Early Mamluk Sultanate 1250–1383* (Carbondale: Southern Illinois University Press, 1986), 125–29.

12. Ibn Hajar al-ʿAsqalani, *al-Durar al-kamina*, 1:296.
13. Uebel, "Re-Orienting Desire," 241–42.
14. Scattered innuendo in the sources about Edward's predecessors William II and Richard I notwithstanding.
15. I have relied on Ibn al-Tuwayr, *Nuzhat al-muqlatayn fi akhbar al-dawlatayn*, ed. Ayman Fu'ad Sayyid (Beirut: Franz Steiner, 1992), 61–68; Ibn Khallikan, *Wafayat al-aʿyan*, ed. Ihsan ʿAbbas (Beirut: Dar Sadir, 1968–1972), 1:237–38; and al-Maqrizi, *Ittiʿaz al-hunafaʾ bi-akhbar al-aʾimma al-Fatimiyyin al-khulafaʾ*, ed. Muhammad ʿAbd al-Qadir Ahmad ʿAta (Beirut: Dar al-Kutub al-ʿIlmiyya, n.d.), 2:270–73. See also Ibn Muyassar, *al-Muntaqa min Akhbar Misr*, ed. Ayman Fu'ad Sayyid (Cairo: Institut Français d'Archéologie Orientale du Caire, 1981), 147–49. For full references and a summary in English, see the *Encyclopaedia of Islam*, s.v. al-Zafir bi-Aʿdaʾ Allah.
16. *Fa-rubbama nataja min al-shabbayn ma la yanbaghi;* al-Maqrizi, *Ittiʿaz al-hunafaʾ*, 2:270.
17. On Usama b. Munqidh, see *Encyclopaedia of Islam*, s.v. He gives his own version of this story in his memoirs, *Kitab al-Iʿtibar*, ed. Philip Hitti (Princeton: Princeton University Press, 1930), 18–21, trans. Philip K. Hitti, *An Arab-Syrian Gentleman and Warrior in the Period of the Crusades: Memoirs of Usamah Ibn-Munqidh* (Princeton: Princeton University Press, 1929), 42–46.
18. Al-Maqrizi, *Ittiʿaz al-hunafaʾ*, 2:272.
19. Ibid.
20. Ibn Khallikan, *Wafayat al-aʿyan*, 1:237.
21. Ibid., 1:238.
22. For the crucial distinction, in the eyes of medieval Islamic societies, between active and passive partners in male homoerotic relationships, see my "The Categorization of Gender and Sexual Irregularity in Medieval Arabic Vice Lists," in *Body Guards: The Cultural Politics of Gender Ambiguity*, ed. Julia Epstein and Kristina Straub (New York: Routledge, 1991), 50–79.
23. On Ayaz, see *Encyclopaedia Iranica*, ed. Ehsan Yarshater (various publishers, 1982–), s.v., and references there; also Michael Glünz, "Das männliche Liebespaar in der persischen und türkischen Diwanlyrik," in *Homoerotische Lyrik: 6. Kolloquium der Forschungsstelle für europäische Lyrik des Mittelalters*, ed. Theo Stum-

mer (Mannheim: Forschungsstelle für europäische Lyrik des Mittelalters an der Universität Mannheim, 1992), 119–28.

24. Sibt Ibn al-Jawzi, *Mir'at al-zaman fi ta'rikh al-a'yan*, section on the Seljuqs, ed. Ali Sevim (Ankara: Türk Tarih Kurumu Basimevi, 1968), 84–85, cited and discussed in Ayalon, *Eunuchs, Caliphs and Sultans*, 153–56. The exceptional status of eunuchs within the system of strict gender segregation observed by (elite) medieval Muslims was the basis for the development of the eunuch institution.

25. Ayalon, *Eunuchs, Caliphs and Sultans*, 166–67, with references.

26. Ibid., 320, citing Sibt Ibn al-Jawzi, *Mir'at al-zaman fi ta'rikh al-a-'yan* (Hyderabad, 1951), 8:318–20 (inaccessible to me).

27. Ibn al-Athir, *al-Kamil fi l-ta'rikh*, ed. C. Tornburg (Leiden: Brill, 1853), 12:496–97, cited in Ayalon, *Eunuchs, Caliphs and Sultans*, 241, 318.

28. Ps.-Ibn al-Fuwati, *Kitab al-Hawadith*, ed. Bashshar 'Awwad Ma'ruf and 'Imad 'Abd al-Salam Ra'uf (Beirut: Dar al-Gharb al-Islami, 1997), 134–35.

29. Ibn Shakir al-Kutubi, *Fawat al-wafayat*, ed. Ihsan 'Abbas (Beirut: Dar Sadir, 1974), 3:6–12. See also Abu Shama, *Tarajim rijal al-qarnayn al-sadis wa-l-sabi'*, ed. Muhammad al-Kawthari (Cairo: Dar al-Kutub al-'Ilmiyya, 1947), 180; Ibn Kathir, *al-Bidaya wa-l-nihaya* (Beirut: Dar al-Fikr, 1978), 13:173–74; and the discussion and references in Pouzet, *Damas*, 367–68.

30. Al-Subki, *Tabaqat al-Shafi'iyya al-kubra*, ed. Mahmud Muhammad al-Tanahi and 'Abd al-Fattah Muhammad al-Hulw (Cairo: Dar Ihya' al-Kutub al-'Arabiyya, 1964–1976), 8:173. See also al-Safadi, *al-Wafi bi-l-wafayat* (Wiesbaden: Franz Steiner, 1962–), 18:180; and Pouzet, *Damas*, 109 n. 10.

31. Ibn Kathir, *Bidaya*, 14:18. See also Ibn Shakir al-Kutubi, *Fawat*, 1:152–53; al-Safadi, *Wafi*, 8:158–59; and Pouzet, *Damas*, 366. Pouzet follows Ibn Kathir in reading "al-Thaqafi," but the other sources confirm that the correct reading is "al-Baqaqi."

32. Ibn Taghri Birdi, *Nujum*, 9:113–19. For a full discussion of al-Nashw's career, including attention to these incidents, see Donald P. Little, "Notes on the Early *nazar al-khass*," in *The Mamluks in Egyptian Politics and Society*, ed. Thomas Philipp and Ulrich Haarmann (Cambridge: Cambridge University Press, 1998), 235–53.

33. The literature on this phenomenon is abundant but widely scattered. For general access, see the *Encyclopaedia of Islam*, s.v. *saki* (cupbearer).

34. See Li Guo, "Paradise Lost: Ibn Daniyal's Response to Baybars' Campaign against Vice in Cairo," *Journal of the American Oriental Society* 121 (2001): 219–35 and references there.

35. Ibn Hajar al-'Asqalani, *Inba' al-ghumr bi-abna' al-'umr*, vol. 3, ed. Hasan Habashi (Cairo: al-Majlis al-A'la li-l-Shu'un al-Islamiyya, 1972), 399–400.

36. Ibn Iyas, *Bada'i' al-zuhur fi waqa'i' al-duhur*, ed. Muhammad Mustafa, 2nd ed. (Wiesbaden: Franz Steiner, 1963), 3:96. Castration for such an offense (or any offense) flew in the face of Islamic law but could have been justified on the basis of *siyasa*, overriding state interest (as were many or most penal measures). Ibn Iyas specifies that the operation was carried out in Old Cairo, probably implying that it was performed by a Christian, and adds that at this time a Jew appeared who was an expert in castration and who subsequently performed the operation on "many people," who, like the Turk, survived it (which is what appears to surprise Ibn Iyas). There were large numbers of eunuchs in Cairo at this time, but theoretically they had all been castrated outside Islamic territory and then imported (as slaves), and certainly the operations were carried out by non-Muslims.

37. Ibid., 4:278–79.

38. Over the course of the Mamluk centuries, the predominance of ethnic Turks among the imported *mamluk*s gradually yielded to Circassians. A number of other ethnic groups were always included, however.

39. Al-Maqrizi, *Suluk*, 3:618. He adds that female prostitutes, due to the bear market in which they found themselves, were obliged to imitate boys, presumably in dress, as elaborated on below.

40. Al-Maqrizi, *al-Mawa'iz wa-l-i'tibar bi-dhikr al-khitat wa-l-athar* (generally referred to as *al-Khitat*) (Bulaq: Dar al-Tiba'a al-Misriyya, 1853), 2:204.

41. Ibn Kathir, *Bidaya*, 13:326, reading *min al-lutiyya* for *wa-l-lutiyya* and *shabbaba* for *shabbaha*; cited by Pouzet, *Damas*, 366 n. 147.

42. Ibn Taghri Birdi, *Nujum*, 8:18; "show off" is *yuli'*, for the text's *yuligh*, "to give (a dog a bowl) to lick," which is in fact impossible despite its perhaps apparent plausibility; but neither reading is sat-

isfactory. According to al-Maqrizi (*Suluk,* 1:792–93), al-Ashraf's assassin later attempted to justify his deed by claiming that the sultan drank wine in Ramadan, committed immoral acts with beardless boys *(yafsiqu bi-l-murdan),* and neglected to perform his prayers (in that order).

43. Levanoni, *Turning Point,* 37–40.
44. Ibn Taghri Birdi, *Nujum,* 11:290–92.
45. See the biography of him in Ibn Hajar, *Durar,* 4:358–59.
46. Ibn Taghri Birdi, *Nujum,* 9:300–02.
47. Ibn Hajar, *Durar,* 1:477–79.
48. Ibn Taghri Birdi, *Nujum,* 14:111. The other anecdote describes how Ibn Taghri Birdi's own father, in attendance on the sultan, offered a clever aside to him on the attractiveness of one of the young men present in the room, which the sultan much appreciated.
49. Ibn Taghri Birdi, *Nujum,* 14:207–10.
50. The dynasty preceding the Mamluks, 564–650/1169–1252, founded by Saladin.
51. Ibn Taghri Birdi, *Nujum,* 15:454–59.
52. Ibn Taghri Birdi, *Nujum,* 16:157–60.
53. Al-Jahiz put forth this theory in a work *On Schoolmasters (Fi l-mu'allimin),* now lost, but the relevant passage was widely copied, most notably by Hamza al-Isfahani in his recension of the poetry of Abu Nuwas. See Abu Nuwas, *Diwan,* vol. 4, ed. Gregor Schoeler (Wiesbaden: Franz Steiner, 1982), 141–42.
54. Ibn al-Dawadari, *Kanz al-durar wa-jami' al-ghurar,* vol. 9, ed. H. R. Roemer (Wiesbaden: Harrassowitz, 1960), 74–75.
55. For an overview of the Iranian situation, see Ehsan Yarshater, "Love-Related Conventions in Sa'di's *Ghazals,*" in *Studies in Honour of Clifford Edmund Bosworth,* vol. 2, *The Sultan's Turret: Studies in Persian and Turkish Culture* (Leiden: Brill, 2002), 420–38.
56. David Ayalon, "The Wafidiyya in the Mamluk Kingdom," *Islamic Culture* 25 (1951): 89–104; S. M. Elham, *Kitbuga und Lagin: Studien zur Mamluken Geschichte nach Baibars al-Mansuri und an-Nuwairi* (Freiburg: Schwarz, 1977), 77–78.
57. Al-Maqrizi, *Khitat,* 2:22–23.
58. Ibn Shakir al-Kutubi, *Fawat,* 2:196–206.
59. For the literary tradition of chaste love, known as *'udhri* (after the name of an Arab tribe celebrated for it), see *Encyclopaedia of Is-*

lam, s.v. *'udhri;* for love theory, Lois Anita Giffen, *Theory of Pro-fane Love among the Arabs: The Development of the Genre* (New York: New York University Press, 1971).

60. Al-Safadi, *Wafi*, 15:341–42, cited by Nasser Rabbat, "Repre-senting the Mamluks in Mamluk Historical Writing," in Kennedy, *The Historiography of Islamic Egypt*, 69 and n. 28; al-Safadi ex-plicitly compares this to al-Saruji's verse. The poem also appears in Ibn Shakir al-Kutubi, *Fawat*, 2:199–200 (in the entry on al-Saruji), with variants in the Turkish lines, which I am not qualified to at-tempt to decipher.

61. Al-Safadi, *al-Ghayth al-musajjam fi sharh Lamiyyat al-'Ajam* (Bei-rut: Dar al-Kutub al-'Ilmiyya, 1990), 2:19. On the poetic topos of "narrow" Turkish eyes, see Thomas Bauer, *Liebe und Liebes-dichtung in der arabischen Welt des. 9. und 10. Jahrhunderts* (Wiesbaden: Harrassowitz, 1998), 285–86. Relying on al-Safadi, Bauer suggests that the shift is first detectable in the early sixth/ twelfth century, but it can be pushed back about a hundred years earlier, as illustrated, for example, in lines by al-Bahhathi (d. 463/ 1071) preserved in al-Tha'alibi, *Tatimmat al-Yatima*, ed. 'Abbas Iqbal (Tehran, 1934), 2:32:

> I have been afflicted by a hunter of lions, himself a gazelle fawn
>   Of the Turks, whose childhood amulets have not yet been
>   removed.
> I find the earth narrow about me because of his narrow eyes,
>   And his black curly hair *(sha'r)* exhausts the wellsprings of my
>   verses *(shi'ri).*

62. *Al-liwat wa-l-fisq wa-qillat al-din:* Ibn Kathir, *Bidaya*, 14:161.

63. For discussion and references, see my article "Two Homoerotic Narratives from Mamluk Literature: al-Safadi's *Law'at al-shaki* and Ibn Daniyal's *al-Mutayyam*," in *Homoeroticism in Classical Arabic Literature*, ed. J. W. Wright, Jr. and Everett K. Rowson (New York: Columbia University Press, 1997), 158–91. The attri-bution of the *Law'at al-shaki* to al-Safadi is uncertain.

64. Ibn Taghri Birdi, *Nujum*, 9:301–2.

65. Ibn Taghri Birdi, *Nujum*, 10:105–6; al-Safadi, *Wafi*, 9:366–69; Ulrich Haarmann, "Arabic in Speech, Turkish in Lineage: Mamluks and Their Sons in the Intellectual Life of Fourteenth-Century Egypt and Syria," *Journal of Semitic Studies* 33 (1988): 81–114.

66. Al-Maqrizi, *Khitat*, 2:214, cited by Ayalon, *Eunuchs*, 55. "There would be hell to pay" renders *ja'ahu l-mawt min kull makan,* literally, "there would come to him death from every place." Ayalon has mistranscribed *makan* as *hal* ("circumstance") and translated "would be executed under any condition," but I am not convinced that the phrase is to be taken so literally.

67. Al-Subki, *Mu'id al-ni'am wa-mubid al-niqam,* ed. Muhammad 'Ali al-Najjar et al. (Cairo: Maktabat al-Khanji, 1993), 40.

68. Ibid., 35–36.

69. An example of the former is al-Dhahabi's (d. 748/1348) survey of major sins, *Kitab al-Kaba'ir,* ed. al-Sayyid al-'Arabi (al-Mansura: Dar al-Khulafa' li-l-Nashr wa-l-Tawzi', 1995), in which sodomy *(liwat)* appears as the sixteenth (pp. 55–63) in a list of seventy. Exactly contemporary are Ibn al-Wardi's (d. 749/1349) *al-Kalam 'ala mi'at malih* (Discourse on one hundred pretty boys, unpublished) and al-Safadi's *al-Husn al-sarih fi mi'at malih* (Manifest beauty on one hundred pretty boys, ed. Ahmad Fawzi al-Hayb [Damascus: Dar Sa'd al-Din, 2003]). On the genre, see Franz Rosenthal, "Male and Female: Described and Compared," in Wright and Rowson, *Homoeroticism in Classical Arabic Literature,* 24–54.

70. A fuller contextualization of elite behavior in this regard would have to deal with homoeroticism among the Sufi mystics, a topic touched on in some of the anecdotes cited here but in need of more detailed treatment.

71. Three centuries earlier, in a celebrated Persian "mirror for princes" addressed to his son and heir, the ruler of Jurjan (on the southeast coast of the Caspian Sea) had warned against the dangers a monarch incurs through passionate love—for either sex, but the accompanying anecdotes are exclusively homoerotic. In a separate chapter on "pleasure," he strongly advocated that his son's (moderate) pursuit of sexual enjoyment be directed at both sexes, invoking medical reasons for recommending that he turn to boys in the summer and women in the winter (Kaykawus, *Qabusnama,* ed. Ghulamhusayn Yusufi [Tehran: Sharikat-i Intisharat-i 'Ilmi wa-Farhangi, 1988], 80–87; trans. Reuben Levy, *A Mirror for Princes: The Qabus Nama* [New York: Dutton, 1951], 70–78). I have not seen this "seasonal" theory proposed elsewhere in Islamic sources, but it does turn up, surprisingly, in the *De planctu naturae* (The complaint of nature) of Alan of Lille (d. 1203 CE); for a discussion

of this work (but omitting the references to seasons), see Mark D. Jordan, *The Invention of Sodomy in Christian Theology* (Chicago: University of Chicago Press, 1997), ch. 4.

72. These are actually two different, if related, aspects of sexual segregation—the unavailability of women because of societywide sexual segregation and the all-male environment of the Mamluk barracks.

SEVEN

"In Spirit We Ate Each Other's Sorrow" Female Companionship in Seventeenth-Century Safavi Iran[1]

Kathryn Babayan

This chapter interprets a widow's "inscription" of herself in a journey of loss and separation in late seventeenth-century Isfahan.[2] My reading of the author's poetic narrative has taken liberties in understanding her suffering because human beings share emotions of grief, though temporal and cultural forms of expression may separate them. Such emotional sensibilities have colored my rendition of her decision after her husband's death to travel and perform the pilgrimage to Mecca. I locate her poem as a singular female expression of sorrow and more generally as a source about death and love within certain textual and social milieus. This Isfahani widow's choice to "cure" her melancholy through the writing of a mystical journey toward God reveals how piety and life experiences kindled her desire to circumambulate the Ka'ba.

To imagine this widow's social world, I focus on Isfahan where she lived and on the Ka'ba to which she traveled as devout pilgrim. I analyze the Isfahani widow's narrativized experiences through the symbols and words she used to translate her personal and social realities and endow them with meaning and power. In situating the ways in which gender and sexuality figure in the writing of the widow's mourning, I encapsulate the social history of elite women in early modern Isfahan and reflect on the relations between social and cultural structures and historical processes. This widow's writing experience illustrates how her subjectivity was formed by dominant discourses on desire and local practices of sworn friendships. In the process of grieving, the widow divulges her love for a female companion *(yar)* from the past. She exposes a feminine space in Isfahani society that was established through a ritual of sisterhood or companionship *(khwahar khwandagi),* which made use of religious connotations and the language of mysticism to express female love and friendship. The freedom awarded by travel, specifically by the experience of pilgrimage, to temporarily rearrange the disciplinary spaces prompts us to reconsider female homosocial spaces in Islamicate societies of the past.

If women did write about their lives in the premodern Islamicate world, these writings have yet to be discovered. Men penned the majority of extant sources, focusing on male circles where women surface in a limited variety of roles as wives, dominant mothers, and beguiling seductresses. Women remain on the margins of recorded premodern Islamic history, and so their experiences are often obscured. But this does not mean that elite women were illiterate, for examples exist of their poetry, calligraphy, and patronage of the literary and visual arts. The Isfahani widow was born into a privileged literary Urdubadi family of penmen, and according to the scribe's introduction to her poem, she was the widow of Mirza Khalil, the *raqamnivis* of the divan, who penned royal decrees for the last Safavi king, Shah Sultan Husayn (1694–1722). It is certainly due to her family's sociopolitical status that the Isfahani widow could perform the Hajj, which was an expensive and dangerous venture in her days. It is also thanks to her elite status that she was educated and that her narrative entered the annals of recorded history. We know that women born into families of religious scholars were learned for it was common to include chapters on women in *'ulama*'s biographies, the majority of which state that they studied with their fathers.[3] The Urdubadi family scribe introduces our author as the Bilqis and Khadija of the age *(Bilqis al-avani va Khadija al-dawrani)*.[4] Praising and comparing the widow with the two wise and powerful female icons of the prophet's wife and the queen of Sheba, the scribe includes her long poem (1,200 verses) in an anthology of letters, decrees, poems, and essays that he probably compiled during his tenure at her family library. These types of anthologies (*jung* and *majmu'a*) are numerous and can certainly serve as archives, yet they remain untapped repositories for the writing of the social and cultural history of Safavi Iran.

Hoping to replenish the void created by her husband's death, the widow sets off on a pilgrimage to Mecca from Isfahan, the capital of the Safavi empire (1590–1722). It is the end of the seventeenth century. At the beginning of her story, she informs the audience of her decision to make the Hajj, and she narrates her pious journey in verse. "Since the wiles of fortune [*charkh-i hilah pardaz*] left my heart burning with sorrow due to the absence [*firaq*] of my intimate companion [*yar*] . . . I vowed to circumambulate the holy Ka'ba," she states, and continues: "I tied myself around the holy Ka'ba," perhaps turning her bodily self into a vow.[5] She tells of her sleepless nights and tormented days: "I saw no solution other than travel [*siyahat*]."[6] The language she employs is mystical, and in fact its poetic form, the *masnavi*, is the privileged medium of Sufi expression and the preferred choice of her favorite medieval poet, Nizami. Travel and circumambulation are the central themes of writing and healing that mark the tone of our widow's poem. The form of this chapter echoes her circular rhythm to communicate the affect of her narrative and to employ it as a tool for leaving and then returning to the widow's melancholy. Each detour hopefully provides for the reader different layers of social and cultural meanings.

The Isfahani widow refers to her husband and God with the same Sufi terms *rafiq* and *yar*, defined as "companion" by the prevalent culture of chivalry that places loyalty and generosity at its heart, expecting a level of sharing both in matters spiritual and material. Her impulse to travel, or *siyahat,* locates her on the Sufi path toward self-knowledge that ultimately leads to unicity, a stage mapped within the monist quest for union with the divine. The ubiquitous mystical sensation of separation *(firaq)* from the object of desire infuses her narrative with an air of gloom and desperation that, according to tradition, prompted mystics to break from society and wander in pursuit of illumination and truth. For some mystics, death offered the only relief from the melancholic state of separation from their beloved, God. Sidestepping eschatology, they desired to release their selves from worldly captivity. Their yearnings were portrayed in mystical poetry with profane articulations of *ʿudhri* love ideals in which the unsatisfied lovers were driven inevitably to death.[7] And yet some mystics sought solace in the continuous contemplation of God through the recitation of his speech (the Quran) and his names or before the sacred space of the Kaʿba, his abode.

This widow chooses to fill her absence with the fullness of God at the Kaʿba, to walk through the spaces that the prophet Muhammad and his children had inhabited, and there to unite with the truth. A persistent call that she hears (and describes at moments as a song) draws her toward Mecca, filling her with an excitement that propels her forward along the arduous terrain from Isfahan, northward to the Caucasus, through eastern Anatolia, Syria, and ultimately southward to Arabia. The pilgrim, aware of the difficulties of the journey, is afraid. But as is the case for fellow Sufi devotees on the path of the unknown, her fear must be conquered, and so she, employing the language of chivalry at the start of her mystical journey, "tied her belt and wore her armband." We admire her decision taking: "I washed my heart from the fear of danger. I wrote the divination of my trip as auspicious."[8]

In the process of telling her story, the traveler reveals another, earlier experience of loss that as a respectable married woman in Isfahan she had borne secretly for many years—a forced separation from another *rafiq* and *yar,* a woman. I argue here that the women's relationship, which was deemed illicit by social, religious authorities, is significant to the widow's decision to perform this holy pilgrimage after her husband's death and to repent of her "sins and crimes" at God's abode. The tensions between profane and sacred love torment this widow, stimulating the journeys toward God and her companion from the past. The tensions at times merge in the language of mysticism but are never fully reconciled.

By the seventeenth century, Persianate poets had versified the experience of the Hajj, though no singular poetic form seems to have been favored to depict the travels. Pilgrimage narratives varied not only in choice of form—*masnavis* (rhymed couplets for didactic, romantic, and Sufi expressions) and *qasidas* (lyric poetry) being used alternatively—but in content as well. It is safe to assume that the Isfahani widow was familiar with these literary practices and exercised the freedom to choose the form and content of the written account of her Hajj. The literature describing the pious act of worship and reverence toward God at the holiest of Muslim shrines relied on a language full of symbols and tropes evoked particularly by poets who understood the Hajj as a mystical journey toward God. The widow's own account of the Hajj demonstrates her knowledge of the modes of representing the pilgrimage's sacred geography and vividly illustrates the common themes of lamentation, absence, separation, and longing for the beloved to recount her personal circumstances and the exercise of piety. Pilgrimage narratives, like the twelfth-century poet Khaqani's *Tuhfat al-'Iraqayn* (Gift of the Two Iraqs), draw on the genre of complaint literature *(shakwiyat)* wherein the state of anguish and sorrow sets the narratives' tone. Communicating his reasons for circumambulating the Ka'ba, Khaqani begins his narrative with a lamentation in which he complains that his contemporaries do not heed the signs of an imminent apocalypse.[9] The causes of grief in complaint literature are unrequited love, the world's transience, destiny's fickleness, and friends' unreliability. All of these themes are present in the Isfahani widow's narrative and situate her pilgrimage narrative within the genre of complaint literature. Hence, the widow begins her poem with a complaint against the wiles of fortune, which have left her heart burning with sorrow due to the absence *(firaq)* of her intimate companion.

The absence and longing for a friend, the illness stage as part of the curative process of purification and transcendence, and messages from the divine in the guise of a birdsong, musical instrument, or natural phenomenon like the wind are literary motifs suffusing the widow's language. Her spiritual quest will be solitary, for none of her relatives will accompany her travel: "Not one became my friend [*yar*]." But she reminds and comforts herself: "Who needs a human companion? God is the *rafiq* of the forlorn."[10] Hurt by relatives' betrayal *(khwishan u azizan),* she leaves Isfahan like a "violent wind [*sursur*]." Using the trope of Majnun (Madman), who, destitute and deprived of his beloved Layla, wanders the desert, the widow writes, "Alone I rode off to circumambulate the House of the Dispenser of Justice."[11] Audiences familiar with this epic romance would certainly sympathize with Majnun, who was refused for a son-in-law by Layla's father and whose own father then urged him to go on the Hajj to remedy his lovesickness. Pressing him to embrace God, the supreme patriarch with the ultimate authority to decide the fate of human lives, Majnun's father attempts to dissuade his son from earthly love and urges him to recite a prayer at the Ka'ba asking God to cure him of his love for Layla.

In their versions of the Layla and Majnun story, famous medieval poets like Nizami and Jami cast the Ka'ba in the image of a woman and used the female figure to symbolize the dilemma between formal and mystical experiences. The consummation of love is portrayed as a choice between the sacred and the profane—between the *Shari'a* (divine law) and the *Tariqa* (mysticism). The male poets' vacillations between the two Ka'bas were relevant to our widow, for as a fellow mystic she too must confront the tensions between the exoteric and the esoteric. Perhaps our widow journeyed to resolve this dualism, to merge between this and the other worlds. But these tensions and the mentalities behind them clashed against the backset of Isfahani daily life. The tensions between mystical and Shari'a-minded modes of thinking and feeling led to the imperial-level project of regulating the sexuality of Isfahan's subjects. The Isfahani widow is writing at an important time—at a moment in Safavi history when the courtly and religious patriarchy was taking measures to govern domestic spheres by sanctifying, with the force of divine law, heterosexual marriage and attendant social and religious norms. The desire-disciplining discourses must have weighed heavily on our widow's dear friendship and homoerotic desires, provoking ambivalence and shame. Does she feel caught in a predicament that is similar to Majnun's?

Though she relies on conventional rhetoric and dilemmas to explain her situation, the Isfahani widow unconventionally "inscribes" her narrative with a male-dominated poetics. I argue that in her capacity to become a historical subject, she deliberately intervenes in changing and shaping the masculinist language, moving between the discursive possibilities and her own experience and condition. She constantly enters and exits the tradition of *hajjnames* to particularize her experiences and attitudes. Our widow's decision to embark on the pilgrimage, her personal language, and her self-association with Majnun all manifest the contours of her repentance, which she hopes will provide the "cure" for her love toward another woman, which is condemned by Islamic law and Isfahani society. Love *('ishq)* and melancholy *(malikhuliya)* have been classified as twin maladies in Islamicate medical and ethical literature.[12] But what to make of the penitent's evocation of the example of Majnun, who has failed his endeavor to repent from loving Layla? This pilgrim also seems to have been unsuccessful. Only when circumambulating the Ka'ba and encountering God does she feel lightened and cleansed of this forbidden love, for the moment she leaves the Ka'ba, her grief and longing return to haunt her. Unlike in the *Layla and Majnun* story, the Isfahani widow evokes not one but three beloveds—God, her husband, and her female companion. She wishes to relinquish the love she had for her old companion, but her pilgrimage is also prompted by the death of her husband and by the complex feelings of grief and liberation that she experiences. Is the husband's appearance in the narrative something of a "social requirement" and pretext that preface the account of her female friend? I do not think so: for the Isfahani widow love was an emotion, albeit problematic, that she felt truthfully and genuinely for both companions in her life. But the textures of these loves seem different.

On her way out of Isfahan, she stops first at her husband's grave, her friend's *(yar)* "rose garden." Tears pour from her eyes, "turning into a stream of blood." When she walks away from his tomb, "a wail sounded off my bones like a reed flute" and cried, "Since you are deprived of union with your dear friend, become a nightingale in his rose garden."[13] So she stays the night, like the symbolic nightingale that sings in the secret language of divine love. There, beside her husband, she sleeps peacefully until dawn, when she weeps aloud like the nightingale. Heavy-hearted, she picks herself up and begins the journey of pilgrimage. This is the last time the widow mentions her deceased husband.

The journey to Mecca and Medina was arduous and challenging for pilgrims, requiring them to travel through strange and rough terrain—mountains, highlands, rivers, and finally deserts in territories held by the hosts of the Hajj, the rival Ottomans. After entering the Ottomans' domains, the grieving widow relates feeling out of place and voices nostalgia for Iran and Isfahan. In this narrative of separation and longing, the widow's "self" is represented with mystical themes, symbols and metaphors in both familiar and foreign landscapes. How does the consistent use of Sufi terminology related to absence and longing configure her subjectivity, her religious experiences, her nostalgia for Isfahan, the revisiting of her birthplace, Urdubad, and the discovery of new and strange cities like Aleppo? During her travels in the domains, the Isfahani widow writes about her relationship to different spaces (whether sacred, social, gendered, or sexual) and displays cultural, linguistic, and religious opinions.

Her preferences and aversions resist easy binary categorizations between Sunni and Shiʿi, Safavi and Ottoman, local and imperial, elite and popular, hetero- and homosexual, private and public.

Though seemingly a lone traveler until she joins the caravan of Persian pilgrims in Erevan (in Eastern Anatolia), the widow must have been traveling with at least one slave.[14] Her colorful and detailed verse is riveting. Readers easily follow the rhythms of her camel litter as it crosses lush prairies and lofty mountains and rests in villages and cities, and they keep her reflective company on strolls through rose gardens. She communicates with a striking ease with men, from local dignitaries to farmers, who are all gracious hosts along the journey. They protect her from highway robbers and save her boat from capsizing. The men she encounters are both youths and adults, and every one is described with the language that is employed to characterize chivalry. They are gallant man (javanmard) who perform their roles with bravery and generosity. Hers is not a gender-specific language for chivalry, for she remarks that she and her female hostesses also live by the same codes of behavior. She emphasizes the "intelligence and discernment" of the good-natured (niku khuy) farmer in whose house she spends a night.[15] Her relationship to these gallants is inescapably gendered; they are like her sons (farzand), and she praises the mothers who have nurtured such peerless men. They are kind hosts who follow the culture of etiquette that requires greeting (pishvaz) guests even if they are female pilgrims, feasting with them, and escorting (badraqah) them to the outskirts of their dwellings. On her way from Qazvin to Sultaniyyeh, she encounters a wise youth (nawjavan) in Dawlatabad who invites her into his "Kaʿba of brotherhood [ikhwan]" and prepares a feast in her honor. She says the javanmard, or gallant youth, treated her with a kindness "I had not seen from relatives except when I was in Isfahan."[16]

The familiarity and kinship that she feels with people on her long journey create a comforting security in the "domains of the Shah of Iran."[17] This security is lost when she leaves behind Iran,

where "we are like valiant lions [*shir-i jiyan*]," and enters the
Ottoman lands, "where in fear we turn into mice [*mush*]."[18]
Her status as pilgrim and widow as well as her prominent
Urdubadi ancestry certainly color her journey through Safavi
Iran. Though courted and pleased by the attentions of a few
suitors, particularly of the governor of Kharvanaq, a distant relative possessed with the "face of a beautiful child [*tifl*] and the
knowledge of Aristotle," she remains nevertheless free to move
in and out of both public and private gendered spaces, her honor
untarnished.[19] Moreover, she seems to command the respect
that allows her to draw the lines between herself and these men
in her role as mother, widow, and pilgrim.

En route to Damascus, where she was to join the Ottoman
caravans headed for Mecca, she makes a detour. Perhaps in a
passionate moment, feeling freed of her husband and liberated
through her journey, she decides to travel north to the Caucasus
and visit her old friend and distant relative. With the story's unfolding, it becomes clear that their separation had been forced
due to rumors in circulation about the two women long ago
when they were both still resident in Isfahan. Now she travels to
reunite with her other lost love, whom she describes with terms
of endearment that are meant for her husband and God *(yar u
rafiq)*.

In Tabriz, a previous capital of the Safavis located in north-
western Iran, she is drawn by the proximity of her homeland
and longs for her birthplace, Urdubad. There is a consistent
sense of the power of space associated either with the holy house
of God or that of her birthplace. The sacred and profane sites
alike stimulate in her the physical pull, merging in a sanctifying process and providing momentary relief from her melancholic state. She travels by boat across the Aras River to
"my Urdubad." Having heard of her arrival, relatives and
acquaintances—old and young, men and women—have assem-
bled along the banks of the river *(pishvaz)*: "With kindness and
affection my relatives greeted me and took me to the house of

my generous companion [*rafiq*]." Later she will write about the relationship:

> Together in Isfahan, we had been companions *(yar)*.
> In spirit, we ate each other's sorrow [or we were each other's companions in sorrow].
> She was a relative better than any sister,
> kinder than any of my other relatives.
> But suddenly heaven's playful tricks
> appeared on the stage of deceit,
> So much so that it [heaven] hid from my gaze that kind one
> as a body is separated from its soul.
> Forty houses they placed between us
> and inflicted separation between our two bodies.
> For our hearts, no cure save constraint;
> in separation [*hijran*], both of us have waited a century.
> Until at last, the end of the night of torturous separation
> turned into the morning of spiritual union.
> After a century, I saw the face of that friend [*yar*],
> and I threw the baggage into her house.
> The remedy [*da'va*] for the incurable [*bidarman*] pain of separation,
> o dear one, was patience and endurance.[20]

What was the context for this forbidden friendship, and what social life did it have? Why would it have provoked such a reaction as to cause the widow's companion to leave Isfahan and resettle in her ancestral homeland? Let us move momentarily to Isfahan, where the widow and her old friend lived and where their friendship was nurtured but reduced to scandal later.

Although the Muslim culture of veiling and seclusion intended partly to protect male honor, in seventeenth-century Isfahani society husbands did not feel so certain or comfortably secure and in fact felt threatened by their wives' female friends. *'Aqa'id al-Nisa'* (The beliefs of women) was a contemporaneous social critique of "female superstition" by the clergyman Aqa Jamal Khwansari (d. 1710), and it refers to the practice of *siqah-*

yi khwahar khwandagi, which involved a vow of sisterhood that two women exchanged with each other.[21] Aqa Jamal enjoyed enviable access to the courts and persons of the Safavi Shah Sulayman and Sultan Husayn, and he would have certainly been acquainted with the widow's husband, Mirza Khalil, who penned official decrees for the king in the chancellery. Courtly circles were small and thrived on gossip and rumors; it is likely he caught wind of the scandal that led to the separation between Mirza Khalil's wife and her female companion. But this cleric's satire on local female culture suggests that intimate friendships between Isfahani women, which he derides, were sufficiently prevalent to cause general male anxiety. I use this satire to interrogate the practice of friendship in Isfahan. Satire ridicules and mocks with the intention of injuring; without a basis in social practice, satire would lose its rhetorical poignancy and affect. So I use this satire to enter Isfahani society's universe of symbols and attitudes. By juxtaposing these two texts, I hope to shed light on the broader social circle that encompassed elite women and men like Aqa Jamal and Mirza Khalil's widow in the late seventeenth-century period when their society was being gripped by increasing inflexibility.[22]

'*Aqa'id al-Nisa'* was written around a decade before the accession of the last Safavi shah, Sultan Husayn (1694–1722). His reign ushered a radical shift in mood for Isfahan.[23] By the early seventeenth century, the Shi'i clerical establishment, under the auspices of the Safavi monarchy, had initiated a normative project of regulating sexuality. After the Safavi revolution had succeeded (1501) in shoring support for its ideas throughout the Iranian domains, the Safavi mystic-king Ismail proclaimed that Shi'ism would be the official religion of his imperium, upsetting the political balance in favor of Shari'a-minded clerical governance. Under the guise of a moral campaign that relied on decrees and ethical treatises to assert the law and rule of the Shari'a, Shi'i jurists effected heteronormative subjects through the control of their religious and sexual practices. I do not elaborate here the complex historical conditions that led to this conservative impulse. Sufism, or Islamic mysticism, was a pervasive, popular mode of religiosity that competed with Shi'ism, the newly established religion of the Safavi state. Against the backdrop of competing Sufi and Shi'i claims to intimacy with God the king and with the believing denizens of the Safavi realms. Shi'i clerics devoted much attention to inscribing certain forms of sexuality and spirituality as their twin objects of discipline.

By the time Aqa Jamal wrote his satire, a strict, orthodox interpretation of the Shari'a was in force. Shah Sultan Husayn (1694–1722) issued decrees concerning the legal (virtuous) and illegal (virtueless) habits and conducts of life under Safavi rule, and the clergy happily signed their endorsements of the shah's decrees.[24] In a grandiose public show of repentance, the king ordered his men to clear several thousands of wine bottles out of his court cellars and to smash them in Isfahan's central square. Men and women's clothing was regulated to conform to ever stricter notions of Islamic "modesty." Guests at weddings and other social events where both sexes gathered could no longer be entertained with music and dance, and gender segregation was enforced at every private and public event. Sodomy, adultery, prostitution, and gambling were banned. Opium and hashish were declared illegal, and coffeehouses, taverns, and Sufi lodges—all considered dens of Sufi fomentation—were forcibly closed. Under the Safavis' patronage of Shi'i scholars and institutions, mosques, seminaries, and individual clergymen could have their say in politics. Everyone awaited the Mahdi, also known as the Twelfth and Hidden Imam, to instate divine justice on earth and rid the people of the social miseries and injustices they had too long suffered. But the Imam had not yet revealed himself, and in the meantime Shi'i scholars were the authorized intermediaries between the believers and God since they were the specialists in divine law and, Sufi mystics, albeit admittedly charismatic and popular with the crowds, were not.

'Aqa'id al-Nisa' (referred to also as *Kulthum Nane*) was composed at this junction in Safavi history, on the eve of the rationalization of power and fear of independent Sufi expressions of sexuality and religiosity. Comparable to the cultural disciplinary effects that edicts and religious treatises on ethics and morals intend to provoke, '*Aqa'id al-Nisa*' endeavors to effect similarly through the injurious bite of satire. But luckily the text helps us to piece together images of female denizens in seventeenth-century Isfahan and their friendships within their social arenas prior to the rise of rationalism and patriarchy at court and the theological seminaries. '*Aqa'id al-Nisa*' constitutes an attempt to impress such forms of religiosity on the minds of Isfahan's audiences in public arenas and in the privacy of households.

Whatever Aqa Jamal's intention, it did not curtail the range of responses when he poked fun at five women—Kulthum Nane, Bibi Shah Zaynab, Khaleh Jan Aqa, Baji Yasaman, and Dede Bazmara. These trusty practitioners of local custom represented a broader female urban culture, attested to by the author's wry comment that "besides these five individuals, there are many specialists like them, but their mention would give way to wordiness."[25] Inasmuch as the author of this social satire was a prominent religious authority mocking popular beliefs, he gives details about local customs and attitudes that had synthesized with Islamic norms and practices. In his opinion, ritual obligations were too often neglected. Aqa Jamal describes rituals that, despite countering the spirit and laws of the Shari'a, women continued to perform as part of their daily spirituality. In his preface, he delineates his object of criticism: "any woman of age [*ki sini dashtah bashad*] and inclined to superstition [*khurafat*]."[26] Soon we shall see what he meant by "superstition." '*Aqa'id al-Nisa*' belongs in the genre of essays *(risalah)* by religious scholars *(mujtahid)* who were emulated by seminary students *(talib)*. Members of the community of believers also composed these essays to clarify practice for those believers who questioned how the Shari'a affected daily life.[27] Aqa Jamal's language and style reflect this genre of essays. "This is a summary," he writes, "of the sayings and actions [*aqval va afal*] of women, and what they consider their obligations [*vajibat va mandubat*] and prohibitions [*mahrumat va makruhat*]."[28] The five Isfahani women, "experts" in "superstition," are often mockingly called *'ulama,* religious scholars, by Aqa Jamal.

The author allocates sixteen chapters to the universe of the female gender, from ritual obligations like ablutions, prayer, and fasting to marriage and childbirth.[29] He enters the female homosocial spaces of public baths *(hammam)* and gatherings that were entertained with live instrumental music and the magical spheres of amulets and talismans. Delineating in one chapter what the five women consider "proper" behavior, he describes the fluidity of the boundaries that women observe in their daily activities of, for instance, food and clothes shopping. Women consistently break the rules of seclusion, improperly exposing themselves in *hammams,* neglecting to put on modest demeanors in the presence of men outside their families, and only laxly observing their ritual obligations. Aqa Jamal ends his book with two chapters on female friendships, relationships portrayed to have involved more passionate emotions than matrimony itself has. Here he expresses political antagonism against and fear of a feminine culture tightly knit with love, loyalty, passion, and even sexual desire through vows of sisterhood. The cleric's rejection of these practices as "superstition" carries larger general significance. The women he ridicules may be stock figures, but their beliefs and rituals undoubtedly represent the larger collective culture that impinged on the rationalist religious establishment's project of transforming the mental, emotional, and sexual universe of Isfahan's denizens. The Isfahani widow's self-representation illustrates the conditions of the project and its pressures on society.

With a heavy tone of moralism and sarcasm, Aqa Jamal distorts the practice of sisterhood. According to the female experts on local culture, whose identities the cleric impersonates in the text, every woman should have an avowed sister *(khwahar khwahdah)* for, "what hope does a woman have if she dies without one?"[30] One female expert asserts that friends who spend all their time together will on the day of reckoning be free of judgment and will go directly to heaven. Women who reject this practice, adds the character of Bibi Shah Zaynab, are sinners *(gonahkar)* who will die as Jews or Christians.[31] Aqa Jamal designates Bibi Shah Zaynab to deride sins *(gonah)* of the kind that the widow would want to repent of in her pilgrimage to the Ka'ba. In these ways, the cleric shows that female practices like the ritual of sisterhood countered sacred law and repentance and ridicule were complementary disciplinary technologies for the production of heterosexual subjects.

In the process of an early and new reading of a corpus of Safavi sources housed in Persian manuscript catalogues in Iran and termed "anthologies" *(jung* and *majmu 'a)*, I have been intrigued to discover numerous texts on vows of brotherhood, *siqqah-yi ikhwat,* and vows of sisterhood, *siqqah-yi khwahar khwandahgi.* The vows' language situated participants in a shared spiritual communitas that was often represented in chivalry manuals being circulated within craft circles. The friendships entailed partnerships in this world and the hereafter between two brothers or sisters who pledged themselves to one another for the sake of God. In the context of Shi'i law and practice, *siqqah* designates temporary marriages. Here follows a sample text of the vows. On the anniversary of Qadir Khum, the day on which Muhammad purportedly chose Ali as his brother and successor, two "brothers" take each other's hands and the older "brother" *(baradar-i buzurg)* declares: "I seek protection for you in God, I shake hands with you before God, I pledge myself to you for God, and I pledge myself to God, His angels, [His] books, messengers, and sent prophets. And praise be to God, Lord of the Two Worlds." To which the younger brother *(baradar-i kuchak)* replies: "I accept and forfeit all the rights of the brotherhood in favor of proximity to God." The sisterhood vows are similar save for the phrase that the sister adds: "I take you as a sister before God."[32]

Within the body of anthologies that I have just mentioned and consider an archive, legal condemnations of same-sex intercourse abound, and seventeenth-century translations into Persian of medieval Arabic Shi'i texts, like *al-Nihaya* by Shaykh Abu Jafar al-Tusi (d. 1067), affirm the legal prohibitions' relevance to Safavi society.³³ *Al-Nihaya* devotes a chapter to the punishments *(hadd)* for homosexuality—for male *(liwat)* and female *(musahiqa)* homosexual practices. "Like sodomy [*liwat*], which entails a man being sexually intimate [*nazdiki*] with another man, . . . *musahiqa* concerns a woman being sexually intimate [*nazdiki*] with a woman."³⁴ The legal categories are similar to those traditionally used to weigh cases of same-sex intercourse between men in which age difference, social status (free or slave), religious affiliation (*Muslim* or *kafir*), and the extent of activity or passivity of sex roles determine the degree of the offense.³⁵ Women like our widow who "have sex" with other women who are their equals in social and religious status are pathologized: they are *majnun* (crazy).

Within the confines of the practice of sisterhood, a certain female intimacy—whether platonic, romantic, or sexual—emerges outside the contours of Islamic law. The rituals and conventions that Aqa Jamal delineates demonstrate the independence of the milieu of sisterhood, which he finds threatening. Aqa Jamal writes that a reputable *(mu'tabar)*, trustworthy woman—a kind of intermediary *(pasabz)*—would prepare a wax doll called the *aruschak* (little bride) and place it on a decorated platform, which she would then send to a prospective sister *(khwahar khwandah)*. The character of Kulthum Nane explains that the term *aruschak* was originally *arus-i kuchak* (little bride) but was abbreviated with frequent usage.³⁶ The term has obviously been transported from the context of heterosexual marriages to that of female-female conjoining. Accepting an offer of sisterly marriage entailed returning the *aruschak* crowned with a necklace and rewarding the *pasabz* with an honorary robe *(khilat)*. If the offer was refused, a black veil instead was wrapped around the head of the doll before it was sent back. According to Aqa Jamal, the practice could occur between two women unknown to one another. He makes no mention, how-

ever, of their marital status. The Isfahani widow's example
shows that female unions occurred not only between acquaintances but also between members from the same extended families who were "sisters" in more ways than one.

According to Aqa Jamal, the bonds were officiated on the anniversary of Qadir Khum as well. Sisters-to-be visited the shrine
of one of Prophet Muhammad's descendants through his daughter Fatima and cousin Ali *(imamzadah)* and announced their intended union. At the shrine they declared their vows: "In the
name of Ali, the shah conqueror of Khaybar [*bi haqq-i shah-i
khaybar gir*], O God, accept and fulfill our desire [*khudaya mat-
lab ma ra bar avar va bipazir*]."[37] Dancing and sherbet drinking
were customary celebrations. Ali's central to Shi'ism is common
knowledge, but among Sufis and craftsmen he also plays the important role of the model saint and "perfect individual" *(insan-i
kamil)*. His figure is ubiquitous in female rituals of the Safavi period, and the female version of the Sufi practice tied disciples together in a companionship founded on loyalty and devotion to
Ali. In early modern Safavi Iran, Sufi brotherhoods were a common feature of town life and prominent centers of religious, economic, and political vigor and stability. Voluntary associations,
they coordinated and directed much of religious life and public
charitable activities in their communities. Their diversity and variety notwithstanding, they shared rituals, like voluntary friendship, that marked people's daily experiences of urban life. In
manuals of chivalry, the love guiding the disciple in the order is
the love for God, attainable *only* through a friend and experi-
enced through mutual sharing and caring between two brothers.
A brother will meet his friend on judgment day, and his friend
will be his witness before God, vouching for his entry into paradise. This is a powerful, threatening paradigm for the Shi'i
clergy, who were attempting to consolidate their roles as the exclusive intermediaries between God and the community of Muslim believers.

The language of love that the widow uses to describe her female friend places her within the semantic field of mysticism.

Though Persian mystical poetry was a male-centered domain whose object of desire was conventionally configured male and young, there was room for ambiguity between masculine and feminine and between human and divine.[38] It was possible for reading audiences to imagine the beloved as male or female because Persian is a gender-neutral language and the aesthetics of Sufism drew the beloved with beauty markers that did not distinguish one particular gender. To declare the love she feels for every one of her companions (*yar* or *rafiq*)—her deceased husband, her "adopted" sister, and God—our widow appropriates the poetic form of the *masnavi*. Consistent with the genre, she describes her religious experiences and the reawakening of her friendship with Sufi idioms for absence and longing. But in her engagement with the canon, does the widow speak a "female" language that is distinct from the mystical language of men? How does she employ Sufi tropes for divine love and yet feminize her writing within the male discourse on love? Does the rhetoric of "absence," so necessary for writing about the experience of pilgrimage, suffuse the widow's text to the extent that interpretation is clouded and hesitant and separation and mourning are reduced to stock emotions and themes in a woman traveler's narrative of pilgrimage?

Based on a cursory reading of *Tuhfat al-'Iraqayn, Nur al-Mashraqayn,* and *Futuh al-Haramayn*—three pilgrimage narratives composed by the respective male poets Khaqani, Bihishti Haravi, and Lari—I note that our traveler's distinctiveness resides her inclusion of personal episodes and submerged discourses in her poem. As narrator, our widow allows us to inhabit her and to move with the rhythms of her encounters. The language of mysticism is the language for expressing her individuality and singular female experience, but her narration of individual and uncommon experiences in the course of the journey relies only partly on the common themes of longing, grief, and lamentation.

The distinctive conventions of sisterhood, of symbol-laden communication, and of the dress customs of the friendship-based society of women that were ridiculed and condemned by larger society's cleric guardian sum up in twentieth- and twenty-first-century Iran the identity associated with "lesbianism." In modern (1950s) Persian literary usage, the term describing these friendships—*khwahar khwandah* (adopted sister)—came to also suggest a *tabaq zan* (a lesbian). Mindful of this modernist consciousness, I had initially resisted reading lesbianism between the lines of Aqa Jamal's early modern *'Aqa'id al-Nisa'*. The argument seemed to be based on no more than fearful male fantasies. But now the discovery and juxtaposition of the Isfahani widow's contemporaneous pilgrimage narrative permits the identification of a complicated (at least in the widow's example) same-sex erotic desire between female companions in the Safavi period.

Aqa Jamal relates that even from the confines of their homes these kindred female spirits communicated their most personal and intimate thoughts. He characterizes the women's friendships with double entendres alluding to eating, rubbing, and pounding that in both Arabic and Persian textual renditions of female sexual intercourse were associated with tribadism *(musahiqa)*.[39] Using the semiotics of food the women sent one another messages. A walnut *(juz)* conveyed the message, "I am yours, do not worry"—literally, "do not eat sorrow [*gham makhur*]." A walnut grated one side *(juz-i yiktaraf sayidah)* meant, "I am in pain and weak. I have rubbed this. Do the same!"[40] Saffron signified, "You have made me yellow [melancholic] like pounded saffron. How long shall I eat of your useless sorrow?" An unsalted hazelnut meant, "I have eaten and will continue to eat of your sorrow." A salted hazelnut conveyed the message, "Still I desire you all over." A whole cardamom seed means "I am patient [*hilm*]," but a cracked one means "I am in agony [*halakam*]." A clove means "I am burning [*kababam*]," a cinnamon stick "I adore you [*qurbanat shavam*]," sandalwood "I smell you constantly [*hamah vaqt mibuyamat*]." And in occasions of jealousy perhaps, a particular seed *(anchuchak)* meant "God damn you [*la'nat bar tu*]." The cryptic codes between friends for passion, intimacy, and lovesickness underscore the significance of natural medicine and medical practices to women's social domains of power and the contestation of them.[41]

Now that we have a more textured appreciation of the practice of friendship between women in early modern Isfahan, let us return to the widow's melancholy and forbidden love. In the encounter, the widow collapses. She "throws [down] her baggage in her friend's house" and shows at least her physical vulnerability. She shifts often from first to second and third persons when addressing her audience and friend, as if boundaries between her self, her beloved, and society blur:

> Happily, I spent some time at my hostess's, that Isfahani companion of mine. O kind friend, o old companion: you did not deny me your sweet soul. I was so nurtured by you, as though fallen from the heavens. But my fortune did not comply. I was exhausted [khastah]. The whole time I was suffering [ranjur]. I was afflicted with fever [tab] and torment [azar]. Not for a moment was I able to be her partner in conversation/soul/sex [ham suhbat].[42] I did not become physically intimate [ulfati] with that good-natured one.

The widow is sick and aloof, unlike her friend, who is openly emotional, expressive, giving. "I was ashamed in front of my friend. You bore pain constantly on my behalf. You grieved over my suffering, you became even more broken-hearted because of my distance [duri]."[43]

In the reunion with her former beloved, the widow undergoes a reversal in roles: she relinquishes her narrative persona as lover ('ashiq), transforming herself into the object (mahbub) of her companion's desire.[44] But on the day of departure, after hearing the nightingale's song, her loyal companion reverts to the status of beloved, sinking into sorrow: "That day, until dinner that dear one had no bread, water, or any other food. You hid the world-illuminating love by drowning your face in the abyss of the deep sea. She cried bloody tears—purple tears poured from her eyelashes like rain onto her skirt. She cried so much, that loyal relative, a new grief befell me [*matam-i naw shud padidar*]." Withdrawing, our widow falls short of her duties as friend. Instead, her female relatives commiserate and comfort *(yari namudand)* the aggrieved beloved; together "they cried over my departure."⁴⁵ Why this cold impassiveness toward her old companion, especially when the widow admits her renewed grief? Was she afraid of divulging the extent of the love she felt for her friend, particularly in her relatives' presence? Maybe she wants to publicly deny the old rumors, declare her renunciation of this illicit love, and traverse the stage before repentance and union with God the true companion. Though women clearly support one another, as the widow's narrative shows, her reconciliation is not whole and satisfactory. Is she ambivalent about leaving her friend, about continuing on the pilgrimage despite her vow? Does grief so rekindle the widow's love for her old companion that it casts doubt on the real object of true love? Or is her grief part of the trope of longing and separation constituent of the pilgrimage experience and of mystical Persianate writing about love?

The widow reveals how much she loves her friend the minute she leaves her, her family, and her native land of Urdubad. Although she has missed Urdubad and voices joy at seeing her family again, her focus is now on her friend. Once she leaves Urdubad, she resumes the role of amorous lover *('ashiq)*. She does not sleep well that night, and the next day she cannot enjoy a stroll in a beautiful garden: "What good is it for me to seek pleasure in a rose garden empty of the ultimate soul? I saw no rose nor plucked one from that garden. I only cried there from loneliness and separation."⁴⁶ But the song that from the very beginning has drawn her out of Isfahan pulls her again toward the Ka'ba: "Since you have become saddened after the separation from your companion, go toward the House of Truth. Do not be gloomy due to the parting from your sweetheart. Hurry up, ride your camel, place your load atop the melancholy [*sawda*] of separation from your friend [*yar*]."⁴⁷

She finds immediate relief when she first espies from a distance the holy cities of Mecca and Medina, pays her respects at the tombs of the prophet's daughter and children, and at last circumambulates the Ka'ba. Her ecstasy is almost palpable: "The night of separation between spirits has ended. Eyes have been illuminated in union with the Friend. Everyone has washed their hearts from Satan's whispers, they have expelled the kindness of friends from their chests. Toward the Ka'ba's stone they all face. Sorrow and grief they cast away."[48] The medieval Sufi poet Nizami's verse comes to mind: "How wonderful it is after a wait for the hopeful one to attain a desire [*umid*]."[49] Her "fortune came to such fruition that from the excitement [*shawq*] of union I lost consciousness." She steps through the Gate of Peace *(salam)*—the first entryway to the Ka'ba—sets her eyes on the house of God, and begins to weep, beyond words to describe the holy site. She cannot utter a word to thank God *(khudavand)*, nor does she have the presence of mind to laugh and be happy. She faints, and though regains consciousness after an hour, remains speechless. But once able to "untie the knot that had restricted her tongue," she begins her surrender to God, praising his omnipotence, knowledge, and endless grace. She thanks her creator for the favor *(tawfiq)* he has granted: "You gave me both wealth and life. You brought me to my goal [*maqsad*] and my desire [*matlub*]."[50] Cloaked in black with a golden belt tied around its waist, its face covered with the kisses of pilgrims, the Ka'ba is the beloved.[51] Though she claims its incomparability, she compares it to a youth *(nujavani)* and a lofty flowing cypress tree *(sarv-i ravani)*, using some of Sufi poetry's ungendered metaphors for divine beauty.

I would like to shift focus for a moment to the female engendering of the Ka'ba in the *hajjnames* versified by men to understand how our writer situates her poetic persona within the masculine genre of pilgrimage narratives. Khaqani's *Tuhfat al-'Iraqayn* (Gift of the two Iraqs), written about mid-twelfth century, provides an early example from Persian poetry that links the Ka'ba to womanhood. The Ka'ba's attributes that were favored by male medieval poets like Khaqani and the subsequent poets Nizami, Sa'di, Hafiz, and Jami were all feminine, and the edifice's architectural features were often compared to a chaste woman's physical ones. Furthermore, the pilgrim's relationship to the Ka'ba is one of love, and the beauty of the Ka'ba is the explicitly human and feminine beloved's. I am relying here on A.L.F.A. Beelaert's excellent study, *A Cure for the Grieving*, of Khaqani's court poetry. Her scholarship discusses the Ka'ba's feminine imagery and concludes that it has yet to see it personified as or compared to a young man or boy in Persian poetry.[52] *Tuhfat al-'Iraqayn* personifies God's sacred abode thus:

> You resemble a bride behind a curtain [*arus-i hijlah*]
> sitting in a quadrangular [*chaharsu*] bridal chamber.
> You are like an houri wrapped in *'abraqi* cloth
> like a king [*shah*] with a mantle [*davaj*] on his shoulders.[53]

The term *arus* referred in early modern Persian usage to both grooms and brides, but it was more commonly used for brides. For Khaqani, the Ka'ba is a hidden bride and heavenly virgin *(huri)*, but alternatively it possesses kingly majesty. The process of the inanimate, sacred object's becoming sexually enlivened deserves further attention and examination. The *huri*, veiled bride, and just king point to the coexistence of gendered attributes in Khaqani's imagery. Another physical, material marker that stands for genderless beauty is the black stone:

> This golden stone, quintessence of the creed,
> is on the face of the Ka'ba a musk-colored mole.[54]

But then Khaqani reconfigures the description of the bride and complicates his and other pilgrims' relationship to the female sex, the Ka'ba, pilgrimage, and formal religion. He problematizes as well pilgrims' mystical relationship to God and his iconic manifestations through the ritual of the Hajj:

> That old and virginal Indian woman
> [who] was given as a bridal present to God's creatures:
> People clasped her against their bosom
> and kissed her, but nobody perforated her.[55]

Khaqani purifies and purges the holy abode of the poet-pilgrim's sexual desires by denying the possibility of penetration. Despite attempts to desexualize the ritual kissing of the Ka'ba, his imagination (re)sexualizes his relationship to the Ka'ba and by extension to women, who interfere with and obstruct his devotion to God. This represents the persistent predicament of men, who are torn between the two Ka'bas of physical and metaphysical love.

Let us return to the Isfahani widow's description of the Ka'ba. She would have been familiar with Khaqani's poetry and repertoire of images. She has already shared her feelings of same-sex desire translated into spiritual friendship *(yar)* with God and her deceased husband. How does the Isfahani widow envision the house of God *(bayt allah, khana-yi yazdan)*? Her term for *beloved* is less gender-specific than Khaqani's. The appellation of *youth (nawjavani)* for the Ka'ba has already referred to the gallant men who have occasionally hosted her along the journey to Mecca.[56] And since the widow does not attribute the culture of chivalry to men exclusively, *nawjavan* can mean "gallant women" as well. She values the chivalric virtues of generosity, courage, and loyalty and praises their display by her friend, mothers, relatives, dervishes, and officials. Male poets have historically treated *nawjavan* as an exclusively masculine noun. The widow's own gender-neutral usage of *nawjavan* for chivalrous youth opens up a semantic possibility. To refer to a young male host, she adds the masculine adjective *mard-i* to *nawjavan* (youth), and the added information brings clarification rather than redundancy.

As a woman composing poetry, she chooses not to call the Ka'ba by the conventional epithet of "bride," perhaps to avoid association with the ritual of sisterhood that involved the exchange of a little-bride wax doll, an *aruschak*. Her description instead borrows Sufi poetry's representation of divine beauty on earth, the chivalrous and beautiful youth, to represent the sacred house's purity and to suggest the mystic pilgrim's relationship to the Hajj and God. Could it be that the Ka'ba's gender does not matter to this widow? The effect of the Ka'ba-sexed male is produced when she imagines the youth wrapped in a cloth *(daman)* that hugged his loins *(miyan)*. Do the golden belt tied around the edifice and the black stone that protect the Ka'ba ward off also illicit desires, shame, and humiliation from besetting the hearts and souls of female pilgrims? Does the widow renounce her feelings of same-sex desire for the old friend and companion when she too "girds her loins" and set off on the long, arduous journey to the holy lands?

> Standing before the Ka'ba, she cannot tell if she is dreaming or awake: Carrying the weight of a hundred tons of crimes and sins, I turned my face toward the circumambulating God's [*yazdan*] Alley. After seven circles, my shoulder became lightened from the weight of my sins [*gunah*]. As I began to enumerate my transgressions [*chu dadam bar qalam-i isyan khud ra*], I emptied my leather bag all the way to the bottom. With water from my eyes, I cleansed my crimes [*jurm*]. My sins were numerous, and the path very short. On the seventh turn of my guilt, I repaired my ruined heart. I sought the road of forgiveness and washed away my filthy crime. I drank a sip of Zamzam's water. Sorrow, pain, and affliction were all forgotten. The water's purity enlivened my body and cured my diseased [*bimar*] heart. At the house of God, I apologized for my crime. Like a beggar, I began to cry. What shall I say? In negligence, my life was wasted. In your abode, no honor remains for me. Woe upon me if you do not forgive my crime. Hell shall be my dwelling place. Since performing the "pilgrimage of women," I have kicked Satan's face. My heart has been cleansed of his whispers. I shall not allow my heart to engage in bad deeds [*afal-i bad*].[57]

Was her heart "diseased" with the malady of desiring another woman, and was loving her one of the satanic crimes she repents of? We cannot be certain, but we do know she demonstrates repentance by having her hair cut and arranging for a camel's sacrifice.

The following provides the social and religious background for the widow's *hajjname* and Aqa Jamal's *'Aqa'id al-Nisa'*. In Safavi times, Shi'i clerical responses to the perceived dangers that emanated from Sufi circles included polemically labeling the Sufi and sodomite as figures of heretical "excess." Shi'i discourse condemned the practices of celibacy and sodomy in favor of heterosexual marriage modeled after the prophet Muhammad's own conjugal unions. Boy gazing was one of the stages that Sufi devotees had to traverse in their mystic journey toward union with God. Characterized often in textual sources as an older man, the one performing the mystical ritual of gazing would look at a beautiful male youth who represented the divine on earth. The ritual of boy gazing, which provoked simultaneous sensations of separation from and longing for the object of desire, was intended to test as well as aid the mystic's self-disciplining of carnal desires. Since he actually sought and loved God and not the youth, the mystic was forbidden from acting on his physical desire. Gazing and celibacy in this context complemented one another, for the gazer had to remain in a state of celibacy before he could truly be an ideal lover on the mystic path. Within Sufi contexts, celibacy and boy gazing signified the sacred, but Shi'i polemics came to cast the two practices as contradicting Muhammad's teachings and hence God's will. Sexual activity within matrimony—not abstinence and celibacy—became sacred. Drawing from the Muslim sacred texts of the Quran and Hadith, Shi'i clerics offered up the sanctity of marriage as the worldly path to God, bolstering state-level Safavi efforts to centralize and govern.

Anxieties about sexual behavior in Sufi circles revealed as well the Shi'i clergy's fears that intimacy between spiritual brothers and friends could easily lead to political solidarities strong enough to resist clerical—perhaps even imperial—authority. In 1550, the Safavi king Shah Tahmasb issued the first in a series of decrees about "proper" and "improper" Muslim behavior that prohibited wine, sodomy, and beard shaving.[58] Besides calling for set prices and secure roads throughout the empire and for the welfare and education of orphans, the first decree laid down a set of ethics detailing appropriate gender roles and displays of sexuality in public spaces. The decree went on to caution Safavi subjects against celibacy, long associated with Sufi ways of life, and exhorted the male populace to be both sexually and socially productive. Vacationing, relaxing, and comfort-seeking were disfavored pastimes since they reduced men to a state of inactivity, making them no better off than women and the dead. Beardless youth *(amrad)*, the objects of male desire in Sufism's conceptualization of spirituality, and women were not allowed to congregate at public events *(marika)* that included storytelling and acrobatics put on by chivalric clubs.

According to the decrees, which were engraved on mosque walls, a beardless youth would be punished by the law if he prostituted himself in a *hammam* (a public bath). The scrupulous proscriptions on social and sexual behaviors also applied to beards, the visible emblems of manhood. When it was practiced within the specific conditions of an older man's penetration of a youth discreetly and behind closed doors, sex between men had been tolerated in Safavi society. But the first sign of a beard—stubble—heralded manhood, at which stage sodomy became taboo. And if a man persistently shaved his beard, "delaying" his entry into manhood with its responsibilities of work, marriage, and children, he was a serious threat to social order in the Safavi imperium. The set of moral significations to beards and their removal deserved discussion in the anti-Sufi discourses penned by Shi'i clerics during the seventeenth century. Devoting fourteen chapters to various aspects of daily life, Muhammad Baqir Majlisi's (d. 1699) normative manual on Shi'i mores and ethics delineated the proprieties of dress, makeup, sleep, marriage, prayer, fasting, pilgrimage, and so on.[59] Though Majlisi Jr. stated that it was well known that clerics had forbidden beard shaving, he nevertheless included a section on the different ways to shave facial hair. But his view that a beard signified sexual virility and even patriarchy was unequivocal throughout the manual. He cited the following originary event, supposedly related by Prophet Muhammad himself. On the day God accepted Adam's repentance for having tasted the apple of knowledge, Adam declared, "O God, make me more beautiful." So God gave him a thick black beard. But having never seen a beard before, Adam asked God, "What is this?" "This is your ornament," replied God, "and that of your sons till eternity."

In his chapter on the virtues of marriage and the vices of celibacy, Majlisi Jr. reiterated the norm of heterosexuality based on the authoritative report that the prophet Muhammad, who was the exemplar for all of humankind, loved women. He proceeded to list examples that confirmed the Imams' heterosexuality and the religious obligation at the core of piety—taking a wife. Like other contemporaneous literature, the manual of mores represented the prophet as having demarcated Muslim men's faith and religious beliefs on specific grounds of sexuality: a true Muslim could not have sexual intercourse with members of his sex, bearded or not. When some women allegedly complained to Muhammad that their husbands avoided sexual relations with them, the prophet condemned the men thus: "They are not of my followers." It is necessary to pause and reflect on the reasons that heterosexual conjugality received such voluble advocacy from Shi'i clerics. Too many Sufi mystics were eschewing the more ordinary unions of marriage to female mortals in favor of the more rarefied, transformative unions with God. And these unions that they pursued so ardently were undermining the project of making socially and sexually disciplined and productive Safavi subjects.

Majlisi Jr.'s normative manual narrates that Imam Jafar once chided a devotee who rejected the material world and turned ascetic and celibate that wife taking constituted one half of a believer's religious duties. Sufi spirituality's fundamental tenet that union between the human and the divine can be attained through a man's mystical love for his male beloved effectually collapsed the distance between the believer and God that the rationalist clerics were attempting to create. Based on a preliminary reading of the religious treatises on Shi'i ethics, I have observed that legitimate sexual acts in marriage are differentiated from the illegitimate, extramarital acts of adultery and sodomy that transgress the Shari'a and social norms. Same-sex desire be-

tween women receives the silent treatment in the religious treatises on ethics; in fact its only treatment is Aqa Jamal's satire, *Beliefs of Women.* Once celibacy, gazing, and same-sex friendships
within Sufism had signified the sacred, but the clergy, intent on
redrawing the boundary between the sacred and the sexual,
preached that these practices contradicted Muhammad's teachings and hence God's will. Sexual activity was limited to matrimony.[60] It is likely that these sexual politics provoked the rumors in Isfahan about our widow's relationship with her
companion and forced them into the long and silent separation.

Aqa Jamal writes of the trouble that wives have suffered because their husbands were uninterested in sexual intercourse
with them. His satire describes the female rituals of shrine visita-
tion and fasting associated with Ali. One of the fasts of Ali
(ruzah-yi mortaza Ali), for example, was particularly recommended for girls who wanted good and dutiful husbands. The
local expert Kulthum Nane recommends that eligible women
visit the famous minaret of *Kawn Birinji* (Brassy base) and recite
the following verse:

> O Minaret of Kawn Birinji,
> I shall utter something, but do not be offended.
> My loins want a handle in them [*miyun-i man dastah
>   mikhwad*].
> They want a man of commitment [*mard-i kamar bastah*]!

I have previously seen visitations to this minaret as instances of a
fertility ritual, but Afsaneh Najmabadi has offered a second
layer of interpretation that within the context of the politics of
matrimony, sodomy, and celibacy is compelling. The women
carry out the rituals and recite the verse because they fear that
what impedes pregnancy and procreation is not male infertility
per say but seed-spilling as a result of sexual acts with other
men. A "man of commitment" in this context could be a virgin
not sodomized *(amrad)* during youth by an older man. As
Najmabadi suggests, *kamar bastan* (knot tying) was perhaps intended to discourage adolescents from developing a sexual pref-

erence for other men. Aqa Jamal hints at the similar threat posed by women who avoided their husbands, preferring the company of "sisters." When a man sent one sister a golden jug *(tung-i tala'i)*, he was demanding:

> You who drink wine from the golden jug, why do you not drink from the tip of my penis [*sar-i surna*]?[61]

Aqa Jamal's male anxiety focuses not only on sisterhood but on other feminine spheres, including public baths, where he imagines that women engage with one another in sexual intimacies. The five experts urge them to sit in a circle, reveal their genitals *(kashf-i awrat)*, depilate each other, and "mix" (the term *ikhtilat*, like *suhbat*, is a double entendre meaning to converse as well as "have sex").[62] In his discussion of female participation in wedding rituals, Aqa Jamal expresses his fear about marriage. In his opinion, only fortunate women should prepare the bride's and groom's bed on the wedding night, and he specifies three kinds of women whose participation should be rebuffed: those who share their husbands with rival wives *(havu)*, those who have remarried, and those who are not husband-lovers *(shawhar dust)*, whom we may categorize "lesbianlike."[63] The fate of the newlywed couple should be protected right away from contamination by objectionable social practices like polygamy and female homoeroticism.

These kinds of technologies that regulated subjects' gender and sexuality would have discredited our widow's relationship with her companion and led to the latter's banishment to the distant northern region of Urdubad. Confronted by the overriding moralism that views same-sex unions with horror, "girding her loins" at the outset of the pilgrimage to the holy lands, does our widow vow to repent of her youthful love? Has she rejected her vows of sisterhood and the obligations and protocols of friendship? Her illicit feelings of same-sex desire for another woman must be part of the one hundred tons of crimes and sins that weigh on her during circumambulation,[64] but maybe her inaction, the result of restraint and abstinence in the face of rekindled erotic desire, makes possible her active pursuit of union with God at his holy abode.

Her pilgrimage completed and her "diseased" heart cured, the traveler turns around and heads back toward Isfahan. But in Aleppo, the pain of melancholy reinhabits her, and she realizes that only in God's holy places of Mecca and Medina did she feel at peace. Woefully she cries, "How pleasant was the Ka'ba! How worthy was the going, and how empty is the return."[65] And she does the only thing she can—continue the journey.

NOTES

1. I would like to thank Dina Al-Kassim, Rima Hassouneh, Afsaneh Najmabadi, Helmut Puff, and Valerie Traub for their invaluable suggestions and critical reading of earlier drafts of this chapter.

2. *Safarnama-yi Manzum-i Hajj,* ed. Rasul Jafarian (Qumm, 1995).

3. For example, see the late seventeenth-century biography of religious scholars *('ulama)* in Safavi Isfahan, Afandi, *Riyaz al-'Ulama wa Hiyaz al-Fuzala,* ed. A. al-Husayni, 6 vols. (Qumm, 1980).

4. *Safarnama-yi Manzum-i Hajj,* 9.

5. Ibid., 23. I would like to thank Afsaneh Najmabadi for suggesting this reading based on the practice of women tying a piece of cloth around shrines to symbolize their vow-taking.

6. Ibid.

7. I would like to thank Franklin Lewis for his generous response to the query about lovesickness and melancholy in Islamicate literature that I posted on *Adabiyat H-NET* (August 6, 2003).

8. *Safarnama-yi Manzum-i Hajj,* 23.

9. See A.L.F.A. Beelaert's study, *A Cure for Grieving* (Leiden: E. J. Brill, 2000), of Khaqani's *Tuhfat al-'Iraqayn.* My understanding of Khaqani relies on Beelaert's sensitive reading of the twelfth-century Persian poet.

10. *Safarnama-yi Manzum-i Hajj,* 23.

11. Ibid.

12. See, for example, Hans Hinrich Biesterfeldt and Dimitri Gutas, "The Malady of Love," *Journal of the American Oriental Society* 104, no. 1 (1984): 21–55; and Ali Asghar Seyed-Gohrab, *Love,*

Madness and Mystic Longing in Nizami's Epic Romance (Leiden: Brill, 2003).

13. *Safarnama-yi Manzum-i Hajj*, 24–25.

14. On the pilgrimage to Mecca during the early modern period and the possibilities of different routes, see Suraiya Faroqhi, *Pilgrims and Sultans: The Hajj under the Ottomans 1517–1683* (London: Tauris, 1994); M. N. Pearson, *Pilgrimage to Mecca: The Indian Experience 1500–1800* (Princeton: Markus Wiener, 1996); Sanjay Subramanyam, "Persians, Pilgrims, and Portuguese: The Travails of Masulipatnam Shipping in the Western Indian Ocean, 1590–1655," *Modern Asian Studies* 22 (1988): 503–30; and R. D. McChesney, "The Central Asian Hajj-Pilgrimage in the Time of the Early Modern Empires," in *Safavid Iran and Her Neighbors,* ed. Michel Mazzaoui (Salt Lake City: University of Utah Press, 2003), 129–156.

15. *Safarnama-yi Manzum-i Hajj*, 39.

16. Ibid., 31–32.

17. She calls the Safavi dominion the *vilayat-i 'ajam* and the *sarzamin-i shah-i Iran, Safarnama-yi Manzum-i Hajj*, 47.

18. Ibid.

19. Ibid., 39.

20. Ibid., 41.

21. Aqa Jamal Khwansari, *'Aqa'id al-Nisa'*, ed. Mahmud Katira'i (Tehran, 1970). For a discussion of this text, see my chapter "The *'Aqa'id al-Nisa'*: A Glimpse at Safavid Women in Local Isfahani Culture," in *Women in the Medieval Islamic World,* ed. Gavin R. G. Hambly (New York: St. Martin's Press, 1998), 349–81.

22. See my article on *'Aqa'id al-Nisa'*, where I place this satire within the larger context of gender and politics at the Safavi court in Isfahan.

23. According to the editor Mahmud Katira'i, *'Aqa'id al-Nisa'* was written during the reign of Shah Sulayman (1666–1694).

24. Abu Talib Mir Findiriski, *Tuhfat al-'Alam*, Tehran University (manuscript 4955), f206a.

25. Khwansari, *'Aqa'id al-Nisa'*, 1.

26. Ibid.

27. This point is made by the editor, M. Katira'i. Ibid., 7–8.

28. Ibid.

29. The sixteen chapter subjects in *'Aqa'id al-Nisa'* are ritual ablutions,

ritual prayer, fasting, marriage, wedding nights, childbirth, bath-houses, musical instruments and their occasions, marital relations, the foods used in vows *(nazr)*, amulets and talismans, men who are accessible *(mahram)* and inaccessible *(namahram)* to women, conditions that make auspicious women's prayers, house guests, vows of sisterhood, and the items sisters would exchange.

30. Khwansari, *'Aqa'id al-Nisa'*, 35.

31. Ibid.

32. Malek Library (manuscript Majmu'a 5085) dated seventeenth or eighteenth century CE and compiled by the poet Abd al-Azim b. Mirza Ali Khoi, known as Shuridah.

33. Shaykh Tusi's *al-Nihaya fi Mujarrad al-Fiqh wa'l Fatawa* was translated into Persian in the late seventeenth century. A copy, recorded and dated fifth of Zul Qadah 1052/1643, is at the Malik Library (manuscript Majmu'a 3624).

34. Ibid., f284b.

35. See Everett K. Rowson's essay on the legal condemnation and literary celebration of male homoeroticism, in which he delineates the symmetries and asymmetries of such sexual conduct in Sunni legal discourse: "Homosexuality in the Medieval Islamic World: Literary Celebration vs. Legal Condemnation," *Princeton Mellon Seminar,* May 1995.

36. Khwansari, *'Aqa'id al-Nisa'*, 37.

37. Ibid., 36.

38. Carla Petievich makes this point about Urdu poetry in her chapter "The Invention and Subsequent Erasure of Urdu Poetry's 'Lesbian' Voice," in *Queering India: Same-Sex Love and Eroticism in Indian Culture and Society,* ed. Ruth Vanita (New York: Routledge, 2002).

39. The verb *khwardan* enjoys a wide semantic field of meanings signifying to *eat, drink, gnaw, corrode, receive, suffer, appropriate, hit* or *strike,* and *touch.* The word's etymological roots are Pahlavi (Middle Persian) and mean *eating* and *consuming. Khwardan* comes to be used as a compound verb in Persian, as in the case of *'gham khwardan'* (to grieve or feel grief and be sorrowful, literally, "to eat sorrow"). I have deliberately chosen to emphasize this literal translation because I think the authors here, Aqa Jamal and the Isfahani widow, play on the erotic layer of *khwardan.*

40. The entry in the contemporary Persian dictionary *Burhan-i Qati'*

defines *juzaak* thus: "to worry and become anxious" *(anduhnak)*. The etymology reveals the relationship between food and humors.

41. All the food elements (jujube, saffron, sandal, cloves) enumerated here have therapeutic value in the realm of natural medicine. See, for example, the late seventeenth-century Safavi medical text, *Tuhfat al-Mu'minin,* by Muhammad Mu'min al-Husayni al-Tunakabuni, Bibliotheque Nationale (manuscript: Persan Supp. 1287).

42. On the double meaning of *suhbat,* see Khwansari, *'Aqa'id al-Nisa'* for the contemporaneous use of *suhbat* to mean "intercourse" in heterosexual matrimonial contexts.

43. *Safarnama-yi Manzum-i Hajj,* 42.

44. I would like to thank Carla Petievich for suggesting this reading of mystical transcendence through role reversal between Isfahani widow and companion in Urdubad. Carla Petievich, Response to "In Spirit We Ate Each Other's Sorrow," Crossing Paths of Middle Eastern and Sexuality Studies: Challenges of Theory, History, and Comparative Methods, conference at the Radcliffe Institute for Advanced Study, May 2003.

45. *Safarnama-yi Manzum-i Hajj,* 42.

46. Ibid., 43.

47. Ibid.

48. Ibid., 74.

49. Ibid., 75.

50. Ibid.

51. Ibid.

52. Beelaert assumes this may be a vestige of the feminine genderization of the word *Ka'ba* in Arabic. In the less common cases of the Ka'ba's masculinity, it is not a beloved but a king or sultan (as in one of Nizami's *qasidas*); this portrayal appears in courtly rather than mystical milieus. The Ka'ba as queen does appear in Khaqani's pilgrimage *qasidas,* but the image of the chaste bride-Ka'ba dominates the tradition of feminizing the edifice.

53. Beelaert, *A Cure for Grieving,* 143.

54. Ibid.

55. Ibid, 143–44.

56. I would like to thank Franklin Lewis for his observation that *nawjavan* could be "an androgynous being, like the *ghulam* in the Quranic paradise, assuming a physical form according to the plea-

sures of the onlooker[.] . . . *nawjavan* may be a claque on the Quranic *ghulam,* or at least have as its possible archetype the young Joseph representing physical beauty, object of jealousy to his brothers, possible illicit object of desire for the male who purchases him, definite illicit object of desire for the wife of 'Aziz and her female companions, and idealized object of lost love for Jacob, his father" (e-mail exchange on August 6, 2003). However, the widow's modification of *nawjavan* to signify a male youth represents the prevailing attitude that masculinized *nawjavan*.

57. *Safarnama-yi Manzum-i Hajj,* 78.

58. "Ain-i Shah Tahmasb," ed. M. T. Danishpazhu, *Barisiha-yi Tarikhi* 7 (1972): 121–42.

59. Muhammad Baqir Majlisi, *Hilyat al-Muttaqin* (Qumm, 1992).

60. Here I have been inspired by Helmut Puff's insightful study *Sodomy in Reformation Germany and Switzerland, 1400–1600* (Chicago: University of Chicago Press, 2003), where he eloquently draws out the similar affinities between celibacy, matrimony, and sodomy in Reformation discourse.

61. Khwansari, *'Aqa'id al-Nisa',* 41. The editor writes in note 66 that *sar-i surna* is a metaphor for the penis.

62. Ibid., 54. The editor notes during the Qajar period a certain cleric issued a *fatwa* in Birjand (Aqa Shaykh Husayni) that all women in the hammams wear cloths *(lung)* to cover their vaginas.

63. Ibid., 13.

64. I have come across other contemporaneous representations of sisters haunted by homoerotic desires. For example, the single-page miniature (1645–1650) by Muhammad Qasim depicts a distressed woman, a cup, a water pipe, and a wine jug with a female face painted on it. The poetry framing the miniature, though a later addition, comments on the taboo desire: "The memory of your neck remains with me. A hundred odes in praise of you. . . . Weave another world out of your temperament [*tab'a*]. This [weaving] too is beyond others." See Massumeh Farhad, *Safavid Single Page Paintings, 1629–1666,* PhD dissertation, Harvard University, 1987, 306. I hope to incorporate these examples in my work-in-progress to broaden the evidence for female homoerotic practices in early modern Iran.

65. *Safarnama-yi Manzum-i Hajj,* 82.

EIGHT

Types, Acts, or What?
Regulation of Sexuality in
Nineteenth-Century Iran[1]

Afsaneh Najmabadi

A slave girl was shown to the Abbasid caliph al-Mutawakkil (r. 847–861).
He asked her, "Are you a virgin or what?" She replied, "Or what, O Emir
of the Believers." He laughed and bought her.[2]

Often narrated as an example of a slave girl's wit, I have long
been intrigued by the possibilities of "or what." By its textual
location, it is at first reading a simple negation of the more
definite category, "a virgin." Yet it refuses a definite description.
The wit lies in the girl's saying yet refusing to say, "I am not a
virgin"—in refusing to identify with a "lack" or a "not" by projecting herself onto an indeterminate designation, a "what." I
have found this refusal of the hailing categories useful for studying genders and sexualities in Qajar Iran (1785–1925), where
genders do not respond to "Are you a man, or are you a
woman?" and sexual subjectivities cannot be named homosexual or heterosexual. How do we study these genders and sexualities within a field dominated by categorizations of types and
acts?

Grounded as I was in the modern imperative to think "man"
and "woman," it was indeed an analytical challenge when I

tried to figure out how to think about an *amrad* (a young male adolescent) who is not a man but not a woman. More problematically, adult men who made themselves look like amrads (called *mukhannas* or *amradnuma*) are often "translated" into effeminate. This transposition of *mukhannas* into effeminate is problematic: by reading sexuality through gender, it privileges gender over sexuality. How do we study transformations of gender and sexual subjectivities in nineteenth-century Iran in the context ("under influence") of recent scholarship on "history of sexuality"? Recent studies of Islamicate sexualities have been informed by the broader conversations in this field. Echoing the debates on Roman, Greek, and early Christian sexualities, some scholars have emphasized the utility of the concept of homosexuality. Others have argued that we would be better in tune with the Islamicate cultures' own sensibilities if we focused on sexual practices.[3]

But as numerous authors since Foucault have pointed out, if we pay attention to the disciplinary and regulatory effects of classificatory regimes, then the line between typologies of desires and acts loses its dividing force. Cultures that regulate through typing people into homo- and heterosexual beings have continued to punish acts to varying degrees, and cultures that discipline dominantly through punishment of acts at the same time do on occasion categorize people according to types of desire. In nineteenth-century Qajar biographical dictionaries, histories, and memoirs, often a man's sexual inclination is noted (the subject of these genres are most often men). He may be recorded as a woman lover *(zan'dust)* or ephebe lover *(amradparast)*. He may be described as a man who "is not inclined to women," especially in a context where exclusive and excessive inclination to *amrads* was chastised. The recording of sexual inclination does not record some innate homo- or heterosexuality, as all men are assumed to be sexually inclined to both women and *amrads*. The recording of exclusivity or excess marks the socially unacceptable (failure of one's reproductive obligation) or individually destructive (men who die of excess of love for young males).

Some relations were considered age inappropriate. Adult men past a certain age (often marked by graying of the beard) were reproved for continuing to display an interest in male youth, and sexual acts with very young boys were reported with severe disapproval and often faced punishment. Some instances of recording related to incidents of social transgression—for instance, having a liaison with a youth servant *(ghulam)* belonging to the inner court of someone higher in social standing or competing over youths and committing "crimes of passion."[4] In fact, once we begin to read these historical records beyond a retrieval impulse, we could learn a great deal about the cultural practices and social relations within which these recordings of sexual desires and acts are embedded and the ways in which these narratives of desire transcribe those cultural practices.

I begin with one Qajar source, *Risalah-'i fujuriyah* (An essay on debauchery), written in 1872 by Vali Khan, a Qajar courtier. The text is believed to have been written for the king's entertainment.[5] In this manuscript, Vali Khan records his sexual adventures with twenty-eight Qajar princesses, fifteen female prostitutes, sixty-five *amrads,* twenty-seven male and ten female servants *(ghulam* and *kaniz),* and eight virgins (these are reported in a separate category, since the concern for their virginity is invoked in relation to his practice of anal intercourse with them).

It would be misleading, though tempting, to conclude from these relative numbers that Vali Khan had a preference for male objects of desire. There is nothing in his descriptions that would indicate superiority of the pleasure he took in male liaisons compared to female ones. What he does emphasize, however, is his preference for anal intercourse with men and women alike, a point on which he further elaborates by concluding his essay with an elaboration of superiority of anus over vagina as an object of penile penetration. Contrary to my prior assumption that a preference for anal intercourse meant a preference for young male adolescents, Vali Khan articulates nothing related to "an object of desire," male or female, but something that reads more like a desire for a particular body part, as if this part was dissected from the entirety of the person's body.[6] It reads more as a hierarchicalization of pleasurable body parts.[7]

Vali Khan's hierarchicalization of pleasure focused on erotic localization has a genealogy in the wider Islamicate culture, noted by scholars of *adab* (belle lettres) and medicine. It is as well echoed in theological and juridical literature and in classical satirical sexual literature. The most famous example of the latter genre in Persian is that of Nizam al-Din 'Ubyd Zakani (d. 1370). Many of his anecdotes and quatrains are dialogues between anus and vagina, including debates between the two over which one is superior. Again the debate is not about male versus female objects of desire but about pleasures of anal versus vaginal penetration and pleasures of anus and vagina being penetrated by a penis.[8]

The nature of the hierarchy in the theological and juridical literature, on the other hand, is structured according to degrees of prohibition. Zayn al-'Abidin Khan Kirmani, a prominent Shaykhi leader of late nineteenth-century Iran, for instance, argued that "*liwat* [anal intercourse] is a more serious [*sakht'tar*] offense than *zina* [fornication]. Hazrat Sadiq (PBUH)[9] said that *hurmat-i dubur* [the sanctity/prohibitiveness of anus] is greater [*a'zam*] than *hurmat-i farj* [the sanctity/prohibitiveness of vagina], and truly God killed a whole people because of *hurmat-i dubur*, and he killed not a single soul for *hurmat-i farj*. Therefore, this act and especially to be a *mukhannas* or a *mu'bun* [an adult male who desires/permits himself to be anally penetrated] is worse."[10] Moreover, he distinguishes the female from male anus, elaborating on the difference of opinion among the 'ulama' about anal intercourse with one's wife: "The most accepted [*mashhur*] among the scholars," he writes, "is that it is *makruh* [abhorrent but not forbidden]." It is prohibited only if the woman does not consent: "if she is willing [*razi*, giving consent], there is no prohibition [*man'*]."[11] He also reports that one reason that some scholars at times prohibited husband-wife anal intercourse may have been the fear of decrease in procreative sex.[12] This is the only place where a link between regulation of sexual practices and procreative sex is forged. Many Islamic schools consider anal penetration of one's wife among the forbidden acts. Since women's bodies are assumed to be penetrable, the exclusion of marital anal intercourse, one may speculate, could have something to do with its potential affiliation with a fantasy of male-male anal penetration. In this sense, the female anus would be borrowing its sanctity or prohibition from that of the male.

The overall logic of this explication, in common with that of Vali Khan's essay, seems to be a hierarchy of sacredness for bodily orifices, in which male anus is the most noble (most pleasurable and religiously strictly forbidden to penetrate), female anus next (comparatively less pleasurable and religiously permitted, though not recommended, for penetration), with female vagina as least pleasurable and religiously most recommended.

Where does this body order come from? What work does it perform in the production of notions of manhood (and power relations among men), as well as womanhood and the power between man and woman? What ideas about the perfect man does it craft? What medical, biological, and philosophical discourses inform this order of bodily orifices? What other webs of meaning intersect to produce this hierarchization of body parts?

These are questions that need to be addressed by historical research. Mary Douglas suggests that "many ideas about sexual dangers are better interpreted as symbols of the relation between parts of society, as mirroring designs of hierarchy or symmetry which apply in the larger social system. . . . Sometimes bodily orifices seem to represent points of entry or exit to social units, or bodily perfection can symbolise an ideal theocracy."[13] This suggestion may constitute a direction for further analytical speculation. For similar interdictions against male anal intercourse in Judaism, Daniel Boyarin has argued that the Torah's interdiction can be understood as the general taboo in Hebrew culture against mixing of kinds—that is, anal penetration turns a man into a woman: "The Torah's language is very explicit; it is the 'use' of a male as a female that is *to'eba,* the crossing of a body from one God-given category to another, analogous to the wearing of clothes that belong to the other sex, by nature as it were."[14]

Persuasive as this may be for Talmudic culture, it does not quite work for Islamic early modern cultures. First, sexual and gender dimorphism is a problematic assumption. As Dror Ze'evi has argued for the Ottoman empire, in dominant Islamic discourses (medical as well as juridical) woman was considered an imperfect man rather than a separate type of being.[15] In terms of gender assignation, the categories of woman and *mukhannas* were distinct though "neighboring" categories. *Amrads* were distinct from adult men, but that did not make them women. To the extent that bodily integrity may constitute a core idea for masculine selfhood and thus that made penetration of a male body forbidden, the association would be that penetration would turn him into a *mukhannas,* a *ma'bun,* not into a woman. Correspondingly, what was considered socially unacceptable and a sign of unmanhood was for an *adult* man to be penetrated by another man. In this, there is perhaps more affinity between Islamic and Hellenic culture than with Talmudic culture.

At this point, however, I want to suggest that perhaps the problem has been the search for a singular logic—mixing of kinds, crossing of body boundaries, incest taboo, whatever—for making sense of nodal complexities that have produced the meaning of gender and sexual differences. The search for one logic of structuring hierarchies may obscure the contingent intersection of several webs of meaning that have mapped out the hierarchy of bodily parts and associated pleasures and prohibitions. For instance, within the religious and sexual ethical writings, there is yet another concern. The problem of male anal intercourse is linked with the issue of "incest effects." In a mid-nineteenth-century work, the respected Shaykhi leader Muham-

mad Karim Khan Kirmani argues that the sister of the penetrated man becomes forbidden to the penetrator, in similar
terms to the prohibition on marrying two sisters, though if a
man is already married, penetrating his wife's brother does not
annul the marriage.[16] The argument is similar to the effect of
zina (adultery) as well.[17]

Within the broader discussion of marriage prohibitions in Islamic jurisprudence, two sets of arguments have been advanced
for the grounds of such "incest effects." One line of argument
has pointed out the equivalence of assumed effects for transfer
of bodily fluids, such as milk or semen. Any such transfer is said
to be productive of close kinship and prohibitive of marriage
(the most commonly accepted and recommended form of sexual
relation within the jurisprudential literature). Yet this explanation runs into its limits immediately as we note that not all transfers are seen to effect such prohibitions. Saliva has not been paid
any attention; blood transfusions and more recently milk banks
have been declared free of such consequences. One could speculate that the singling out of milk and semen may have something
to do with their homologous relations to erotic localizations.

A second line of argument emphasizes the notion of ownership or quasi-ownership that makes specific sexual relations allowed or prohibited.[18] Though it is tempting to use this argument for an understanding of forbidding of any sexual acts
between two Muslim men (neither could own or quasi-own the
other), it runs into trouble since sexual acts between a male master and male servant are equally forbidden by Islamic law,
though it is accepted between a male master and his female servants and forbidden between a female master and her male and
female servants. Explanations such as those offered by Colin
Imber construct their scheme by not considering these less tidy
questions and taking male-female sexual relations as the primary subject of law. I am not suggesting that some concept of
ownership did not become commonly understood as providing
the legal, and not only legal, grounds for working out what is

forbidden and what not. To take one example from Vali Khan's *Essay on Debauchery,* his first "famous prostitute woman." Here are the few lines in full:

> The first is Shams Jahan, *sighah* [temporary wife] of Mahdi Khan. When we were meeting in the night, he had been informed and entered unexpectedly. He became very upset; eventually I had a talk with him, slowly his anger subsided, he drank a few cups of 'araq and accepted (to settle for) fines—one tuman from the lady and two tumans from me.[19]

What else would be the logic of settling for fines (twice for the transgressing man compared to the woman) if not as a compensation for the abuse of his quasi-ownership over the sexual benefits of Shams Jahan? Yet to expect this notion to do overarching explanatory work runs into the kind of inconsistencies I have already pointed out. It seems to me that bringing out as many possible directions of meaning can illuminate the complex node at which notions of gender and sexuality are worked out, without seeking a singular logical underpinning.[20] And this would imply that we cannot make the kind of neat break that is often made between sexual practices and erotic desire or the sharp delineating line that is often drawn between homoerotics and same-sex practices. If we consider pleasures and prohibitions as connected in a complex way to the production of notions of masculinity and of the perfect man, then not only acts or body parts but also discourses of desire and love have much to do with the construction of masculinity. Love as slavery, love as illness, and love as the state of total submission (often reported not to be identified with but to recognize as excessive and unacceptable in man) are some of the issues that need to be brought into these considerations.[21]

One of the major problems I faced in studying Qajar Iran was the relatively rapid disappearance of the figure of *amrad* from Iranian cultural imagination. Although this figure was already under pressure in the last decades of the nineteenth century, within a relatively short period (the first three decades of the twentieth century) the *amrad* changed from a desired figure to one of abjection and ridicule. Correspondingly, the practice of *amradbazi* changed from an acceptable social practice to a despicably shameful one. This transformation was intimately linked with a radical cultural change in perceptions of adult male attraction, love, and desire for an *amrad*. Once considered a *divine production* (God created men thus)—even though engaging in certain sexual practices out of that desire may have been considered forbidden—now such attraction, as well as acts, became recoded as *unnatural*.

Moreover, this change in the "nature" of sexual desire (and here I note that there is a corresponding change from *fitrat* to *tabi'at* as the relevant concept for nature, the first correlating with creation and the second with material embodiment) did not happen under the kind of "biopower" transformative mappings that Foucault had suggested for modern Europe. That is, Iran's "long" nineteenth century, a period of enormous transformations of sexual sensibilities and gender readability, was *not* driven largely by the production of governable citizens. Not until perhaps the late 1920s was the government intensely invested in regulating its subjects.

That Qajar sociocultural transformations did not take the form of sustained projects of centralized state building or national consolidation can be seen on many levels, but for my purposes here it can be seen in the relative inchoateness of development of the legal, disciplinary, and educational institutions. Historians of the Ottoman domain have studied the connection between the legal transformations and regulation of sexuality in the nineteenth century compared to earlier periods.[22] Qajar legal developments seem to have been very different. The newly established citywide police were only marginally interested in "sex crimes." Police regulations (issued in September 1879) criminalized forced abduction of married women as well as unmarried girls, whether of age or not *(baligh va nabaligh)* but did not make any mention of boys or male adolescents. Only if "an irregular and transgressive act [*bighayr-i qa'idah va khilaf*]" be-

tween a man and a woman or a *bachchah* (a word commonly
used for male adolescents) had taken place in a mosque was a
light punishment imposed—eight days to a month of imprison-
ment and one to fifty tumans in fine to be donated to a religious
fund.[23] The concern was the transgression of the sanctity of a
space of worship rather than punishment of a sexual act. The
Tehran police reports that were compiled on a daily basis (and
that have been published for the period August 1886 to June
1888) indicate a concern with theft, public drunkenness, and
negligence of duty (on the part of members of the new police
force itself) more than any other offense.[24] In 1886, public
coffeehouses were ordered closed "because of corrupt practices
prevalent in these locations,"[25] but the dominant "corrupt practice" of interest to and recorded in the police reports was female
prostitution. Sixty-three cases related to prostitution are reported, and thirty-one prostitutes suffered the most commonly
meted out punishment—expulsion from the city *(nafy-i balad)*.
Only fifteen reports concern male-male sexual practices (with
eight cases recording some sort of unspecified punishment, possibly bastinadoe). A national category of crimes that were specifically named sexual—*jara'im-i jinsi* (as distinct from sinful
acts punishable by religious sanctions—*hudud* and *ta'zir*)—is so
named at a much later date.[26]

From Qajar Iran, we also have extensive records of male-male
sexual practices, including what seems to have been a well-
known practice of adult men "keeping" younger men as their
companions, sometimes referred to as *adam'dari* (keeping a
male). The older man was sometimes referred to as "the cover"
(milhaf) of the younger one.[27] The 1921 city census of Tehran
suggests that the practice of *adam'dari* continued into the twentieth century.[28]

Nor was the Qajar medical discourse on matters sexual focused on categorizing desire or acts as natural or unnatural. The
medieval Islamic medical discourse on sexual practices and dis-
eases were selectively dropped and partially replaced by adaptations of European modern medical treatises. For instance, the

classical presumption that woman's orgasm was necessary for conception was replaced by noting that it was not.[29] For the Ottoman empire, Ze'evi has powerfully argued that while the classical single-sex model of human body—with woman as an imperfect version of man and a single notion of sexual desire that did not differentiate according to the gender of the object of desire—was dropped in the nineteenth century, it was not replaced with one determinate model (such as differences of gender and sexuality read as innate to the human body).[30]

The selectivity of translations and adaptations from nineteenth-century European sexual sciences needs to be studied. In the Iranian medical texts of the nineteenth century, while the figure of the hysteric does appear at length, there is no mention of perverts.[31] While such domains as law and medicine changed in this period, each seem to have followed a logic of its own contingent formation, with little centralizing pull to bring them into any cohesive building of spirals of power and desire.[32] The most important domain in which transformative regulations of sexuality can be said to have taken shape was in the political discourses of dissident intellectuals about nationhood and modernity. Here adult-man and male-adolescent sexual practices *(amradbazi)* became a key site for critiquing prevailing politics and morality of the Qajar state and society.[33]

Mirza Fath'ali Akhundzadah (1812–1878) and Mirza Aqa Khan Kirmani (1853?–1896), two of the most influential modernist sociocultural critics of Qajar state and society, argued extensively against *amradbazi* as a pervasive corrupt sexual practice of their time. Yet by the 1920s and 1930s, such concerns abated, and *amradbazi* seems to have been banished from the public face of Iran's emerging modernity without stoning and burning punishments that sodomy faced in the fourteen through seventeenth centuries in European countries.[34] No similar "defining moments" seem to have marked the modernist transformations of masculinity in Qajar Iran. Iranian banishment of *amradbazi* from publicly visible culture seems to have happened largely through what could be called the shame of backwardness. While Iranians' self-perception of backwardness and the shame of it have been given historical credit (at least in part) for all kinds of transformations—including changing the military and administrative structures of the government, completely transforming the educational system, and bringing about other cultural effects (such as changes in styles of clothes, music, and food preferences)—the materiality of shame for transformations of gender and sexual sensibilities has been largely neglected. Especially for a country that was not formally colonized and therefore did not have these cultural transformations taking place in relation to the structures of a colonial state, the process of identifying with and disavowing particular cultural practices becomes significant for studying the emergence of modern subjectivities.

In the nineteenth century, Iranian men became acutely and increasingly aware that Europeans considered older-man and younger-man love and sexual practices prevalent in Iran and that they considered it a vice. As Iran became identified by Europeans for and by homosocial and homosexual practices, Iranian modernists came to identify with and simultaneously disavow this abject position. This disidentification did not take the shape of codification of homoeroticism into a distinct type of desire and of men engaged in same-sex practices into particular types of beings. Unlike the European scene as mapped in the Foucauldian paradigm, in which an autonomous self located in the bodily contoured individual emerges as the site of modern technologies of subject formation, in the Iranian modernist imaginings the making of sexual practices did not ensue from some inherent quality located within the individual human body. Same-sex sexual practices, Iranian modernists argued, were a result of particular social institutions, most pointedly gender homosociality. As Kirmani argued,

> Men are naturally inclined toward socializing with and enjoying the companionship of women. This is so strongly evident that it needs no explication and proof. If a people is forbidden from this

great blessing and is deprived of this great deliverance, then inevitably the problem of sexual acts with male adolescents and male slaves is created, because young males without facial hair resemble women and this is one of the errors of nature. It is for this reason that in the Iranian people this grave condition has reached saturation. "You lust after men instead of women" can be witnessed in Iran.[35]

And the ground for this situation is the veiling of women that has become established in Iran. Since men's natural desire to see women is frustrated and they are deprived of that blessing, of necessity and inevitably, they turn to sex with male adolescents and making love with boys. Sa'di of Shiraz and the obscene and shameful Qa'ani and other Iranian poets have big collections of poetry that prove my word and relieve me of further explication.[36]

The notion of same-sex desire as a derivative deviant desire, forced on the natural as a consequence of unfortunate social arrangement of sex segregation, distinguishes the process of modern heteronormalization in Iran from that of Western Europe, as proposed by Foucault. In Iran, the modernist project of compulsory heterosocialization was premised on the expectation that once women became "available" to men, homosexual practices would disappear. The success of this project could have produced a tendency to "type" men (and women) who "still" engaged in same-sex practices as anormal, if not abnormal, and stricken with some sort of "illness."[37] A psychomedical discourse of male same-sex desire as illness (through the figure of *ma'bun* and in particular in Ibn Sina's discourse on *'ubna* as illness of will) was available. But the dominant regime of regulating sexuality continued, until recently, to remain centered on practices rather than on inherent forms of desire. The notion of the homosexual as a type did not emerge as a dominant discourse for disciplinary practices or for self-identification. Sexual acts between men continued to be seen as what men did before they settled into heterosexual procreative sex with wives (or even as they so settled so long as they performed their reproductive obligations) and did not mark them as a particular human type.

Yet one should ask: Is the notion that male-male sexual acts are what men do before they settle into procreative sexuality with wives (or what women do when not satisfied with their husbands' performance) not a deferral of recognition of same-sex desire as an erotic preference? Is it not yet another way of denial and disavowal of homosexuality? After all, we are assured that all men will eventually become practicing (if not believing) heterosexuals. Is this not a cultural move to make homosexuality an "unreadable text" and at best a temporally containable phenomenon? It marginalizes same-sex desire through temporal boxing rather than through minoritization. Instead of considering homosexual men a minority of peculiar queer disposition, men are seen to engage in same-sex practices but only for a "minor" period of their life cycle.

Though not linked with disciplinary technologies of producing modern governmentable bodies, Iranian modernist discourse on male same-sex practices was linked with production of modern citizenship in a different domain. Sexual acts that always seemed to enact relations of power (age seniority, class delineation) were seen as disruptive of patriotic brotherhood—which implied a measure of political egalitarianism and homologous subjecthood. For fraternal affective bonds of patriotism to emerge, the banishment of homoerotic desire and same-sex practices seem to have been called for. Patriotic sentiment was linked to gendering Iran (as national homeland) as a female beloved, engendering a regime of patriotic hetero-eros on which modern marital norms and concepts were shaped. In this sense, the nineteenth-century affiliations fashioned among *amradbazi,* gender homosociality (most signally condensed on the veil), and marriage were closer to the kind of affinities that were established between celibacy, matrimony, and sodomy in German Reformation discourse than to the legal, psychological, medical, and scientific discourses in nineteenth-century Europe.[38]

The history of the disappearance of the *amrad* cannot be told without the history of the culture wars over the veil. The modernist expectation was that with heterosocialization of social life and romanticization of marriage *amradbazi* would disappear. Iranian modern citizens, male and female, would become their natural heterosexual heterosocial selves. If we name the social regime of Qajar Iran as one of compulsory homosociality combined with procreative heterosexuality that left the structure of sexual desire indeterminate, we can say that Iranian modernity insisted on a regime of compulsory heterosociality that was to underwrite normative heterosexuality. The Islamic Republic, on the other hand, has been trying to preserve the modernist "achievement" of normative heterosexuality while reinstituting compulsory homosociality.

The "modernist optimism" initially worked against mapping of same-sex desire and practices onto minoritization of human types. But the "failure" to produce homogeneously heterosexual modern men and women—despite decades of gender heterosocialization, propagation of the complementarity of two "opposite sexes," and support for romantic marriage—provided the sociocultural space in which two distinct discourses combined to produce a religious, psychological, and medical discourse on "unnatural and deviant" (*ghayr-i tabi'i* and *inhirafi*) sexualities. Classical Islamic discourse on hermaphrodites has combined with a psychomedicalized notion of a biological sexuality (hormonal and chromosomal) that conflicts with socializing norms and produces abnormality and gender disorder, and the emerging discourse sanctions transsexuality and sex-change medical interventions. Such interventions are seen to transform same-sex desire into opposite sex desire, making transsexuality legible while at the same time insisting on abnormality and total prohibition of homosexuality.[39]

Translations across temporal and geographical zones of desire have taken the sexual sciences and biobehavioral sexual studies onto new lands. The emergence of gay/lesbian/bi/trans/queer sexual subjectivities and activism and the remapping of nations through diasporic communities have also produced complex global reconfigurations of sexualities and genders in contemporary Iran—a topic about which that we have just begun to converse.[40]

NOTES

1. An early draft of this work was presented at the Lesbian and Gay Studies seminar at the Humanities Center, Harvard University, Fall 2002. My thanks to the chairs of the seminar, Brad Epps and Heather Love, for providing me with this occasion for critical engagement. Dina Al-Kassim's response to my paper at the Radcliffe seminar as well as all participants' suggestions were immensely insightful and helped me to rethink some issues. Kathryn Babayan's and Valerie Traub's critical comments and supportive urgings made me rewrite rather than abandon this paper.

2. A popular anecdote in the *adab* corpus on women. For an insightful analysis of this and related anecdotes, see Fedwa Malti-Douglas, *Woman's Body, Woman's Word: Gender and Discourse in Arabo-Islamic Writing* (Princeton: Princeton University Press, 1991), 35–37.

3. For a review of these issues, see Frédéric Lagrange, "Methodologies, Paradigms, and Sources for Studying Women and Islamic Cultures: Sexualities and Queer Studies," *Encyclopedia of Women and Islamic Cultures* (Leiden: Brill, 2003), 1:419–22.

4. For a fuller discussion of these reports in nineteenth-century sources, see chapter 1 of my book *Women with Mustaches and Men without Beards: Gender and Sexual Anxieties of Iranian Modernity* (Berkeley: University of California Press, 2005).

5. Vali Khan ibn Suhrab Gurjistani, *Risalah-ʾi fujuriyah*, Kitabkhanah-ʾi milli (National Library), Tehran, manuscript 1425/F. Among the readers was Nasir al-Din Shah himself. See Iʿtimad al-Saltanah, *Ruznamah-i khatirat,* ed. Iraj Afshar (Tehran: Amir Kabir, 1966), 577, 831.

6. For a critique of our "habitual condensation" of acts or "erotic localizations" onto the gender of object-choice in a different context, see Eve Kosofsky Sedgwick, *Epistemology of the Closet* (Berkeley: University of California Press, 1990), 35.

7. This is not unique to Iran or the nineteenth century. David Halperin, in his discussion of pseudo-Lucianic *Erôtes,* a familiar stag-

ing of preferences for ephebes versus for women, suggests, "Such passages leave one with the distinct impression that what endears boys to Callicratidas and women to Charicles is not a preferred sex or gender but merely certain favorite parts of the human anatomy." David M. Halperin, "Historicizing the Subject of Desire: Sexual Preferences and Erotic Identities in the Pseudo-Lucianic *Erôtes,*" in Jan Goldstein, *Foucault and the Writing of History* (Oxford: Blackwell, 1994), 29. Yet after a page and a half of discussing this issue, Halperin reverts back to the "habitual condensation" of "erotic localizations" onto "boys and women." Sidestepping the commonality of erotic localization makes it possible to distinguish neatly between the two contestants of this dialogue according to typologies of objects of desire and forestalls the question of what other webs of meaning intersect in this production of notions of pleasure focused on "favorite parts of human anatomy." For debates between lovers of young men and lovers of women in the Ottoman context, see Selim Kuru, *A Sixteenth-Century Scholar Deli Birader and His Dafi'u'l-gumum ve rafi'u'l-humum,* PhD dissertation, Department of Near Eastern Languages and Civilizations, Harvard University, 2000.

8. See Nizam al-Din 'Ubyd Zakani, *Collected Works,* ed. Mohammad-Ja'far Mahjoub (New York: Bibliotheca Persica Press, 1999). For a discussion of desirability of anal penetration in Arabo-Islamic culture, see Abdelwahab Bouhdiba, *Sexuality in Islam,* trans. Alan Sheridan (London: Routledge, 1985), 202–03.

9. Ja'far al-Sadiq (ca. 699–765), Shi'ite sixth Imam. The dominant school of Twelver Shi'ite jurisprudence takes its name from him.

10. Zayn al-'Abidin Khan Kirmani, *Risalah-i haftad mas'alah dar javab-i Saqat al-'Ulama Salmasi az masa'il-i mukhtalafah* (Kirman: Sa'adat, 1959), 130. Note that *hurmat* means "reverence, sanctity," which is the grounds for prohibiting something that breaks down the sanctity.

11. Ibid., problem number 17, 145–49.

12. Other Islamic sources concur on the permissibility of anal intercourse between husband and wife as a "birth control" technique. The condition of woman's consent is noteworthy, as that is usually not considered a requirement for vaginal intercourse.

13. Mary Douglas, *Purity and Danger: An Analysis of the Concepts of Pollution and Taboo* (London: Routledge, 1966), 3–4.

14. Daniel Boyarin, "Are There Any Jews in 'The History of Sexuality'?," *Journal of the History of Sexuality* 5, no. 3 (1995): 333–55. He further argues that "The issue is gender (as the verse of the Bible explicitly suggests) and not 'homosexuality,' and gender is conceived around penetration and being penetrated" (344). And further: "The very word for female, *neqeba* in both biblical and Talmudic Hebrew, as well as Talmudic Aramaic, means 'orifice bearer,' as if male bodies did not possess orifices" (345).

15. Dror Ze'evi, *Producing Desire: Changing Sexual Discourse in the Ottoman Middle East 1500–1900* (Berkeley: University of California Press, 2006). Today's Islamic discourses are based on presumption of created complementary differences between man and woman. This is a modernist development in Islamic thought, an effect of nineteenth-century abandonment of the idea of woman as imperfect man and the need for a different ground for generating legal gender differences.

16. Muhammad Karim Khan Kirmani, *Majma' al-fatavi-i Hajj Muhammad Karim Khan Kirmani,* ed. Hajj Zayn al-'Abidin Kirmani (Kirman: Sa'adat, 197?), 193.

17. "An effect of *zina* in family law is to create affinity, which acts as an impediment to marriage: 'If a man commits fornication with a woman, her mother and daughter are forbidden to him.' The same rule applies even without intercourse: 'If a woman touches a man with lust, her mother and daughter are forbidden to him.'" Colin Imber, *Studies in Ottoman History and Law* (Istanbul: Isis Press, 1996), 178–79. The stronger effect of woman's lust is worth considering here. I would also suggest that it may be productive to revisit many Islamic regulations through the angle of anxieties over the effects of marriage prohibition of particular practices. For instance, the Quranic verses often referred to as the *hijab* verses are explicitly formulated in conjunction with marriage prohibition. Those toward whom one ought to practice rules of modesty are those whom one is not prohibited to marry. This line of thinking I owe to reading an essay about Afghan practices of public modesty, including men turning their eyes away from women in public, by Jon W. Anderson in which he noted that the most common answer he was given when asking for the reason of this practice was that if women and men saw each other too frequently they would become like siblings and prohibited from marriage. See Jon W. Anderson,

"Social Structure and the Veil: Comportment and the Composition of Interaction in Afghanistan," *Anthropos* 77 (1982): 397–420.

18. See Imber, *Studies in Ottoman History and Law,* 176–77, for the invocation of ownership and quasi-ownership as grounds for discussion of *zina* in Ottoman law.

19. Vali Khan, *Essay on Debauchery,* manuscript 14.

20. For a rich example of this kind of multilevel approach, see Tamer al-Leithy, "'Of bodies chang'd to various forms . . .': Hermophrodites and Transsexuals in the Medieval Middle East," unpublished manuscript.

21. See Sunil Sharma, "Women, Gender, and Pre-modern Discourses of Love," in *Encyclopedia of Women and Islamic Cultures,* vol. 5 (Leiden: Brill 2007); and Indrani Chatterjee, "Alienation, Intimacy, and Gender: Problems for a History of Love in South Asia," in *Queering India: Same-Sex Love and Eroticism in Indian Culture and Society,* ed. Ruth Vanita, 61–76 (New York: Routledge, 2002). See also Daniel Boyarin, "Homotopia: The Feminized Jewish Man and the Lives of Women in Late Antiquity," *differences* 7, no. 2 (1995): 41–81, for a discussion of cultures in which submissiveness, modeled after one's submissiveness to God, is valued.

22. See Dror Ze'evi, "Changes in Legal-Sexual Discourses: Sex Crimes in the Ottoman Empire," *Continuity and Change* 16, no. 2 (2001): 219–42.

23. Count de Mont Fret, *Kitabchah-i qanun* (n.p., 1879), 10–12, 20. The full text was serialized in the emigré paper (published in Istanbul) *Akhtar* 6, no. 6 (21 January 1880): 50; no. 7 (28 January 1880): 58; no. 8 (4 February 1880): 67–68; no. 9 (11 February 1880): 74–75. Criminalization of abduction appears in number 7 and the mosque regulation in number 9.

24. Anisah Shaykh Riza'i and Shahla Azari, eds., *Guzarish-ha-yi nazmiyah az mahallat-i Tihran,* 2 vols. (Tehran: Sazman-i asnad-i milli-i Iran, 1998).

25. Ibid., 1:99.

26. Mas'ud Ansari, *Jara'im va inhirafat-i jinsi* (Tehran: np, 1961). The use of the word *jins* (meaning "kind, species," as well as "grammatical gender") to mean *sex* is itself of recent origin. I have come across a couple of references in the 1920s, a few more in the 1930s, and a lot more in the 1940s. The usage really takes off in the 1950s, and by the 1960s it becomes used widely, except that in

medical discourse (excluding psychology texts) it is still not the dominant word. The usage of *jins* for *sex* seems to have come into Persian from translated marriage manuals and books on child rearing and from the increasing popularity of psychology and psychoanalysis from the late 1950s onward. Its usage in Arabic and Turkish seems to be of a similarly recent origin. Private communication with Dror Ze'evi, 31 July 2004. See also Sima Shakhsari, "From Hamjensbaaz to Hamjensgaraa: Diasporic Queer Reterritorializations and Limits of Transgression," forthcoming paper and my "Sex in Change" a two-volume project, work-in-progress.

27. See, for example, I'timad al-Saltanah, *Ruznamah,* 90, 238. An article on prostitution in Iran by the Viennese doctor, Jakob Eduard Polak (1818–1891, in Iran 1851–1860) had one lengthy section devoted to discussion of male-male sexual practices and a much briefer section on female-female sexual practices in Iran. Jakob Eduard Polak, "Prostitution in Persia," *Wiener Medicinische Wochenschrift,* nr. 32, 1861, Persian trans. by Kjell Madsen, George Warning, and Mansour Saberi, in *Homan* 13 (1998): 13–18. I have come across the word *milhafah* (feminine for *milhaf*) used for a woman in one instance (Shaykh Riza'i and Azari, *Guzarish-ha,* 2:479), perhaps connoting a similar meaning (older woman who "keeps" younger woman for companionship including sexual). In more recent times, such women were referred to as *baruni* (literally, "raincoat").

28. See Ja'far Shahri, *Tarikh-i ijtima'i-i Tihran dar qarn-i sizdahum,* 6 vols. (Tehran: Mu'assisah-i khadamat-i farhangi-i rasa, 1990), 1:88, where he says that according to the Tehran census, some 5 percent of the (male?) population were "same-sex keepers." See further 1:536–37, 4:697, 5:247, and 4:17 for a photograph of "tough men with their beardless *bachchahs.*" He also reports that the rate of same-sex desire among women was 1.5 in 1,000. It is not clear how he has arrived at these figures, and I have not had access to the 1921 Tehran census. Women had several "public" forms of partnership. These included "vows of sisterhood" and arranging to be married as cowives to the same man, presumably without his knowledge of their relationship. Polak (1861/1998) assumed that all vows of sisterhood were pacts of lesbian relationships.

29. See, for instance, 'Ali ibn Zayn al-'Abidin Hamadani, *Javahir al-tashrih* (Tehran: Dar al-funun, 1888), 941–42.

30. Ze'evi, *Producing Desire.*

31. These are preliminary observations that were made on the basis of looking at a small number of nineteenth-century medical manuscripts. This is a topic about which very little research has been done. My thanks to Mohamad Tavakoli-Targhi and Gholamreza Salami for making some of these manuscripts available to me.

32. This is again a tentative preliminary observation. Works on legal and judicial transformations in Qajar Iran have not investigated regulations of sexuality. This remains a topic for future research. Recent scholarship by Kathryn Babayan (1998, 2003, and in this volume) on Safavi Iran provides us with an excellent historical context for the Qajar period.

33. In a different historical context, Helmut Puff has persuasively argued that "sodomy—the topic generations of historians have marginalized as beyond history proper, censored as inappropriate for the historically minded public, or condemned as monstrous—was inextricably woven into the cultural matrix of the German-speaking lands during the fifteenth and sixteenth centuries. Like few other concepts, sodomy touched mightily upon honor, both personal and communal—a nexus which turned this sexual sin into a social one and transformed suspicions of sodomy into perceived and strategically deployed threats to the body politic." *Sodomy in Reformation Germany and Switzerland 1400–1600* (Chicago: University of Chicago Press, 2003), 2. One could make a similar argument about *amradbazi* in late nineteenth-century Iranian modernist discourse. For a fuller discussion, see my *Women with Mustaches.*

34. See Puff, *Sodomy;* Alan Bray, *Homosexuality in Renaissance England* (New York: Columbia University Press, 1982).

35. This sentence appears in Arabic in the original and is a partial text of Quranic verses, 7:81 and 27:55, both in the context of narrating the story of Lot and his people.

36. Mirza Aqa Khan Kirmani, *Sad khatabah,* manuscript in Edward G. Browne Collection, Cambridge University Library. Selections in *Nimeye Digar* 1, 9 (1989): 101–12; quote from manuscript 137b (*Nimeye Digar,* 111). See also Mirza Aqa Khan Kirmani, *Sih*

maktub, ed. Bahram Chubinah (n.p.: Mard-i imruz, 1991), 72–73, 83–87.

37. Classical Islamic medical and legal treatises categorized *'ubna* as illness. In the modernist redefinition, the concept of same-sex desire as abnormal (while not a dominant concept in late Qajar period) became inclusive of both desire and act *and* covered both partners to the act and desire. The concept of abnormality has become a more dominant paradigm in Iran in recent decades. See Sima Shakhsari, "Naqdi bar kitab-i *Jinsiyat-i gumshudah,*" *Homan* 18 (2001): 34–36.

38. As Puff argues, "The relationship between sodomy and marriage . . . can also be cast as mutually constitutive in forms other than inversio. . . . [S]odomy became legible through matrimony as much as matrimony achieved legibility through its supposed sexual opposite" (*Sodomy,* 167). In other words, "[S]odomy is traceable through marriage" (168). *Celibacy* here was a critical term as the originator of the closely affiliated sexual sins of "'adultery, whoredom, and sodomitical sins'" (170). In a cultural context where a large part of the population never married or married late in life, celibacy became marked as responsible for sodomy, and there was an expectation by Protestants that sodomy would be left behind by embracing matrimony (180). But there are important differences here as well. Marriage in Iran was a reproductive contract that complemented "sodomitical sins." Celibacy in the fifteenth- and sixteenth-century European discourse seems to have done the same cultural work as gender segregation and the veil in a nineteenth-century Iranian context—as originators of sexual sins. Qajar discourses on sexual practices were not linked to marital and reproductive sex. Whether in texts of entertainment or of religious sexual ethics, categorization of sexual practices does not follow a prioritization that places referentiality onto marital sex.

39. See my manuscript "Transing and Transpassing across Sex-Gender Walls in Contemporary Iran" for further discussion of these issues.

40. On this topic, see Sima Shakhsari, "The Discursive Production of Iranian Queer Subjects in Diaspora," MA thesis, San Francisco State University, 2002.

Epilogue:
Sexual Epistemologies, East in West

Dina Al-Kassim

SEXUAL EPISTEMOLOGIES,
INTRACTABLE ORIENTALISMS

This volume is the result of a provocative proposition: can a group of area studies specialists, historians, literary scholars, and queer studies specialists come together to query the disciplinary assumptions of queer historiography while focusing critically on the project to queer Middle Eastern studies? The resulting collection engages issues of gender and sexuality in a diverse array of Arabic, Persian, French, Spanish, Christian, and Islamic contexts, while each contribution reflects on the methodological limits raised by their distinctive archives and the framing of sexuality studies in recent years.[1] To pursue the question of desire outside the conventions of the area studies fields represented by these rich and insightful essays affords us a welcome opportunity to explore the deployment of sexuality beyond the bounds of its more familiar exercise in premodern and modern Europe.

Such work is needed for many reasons, not the least of which is to locate the present conditions of feminism and feminist scholarship in its global frame by historicizing categories like gender, often naturalized as traditional practice. Another important effect of this work is to extend the analysis begun by Foucault well beyond the European example to the modern postcolonial, neocolonial, and developing states for which the deployment of modern sexuality is very much underway (though unevenly) as a mode of power haunted by an archaism or traditionalism, alternately disavowed and embraced but poorly understood.

We see this potential most explicitly in Asfaneh Najmabadi's work on the origins of Iranian modernity, but this thought of the present disastrous fiction of East against West echoes throughout the chapters and recurs as an unanswerable question about the limits of knowing and naming the desire that we moderns hear in the archive. Hearing voices might be a figure for archival research of this kind, which is always incomplete and rarely a disinterested pursuit; haunting seems to me the best figure for the kind of history that can emerge from within queer studies.

This methodological concern is immediately foregrounded in Najmabadi's "Types, Acts, or What? Regulation of Sexuality in Nineteenth-Century Iran" (chapter 8), which proposes a working apparatus for approaching the different threads of sexual regulation, politics, and desire in Iranian modernity from the nineteenth century to the present. Rejecting the notion of a univocal structure of gender and sexual practice, Najmabadi advocates an analytic strategy that reads for the sedimented and contradictory logics haunting the historical texts she examines. This analytic work asks us to consider the dynamic field of internalization proper to the success of sexual commandment or recruitment to particular sexual norms, gender identities, and exceptional desires.

Questioning the epistemologies within queer historiography while simultaneously urging us to theorize the subjectivities and identities in the historical record, this collection breaks with the confining methodological habits of queer studies and area studies, which risk flattening the archive or cutting sexual practice out of the discursive web of its production. From this renewed perspective, we might pursue several questions around the same theme: Can queering Middle East studies redress the confabulations of tradition that continue to wrest the future from the present in the Middle Eastern states? Can queer studies offer us a more complex understanding of temporal relations that does not indulge the fantasy of progressive development? Can queer historiographies provide a critical advantage in our efforts to unravel the phobic and injurious—masculinist, Orientalist, heterosexist, fundamentalist (and here I include the many American fundamentalisms)—effects of power that we moderns live? And finally, given that the East/West divide is both profitable and not likely to recede soon and given that the modern state regulates as much by dealing death to its enemies both within and beyond its borders as it does by inciting commerce with the norm, can a field as fragile as queer Middle East studies find the tools to analyze the power and pleasures that have invested the psychosocial body of traditional and modernizing cultures of the region?

Seven years ago, the editors of the volume *Premodern Sexualities* drew the contours of a problem that continues to frame historical approaches to sexuality studies when they argued that queer theory's more nuanced understanding of the mechanisms of identification could contribute

in general to the notion that, in studying the specificity of a particular "moment," it might, precisely, be more pleasurable *and* ethically resonant with our experience of the instabilities of identity-formation to figure that "moment" as itself fractured, layered, indeed, historical. It seems symptomatic of how alterity is too often now used to stabilize periods or epistemes that the academic reception of Foucault has tended to emphasize the radical difference of one episteme from another and to de-emphasize those aspects of Foucauldian thought engaged with multiple time lines. In contrast, we might point to Foucault's own emphasis, however ambivalent, on the ways in which the "confessional regimes" he

traces to early Christian forms of truth-telling and expiation continue to operate in modern institutions of power-knowledge such
as medicine, therapy, and education.[2]

The thrust of their intervention—which they claim for queer
theory in general but also potentially as the unfinished task of
the new science—calls for both a renewed self-reflection on the
part of the historiographer and a more nuanced, speculative encounter with the conceptual apparatus that guides the prevailing
historical insight that sodomy and homosexuality represent distinct, temporally and geographically noncontiguous regimes of
desire, discipline, and regulation. This epistemic distinctiveness
rides on the often incoherent division of acts from identities. It is
incoherent because the performative character of identity cannot do without its acts anymore than the premodern obsession
with masculine (and perhaps feminine; cf. Babayan's exploration of excessive female mourning) temperance (the balance of
appetite and excess) allows one to suppose that economies of
sodomy are free of identity or that they are not dominated by
the specter of identity. This difference of episteme guarantees the
modernity of the modern against the now utopian, now primitive unfinished past. This axiomatic difference guards each historical epoch from the other to confer on them the status of
fields.

If there is an uncanny within queer studies (which claims for
itself a freedom from repression), it is this repeated return of
sodomy and homosexuality as the inseparable but completely
incompatible axis of historical analysis. The premodern and the
Eastern are thereby always defined by an opposition that secures
their uniqueness by saving them from modern disciplinary projections. As some contributors have noted and as we learn at
length from Najmabadi, this insistence has the effect of prescrib-
ing a descriptive apparatus even where it may not be sustained
by historical detail. As an argument for alterity *that has become*
an institutional and disciplinary production of knowledge, this
"hard distinction" is troubled throughout Najmabadi's discus-

sion of Qajar Iran even as it supplies much of the conceptual frame from which she seeks to depart. That this hard line has formed on the authority of Foucault's studies of modern regulation via sexuality is something of an irony given his warning against "'histories of mentalities' that would take account of bodies only through the manner in which they have been perceived and given meaning and value."[3]

There is a certain irony in the fact that when queer literary and cultural studies borrow from anthropology or other social sciences, they sometimes essentialize cultural models in the name of accurate and fair representation of "other" cultural norms and practices. In the general field of Middle East studies, this is nowhere more evident than in the use and abuse of the so-called Mediterranean model, a common reference point of sexuality studies of North Africa, the Middle East, and western Asia. This epistemological organization of practice and desire is of ancient provenance and characterizes the world of classical Greece and Rome. According to this regime of same sex acts, "homosexuality" (which is also said not to exist as such within this sexual regime) does not attach to the active partner in homosexual intercourse but falls exclusively on the passive partner. Further, because the term *homosexual* and the discrete form of subjectivity to which it is attached are of nineteenth-century European provenance and because this social type emerges as a main axis of demographic rationality in the modern state, "homosexuality" poses particularly difficult semantic, political, and methodological problems in non-Western and premodern studies of the imbrication of sexuality and culture. For these reasons, scholars of these fields have seized on the acts and identities distinction (and the attendant distinction of sodomy from homosexuality) as a way of taming the risk of historical anachronism.

As a counterpart to this scholarly caution within the field, another gesture has become commonplace. The Mediterranean model is now cited as a fact of difference between the "two" cultures, East and West. In the field of modernist studies of North African literature and culture, for instance, this cultural feature is used to describe and explain aspects of literary explorations that are often critical of existing national and societal norms, as if sexuality in the region had remained unchanged for eons.[4] The acts and identities dichotomy sanctions the contemporary use of the Mediterranean model as an absolute difference between the sexual epistemologies of the East and West and the distinct subjectivities arising along this declivity. Those working in queer studies invoke this civilizational model when we caution each other to avoid projecting our own cultural norms where they are held to have no historical, political, or epistemological purchase. In the name of cultural difference, the East is asked to produce its difference from the West across all periods because cultural difference is assumed to be a mark of distinction, even where no salient difference or no univocal model dominates the multiform logics braided together in a given period or region. The Mediterranean model provides a salient example of this desired production. Now a watchword of queer studies, the invocation of the Mediterranean model serves to simplify rather than explain the play of putative license and prohibition in cultures as complexly diverse as those of the Mediterranean and the Islamicate cultures beyond. The papers collected in this volume contest such an easy assimilation of the history of sexual practices, desires, and social regulation in the Middle East to the simplicity of the active/passive dichotomy or the Mediterranean model. Eschewing the dependence on singular logics, these investigations share in their generosity toward the heterogeneous character of the archives they study.

In an excellent example of this orientation, Sahar Amer's "Cross-Dressing and Female Same-Sex Marriage in Medieval French and Arabic Literatures" (chapter 3) troubles the received wisdom of the Mediterranean model by taking up the representation of lesbian desire and acts, which are often ignored in the acts and identities debate. Amer argues that the invisibility of the Western lesbian is a product of a prior erasure of cross-cultural inspiration. Using the French medieval epic *Yde et Ol-*

ive, Amer shows that the tale of lesbian love transubstantiated into Christian heterosexual piety hides within its normative resolution of the lesbian romance and in this case, marriage, its own origins in translation, scandalously rooted in a non-Christian and Arabic text, *The Thousand and One Nights.* While the source text (the cross-dressing tale of Qamar al-Zaman and Princess Budur and its story of a lesbian and possibly male homosexual love triangle) disappears in the French retelling of the tale, what is lost most decisively in translation is the legibility of lesbian preference itself. *The Thousand and One Nights* does not recuperate female same-sex desire to heterosexual ends but allows for a ménage à trois that shelters a lesbian, heterosexual, and male homoerotic triangulation of desire and acts. The repression of lesbian preference as a possible telos for desire rather than as a fantastic detour of the convention is acted out in the interstices of translation to domesticate errant desires under the sign of a Christian heterosexual norm. What Amer discovers in the complex textuality in play is a mechanism of discipline that harnesses poetry to the ends of social regulation. Her interpretive strategy is thus amply informed by queer feminist, postcolonial, and Foucauldian approaches, but the epistemologies that are held to be axiomatic for sexuality studies of the Middle East and for studies of East-West comparisons do not dominate the reading underway.

In "Homoerotic Liaisons among the Mamluk Elite in Late Medieval Egypt and Syria" (chapter 6), Everett K. Rowson approaches larger questions of the field by considering a rumor that has come down to us in the archive and that still operates in various forms. Using the caricature of sexual practices and mores in Islamicate culture found in a fourteenth-century French text, Rowson examines Mamluk sexuality and social organization to explain the practices that might lie beneath the European slander. Tracking parallel political scandals involving resentment at a ruler's obsession with a male favorite in fourteenth-century England and in Egypt, Rowson argues that the Orientalist slander, which acts in his essay as a representative for Western prejudice toward Eastern culture, substantially misrepresents the complexity of practice and law relevant to sexual conduct under the Mamluk reign. This historical approach provides a context that reveals cultural distortions in the East/West encounter while affording us a speculative space to test several hypotheses about the construction of practice and difference in Mamluk Egypt. Rowson asks whether contemporary fourteenth-century perceptions of homosexuality attributed its provenance to a foreign influence, what he calls the "importation" theory of sexual origins, or whether the same-sex practices of the Mamluk elite represented a common, if not commonly praised, set of accepted behaviors and desires.

Both Amer and Rowson pursue the thread of comparative analysis to offer convincing evidence of interdependence and transcultural borrowing, even if in the negative form of a slander, in medieval and early modern periods between East and West. These indications of a shared history that crosses the imaged divide between worlds throw into stark relief the confidence with which the East/West distinction is deployed today to justify countless forms of Orientalism.

Along similar lines, a recent critic of gay scholarship and gay, lesbian, bisexual, and transgender (GLBT) human-rights discourse diagnoses the free-floating Orientalism of gay cultural production from touristic guide books to some academic publications.[5] In an essay of many valid and even vital observations, Joseph Massad attempts to extend a Foucaultian analysis to a contemporary situation, but in doing so he reifies cultural difference to such a degree that he winds up arguing for the clarity and distinction of the East/West divide in ways that resonate with the very Orientalism he critiques. The example concerns the Cairo 52, a group of Egyptian men rounded up in a series of vice raids that began in 2001 and continue to the present. For Massad, the key issue revolves around an ideological consensus on the part of GLBT activists to disseminate their assumptions about GLBT identity around the globe, and he highlights particularly egregious criticisms of Arabic countries in the comments and strategies of key GLBT human-rights organizations and political figures.

To make the legitimate criticism that GLBT organizations act without an informed awareness of different cultural practices of sexuality, of the imperialism of the West, or of the role that charities and human-rights organizations have played in the exercise of imperialist policies, Massad deploys the Mediterranean model. On the basis of the model, he then argues that the "gay international" incites repressive homophobic legislation and thereby disseminates its key category of influence—namely, Western identity based homosexuality. The problems with Massad's own complicity in a sexual and epistemological essentialism are manifold. A critique that is content to halt with a righteous indictment of Orientalism, however just and justified, cannot hope to illuminate the complexity of the deployment of sexuality and falls into the trap of essentializing cultural difference through a prior essentialisation of epistemology.

As an illustration of the extremes to which theorization on the axis of the acts and identities distinction remade as the history of a sexual economy from sodomy to homosexuality will go, Najmabadi offers numerous examples of what she brilliantly diagnoses as a counting mania in the case of Walter Penrose, whose drive to catalogue every conceivable variation of so-called gender leads him to create an incoherent category—a borgesian library—for those who resist classification. This scholarly mania describes an impasse that results when multiplicity becomes its own mandate such that reiteration of the "hard distinction" between types demands the proliferation of names and therefore types. Invoking the Mediterranean model of same-sex acts that do not confer identity on the doers, Najmabadi asks whether comparative typologies do not also force naming onto acts even with the alibi of presenting multiplicity. Instead of extending the list of types, she proposes the far more useful project of "critical studies of regulatory technologies of gender and sexuality" that can reflect on the disciplinary effects of typological study itself.

Najmabadi's synthesis of the debate around the distinction between worlds of the type and worlds of the act results from her concern for the way that "classification whether as type or act contributes to the production of sexuality and gender." It culminates in a translation of terms that takes us a step further from the acts and identities impasse toward an analysis of the psychosocial field of internalization and reproduction of social commandment or injunction in ways that promise to reread the archive for the trace of historical shifting and folding, haunting and translation, that cannot be described simply as epistemic break.

"How do categories become commandments?" This question attempts to move the field of sexuality studies—which so believes in the significance and extent of distinction (acts/identities, act/object, premodern/modern, Christian/Muslim, West/East, young/old, passive/active, male/female, male/not-yet-male) that it risks losing both the premodern and the postcolonial as relevant or interesting sites of social and sexual organization—beyond prohibition and its excess. Noting the absence of other clear conceptual markers of distinction between people of the type and people of the act, Najmabadi describes the shared exercise of penal codes to police normativity. The example of the nineteenth-century Qajar biographical history is an interesting case of how sexual preferences are catalogued and recorded only because of an excessive, exclusionary, and therefore suspect sexuality. In short, Najmabadi's work argues that residues of historical changes and competing logics of pleasure and prohibition are layered in any single text or historical moment found in the archive.

This welcome complication of the epistemic model is something that I see emerging in these chapters. In volume 1 of his *History of Sexuality,* Foucault describes the development of confession as a technology of the self and of the state. He describes a mode of instruction and initiation (what he calls an Eastern *ars erotica*) that is transmitted via the mentorship of a learned authority, whose knowledge of sex and pleasure derived from practice and who taught by example. Explicitly situated in the Far East and Islamic cultures, *ars erotica* cultivates the individual as the embodiment of a practical teaching to which he is first apprenticed. Christian confession breaks with this transmission of truth and pleasure by reversing the hierarchy of value such that the unknowing, lowly subject who is in need of absolution confesses the truth of his experience and his practices to the skilled listener. For Foucault, the key distinction between the premodern, Eastern mode of pleasure and the modern deployment of sexuality lies in the difference between a cultivation of the self via mentorship and the structure of subjection produced by the confessional scene that underpins what he calls the juridical subject. Modern subjection is effected by a translation of the technique of confession into the *scientia sexualis* via a system of scientific classification that is capable of diagnosing the social, moral, and medical types. In short, the modern confessional subject is endowed with a sexuality that emerges analytically in Foucault's work through a distinction of East and West, where the latter is not only a geographical territory but a particular modern configuration of social life that is understood as the normative regulation of subjects through the juridical model of power. The chapters in this volume contest this East/West divide by showing that in the East the policing of the state's citizenry proceeded via the institution of heterosexual norms that sought to establish particular types of subjects whose styles of speech, action, and expression could be regulated through the invocation of the pathological type. Thus, the investigations in cultures where same-sex practices are regulated according to a system of acts seems to yield an unexpected conclusion—namely, that to be defined by an act is to become a type.

According to the *History of Sexuality*, the *ars erotica* did not entirely disappear in the West as it was displaced by a newer form. Rather, it lingers, converting practice into styles of subjectivation:

> The phenomena of possession and ecstasy, which were quite frequent in the Catholicism of the Counter Reformation, were undoubtedly effects that had got outside the control of the erotic technique immanent in this subtle science of the flesh and we must ask whether, since the 19th [century], the *scientia sexualis*—under the guise of its decent positivism—has not functioned, at least to a certain extent, as an *ars erotica*. Perhaps this production of truth, intimidated though it was by the scientific model, multiplied, intensified, and even created its own intrinsic pleasures.[6]

Excess within the heart of the scientific will to knowledge the *ars erotica* may come down to us as a queerness we find within the modern discourse of sex—"a pleasure in analysis" of things sexual. Such a vestige or subtle sublimation of a lost tradition folds the former epistemic order into its successor.[7] One might say that the *ars erotica* haunts the *scientia sexualis* but not in its native guise or original form. The lost tradition is reworked to release the old function in the new form, as knowledge artfully secured to intensify pleasure and with a subtle rearrangement of the norm.

Here, we might take Leyla Rouhi's elegant reading of Cervantes's practice of cultural translation back to Foucault. In "A Handsome Boy among Those Barbarous Turks: Cervantes's Muslims and the Art and Science of Desire" (chapter 2), Rouhi considers what it means to attribute homosexualities to translation. As her comparative analysis shows, the theme of cultural exchange is intimately allied to sexuality. The trope of translation returns us to the difficult figure of historical time in the transformation, translation, and reconstruction of *ars erotica* to the science of sex. What Foucault really offers us is a model of the many "nows" contained and reworked in the same present. These many histories shift and fold back on one another in an endless work of translation and retranslation or (as another psychoanalytic scholar would argue) in a process of never completed metabolization.[8]

The notion of a haunting excess that escapes the control of erotic technique and state regulation complicates efforts to distinguish premodern from modern sexualities as much as it complicates the task of locating the threshold of the modern. Kathryn Babayan's discussion of sodomy and heresy proves enlightening on this score, for her essay "'In Spirit We Ate Each Other's Sorrow': Female Companionship in Seventeenth-Century Safavi Iran" (chapter 7) does more than provide an access to early modern Safavi society. Her analysis of the polemical discourse surrounding figures of unregulatable excess shows that a project of normative regulation via sexuality was begun in the sixteenth century.

At that time, Shi'a jurists were intent on controlling the religious and sexual practices of the population, and they instituted through the writing of ethical treatises and manuals of sovereignty the kinds of behaviors (namely, those of heteronormative subjects) that would reproduce the sexuality of marriage uncontaminated by any supplementary excess. Sufism and the practice of hypnotic boy gazing, wherein the practitioner stares at a lovely youth until achieving transcendence, were gaining ground as a popular spiritual competitor to official religion. By the end of the seventeenth century, the political balance had tipped so steeply in favor of the state religion that, in the guise of a morals campaign, Shah Sultan Husayn could issue decree after decree announcing the rule of Shar'i as interpreted by the conservative clericy.

This landscape of sexual regulation expanded to such an extent that the mere rumor of lesbian sexuality inspired both a semipublic masculinist satire and forced the separation of the two female companions narrated in the melancholy pilgrim's tale that Babayan retrieves for our consideration. When read against the background of a political battle for hegemony and resistance to heteroglossia, such an example of a legible lesbian threat (or anxiety concerning such a threat) poses an epistemological problem for the queer historiography we inherit. In the context of Foucault's schematic distinction between an Eastern *ars erotica* and a Western social mechanism of regulation through the production of subjects who are endowed with sexuality and legible according to the categories of normative classification, the opposition of Sufi boy gazing to heterosexual marriage in emulation of the prophet suddenly complicates the caricature of the East that is so productive for Foucault's argument. Instead, we find that in sixteenth- and seventeenth-century Safavi court culture and public policy, procreative, consummated heterosexual marriage assumes importance because it can be upheld as an institution secured by the subjects of gender.

The interrelations of heterosexual marriage and the threats to that marriage that are constituted by celibacy and boy gazing suggest a number of possible modifications of Foucault's historical narrative, but beyond that Sufi excess could be seen in its very inaction. The historical transformation of Sufism provides the framework of what appears to be a secularization of the sacred simultaneous with a sacralization of the heteronormative family. To quote Babayan, "Within Sufi contexts, celibacy and boy gazing signified the sacred, but Shi'i polemics came to cast the two practices as contradicting Muhammad's teachings and hence God's will. Sexual activity within matrimony—not abstinence and celibacy—became sacred." The Sufi sacred, like Sufi sexuality, constituted an unregulated excess chiefly because its mode of intelligibility revolved around a single mark of distinction (youth) and not around consolidated subject positions—hence, the necessity to police the border of the beard, for youths turn into men, whose sexual inaction converts into spiritual action or unity with God. Mystical union with God, like the exquisite cultivation of the *ars erotica,* transforms the participant but cannot produce the socially regulatable, reproductively intelligible citizen or subject. Marriage, on the other hand, offers a worldly path to God because the distinction of gender (unlike youths, women will not turn into men) secures a secular and juridical subject that is produced in and by man's law.

Further, if the Shiʻa clergy are forced to include heterosexual marital union as both normative and ideal within the divine order, then this material suggests that an historical shift may be afoot. Same-sex desire, acts and inaction, are problems to be disciplined, regulated, and reformed precisely because homoerotic religious practices sublimate the worldly order and thus threaten to dispossess the sovereign of his divine sanction. The identity secured by these erotic acts is seditious and theologically counterhegemonic. According to Babayan, "Once celibacy, gazing, and same-sex friendships within Sufism had signified the sacred, but the clergy, intent on redrawing the boundary between the sacred and the sexual, preached that these practices contradicted Muhammad's teachings and hence God's will. Sexual activity was limited to matrimony." Given this imperative to consolidate political and theological hegemony by instituting heterosexuality as a sacred norm, it is entirely plausible that the mourning Isfahani widow who was stricken with guilt by the resurgence of her youthful lesbian love would choose to figure her passion by referencing the Sufi action of inaction and through a rhetoric of lovesickness and fainting. As Babayan persuasively suggests, the Isfahani widow takes up these "Sufi" signs to write a legibly lesbian desire into a heterosexual pilgrimage. In such a densely woven text, the distinction between acts and identities seems far less important than the psychic writing of hysteria, a poetic practice that makes signs of bodily postures while attesting to the tension of competing erotic logics that both form and thwart desire.

One last observation in this connection: in *Rethinking Islam: Common Questions, Uncommon Answers,* Mohammed Arkoun suggests that a major obstacle to the progress of modern secularization in contemporary Islamic cultures and states derives from what he calls a sacralization of kinship that is fundamental to the structure of the family.[9] Arkoun mounts this argument in the service of a progressive project that clearly has a feminist dimension. However, one might wonder if the example of Savafi society (in its normative identification with Sufism and sodomy as the necessarily repudiated ground of married life) might also contest Arkoun's claim for the sacralization of kinship, both as an historical fact and as a structuring obstacle to modernity. Babayan's reading of the Isfahani women's prayer for penetrating husbands offers an alternative to a conventional understanding of the prayer as a fertility ritual. It would seem to suggest that the sacralization of kinship is only an appearance that masks the complex economy of identification and disavowal that subtends the normative genders[50] newly constituted through what we could view as a secularization of the sacred. If this hypothesis proves convincing, it stands to reconfigure a staggering set of assumptions regarding the "tradition" of women's folk practices and customs, but a perhaps more far-reaching implication of Babayan's research lies in the complication of the naturalization of heterosexuality that is assumed to underlie a "traditional" sacralization of kinship. If heterosexual marriage had to be instituted as a corrective to the political threat posed by Sufi sexuality and perhaps Sufi homosexuality, then the traditional nature of heterosexual kinship in the Islamicate world might be rethought as the effect of a collusion among modern statecraft, clerical authority, and Sufi populism.

When one complicates the picture of perception and imagined meaning of an action or inaction by situating the juridical and theological literature on sexuality in its political frame, acts and identities become blurred. I can most clearly make this claim by referring to Leslie Pierce's work on the institution of vice codes where none had held before.[10] Pierce extends Babayan's excavation of normative regulation in sixteenth-century Iran to the Ottoman expansion of criminality in Aintab with the institution of a new moral code. Again, the juridical model of law acts as a productive incitement to adopt a highly stylized subject position via the category of sexual deviance. Pierce argues that while this "politicization of sexual behavior" sought to achieve an unprecedented level of moral and cultural homogeneity, her case study of Aintab reveals a diverse array of negotiations with the normative pressure of the law as well as a social activity that seems to generate discrete subjective distinctions (for instance, between those who police their neighbors and those who must deny accusations in court). As Pierce describes, interactions between the sexes became objects of intensive police scrutiny, and members of the local community were employed to enforce through elaborate surveillance the purview of the foreign moral code. In effect, the law proliferated its norms through the sudden proximity of all to criminality. The entire populace became suspect, and their normative claims and identification were pursued in this intimacy with deviance.

As I have hoped to show in these short summaries, arguments for autochthonous traditional kinship and sexual norms and practices will have to contend with historical research like that of the contributors. The belief that a Mediterranean model governs contemporary homoerotic investments in an unbroken chain since the classical period has been dealt a mortal blow by historians who are even now proving that the sexual practices of the region have been and continue to be the product of a complex disciplinary and regulative industry.

ANAL ECONOMIES

Najmabadi returns to some of this terrain in her survey of what she calls the second stream of sexuality studies, within which historical studies of premodern cultures fall into two camps—one that understands prohibition via the typology *homo/hetero* and one that understands prohibition via same-sex acts. Here Najmabadi begins to radically distinguish nineteenth-century Iran from the picture of the modern state that is central to Foucault's analysis, for unlike its European contemporary Qajar Iran did not generate the centralizing regulations that are associated with industrial capital. Discipline and regulation must take a different form. Consequently, the study of sexual commandment requires the development of a different analytic strategy. Najmabadi turns not to scientific manuals on sexual type. It appears that the medical literature did not produce a counterpart to Krafft-Ebbing, though she cautions that more research must be done. Instead, she turns to the nineteenth-century Islamicate equivalent of the libertine literature of the Middle Ages, Vali Khan's "An Essay on Debauchery." Reading Iranian modernity via an *ars erotica* tradition, she asks how commandment was translated, repeated, and invested.

Uncovering a hierarchy of organ pleasures in Vali Khan, Najmabadi exposes pleasures that are not only acts and not fully an identity. This field of desire and pleasure is imperceptible to any scholarship that focuses exclusively on counting gendered acts without foregrounding its own conceptual framework. Corroborating the libertine's view of anal pleasures but in reverse, the literature of the clerics and the law takes a dim view of anal intercourse whether within or outside of marriage. Thus, in the clerical literature the anus is more prohibited than the adulterous vagina, and the male anus is most prohibited of all. Prohibition of profane bodily orifices reveals a descending scale of the sacred, where the profane male anus is the most sacrosanct because pious masculine virility represents the highest ideal. Does the scale of profane and increasingly inviolable orifices reveal merely the sacralization of the heteronormative? Or does the model of masculinity have other sources and origins? Why would the clerics raise up a normativity that does not derive from the religious domain? And if Najmabadi is right to suppose, on the strength of textual proofs, that anal intercourse with a woman, even one's wife, is dangerously suggestive of the same act with a man, is this the paranoid legacy of that earlier transformation of state power and family life that Babayan sketches for us in sixteenth-century Iran, where the Shi'a clerics prohibit Sufi sexuality on the grounds of its nonprocreativity? In short, is the nineteenth-century hierarchy of the anus, which became a commandment to heteronormative procreativity, a residue of a prior clerical disciplinary regime? Is this modern anality a resistant relic of a disciplinary regime begun three centuries before? What figure of historical time can account for this belated and haunting reconstruction of a prior political struggle? Can we read the inscription and investment of the body as a trace of a prior erasure that lingers in the form of subtle sublimation or incomplete translation?

I want to second Najmabadi's striking resolution to the emerging picture of sexual and gender diversity in her discussion—that "[t]he search for one logic of structuring hierarchies may obscure the contingent intersection of several webs of meaning that have mapped out the hierarchy of body parts and associated pleasures and prohibitions." This statement is very much in keeping with the complication of epistemic series that we suggest today on the authority of an idea presented but not pursued by Foucault. Haunting—a sublimated version of a lost tradition—may be a model for understanding attitudes toward anal eroticism that are found in the archive.

EPISTEMOLOGY OF THE INSULT

These considerations offer haunting as a figure for the archive, for the production of knowledge on the authority of the archive, and for the simultaneously sedimented and embroidered character of regulation we see emerging in the various analyses of legal and theological institutions. We might extend this figure beyond the historical model sketched here by reflecting on the textual dimension of the archive as well. Frédéric Lagrange (chapter 5) proposes that we consider the performative and rhetorical possibilities of a genre of the *adab* tradition for the implication of identity that it puts in play. In the conclusion to "The Obscenity of the Vizier," Lagrange sets out the central challenge of queer Middle East studies when he asks how a tenth-century male subject might resolve the contradiction of a norm that includes attraction to youth, with a strong dichotomy between two types of homoerotic relation. The answer he offers pits an ideal against a right by proposing "that occasional and discrete affairs with young men fit into or indeed reinforce masculinity, but that the affirmation of a right to this kind of relationship or even of its repeated evocation (implying a suspicious interest, a preference, or possibly even an exclusive preference) takes the author dangerously close to the limit." Although it might be argued that rights can come to figure as ideals, Lagrange's essay proposes a right that is figurable in its absence through the genre of insult and only through the further implication that the reviled and insulted have no right to that of which they have become the sign. Brilliantly seizing on the insult as the rhetorical form that is equipped to reveal this paradox of simultaneous inscription and erasure (what some critics would call a fetishism),[11] Lagrange attempts to forge a theory of ritual and transgression from generic criticism, itself indebted to a language of typologies. He argues that the form of the insult provides the "idea of homosexuality based on preference of gender and not role," an idea that is, according to this convention of generic studies of Arabic literature, inexpressible and historically inarticulable. Thus, homosexual desire that is not shaped by the distinction passive and active and is not framed by pederastic mentorship "finds its expression in the insult." For the insult is not merely the mode of expression of unthinkable desire; it is credited with "constructing the field of the homosexual." What, then, do we know of the insult? How might it be held to avow what it disavows? What rhetorical strategies of reading should we invoke to separate the stigmatization from the emergent image of a love that never speaks at all, let alone constitutes itself in the mode of rights? What is revealed by and in the insult? Before turning to the theoretical implications of Lagrange's dense and provocative work, we might begin to consider what we know of the insult with a few lines from a distinctly modern perspective the better to situate our own practice of queer scholarship.

KNOWING NO BAD LANGUAGE

But as he knew no bad language, he had called him all the names of common objects that he could think of, and had screamed: "You lamp! You towel! You plate!" and so on.[12]

The first human who hurled an *insult* instead of a stone was the founder of civilization.[13]

Between civilization (a product of mediation and of the sublimation of murderous impulses) and ignorance or lack, we find ourselves in a zone that is familiar to the scholar of sexuality who seeks to complicate the received wisdom of Western queer studies by extending the analysis of sexuality into the premodern and well beyond the occident. Amply equipped with cautions to avoid the pitfalls of anachronism and homophobia, such work struggles to conceptualize same-sex desire in modes that are not already mediated by a modern deployment of sexuality that claims for sex the status of a truth to be verified transhistorically and everywhere. On the one side lies the risk of projecting simultaneously into the past and across the globe a similitude—a desire identical to the one that drives our own impulses and normatively frames, even through opposition, our emancipatory aspirations. At a close remove, we find the equal risk of obliterating a legible but not quite translatable desire, especially when encountered in the archive, for fear of this very risk of projection. Between, on the one hand, the sublimation of impulse and the normative structure that all sublimations imply and, on the other, the imperfect mastery of an individualized but ritual exercise of language and desire, "queering" as a diverse, heterogeneous set of intellectual endeavors finds its common place if not a common purpose.

In Freud's example of the child's invective, the insult is legible to us even without a "proper" reference, for we understand the child's speech ("You lamp! You towel! You plate!") as a catechresis of the common object put to abusive purpose. The convention is easily read. The emotions are if not transparent then at least evocative, and the desire of the speaker can be registered despite his incompletely disciplined and not quite regulated speech. Cursing without knowing how suggests that the form can work without a subject of mastery and that when one curses one may not know what one says even in the throes of passionate rebuke. The unsovereign subject who hurls household goods as specific epithets does not even know language "properly" before knowing that he curses, for there is an unconscious dimension to the insult even as it vehiculates a host of disciplinary sanctions and prohibitions. As a figure for knowledge that is not yet possessed of its sovereign right to confess and determine its own claims for truth, we might see in the situation of "possessing no bad language" the condition to which our scholarly evocations of homosexual desire in premodern and non-Western social forms are relegated.

Dispossessed of the key terms *hetero-* and *homosexual* and yet endowed with scientific erudition and trained in the arts of reading, this lack of an idiom for homosexual desire in the past[14] is, many would argue, essentially linked to heterosexuality. Even today, it is caught up in the entanglements of the sacred and the profane. Even in the West, such a conditioning lack has the perverse effect of relegating "queering" endeavors to a paraleptic formulation of knowledge where the researcher gathers his cautions to himself in familiar formulations, such as "without falling into the trap of an ahistorical essentialism" or "needless to say, this apparently homosexual desire does not give rise to homosexual identity." In this sense, the knowledge produced under the sign of queer studies must go without its certainties into speculative and theoretical reflections that also hold the promise of that "different economy of bodies and pleasures" that Foucault foresaw without telling us how to reach it.

To turn a stone into a word is a magical act—a sublimation that translates impulse, drive, or unmediated pleasure into a socially valued gratification. Each sublimating detour yields another as the transubstantiation of stones to words reworks the conditions of relation, transforming passions one after another beyond reckoning to train desire on another satisfaction. Sublimating rage, the "first human" of the fictional scene originates a narrative, founds a civilization through an impossible temporal sleight of hand for before disciplining the other, and thereby regulating the world, he disciplines himself. Civilization before civilization, the logic of founding finds result before the cause. In another context, Freud argues that sublimation that renounces lusts of all kinds but primarily those satisfactions that seem to hold at least the vestige of homosocial and homoerotic play (such as micturation on the fire) lifts humans above other animals and carries them toward an ideal.[15] As we pursue Frédéric Lagrange's argument for the disclosure of the field of the homosexual through the rhetorical detours of the insult and the phobic homosociality that such detours seem to command, let us keep in mind Freud's fable of normative sublimation and renunciation at the foundation. When a belle-lettrist such as al-Tawhidi hurls the insult because he cannot hurl the stone, he sublimates his rage the better to save an ideal. But what if this salvation operation were a kind of gratuitous foundation that includes among its perhaps unconscious aims the preservation of a gender hierarchy that folds males into the abject ranks of women and children?

UNTRANSLATABLE

> We might understand queerness as that which normativity—in this case, a cultural normativity—must reject or conceal in order to exist. Its presence is always palpable in the incongruities, excesses, or anxieties of normative discourse, but it is only exceptionally given expression, and this only at the margins.[16]

The field of Spanish peninsular studies (cited several times in this volume) invites us to hear queerness as a secret that whispers in the margins of cultural normativity—a norm that appears to gather its force precisely where it has banished its most sustaining resource. A secret loudly denounced and a mystery concealed in the light of day, queerness is charged with the burden of resistance, which we learn from Foucault to be an internal deformation of power. It is the one housed in the very systems of discipline and regulation that are designed to deny it life. Whether excess or anxiety, something within the norm divides the norm, and at its source for *Queer Iberia,* and so many similar interventions into the fields that we inherit, conceives the queer as a noise or buzz in the machine, one that only exceptionally becomes an "expression." Despite this avowedly liberatory model of the queer, it is not so easy even for queer theorists to reconcile themselves to queer resistance when it breaks out in unwelcome ways. As Rouhi shows in her discussion of the problem of translation posed by the title of *Queer Iberia*, the problem is eventually resolved by allowing the English word to linger as a failed translation that is accused of cultural imperialism. This scandal of translation is another version of the injunction against mixed productions that seems to shadow studies of gay and lesbian figuration in the form of a warning to avoid anachronistic projection and that, at least in the case of this title, may reveal more about fears of gay dissemination than any actual threat of gay hegemony.

Walking a fine line between the purism of the constructivist typological imperative and the historically flattening prospect of a gay-male essentialism, Lagrange also approaches the unavowable homosexuality of the tenth century via a paradox of secrecy "expressed at the margin" when he tells us that the contours of a field of homosexuality are disclosed in the paralepsis of the insult, which says it but says that it is not *it* that says it: "What is important is that the insult may accidentally construct what it denounces: it may build this field of homosexuality, which remains an unthought-of in theory." These possibilities—that one could insult another by writing that the other is an effeminate passive pederast and by accusing him of being deeply emasculated (with an accumulation of the feminine attributes, such as soft, lazy, talkative, indiscrete, passive in sex, and intemperate when roused)—produce and provide a field of nascent, faintly possible homosexuality constructed through the availability of profanation. But what of the "field" of homosexuality?

I would contend that this line of argument is itself unable to guarantee the historicist and methodological cautions of the author. If there is a field of homosexual desire and identity (what Lagrange calls "the uniqueness of a man who is drawn to individuals of his same constructed gender) rather than a more loosely organized *ars erotica* and if this identity or uniqueness is made available through the social consensus that is implied in the themes of emasculation and virility via the dichotomy passive/active but embroidered through other marks of a gendered difference, then it is a ghostly presence that can always disappear in disavowal. If homosexual preference is only a potentiality of rhetoric, then it is always unstable. This instability of the never articulated offers no promise of ever repeating it, and for this reason, while derogation does construct its field, it lies open to other risks. A poem lamenting the appearance of the crow's wing on the beloved's cheek can signal both the conventional notes to be played but not taken for love's true letter *and* the possibility of a perverse reading, and this possibility hides within the very field of its own derogation. According to Lagrange's reading, there could be no prospect of emasculating insult without the conditioning possibility of homosexual desire, but this possibility cannot summon its own repetition or call for its own articulation.

Such a paradox suggests two amendments to the reading of the archive of invective and social power. The first concerns the proliferation of positions, personae, dispositions, genders, and other identities across the many terms we find in Lagrange. Are there so many simply because the modern deployment of sexuality has not subjected an archive of positions and dispositions to its normative imperatives, as a cultural constructivist might argue? How do we understand the hierarchy of gender and role that is played out in the proliferation of sexual types for which there are so many distinguishing names? How might this complexity of names fluctuate with historical changes? I note Lagrange's sensitivity to the historical shifts of terms, as when he tells us that *ma'bun* replaces *hulaki* after the Umayyad period. But the speculative argument he makes—about a same-sex gender preference that is based on a gender system of masculinity versus effeminacy wherein women do not figure—would need to organize the larger case of sexual types and translate them into their "gender" equivalents. Gender of object choice appears insufficient to account for the complexity of identities in play. It is useful to recall Najmabadi's caution to avoid forcing a univocal structure on a field of evidence where several differing and even opposing logics seem to coexist. Nonetheless, if we are to locate a desire based on *gender of object choice* in the tenth century, we will need further corroboration from the archive or to conduct a comparative analysis that follows the beloved, male and female, through a number of settings.

This taxonomic concern leads to a further problem with the effort to produce the "homosexual field" out of historical material for which there may be no heterosexual field either. It would seem that a picture of the social norms organizing this premodern world would have to provide some account of how gender, sexuality, and the idealized hierarchy of social values are bound together. To anchor this problem, let us consider the question of what may be gender as it emerges within the example of al-Tawhidi and his time. Early in his argument, Lagrange characterizes the place of homoeros in tenth-century court culture by locating it within the deployment of masculinity. On the basis of archival discourses about effeminacy, he argues for the salience of effeminacy as a marker of the homosexual desire that he is tracking. This emphasis on effeminacy as a marker is weighed against a courtly practice of poetic praise for androgeny, specifically the youth of the *amrad* or beardless boy beloved. Claiming that youth's beauty was *ungendered* in the classical Arabic literary tradition, Lagrange writes, "What is turned into an object of desire is not extreme virility but rather its timid blossoming under an androgynous surface." Yet Lagrange derives the possibility of homosexuality in the text from his coupling of effeminacy with homosexuality and goes on to suggest that to accuse the active partner of effeminacy amounts to a shadowy perception of homosexuality. For Lagrange, feminization via insult implies that a feminized masculinity could be imagined within the confines of the sexual regime at hand. This reading of al-Tawhidi's insult suggests that he seizes on a notion of effeminate homosexual preference without yet having the name for it. It is a name that we can confer in hindsight—a bit like saying that he says, "You towel!"

Yet to argue that under the androgynous surface of the *amrad* lies concealed the real object of desire would require an argument that gender is paramount—that the desire for androgynous boys is a desire for effeminate boys and not for androgeny. Inasmuch as all men are supposed to desire to become ideal active penetrating men, in what way does the not yet achieved, not yet masculine, effeminate masculinity of the adolescent boy afford either lover or beloved access to the ideal if not precisely by his failure to be that penetrating man and in his role as the passive actor? It would be difficult to distinguish gender from role in the coitus at hand. What organizes the appearance of multiplicity of the sexual regime if not the very ideal called forth in the insult? All this bad language graphically surrounds the one who is absent. A third-person masculine ideal cannot be *luti* (active), *majin* (rake), *mukhannath* (effeminate), *ma'bun* (passive), *mu'ajar* (whore), or *amrad* (ephebe). What may lie under the surface of the *amrad* may not be *his* masculinity but the absent ideal masculinity of the nameless active man who cannot be contained in the word *luti*. For this reason, neither the term *androgeny* nor *masculinity* is sufficient to anchor gender as the master term of what may not be a system or univocal logic at all.

The second amendment that I suggest also concerns the ways that we might conceptualize a desire that Lagrange so delicately describes in terms of linkage, continuity, and perception but that he gives away by bringing homosexual desire to gender: "As this study reveals, it seems unimaginable to me to deny the perception of a link between active and passive roles within male homosexuality and therefore of a feeling of uniqueness in a man who is drawn to individuals of his same constructed gender, whatever the nature of his practices within the framework of this relationship." The end of this formulation involves an odd return to the notion of gender sameness, even though the argument tends toward gender difference—through distinguishing the beardless boy from his older male lover, effeminate youths (male *and* female) from adults, coquette from serious man, and even those who write court poetry from those who do not. All these differences attest to gender's inability to capture the homosexual imagination—which is over and over again presented in the material that Lagrange collects as languorous, bawdy, salacious, hedonistic, and lingering over the most delicate perfumed detail and which he says shows in negative form the possibility of exclusively homosexual desire. Gender gets us no further as a description of the desire at hand than do terms like *hetero-* and *homosexual* (the categories of normative discipline within the deployment of sexuality) key to the modern. If one is to really theorize the homosexual desire that lies somewhere between al-Tawhidi's invective and Ibn Abbad's abjection, we must analyze the constructions not of homosexuals but of the fantasies and the identifications that give rise to a desire that is described impossible and that calls to us moderns as homosexual. This would lead us to exactly the texts that Lagrange engages—the poetry and prose of a pleasurable exercise, the insult as revenge, the figure of the *majin*, and the gratuitous impudence that he enables through his pranks in his listeners. This cultural field of the jest carries within it a wildness that proliferates gendered positions and personas (Lagrange lists six forms of "homosexual persons"—*muhannath, luti, ma'bun, hulaqi, mu'ajir*, and *amrad*) as a counterdiscourse to that of masculine idealization. The importance of this more extended field of gendered differences lies in the interdependence of homophobia with a denunciation of a kind of effeminacy that does not include women.

Is it possible to read the insult as the taking-place of the homosexual field without reinscribing masculinity as a particular type of heteronormative male? What is the nature of the fantasy that conditions the production of pleasure via insult? What does it conserve, and what does it foreclose as the impossible and unavowable? According to Lagrange,

[Abu Hayyan] al-Tawhidi develops a discourse arguing the legitimacy of his composition of a *kitab* that is entirely dedicated to a satire on two people. What the author attempts to justify is not simply the denunciation of the vices of a prince whose true nature no one dares expose. Abu Hayyan's justification is in fact threefold. First, he sets out to define his project in relation to the classical poetic genre of the *hija* (libel). Second, he seeks to elaborate a moral justification for writing a work based on insult. Finally, he wants to situate himself in a certain literary continuity, even though his work could be seen as the founding of a new genre. Every creation of the heart of the *adab* has to be camouflaged through its location in a preexisting literary movement, a tradition through which one could award oneself predecessors, thereby guaranteeing for oneself a sort of generic *isnad*. Abu Hayyan knows that his enterprise is risqué and reprehensible. Certainly, the rhetorical excesses of invective are tolerated for the same reason that the positive presentation of transgression is tolerated in poetry: in both cases, the excess is ritual.

Given the extreme care with which genre is weighed by al-Tawhidi, it is no stretch to understand the ritual of insult (in his text and generally for the culture of this literary convention) as engaged in the poetics of sublimation, a particular play of fantasy that evaporates its material cause to secure an ideal.

This sublimating activity of idealization can extend itself to obscenity as well. Commenting on a similar use of vulgarity in medieval French courtly love poetry, the psychoanalytic thinker Jacques Lacan offers this observation of the synergy of the insult with the sublimating imagination: "the crudest of sexual games can be the object of a poem without for that reason losing its sublimating goal. . . . On the level of derision, we find the structure of emptiness at the core, around which is articulated that by means of which desire is in the end sublimated."[17] Obscenity can become the source and center of an inventive practice that deflects desire from an immediate but unrealizable satisfaction (sleeping with the high-born lady, destroying the false Ibn Abbad, replacing the undeserving with the worthy, securing

one's literary fame) to turn it back to the assertion of an idealization, which is, in the case of al-Tawhidi, a reinsistance on a masculinity for which avowal of same-sex desire and love is impossible. Further, the ideal prince, who sets the standard against
which the vile Ibn Abbad is measured and found so wanting, is
also caught in the detour of the paraleptic structure—for is it not
the case that al-Tawhidi also attacks the false status of Ibn
Abbad's station in life, which can be reached by the unworthy?
It seems that al-Tawhidi's insult envisions a triumphant masculine worthiness that leaves very little margin for difference of
any kind.

On the subject of idealization, Lacan argues that the filthiest
language can create an image which will provide the means of a
renewed ideal, endowed with the perverse ability to rob the subject of yet another satisfaction. Thus, obscenity creatively implies or generates the ideal, for the sublimation of desire that is
entailed by the war of words kills desire by finding it another
form that is sublimated, conceptual, linguistic, or idealized. For
this reason, insult, invective, and obscenity are never far from
the scene of idealization. Here, we might recall the proximity of
high and low and of sacred and profane as an attribute of so-
called primal words.[18] If the curse of invective poetry works by
invoking the most taboo and if it is possible to curse without
sovereign knowledge of the categories in play, what does the
practice of vulgar derogation tell us about the social consensus
and normative practices that surround and support the production of such profane images? How might the practice of low
speech reaffirm the high ideal? Does the unmasterable practice
of invective always risk the invention of new ideals and new objects of worthiness and desire? And if so, what new ideals or
norms come into view when the unspeakable is so spectacularly
visible? Insult and praise and loathing and admiration are inti-
mates, just as defamation has as its mirror image "the ideal *fama*
that eludes the speaker."[19] As Lacan reminds us, the mirror—of
true telling, of things as they ought to be—is a narcissistic imaginary and can signify as well a moral limit that cannot be

crossed.[20] Yet the moral limit approached by invective truth telling is a limit dangerously crossed by the same practice. While low speech may well uphold the ideal, it cannot master itself and cannot guarantee that its own practice may not give rise to other truths and other images.

We might rephrase a crucial statement from these same pages to read "what needs to be justified is not simply the secondary benefits that individuals might derive from their insults (works) but the originary possibility of a function like the invective (poetic) function in the form of a structure within a social consensus."[21] Poetry miraculates an ideal from out of the empty images of profane desire, and to this end, the conventions of courtly love offer a picture of a social consensus encircling its ideal (the lady, Christian devotion, chastity), which is itself located at the origin of a "moral code, including a whole series of modes of behavior, of loyalties, measures, services, and exemplary forms of conduct." The profane exception slides behind the newly sublimated desire (ground of idealization) with the result that a social norm materializes where there had been only "the crudest of sexual games." What Lacan's brief discursus on courtly love offers is not a model of repressed and taboo desire but rather a psychoanalytic version of a mechanism of translation that sutures social consensus beyond the aims and intents of any individual subject. Like Lagrange's intuition that the insult casts in legible relief the contours of an unthinkable identity, the poetic function of bawdy courtly verse demonstrates the translative powers of derogation and abjection when, as in Lacan's example, the poet devotes his poem to his refusal to fulfill his lady's demand that he put his mouth to her "trumpet." There follows an explicit description of his disgust with female genitalia and an attempt to win credit for his refusal to succumb to a foul challenge that violates the conventions and morals of courtly love. The difference between the courtly love poem of this French medieval tradition and the libertine genre of classical Arabic letters is that the ideal is not a beautiful lady kept ineffably at bay but a man who will not be penetrated and who thereby lives up to his social station as a prince. Can this model of the empty and absent sacred generation of so many profane multiplicities describe the homoerotic imagination at work in the accusation of *ubna*? Can the labor of sublimation install a legibly homosexual potential where the culture cannot name it? Yes, but with a further refinement.

RAILING

To rail at you is to be forced to put up with you away from your misdeeds, even though you derive all of your power from your miserliness. To know you is a dishonor. To break with you is a blessing. Your name is an insult, your execution an offering of worship.[22]

Let us consider again the disregard inherent in the paralepsis suggested by Lagrange: "I do not say what I say" may be understood as "I know very well that I say this, but even so, what a rapture of revenge!" Paralepsis attempts to ward off guilt through a rhetorical move that looks very much like the superstitious disavowal of a fetishist, as the paraleptic assertion magically claims that it disavows what it is in the process of constructing.[23] This rhetorical shiftiness cannot guarantee the certainty of what is half-alleged, and like all magical invocations it threatens to contaminate the very instance of its invocation. Paralepsis risks staining speaker and listener with the trivial, irrelevant, or slanderous, and so this "prophylactic system" (which for at least one psychoanalytic thinker, Octave Mannoni, constitutes the fetishist's disavowal) swears itself to the proliferation of false or magical proofs in the form of testimonies to the thing that the speaker-fetishist is not saying. In the psychoanalytic register, the rhetoric of fetishistic envy works something like this. Gripped with jealousy, the subject recoils from the presentiment of his own deficiency and produces a magical resolution to the imminent threat to himself and to a governing ideal. He produces a fantasy to cover over the risk of losing what is for him the integrity of a world of value. Typically, psychoanalytic critics will speak of fetishism as the result of a clash between a social convention of gender difference and an individual idiosyncratic organization of value and desire that does not conform to gender norms. In the classical texts of psychoanalysis, this castration crisis of the fetishist arises in the male child when he refuses to accept the "fact" of female gender. His refusal protects the idealization of the feminine and accords her the power of a substitute object, the fetish, which then inaugurates a "cultural" regime of signs, memories, objects, acts, and identities that are not in lock step with the dictates of a "reality." Al-Tawhidi's elaboration of a world of the insult, through the sublimative economy of the word, resembles in no small measure this refusal to accord to the vizier the "reality" of his status and instead asserts a counterreality of insufficiency, degradation, and lack. It would be too easy and too anachronistic to accuse al-Tawhidi of projecting a secret homosexual desire onto his object of loathing. Instead, Lagrange offers an economy of envy and ideal that fortuitously engenders an entirely new potentiality of desire.

Lagrange supplies us with the source of al-Tawhidi's resentment in his failure to rise within the hierarchy of writing, bureaucracy, and repute that was well manipulated by Ibn 'Abbad. It comes as no surprise that the idée fixe of al-Tawhidi's overinvestment in the two viziers should mirror the very source of his rage. The accusation of *ubna* or passive and effeminate homosexuality that he levels at those of higher station reflects what the psychoanalyst also finds at the source of fetishism—namely, "a system of protection against castration."

I want to move from this all too brief invocation of the fetish to an examination of another species of fetishism—one that is systematically worked through the idea of renunciation, which might serve as a surrogate for insult. In *The Psychic Life of Power: Theories in Subjection,* Judith Butler argues that gender performance constitutes gender through a set of disavowed at-

tachments that are held to be "unperformable" because to perform these gender acts (to be guilty of *ubna*) would amount to
becoming abjectly illegible: "Heterosexualized genders form
themselves through renouncing the possibility of homosexuality,
a foreclosure that produces both a field of heterosexual objects
and a domain of those whom it would be impossible to love."[24]
What is sexually unperformable becomes so through simultaneous renunciation and identification with the act of renouncing. The sexually unperformable is performed as gender identification through a set of renounced possibilities and attributes at
the emptied center of a continued effort to render them unperformable and to banish them without feeling. If the virility of
male gender attempts to secure itself by means of the sexually
unperformable (namely, through the taboo on *ubna*), this masculinity of acts identifies itself by and through the act that it refuses to perform. But it is also bound to return to the disavowal
of the act that it refuses.

In light of this cultural production of what Butler calls "heterosexual melancholy" (literary conventions of lamentation),
the regret that attends first bloom of the *amrad*'s beard could be
understood as a cultural practice of masculine heterosexual performance. As Butler puts it, "the straight man becomes the man
he 'never' loved and 'never' grieved." Via the analysis of heterosexual melancholia, I am suggesting that masculine performance
within the system of two distinct types of homoerotic relation
enacts a disavowal that inscribes an incoherence at the heart of
its epistemology. It is easily imaginable that the former *amrad*
would simply say yes to a continuation of his relations with his
lover or that pairs of the same type might choose each other. If
multiplicity is key to the scene of sexual type defined by acts,
how do we explain the limits to variation without lapsing into
mere psychological rationalization of the kind demystified in
Rowson's treatment of the importation theory? If the system derives its coherence from the ultimate exclusion of a terrible type,
how do we analyze the psychosocial mechanism of this choice
and this dynamic of the sexually unperformable?

To the extent that homosexual attachments remain unacknowledged within normative heterosexuality, they are not merely constituted as desires which emerge and subsequently become prohibited; rather these desires are proscribed from the start and when
they do emerge on the far side of the censor, they may well carry
the mark of impossibility with them, performing, as it were, as the
impossible within the possible. This is, then, less a refusal to grieve
than a preemption of grief performed by the absence of cultural
conventions for avowing the loss of homosexual love.[25]

Yet in the Arabic classical tradition, there is a genre or convention for an avowal of homoerotic loss by men for whom
masculinity and perhaps heterosexual love is secured by the
androgyny of youth. These are the poems lamenting the advent
of the *amrad*'s beard, a detestable sign that love must end or
shame begin. The unperformable, according to Lagrange's convincing research and analysis, is also locatable within this poetic
convention and as the impossible. While there may be ways,
there is no right to avow (1) the preference of an adult male for
'ubna and (2) the preference of two adult men for each other.
The very convention of lamentation seems to perform the function of ritual that both Butler and Lagrange contend. The loss of
the *amrad* is the gain of normative masculinity and the infinite
renunciation of homosexual and effeminate identity. It has as its
twin goals the production of normative masculinity and the containing of passive identity (as the unperformable, infinitely renounced, passing youth). Through this logic, youth is the exception that can prove the rule of active masculinity and secure
identity for the latter on the condition that there be an identi-
fiable threshold dividing youth from masculinity. This looks
very much like the condition of fetishism in that it narrativizes a
simultaneous structure of inscription and erasure. But the fetish
also gives rise to what we might call a fetish culture—a series of
sublimations or innovations within the fantasy of fetishism and
a renewed stylization of the subject.[26] By engaging in this work
of imagination, fetishistic sublimation dematerializes its sub-
strate to manufacture another regime of the sign—from the

body to the theater, from one masculinity to several, and from one genre of reproach to a field of jest and libertinage.

PSYCHOANALYSIS AFTER QUEER THEORY

Following Rouhi's suggestion, I earlier proposed translation as a model for this figure of reemergent discipline within the form of power that usurps it. However, translation is not only a path of successful transfer, and it does not always subvert. Translation also transfers by leaving something behind or by failing fully to carry over. Psychoanalysis has attended to the failed translation and to the residue of such failure, resistant to meaning, under the sign of repression.[27] Yet psychoanalytic insight has not always been welcomed by scholars who work in the fields of queer studies, especially when those fields have of necessity wrestled with the epistemological frameworks of their ways of knowing. If I have pressed psychoanalytic reflections into the features of historical analysis undertaken by the contributors to this book, it is because the question of how we come to know what desire has been and what it has meant (politically, institutionally, subjectively, rhetorically, juridically, medically, in folk practices, in literature, in translation, in cultural transmission, in heteroglossia of all kinds) requires us to think historically while also attending to the formation of power in the multiple presents sedimented in our archives and in our attitudes. There are countless other good reasons to invoke psychoanalytic reflection in the context of Middle East sexuality studies, for it offers interpretive purchase on the often unconscious inscription of desire in texts. Queer theory owes many debts to psychoanalysis, and queer Middle East studies share these debts. Queer consciousness derives from a modernity that is unthinkable without psychoanalysis, while the putatively Western notion of psyche (a dubious claim when scrutinized) is by now disseminated everywhere and mutating everywhere.

All these reasons, and more, convince me that our tools of historical and social analysis require refinement in a closer negotiation with psychoanalysis. Notice that I do not argue that psychoanalysis will afford us a technical language or a ready-made tool of analysis. Rather, psychoanalysis is a set of reflections on the very objects of our study—desire, relation, kinship, gender, power. As workers in the field of queer studies, we can bring to the encounter with psychoanalysis, among so many other things, our subtle proofs that systems of classification, taxonomies, and the acts/identities imperative that supports a particular regime of East/West relation in the present are themselves a production of power and regulation.

The notion of desire that we bring to the study of sexuality deserves reconsideration in light of the disciplinary effects of our epistemologies on historiography and social diversity. In addition, the ethical work that queering interventions can undertake demands that the scholar engage critically and analytically with our contemporary thinking about desire, identification, attachments, and repudiation in their many dimensions, including their unconscious ones. In line with the numerous endeavors to think psychoanalytically about desire (many of them from within queer studies), I would like to suggest a few propositions about the relation of Foucault's study of sexual regulation and psychoanalysis. These remarks are of a general nature. I offer them in the spirit of overcoming the kinds of caution that foreclose the reading of desire where alterity is allegedly assured, and I seek to trouble that assurance.

At the beginning of this chapter, I cite Foucault's admonition against producing "histories of mentalities" that take account of the body exclusively through perception, meaning, and value. Against this negative model, he proposes a "'history of bodies' and the manner in which what is most material and most vital in them has been invested." Somewhat against the grain of Foucault's avowed attitude toward psychoanalysis, he offers as a counter to an ideological or positivist historiography a kind of history for which the key terms are *body, matter, vitality,* and *investment.* And he does this knowing that psychoanalysis incessantly reads precisely those bodily investments of energy and materiality in symptoms but not only there. His prescribed object of a historical research that could move beyond anachronistic reiteration of power's alibi (the alibi of the sovereign subject) is a kind of psychoanalytic thinking but one that is turned away from the representation of power and from what he calls "sex-desire" and toward the investment of bodies and pleasures. Here is a characteristically complex disavowal of psychoanalysis from the final pages of *The History of Sexuality*, volume 1:

> We can trace the theoretical effort to reinscribe the thematic of sexuality in the system of law, the symbolic order, and sovereignty. It is to the political credit of psychoanalysis . . . that it regarded with suspicion (and this from its inception, that is, from the moment it broke away from the neuropsychiatry of degenerescence) the irrevocably proliferating aspects which might be contained in these power mechanisms aimed at controlling and administering the everyday life of sexuality: whence the Freudian endeavor (out of reaction no doubt to the great surge of racism that was contemporary with it) to ground sexuality in the law—the law of alliance, tabooed consanguinity, and the Sovereign-Father, in short to surround desire with all the trappings of the old order of power.[28]

Viewed from this ambivalent perspective, the error or blind spot of psychoanalysis consists in the fit between Freud's analysis and sovereign power, which according to Foucault is but a representation or fantasy of power that is dominate in the modern period and actualized via sexuality. As he says, psychoanalysis diagnoses the circuits of power and disentangles itself from the web of the perversion, heredity, degenerescence system by supplying a different logic of desire and transmission. Desire is wrested from the biology of a racial discourse and given over to an unconscious and symbolic organization of the body and its investment with subjectivity. This psychoanalytic understanding of sovereignty as an alibi of the subject is echoed by Foucault as he productively supplements and supersedes the Freudian theory of identification—a matter of unconscious investment of the bodily form. For Foucault, power is analogous to the unconscious but derives its logics not from the subjectivity that it generates but through the disciplinary techniques and regulative functions that are already in play.

Psychoanalysis refuses the fixed sovereignty of the subject via the notion of the unconscious and thereby deforms from within the confines of power and a psychiatric dogma of race and perversion, the contours of the given. This resistance of psychoanalysis to its own origins, which can be indexed in Freud's divergence from Charcot, is not absolute and also serves the ends of the dominant. Nonetheless, psychoanalysis has a key role to play in the resolution of a conflict between an older form of life where power and capital were disseminated according to laws of kinship and alliance and the newly developing modernity of a state governance that takes as its object the zoning of life and death via sexuality and race. This war between an inherited system (what Foucault calls the symbolics of blood) and the newcomer that is a product of so many forces of centralization (the analytics of sex) enlists subjectivity and avowal. It translates Christian confession and the pastoral tradition in the new science: "with psychoanalysis, sexuality gave body and life to the rules of alliance by saturating them with desire." For this reason, a psychoanalysis read through the history of its own development would be an invaluable ally in efforts to understand the historical relation of sexuality, gender, and desire to government, discipline, and regulation.

Can there be a psychoanalysis without investing desire with the antique model of the law as the sovereign father when biopower has already shifted the exercise of power beyond the sovereign and into a territory that with Achilles Mbembe we might call the necropolitical?[29] I want to suggest that it is already underway in many approaches to affect and attachment that engage psychoanalytic thinking but from a perspective that is informed by the denaturalizing work of Foucault and others. What is called for at the present moment is a more overt foregrounding of the key concepts of desire that might be borrowed from the psychoanalytic register and reworked to produce a new set of reflections about the complex temporalities that we observe and construct in the archive.

In an essay urging scholars to take up the task of examining what he calls the psychosocial basis of life in Islamicate cultures, Mohammed Arkoun writes, "the code of honor in traditional societies is unwritten; it is lived and internalized in the form of habits that order individual and collective behavior. It is not transmitted by theoretical teaching but instead reproduced through daily life in all its formal, ritual, social and symbolic complexity."[30] This comes close to what I am advocating today—namely, a study of the psychic and social investment of the body in Middle Eastern cultures. When Najmabadi investigates the hierarchy of the anus via the theoretical texts of a cleric's treatise but also through a bawdy tale and a chronicle of conquests, I think she is in the middle of what is "reproduced through daily life in all its formal, ritual, social and symbolic complexity." What remains a challenge for queer theory is to formulate a set of terms that can organize these investments of the body with an analytic knowledge of the regularization of these commandments.

NOTES

Editors' note: As indicated in the Preface, our authors have revised their original papers in response to discussants' critiques and seminar conversations. Since we decided to include these discussants' remarks as integral and rich contributions to this volume, our discussants revised their critiques as well, prompting even further revisions on the part of both discussants and original authors. In this case, some of Dina Al-Kassim's references to other chapters, especially to that of Frédéric Lagrange (chapter 5), may be based on the original presentations, now revised, while the quoted ideas remain relevant to the discussion. We have decided to publish Al-Kassim's Epilogue in this form, as an important summary of the Radcliffe seminar and contribution to the field of Islamicate Sexuality Studies.

1. I thank the organizers, Kathryn Babayan and Afsahneh Najma-badi, of the original Middle East Studies Association (MESA) panel in November 2001, which inspired the May 2003 Radcliffe Institute for Advanced Study seminar, for the invitation to be involved in this project. It is a testament to their originality that they have been able to draw together a distinguished group of scholars who are working in diverse historical periods to consider the questions at hand. That they sought to include a modernist and a theorist working across these languages and geographies underscores the intellectual generosity and imagination at the source of this unusual encounter.

2. *Premodern Sexualities,* ed. Carla Freccero and Louise Fradenburg, with Lathy Lavezzo (New York: Routledge, 1996), ix–xx.

3. Michel Foucault, *The History of Sexuality,* trans. Robert Hurley (New York: Vintage Books, 1990), 1:152.

4. Two examples of the literary exercise of this model can be found in Greg Mullins, *Colonial Affairs* (Madison: University of Wisconsin Press, 2002), and Jared Hayes, *Queer Nations: Marginal Sexualities in the Maghreb* (Chicago: University of Chicago Press, 2000). For a canonical anthropology where the same gesture is in evidence, see Pierre Bourdieu, *La Domination masculine* (Paris: Seuil, 1998).

5. Joseph Massad, "Re-Orienting Desire: the Gay International and the Arab World," *Public Culture* 14, no. 2 (2002): 361–85.

6. Foucault, *The History of Sexuality,* 1:71.

7. Ibid.

8. For a discussion of the tensions between historicist and determinist reading strategies, see Jean Laplanche's essay "Interpretation between Determinism and Hermeneutics: A Restatement of the Problem," in *Essays on Otherness* (London: Routledge, 1999), 138–65.

9. Mohammed Arkoun, *Rethinking Islam: Common Questions, Uncommon Answers* (Boulder: Westview Press, 1994).

10. Leslie Pierce was a member of the original MESA panel in November 2001. This work can now be found in Leslie Pierce, *Morality Tales: Law and Gender in the Ottoman Court of Aintab* (Berkeley: University of California Press, 2003).

11. For an exploration of this understanding of fetishism, see Michael Taussig, "Maleficium State Fetishism," in *The Nervous System* (New York: Routledge, 2001).

12. Sigmund Freud, "Ratman," in *Three Case Studies* (New York: Collier, 1963), 103.

13. Sigmund Freud, *Civilization and Its Discontents,* ed. James Strachey (New York: Norton, 1969), 132.

14. Histories of sexuality and desire in the past are caught up in the present, as I have been arguing throughout this chapter. This shuttling temporality of a haunting sublimation means that the archive risks being perceived through the ideological lens of presentist concerns, like that of the sodomy/homosexuality dichotomy. The figure of haunting also suggests that traditions (say, of sexual taboo) are constructed, deconstructed, and reconstructed in the many presents that they traverse, such that knowledge becomes accountability to this simultaneously retroactive and proleptic (not paraleptic) relation.

15. We can read in Freud's analysis of the homophobic origin of sublimation the keen observation that the insult and the ideal are closely related and may even be engendered by a repudiated homoeros.

16. *Queer Iberia,* ed. Gregory Hutcheson and Josiah Blackmore (Durham: Duke University Press, 1999) 3.

17. Jacques Lacan, *The Ethics of Psychoanalysis 1959–1960 (Seminar of Jacques Lacan)* (New York: Norton, 1997), 161–63.

18. Sigmund Freud, "The Antithetical Sense of Primal Words" (1910), *Writings on Art and Literature* (Stanford: Stanford University Press, 1997).

19. Ibid.

20. According to Lagrange (chapter 5 in this book), "But the author ceaselessly tries to protect himself against the moral condemnation of his project (from which, however, he will not escape), on the one hand, by references to precedents in the field of *adab* prose and, on the other, by a religious defense making the denunciation of the crimes of the unjust prince appear to be a religious duty."

21. Lacan, *The Ethics of Psychoanalysis,* 145, 161.

22. Frédéric Lagrange, "The Obscenity of the Vizier" (chapter 5 in this volume), appendix 5C.

23. For a discussion of disavowal and fetishism as forms of mythic imagination, see Octave Mannoni, "Je sais bien, mais quand même," in *Clefs pour l'imaginaire ou l'autre scène* (Paris: Seuil, 1985).

24. Judith Butler, *The Psychic Life of Power: Theories in Subjection* (Stanford: Stanford University Press), 146–47.
25. Ibid.
26. Gilles Deleuze, *Foucault* (Minneapolis: University of Minnesota Press, 1988).
27. Most famously, in an 1897 letter to his friend Fliess, Freud defines repression as failed translation.
28. Foucault, *The History of Sexuality,* 1:150.
29. Achilles Mbembe, "Necropolitics," *Public Culture* 15, no. 1 (2003): 11–40.
30. Mohammed Arkoun, *Rethinking Islam: Common Questions, Uncommon Answers,* trans. and ed. Robert D. Lee, Westview Press, 1994, p. 118.

Bibliography

Abraham, Nicolas, and Maria Torok. *The Shell and the Kernel: Renewals of Psychoanalysis,* Vol. 1. Edited, translated, and introduced by Nicholas T. Rand. Chicago: University of Chicago Press, 1994.

Abu Nuwas. *Diwan.* Vol. 4, edited by Gregor Schoeler. Wiesbaden: Franz Steiner, 1982.

Abu Shama. *Tarajim rijal al-qarnayn al-sadis wa-l-sabiʿ.* Edited by Muhammad al-Kawthari. Cairo: Dar al-Kutub al-ʿIlmiyya, 1947.

Alexander, M. Jacqui. *Pedagogies of Crossing: Meditations on Feminism, Sexual Politics, Memory, and the Sacred.* Durham Duke University Press, 2005.

Alf layla wa layla [One thousand and one nights]. Edited by Muhsin Mahdi. 4 vols. Leiden: Brill, 1984.

Amer, Sahar. "Lesbian Sex and the Military: From the Medieval Arabic Tradition to French Literature." In *Same Sex Love and Desire among Women in the Middle Ages,* edited by Francesca Canadé Sautman and Pamela Sheingorn, 179–98. New York: Palgrave, 2001.

Anderson, Jon W. "Social Structure and the Veil: Comportment and the Composition of Interaction in Afghanistan." *Anthropos* 77 (1982): 397–420.

Andres-Suárez, Irene, ed. *Las dos grandes minorías étnico-religiosas en la literature española del Siglo de Oro: los judeoconversos y los moriscos.* Paris: Annales Littéraires de l'Université de Besançon, 1995.

341

Ansari, Mas'ud. *Jara'im va inhirafat-i jinsi.* Tehran: n.p., 1961.

Anson, John. "The Female Transvestite in Early Monasticism." *Viator* 5, no. 1 (1974): 1–32.

Antle, Martine, and Dominique Fisher, eds. *The Rhetoric of the Other: Lesbian and Gay Strategies of Resistance in French and Francophone Contexts.* New Orleans: University Press of the South, 2002.

The Arabian Nights. Translated by Husain Haddawy. 2 vols. New York: Norton, 1995.

Archibald, Elizabeth. *Incest and the Medieval Imagination.* London: Oxford University Press, 2001.

Arkoun, Mohammed. *Rethinking Islam: Common Questions, Uncommon Answers.* Boulder: Westview Press, 1994.

Ayalon, David. *Eunuchs, Caliphs and Sultans: A Study of Power Relationships.* Jerusalem: Magnes Press, 1999.

———. *The Mamluk Military Society.* London: Variorum Reprints, 1979.

———. "The Wafidiyya in the Mamluk Kingdom." *Islamic Culture* 25 (1951): 89–104.

Babayan, Kathryn. "'The 'Aqa'id al-Nisa': A Glimpse at Safavid Women in Local Isfahani Culture." In *Women in the Medieval Islamic World: Power, Patronage, Piety.* Edited by Gavin R. G. Hambly. New York: St. Martin's Press, 1998. 349–81.

———. *Mystics, Monarchs and Messiahs: Cultural Landscape of Early Modern Iran.* Cambridge: Harvard University Press, 2003.

Bach, Rebecca Ann. *Shakespeare and Renaissance Literature before Heterosexuality.* New York: Palgrave Macmillan, 2007.

Bauer, Thomas. *Liebe und Liebesdichtung in der arabischen Welt des. 9. und 10. Jahrhunderts.* Wiesbaden: Harrassowitz, 1998.

Beelaert, A.L.F.A. *A Cure for Grieving,* Leiden: Brill, 2000.

Bennett, Judith M. "'Lesbian-Like' and the Social History of Lesbianisms." *Journals of the History of Sexuality* 9, nos. 1–2 (2000): 1–24.

Biesterfeldt, Hans Hinrich, and Dimitri Gutas. "The Malady of Love." *Journal of the American Oriental Society* 104, no. 1 (1984): 21–55.

Bingham, Caroline. *The Life and Times of Edward II.* London: Weidenfeld and Nicolson, 1973.

The Book of the Thousand Nights and One Night. Vol. 2. Translated by Powys Mathers from the French translation by J. C. Mardrus. London: Routledge, 1996.

Boone, Joseph. "Vacation Cruises; or, The Homoerotics of Orientalism." *PMLA* 110, no. 1 (1995): 89–107.

Boswell, John. "Revolutions, Universals, and Sexual Categories." In *Hidden from History: Reclaiming the Gay and Lesbian Past,* edited by Martin Duberman, Martha Vicinus, and George Chauncey, Jr., 17–36, 478–81. New York: Meridian, 1989.

Bouhdiba, Abdelwahab. *Sexuality in Islam.* Translated by Alan Sheridan. London: Routledge, 1985. (Original work *La sexualité en Islam* published in Paris: PUF, 1975)

Bourchier, Sir John (Lord Berners). *The Boke of Duke Huon of Burdeux.* Ed. S. L. Lee. London: N. Trübner, 1882–1884. Reissued New York: Kraus, 1975, 1981.

Bourdieu, Pierre. *La Domination masculine.* Paris: Seuil, 1998.

Boyarin, Daniel. "Are There Any Jews in 'The History of Sexuality'?" *Journal of the History of Sexuality* 5, no. 3 (1995): 333–55.

———. "Homotopia: The Feminized Jewish Man and the Lives of Women in Late Antiquity." *differences* 7, no. 2 (1995): 41–81.

Braunschneider, Theresa. *Maidenly Amusements: Narrating Female Sexuality in Eighteenth Century England.* Ph.D. diss., University of Michigan, 2002.

Bray, Alan. *The Friend.* Chicago: University of Chicago Press, 2003.

———. *Homosexuality in Renaissance England.* New York: Columbia University Press, 1982.

Brewska, Barbara Anne. "*Esclarmonde, Clarisse et Florent, Yde et Olive I, Croissant, Yde et Olive II, Huon et les Geants,* Sequels to *Huon de Bourdeaux.*" PhD dissertation, Vanderbilt University, 1977.

Brown, Catherine. "In the Middle." *Journal of Medieval and Early Modern Studies* 30, no. 3 (2000): 547–74.

Bullough, Vern L. "Cross Dressing and Gender Role Change in the

Middle Ages." In *Handbook of Medieval Sexuality,* edited by Vern L. Bullough and James A. Brundage, 223–42. New York: Garland, 1996.

Bullough, Vern L., and James Brundage, eds. *The Handbook of Medieval Sexuality.* New York: Garland, 1996.

Burger, Glenn, and Steven F. Kruger, eds. Introduction to *Queering the Middle Ages.* Minneapolis: University of Minnesota Press, 2001.

Burshatin, Israel. "The Moor in the Text: Metaphor, Emblem, and Silence." In *Critical Inquiry* 12, no. 1 (Autumn 1985): 98–118.

Burton, Sir Richard Francis, tr., *The Book of the Thousand Nights and a Night, with Introduction Explanatory Notes on the Manners and Customs of Moslem Men and a Terminal Essay upon the History of The Nights,* 10 vols. (Privately printed by the Burton Club, c. 1900).

Butler, Judith. *Bodies That Matter: On the Discursive Limits of "Sex."* New York: Routledge, 1993.

———. *Gender Trouble: Feminism and the Subversion of Identity.* New York: Routledge, 1990.

———. "Imitation and Gender Insubordination." In *Inside/Out: Lesbian Theories, Gay Theories,* edited by Diana Fuss, 13–31. New York: Routledge, 1991.

———. *The Psychic Life of Power: Theories in Subjection.* Stanford: Stanford University Press, 1997

Canguilhem, Georges. *The Normal and the Pathological.* Translated by Carolyn R. Fawcett. New York: Urzone, 1989.

Cascardi, Anthony J., ed. *The Cambridge Companion to Cervantes.* Cambridge: Cambridge University Press, 2002.

Cervantes, Miguel de. *Don Quixote.* Translated by Edith Grossman. New York: HarperCollins, 2003.

Chakrabarty, Dipesh. *Provincializing Europe: Postcolonial Thought and Historical Difference.* Princeton: Princeton University Press, 2000.

Chaplais, Pierre. *Piers Gaveston: Edward II's Adoptive Brother.* Oxford: Oxford University Press, 1994.

Chatterjee, Indrani. "Alienation, Intimacy, and Gender: Problems for a History of Love in South Asia." In *Queering India: Same-Sex Love and Eroticism in Indian Culture and Society,* edited by Ruth Vanita, 61–76. New York: Routledge, 2002.

Chauncey, G. *Gay New York.* New York: Basic Books, 1994.

Cheikh-Moussa, A. "L'Historien et la littérature Arabe médiévale" *Arabica* 43 (1996): 155.

Chejne, Anwar. *Islam and the West: The Moriscos, a Cultural and Social History.* Albany: SUNY Press, 1983.

Cherkaoui, Driss. *Le Roman de 'Antar: Perspective littéraire et historique.* Paris: Présence Africaine, 2000.

Childers, William. "The Captive's Tale and Circumcision." In *Annals of Scholarship: Don Quixote and Race,* edited by Baltasar Fra Molinero. Philadelphia: Temple University Press, 200x.

Clark, Robert L. A. "A Heroine's Sexual Itinerary: Incest, Transvestism, and Same-Sex Marriage in *Yde et Olive.*" In *Gender Transgressions: Crossing the Normative Barrier in Old French Literature,* edited by Karen J. Taylor, 889–905. New York: Garland, 1998.

Clark, Robert L. A., and Claire Sponsler. "Queer Play: The Cultural Work of Crossdressing in Medieval Drama." *New Literary History* 28, no. 2 (1997): 319–44.

Crompton, Louis. "The Myth of Lesbian Impunity: Capital Laws from 1270 to 1791." *Journal of Homosexuality* 6, nos. 1–2 (1980–1981): 11–25.

Cruz, Anne J. "Psyche and Gender in Cervantes." In *The Cambridge Companion to Cervantes.* Edited by Anthony J. Cascardi. Cambridge: Cambridge University Press, 2002. 186–205.

Cruz, Anne J., and Carroll B. Johnson, eds. *Cervantes and His Postmodern Constituencies.* New York: Garland, 1998.

Dean, Tim, and Chris Lane, eds. *Homosexuality and Psychoanalysis.* Chicago: University of Chicago Press, 2001.

Delgado, María José, and Alain Saint-Saëns, eds. *Lesbianism and Homosexuality in Early Modern Spain: Literature and Theater in Context.* New Orleans: University Press of the South, 2000.

Deleuze, Gilles. *Foucault.* Minneapolis: University of Minnesota Press, 1988.

al-Dhahabi. *Kitab al-Kaba'ir.* Edited by al-Sayyid al-'Arabi. al-Mansura: Dar al-Khulafa' li-lNashr wa-l-Tawzi', 1995.

Dinshaw, Carolyn. *Getting Medieval: Sexualities and Communities, Pre- and Postmodern.* Durham: Duke University Press, 1999.

———. "The History of *GLQ*, Volume 1: LGBTQ Studies, Censorship, and Other Transnational Problems." *GLQ: A Journal of Lesbian and Gay Studies* 12, no. 1 (2006): 5–26.

Douglas, Mary. *Purity and Danger: An Analysis of the Concepts of Pollution and Taboo.* London: Routledge, 1966.

Dover, K. J. *Greek Homosexuality.* London: Duckworth, 1978.

Dunne, Bruce. "Homosexuality in the Middle East: An Agenda for Historical Research." *Arab Studies Quarterly* 12, no. 3–4 (1990): 55–82.

Durling, Nancy Vine. "Rewriting Gender: *Yde et Olive* and Ovidian Myth." *Romance Languages Annual* 1 (1989): 256–62.

Elham, Shah Morad. *Kitbuga und Lagin: Studien zur Mamluken Geschichte nach Baibars al-Mansuri und an-Nuwairi.* Freiburg: Schwarz, 1977.

Eng, David L. *Racial Castration: Managing Masculinity in Asian America.* Durham: Duke University Press, 2001.

Epps, Brad. "The Fetish of Fluidity." In *Homosexuality and Psychoanalysis,* edited by Tim Dean and Christopher Lane, 412–31. Chicago: University of Chicago Press, 2001.

———. "El peso de la lengua y el fetiche de la fluidez." *Revista de Crítica Cultural* 25 (2002): 66–70.

Eribon, Didier. *Réflexions sur la question gay.* Paris: Fayard, 1999.

Farhad, Massumeh. *Safavid Single Page Paintings, 1629–1666,* PhD dissertation, Harvard University, 1987.

Faroqhi, Suraiya. *Pilgrims and Sultans: The Hajj under the Ottomans 1517–1683* (London: Tauris, 1994).

Ferguson, Roderick A. *Aberrations in Black: Toward a Queer of Color Critique.* Minneapolis: University of Minnesota Press, 2004.

Fernández, Jaime. *Bibliografía del Quijote por unidades narrativas y materials de la novella.* Alcalá de Henares: Centro de estudios cervantinos, 1995.

Fernández-Morera, Darío. "Cervantes and Islam: A Contemporary Analogy." In *Cervantes y sumundo,* edited by Robert Lauer and Kurt Reichenberger. Kassel: Reichenberger, 2005. 123–66.

Fisher, Dominique, and Lawrence Schehr, eds. *Articulations of Difference: Gender Studies and Writing in French*. Stanford: Stanford University Press, 1997.

Foster, Jeannette. *Sex Variant Women in Literature: A Historical and Quantitative Survey*. New York: Vantage Press, 1956.

Foucault, Michel. *Discipline and Punish: The Birth of the Prison*. Translated by Alan Sheridan. New York: Vintage Press, 1979.

———. *The History of Sexuality*. Vol. 1. Translated by Robert Hurley. New York: Vintage Books, 1990.

Freccero, Carla. *Queer/Early/Modern*. Durham: Duke University Press, 2006.

Freccero, Carla, and Louise Fradenberg, eds. *Premodern Sexualities*. New York: Routledge, 1996.

Freud, Sigmund. "The Antithetical Sense of Primal Words" (1910). *Writings on Art and Literature*. Stanford: Stanford University Press, 1997.

———. *Civilization and Its Discontents*. Edited by James Strachey. New York: Norton, 1969.

——— "Mourning and Melancholia." In *The Standard Edition of the Complete Psychological Works of Sigmund Freud,* edited and translated by James Strachey, 14:239–58. London: Hogarth Press, 1953.

———. *Three Case Studies*. New York: Collier, 1963.

Fuchs, Barbara. *Mimesis and Empire: The New World, Islam, and European Identities*. Cambridge: Cambridge University Press, 2001.

———. *Passing for Spain: Cervantes and the Fictions of Identity*. Urbana: University of Illinois Press, 2003.

Furth, Charlotte. "Androgynous Males and Deficient Females: Biology and Gender Boundaries in Sixteenth- and Seventeenth-Century China." In *The Lesbian and Gay Studies Reader,* edited by Henry Abelove, Michèle Aina Barale, and David M. Halperin, 479–97. New York: Routledge, 1993.

Garber, Marjorie. "The Chic of Araby: Transvestism, Transsexualism and the Erotics of Cultural Appropriation." In *Body Guards: The Cultural Politics of Gender Ambiguity,* edited by Julia Epstein and Kristina Straub, 223–47. New York: Routledge, 1991.

————. *Vested Interests: Cross-Dressing and Cultural Anxiety.* New York: Routledge, 1992.

Garcés, María Antonia. *Cervantes in Algiers: A Captive's Tale.* Nashville: University of Vanderbilt Press, 2002.

García Arenal, Mercedes. *Los moriscos.* Granada: Universidad de Granada, 1995.

Gaunt, Simon. *Gender and Genre in Medieval French Literature.* Cambridge: Cambridge University Press, 1995.

Giffen, Lois Anita. *Theory of Profane Love among the Arabs: The Development of the Genre.* New York: New York University Press, 1971.

Glünz, Michael. "Das männliche Liebespaar in der persischen und türkischen Diwanlyrik." In *Homoerotische Lyrik: 6. Kolloquium der Forschungsstelle für europäische Lyrik des Mittelalters,* edited by Theo Stummer, 119–28. Mannheim: Forschungsstelle für europäische Lyrik des Mittelalters an der Universität Mannheim, 1992.

Goldberg, Jonathan, ed. *Queering the Renaissance.* Durham: Duke University Press, 1994.

Goldstein, Jan. *Foucault and the Writing of History.* Oxford: Blackwell, 1994.

González Echevarría, Roberto, ed. *Cervantes' Don Quixote: A Casebook.* Oxford: Oxford University Press, 2005.

Gopinath, Gayatri. *Impossible Desires: Queer Diasporas and South Asian Public Cultures.* Durham: Duke University Press, 2005.

Graf, E. C. "When an Arab Laughs in Toledo." *Diacritics* 29, no. 2 (1999): 68–85.

Greene, Jody, ed. "The Work of Friendship: In Memoriam Alan Bray." Special issue, *GLQ: A Journal of Lesbian and Gay Studies* 10, no. 3 (2004).

Guo, Li. "Paradise Lost: Ibn Daniyal's Response to Baybars' Campaign against Vice in Cairo." *Journal of the American Oriental Society* 121 (2001): 219–35.

Gurjistani, Vali Khan ibn Suhrab. *Risalah-ʿi fujuriyah,* Kitabkhanah-ʿi milli (National Library), Tehran, manuscript 1425/F.

Haarmann, Ulrich. "Arabic in Speech, Turkish in Lineage: Mamluks and Their Sons in the Intellectual Life of Fourteenth-Century Egypt and Syria." *Journal of Semitic Studies* 33 (1988): 81–114.

Halperin, David M. "Historicizing the Subject of Desire: Sexual Preferences and Erotic Identities in the Pseudo-Lucianic *Erôtes.*" In Jan Goldstein, *Foucault and the Writing of History,* ?–? (Oxford: Blackwell, 1994).

———. *How to Do the History of Homosexuality.* Chicago: University of Chicago Press, 2002.

———. "Sex before Sexuality: Pederasty, Politics, and Power in Classical Athens." In *Hidden from History: Reclaiming the Gay and Lesbian Past,* edited by Martin Duberman, Martha Vicinus, and George Chauncey, Jr., 37–53, 482–92. New York: Meridian, 1989.

Hamadani, ʿAli ibn Zayn al-ʿAbidin. *Javahir al-tashrih.* Tehran: Dar al-funun, 1888.

Hamilton, J. S. "Ménage à Roi: Edward II and Piers Gaveston." *History Today* 49, no. 2 (June 1999): 26–31.

———. *Piers Gaveston, Earl of Cornwall 1307–1312: Politics and Patronage in the Reign of Edward II.* Detroit: Wayne State University Press, 1988.

Hamori, Andras. "A Comic Romance from the *Thousand and One Nights:* The Tale of Two Viziers." *Arabica* 30, no. 1 (1983): 38–56.

———. *On the Art of Medieval Arabic Literature.* Princeton: Princeton University Press, 1974.

Harper, Phillip Brian, Anne McClintock, José Esteban Muñoz, and Trish Rosen, eds. "Queer Transexions of Race, Nation, and Gender." Special issue, *Social Text,* no. 52–53 (1997).

Hawley, John C., ed. *Postcolonial, Queer: Theoretical Intersections.* Albany: State University of New York Press, 2001.

Hayes, Jarrod. *Queer Nations: Marginal Sexualities in the Maghreb.* Chicago: University of Chicago Press, 2000.

———. "Queer Roots in Africa." In *Topographies of Race and Gender: Mapping Cultural Representations,* edited by Patricia Penn Hilden and Shari Huhndorf. Trenton: Africa World Press, forthcoming.

Hayes, Jarrod, William Spurlin, and Margaret Higonnet, eds. *Comparatively Queer: Crossing Time, Crossing Cultures.* Forthcoming.

Hitchcock, Richard. "Cervantes, Ricote, and the Expulsion of the Moriscos," *Bulletin of Spanish Studies* 81, no. 2 (2004): 175–85.

Hodgson, Marshall G. S. *The Venture of Islam: Conscience and History in a World Civilization.* Vol. 1. Chicago: University of Chicago Press, 1974.

Hollywood, Amy. "The Normal, the Queer, and the Middle Ages." *Journal of the History of Sexuality* 10, no. 2 (2001): 173–79.

Hotchkiss, Valerie R. *Clothes Make the Man: Female Cross Dressing in Medieval France.* New York: Garland, 1996.

Hutcheson, Gregory. "Return to *Queer Iberia.*" In Gregory S. Hutcheson and Sidney Donnell, eds., "Forum on Return to Queer Iberia," *La Corónica* 30.1 (Fall 2001). http://www.wm.edu/msll/lacoronica/qi/qimain.html.

Hutcheson, Gregory, and Josiah Blackmore, eds. *Queer Iberia.* Durham: Duke University Press, 1999.

Ibn al-Athir, 'Izz al-Din. *al-Kamil fi l-ta'rikh.* 13 vols. Edited by C. Tornburg. Leiden: Brill, 1853.

Ibn al-Dawadari. *Kanz al-durar wa-jami' al-ghurar.* Vol. 9. Edited by H. R. Roemer. Wiesbaden: Harrassowitz, 1960.

Ibn al-Fuwati. *Kitab al-Hawadith.* Edited by Bashshar 'Awwad Ma'ruf and 'Imad 'Abd al-Salam Ra'uf. Beirut: Dar al-Gharb al-Islami, 1997.

Ibn Hajar al-'Asqalani. *Al-Durar al-kamina fi a'yan al-mi'a al-thamina.* 4 vols. Hyderabad: Matba'at Majlis Da'irat al-Ma'arif, 1929–31.

———. *Inba' al-ghumr bi-abna' al-'umr.* 3 vols. Edited by Hasan Habashi. Cairo: al-Majlis al-A'la li-l-Shu'un al-Islamiyya, 1972.

Ibn Iyas. *Bada'i' al-zuhur fi waqa'i' al-duhur.* Vol. 3. Edited by Muhammad Mustafa. Wiesbaden: Franz Steiner, 1963.

Ibn Kathir. *al-bidaya wa-l-nihaya.* 14 vols. Beirut: Dar al-Fikr, 1978–82.

Ibn Khallikan. *Wafayat al-a'yan.* 8 vols. Edited by Ihsan 'Abbas. Beirut: Dar Sadir, 1968–72.

Ibn Muyassar. *al-Muntaqa min Akhbar Misr.* Edited by Ayman Fu'ad Sayyid. Cairo: Institut Français d'Archéologie Orientale du Caire, 1981.

Ibn al-Mu'tazz. *Tabaqat al-shu'ara'*. Edited by Abd al-Sattar Ahmed Farraj. Cairo: Dar al-Ma'arif, 1968.

Ibn Nasr al-Katib, Abul Hasan Ali. *Encyclopedia of Pleasure*. Edited by Salah Addin Khawwam. Translated by Adnan Jarkas and Salah Addin Khawwam. Toronto: Aleppo, 1977.

Ibn Shakir al-Kutubi. *Fawat al-wafayat*. 5 vols. Edited by Ihsan 'Abbas. Beirut: Dar Sadir, 1974.

Ibn Taghri Birdi. *al-Nujum al-zahira fi muluk Misr wa-l-Qahira*. 16 vols. Cairo: al-Mu'assasa al-Misriyya al-'Amma li-l-Ta'lif wa-l-Tiba'a wa-l-Nashr, 1963–1971.

Ibn al-Tuwayr. *Nuzhat al-muqlatayn fi akhbar al-dawlatayn*. Edited by Ayman Fu'ad Sayyid. Beirut: Franz Steiner, 1992.

Imber, Colin. *Studies in Ottoman History and Law*. Istanbul: Isis Press, 1996.

Irwin, Robert. "'Ali al-Baghdadi and the Joy of Mamluk Sex." In *The Historiography of Islamic Egypt (c. 950–1800)*, edited by Hugh Kennedy, 45–57. Leiden: Brill, 2001.

———. *The Arabian Nights: A Companion*. London: Tauris Parke, 2004.

———. *The Middle East in the Middle Ages: The Early Mamluk Sultanate 1250–1383*. Carbondale: Southern Illinois University Press, 1986.

Jackson, Peter A. "The Persistence of Gender: From Ancient Indian *Pandakas* to Modern Thai *Gay-Quings*." In "Australia Queer," edited by Chris Berry and Annamarie Jagose. Special issue, *Meanjin* 55, no. 1 (1996): 110–20.

Jagose, Annamarie. *Inconsequence: Lesbian Representation and the Logic of Sexual Sequence*. Ithaca: Cornell University Press, 2002.

Johnson, E. Patrick, and Mae G. Henderson, eds. *Black Queer Studies: A Critical Anthology*. Durham: Duke University Press, 2005.

Jordan, Mark D. *The Invention of Sodomy in Christian Theology*. Chicago: University of Chicago Press, 1997.

Katz, Jonathan. *The Invention of Heterosexuality*. New York: Dutton, 1995.

Kaykawus. *Qabusnama*. Edited by Ghulamhusayn Yusufi. Tehran: Sharikat-i Intisharat-I 'Ilmi wa-Farhangi, 1988. Translated by Reuben Levy, *A Mirror for Princes: The Qabus Nama.* New York: Dutton, 1951.

Khwansari, Aqa Jamal. *'Aqa'id al-Nisa'.* Edited by Mahmud Katira'i. Tehran, 1970.

Kirmani, Mirza Aqa Khan. *Sad khatabah,* manuscript in Edward G. Browne Collection, Cambridge University Library. Selections in *Nimeye Digar* 1, 9 (1989): 101–12.

——. *Sih maktub.* Edited Bahram Chubinah. n.p.: Mard-i imruz, 1991.

Kirmani, Muhammad Karim Khan. *Majma' al-fatavi-i Hajj Muhammad Karim Khan Kirmani.* Edited by Hajj Zayn al-'Abidin Kirmani. Kirman: Sa'adat, 197?.

Kirmani, Zayn al-'Abidin Khan. *Risalah-i haftad mis'alah dar javab-i Saqat al-'Ulama Salmasi az masa'il-i mukhtalafah.* Kirman: Sa'adat, 1959.

Kruger, Steven F. "Conversion and Medieval Sexual, Religious, and Racial Categories." In *Constructing Medieval Sexuality,* edited by Karma Lochrie, Peggy McCracken, and James A. Schultz, 158–79. Minneapolis: University of Minnesota Press, 1997.

Kuru, Selim. *A Sixteenth-Century Scholar Deli Birader and His Dafi'u'l-gumum ve rafi'u'l humum.* PhD dissertation, Department of Near Eastern Languages and Civilizations, Harvard University, 2000.

Lacan, Jacques. *The Ethics of Psychoanalysis 1959–1960 (Seminar of Jacques Lacan).* New York: Norton, 1997.

Lagrange, Frédéric. "Methodologies, Paradigms, and Sources for Studying Women and Islamic Cultures: Sexualities and Queer Studies." In *Encyclopedia of Women and Islamic Cultures* (Leiden: Brill, 2003), 1:419–22.

——. "Sexualities and Queer Studies." In *Encyclopedia of Women and Islamic Cultures,* edited by Suad Joseph et al. 6 vols. Leiden: Brill, 2003, 1:419–22.

Laplanche, Jean. "Interpretation between Determinism and Hermeneutics: A Restatement of the Problem." In *Essays on Otherness.* New York: Routledge, 1999.

Laqueur, Thomas. *Making Sex: Body and Gender from the Greeks to Freud.* Boston: Harvard University Press, 1990.

Lauer, Robert, and Kurt Reichenberger, eds. *Cervantes y su mundo*. Kassel Reichenberger, 2005.

Leavitt, David. *Martin Bauman; or, A Sure Thing*. Boston: Houghton Mifflin, 2000.

Lee, Christina H. "Don Antonio Moreno y el 'discreto' negocio de los moriscos Ricote y Ana Fénix." *Hispania* 88, no. 1 (2005): 32–40.

el-Leithy, Tamer. "'Of bodies chang'd to various forms . . .': Hermaphrodites and Transsexuals in the Medieval Middle East," unpublished manuscript.

Levanoni, Amalia. *A Turning Point in Mamluk History: The Third Reign of al-Nasir Muhammad Ibn Qalawun 1310–1341*. Leiden: Brill, 1995.

Little, Donald P. "Notes on the Early *nazar al-khass*." In *The Mamluks in Egyptian Politics and Society*, edited by Thomas Philipp and Ulrich Haarmann, 235–53. Cambridge: Cambridge University Press, 1998.

Lochrie, Karma. *Heterosyncrasies: Female Sexuality When Normal Wasn't*. Minneapolis: University of Minnesota Press, 2005.

López-Baralt, Luce. "The Supreme Pen (Al-Qalam Al-A'Ala) of Cide Hamete Benengeli in *Don Quixote*." Translated by Marikay McCabe. *Journal of Medieval and Early Modern Studies* 30, no. 3 (Fall 2000): 505–18.

Lord, Albert B. *The Singer of Tales*. Cambridge: Harvard University Press, 2000.

Lyons, M. C. *The Arabic Epic: Heroic and Oral Story-Telling*. 3 vols. Cambridge: Cambridge University Press, 1995.

Mahdi, Muhsin. *Alf layla wa layla* [*The Thousand and One Nights*]. Leiden: Brill, 1984.

Mahmud, Ibrahim. *Al-Mut'a al-Mahzura*. London: Riyad al-Rayyis, 2000.

Majlisi, Muhammad Baqir. *Hilyat al-Muttaqin*. Qumm, 1992.

Malti-Douglas, Fedwa. "Tribadism/Lesbianism and the Sexualized Body in Medieval Arabo-Islamic Narratives." In Sautman and Sheingorn, *Same Sex Love and Desire among Women in the Middle Ages*, 123–41.

———. *Woman's Body, Woman's Word: Gender and Discourse in Arabo-Islamic Writing*. Princeton: Princeton University Press, 1991.

Manalansan, Martin F., IV. "In the Shadows of Stonewall: Examining Gay Transnational Politics and the Diasporic Dilemma." *GLQ: A Journal of Lesbian and Gay Studies* 2, no. 4 (1995): 425–38.

Mannoni, Octave. "Je sais bien, mais quand même." In *Clefs pour l'imaginaire ou l'autre scène*. Paris: Seuil, 1985.

al-Maqrizi. *Itti'az al-hunafa' bi-akhbar al-a'imma al-Fatimiyyin al-khulafa'*. Edited by Muhammad 'Abd al-Qadir Ahmad 'Ata. Beirut: Dar al-Kutub al-'Ilmiyya, n.d.

———. *Kitab al-Suluk li-ma'rifat duwal al-muluk*. 4 vols. Edited by Muhammad Mustafa Ziyada. Cairo: Lajnat al-Ta'lif wa-l-Tarjama wa-l-Nashr, 1934–1942.

———. *al-Mawa'iz wa-l-i'tibar bi-dhikr al-khitat wa-l-athar (al-Khitat)*. 2 vols. Bulaq: Dar al-Tiba'a al-Misriyya, 1853.

Marcuse, Herbert. "Repressive Tolerance." In *A Critique of Pure Tolerance*, 81–117. Boston: Beacon Press, 1965.

Márquez Villanueva, Francisco. *Personajes y temas del* Quixote. Madrid: Taurus, 1975.

Martin, Biddy. "Extraordinary Homosexuals and the Fear of Being Ordinary." In *Feminism Meets Queer Theory*, edited by Naomi Schor and Elizabeth Weed, 109–35. Bloomington: Indiana University Press, 1997.

Massad, Joseph. "The Intransigence of Orientalist Desires: A Reply to Arno Schmitt." *Public Culture* 15, no. 3 (2003): 593–94.

———. "Re-Orienting Desire: The Gay International and the Arab World." *Public Culture* 14, no. 2 (2002): 361–85.

Mazaleyrat, J. and G. Molinié. *Vocabulaire de la stylistique*. Paris: PUF, 1989.

Mbembe, Achilles. "Necropolitics." *Public Culture* 15, no. 1 (2003): 11–40.

McChesney, R. D. "The Central Asian Hajj-Pilgrimage in the Time of the Early Modern Empires." In *Safavid Iran and Her Neighbors*, edited by Michel Mazzaoui, 129–56. Salt Lake City: University of Utah Press, 2003.

Miracle de la fille d'un roy. In *Les Miracles de Nostre Dame par per-*

sonages, edited by Gaston Paris and Ulysse Robert, 7:2–117. Paris: Firmin et Didot, 1876.

Mohanty, Chandra. "Under Western Eyes: Feminist Scholarship and Colonial Discourses." *Feminist Review* 30 (Autumn 1988): 61–88.

Molloy, Sylvia, and Robert McKee Irvins, eds. *Hispanisms and Homosexualities.* Durham: Duke University Press, 1998.

De Mont Fret, Count. *Kitabchah-i qanun.* n.p., 1879.

Morris, Rosalind C. "Educating Desire: Thailand, Transnationalism, and Transgression." In Harper et al., "Queer Transexions of Race, Nation, and Gender," 53–79.

Mullins, Greg. *Colonial Affairs.* Madison: University of Wisconsin Press, 2002.

Muñoz, José Esteban. *Disidentifications: Queers of Color and the Performance of Politics.* Minneapolis: University of Minnesota Press, 1999.

Murillo, Luis Andrés. "El Ur-*Quijote:* nueva hipótesis." *Cervantes: Bulletin of the Cervantes Society of America* 1, nos. 1–2 (1981): 43–50.

Murray, Jacqueline. "Twice Marginal and Twice Invisible." In *The Handbook of Medieval Sexuality,* edited by Vern L. Bullough and James Brundage, 191–222. New York: Garland, 1996.

Murray, Stephen O. "Male Homosexuality, Inheritance Rules, and the Status of Women in Medieval Egypt: The Case of the Mamluks." In *Islamic Homosexualities,* edited by Stephen O. Murray and Will Roscoe, 161–73. New York: New York University Press, 1997.

Murray, Stephen O., and Will Roscoe, eds. *Islamic Homosexualities: Culture, History, and Literature.* New York: New York University Press, 1997.

Najmabadi, Afsaneh. "Transing and Transpassing across Sex-Gender Walls in Contemporary Iran." Unpublished paper.

———. *Women with Mustaches and Men without Beards: Gender and Sexual Anxieties of Iranian Modernity.* Berkeley: University of California Press, 2005.

One Thousand and One Nights. Edited and translated into French by Joseph Charles Mardrus. Paris: Laffont, 1999.

One Thousand and One Nights. Translated into English by Pomys Mathers. 4 vols. N.p., Yugoslavia: Dorset Press, 1964.

Ovid. *Iphis and Ianthe.* In Ovid, *Metamorphoses,* translated by Rolfe Humphries, 229–33. Bloomington: Indiana University Press, 1955.

Patterson, Lee. "On the Margin: Postmodernism, Ironic History, and Medieval Studies." *Speculum* 65, no. 1 (1990): 87–108.

Pearson, M. N. *Pilgrimage to Mecca: The Indian Experience 1500–1800.* Princeton: Markus Wiener, 1996.

Perret, Michèle. "Travesties et transsexuelles: Yde, Silence, Grisandole, Blanchandine." *Romance Notes* 25, no. 3 (1985): 328–40.

Petievich, Carla. "The Invention and Subsequent Erasure of Urdu Poetry's 'Lesbian' Voice." In *Queering India: Same-Sex Love and Eroticism in Indian Culture and Society.* Edited by Ruth Vanita. New York: Routledge, 2002.

———. Response to "In Spirit We Ate Each Other's Sorrow," Crossing Paths of Middle Eastern and Sexuality Studies: Challenges of Theory, History, and Comparative Methods, conference at the Radcliffe Institute for Advanced Study, May 2003.

Pierce, Leslie. *Morality Tales: Law and Gender in the Ottoman Court of Aintab.* Berkeley: University of California Press, 2003.

Pinault, David. *Story-Telling Techniques in the Arabian Nights.* Leiden: Brill, 1992.

Polak, Jakob Eduard. "Prostitution in Persian." *Wiener Medicinische Wochenschrift,* Nr. 32, 1861. Persian translation by Kjell Madsen, Georg Warning, and Mansour Saberi, in *Homan* 13 (1998): 13–18.

Pouzet, Louis. *Damas au VIIe/XIIIe siècle: vie et structures religieuses dans une métropole islamique.* Beirut: Dar El-Machreq Sarl, 1991.

Povinelli, Elizabeth A. and George Chauncey, eds. "Thinking Sex Transnationally." Special issue, *GLQ: A Journal of Lesbian and Gay Studies* 5, no. 4 (1999).

Presberg, Charles. "'Yo sé quién soy': Don Quixote, Don Diego de Miranda and the Paradox of Self-Knowledge." *Bulletin of the Cervantes Society of America* 14, no. 2 (1994): 41–69.

Puar, Jasbir Kaur. "Circuits of Queer Mobility: Tourism, Travel, and Globalization." *GLQ: A Journal of Lesbian and Gay Studies* 8, no. 1–2 (2002): 101–37.

Puff, Helmut. *Sodomy in Reformation Germany and Switzerland 1400–1600.* Chicago: University of Chicago Press, 2003.

Ricapito, Joseph V. "Cervantes y la conciencia: 'Yo sé quién soy,' el caballero de los leones y Ricote el Moro." In Lauer and Reichenberger, *Cervantes y su mundo III,* 505–17.

Rich, Adrienne. "Compulsory Heterosexuality and Lesbian Existence." *Signs 5,* no. 4 (1980): 631–60.

Rocke, Michael. *Forbidden Friendships: Homosexuality and Male Culture in Renaissance Florence.* New York: Oxford University Press, 1996.

Rosello, Mireille. "The National-Sexual: From the Fear of Ghettos to the Banalization of Queer Practices." In *Articulations of Difference: Gender Studies and Writing in French,* edited by Dominique D. Fisher and Lawrence R. Schehr, 246–71. Stanford: Stanford University Press, 1997.

Rosenthal, Franz. "Male and Female: Described and Compared." In *Homoeroticism in Classical Arabic Literature,* edited by J. W. Wright, Jr., and Everett K. Rowson, 24–54. New York: Columbia University Press, 1997.

El-Rouayheb, Khaled. *Before Homosexuality in the Arab-Islamic World, 1500–1800.* Chicago: Chicago University Press, 2005.

Rouche, Michel. "L'Age des pirates et des saints (Ve–Xie siècles)." In *Histoire de Boulogne-surmer,* edited by Alain Lottin, 33–53. Lille: Presses Universitaires de Lille, 1983.

Rowson, Everett K. "The Categorization of Gender and Sexual Irregularity in Medieval Arabic Vice Lists." In *Body Guards: The Cultural Politics of Gender Ambiguity,* edited by Julia Epstein and Kristina Straub, 50–79. New York: Routledge, 1991.

———. "The Effeminates of Early Medina." *Journal of the American Oriental Society* 111, no. 4 (1991): 671–93.

———. "Gender Irregularity as Entertainment: Institutionalized Transvestism at the Caliphal Court in Medieval Baghdad." In *Gender and Difference in the Middle Ages,* edited by Sharon Farmer and Carol Braun Pasternack, 45–72. Minneapolis: University of Minnesota Press, 2003.

———. "Homosexuality in the Medieval Islamic World: Literary Celebration vs. Legal Condemnation." *Princeton Mellon Seminar*, May 1995.

———. "Two Homoerotic Narratives from Mamluk Literature: al-Safadi's *Law'at al-shaki* and Ibn Daniyal's *al-Mutayyam*." In *Homoeroticism in Classical Arabic Literature*, edited by J. W. Wright, Jr., and Everett K. Rowson, 158–91. New York: Columbia University Press, 1997.

Rubin, Gayle. "Geologies of Queer Studies: It's Déjà Vu All Over Again." *CLAGS News* 14, no. 2 (2004): 6–10.

———. "The Traffic in Women: Notes on the 'Political Economy' of Sex." In *Toward an Anthropology of Women*, edited by Rayna R. Reiter, 157–210. New York: Monthly Review, 1975.

Sabbah, Fatna A. *Woman in the Muslim Unconscious*. Translated by Mary Jo Lakeland. New York: Pergamon, 1984.

al-Safadi. *al-Ghayth al-musajjam fi sharh Lamiyyat al-'Ajam*. 2 vols. Beirut: Dar al Kutub al-'Ilmiyya, 1990.

———. *al-Husn al-sarih fi mi'at malih*. Edited by Ahmad Fawzi al-Hayb. Damascus: Dar Sa'd al-Din, 2003.

———. *al-Wafi bi-l-wafayat*. 30 vols. Beirut-Wiesbaden: Franz Steiner, 1962–.

Safarnama-yi Mazum-i Hajj. Edited by Rasul Jafarian. Qum. 1995.

El Saffar, Ruth Anthony, and Diana de Armas Wilson, eds. *Quixotic Desire: Psychoanalytic Perspectives on Cervantes*. Ithaca: Cornell University Press, 1993.

Sahib, Abu al-Qasim al-Talqani. *Mustadrak al-diwan*. Edition Muhammad Hasan al Yasin. Baghdad: Maktabat al-Nahda, 1965.

Said, Edward. *Orientalism*. New York: Vintage, 1979.

al-Saltanah, I'timad. *Ruznamah-i khatirat*. Edited by Iraj Afshar. Tehran: Amir Kabir, 1966.

Sautman, Francesca. "What Can They Possibly Do Together? Queer Epic Performances in *Tristan de Nanteuil*." In Sautman and Sheingorn, *Same Sex Love and Desire*, 199–232.

Sautman, Francesca, and Pamela Sheingorn, eds. *Same Sex Love and Desire among Women in the Middle Ages*. New York: Palgrave, 2001.

Savater, Fernando. *Instrucciones para olvidar el* Quijote *y otros ensayos generales.* Madrid: Taurus, 1995.

Schmitt, Arno. "Different Approaches to Male-Male Sexuality/Eroticism from Morocco to Uzbekistan." In Schmitt and Sofer, *Sexuality and Eroticism among Males in Moslem Societies,* 1–24.

Schmitt, Arno, and Jehoeda Sofer, eds. *Sexuality and Eroticism among Males in Moslem Societies.* New York: Haworth Press, 1992.

Schweigel, Max. *Esclarmonde, Clarisse et Florent, Yde et Olive: Dreifortsetsungen der chansun von Huon de Bourdeaux, nach der einzigen Turiner handschrift.* Marburg: Elwert, 1889.

Sedgwick, Eve Kosofsky. *Epistemology of the Closet.* Berkeley: University of California Press, 1990.

———. *Tendencies.* Durham: Duke University Press, 1993.

Seyed-Gohrab, Ali Asghar. *Love, Madness and Mystic Longing in Nizami's Epic Romance.* Leiden: Brill, 2003.

Shahri, Ja'far. *Tarikh-i ijtima'i-i Tihran dar qarn-i sizdahum.* 6 vols. Tehran: Mu'assisah-i khadamat-i farhangi-i rasa, 1990.

Shakhsari, Sima. "Diasporic Performances: Gender, Sexuality, and Nation in the *Sweet Smell of Love* and *Bye-bye Los Angeles.*" Unpublished paper.

Shakhsari, Sima. "The Discursive Production of Iranian Queer Subjects in Diaspora." MA thesis, San Francisco State University, 2002.

———. "From Hamjensbaaz to Hamjensgaraa: Diasporic Queer Reterritorializations and Limits of Transgression." Unpublished paper.

———. "Future of Ghorbat and the Past of Homeland: Subject Formation and Historical Appropriation in Diasporic Imaginations of Iranian.com." Unpublished paper.

———. "Naqdi bar kitab-i *Jinsiyat-i gumshudah.*" *Homan* 18 (2001): 34–36.

Sharma, Sunil. "Women, Gender, and Pre-modern Discourses of Love." In *Encyclopedia of Women and Islamic Cultures.* Vol. 5. Leiden: Brill, 2007.

Shaykh Riza'i, Anisah, and Shahla Azari, eds. *Guzarish-ha-yi nazmiyah az mahallat-i Tihran.* 2 vols. Tehran: Sazman-i asnad-i milli-i Iran, 1998.

Sibt Ibn al-Jawzi. *Mir'at al-zaman fi ta'rikh al-a'yan.* Section on the Seljuqs, edited by Ali Sevim. Ankara: Türk Tarih Kuruma Basimevi, 1968.

Sieber, Diane E. "Mapping Identity in the Captive's Tale: Cervantes and Ethnographic Narrative." *Cervantes: Bulletin of the Cervantes Society of America* 18, no. 1 (1998): 115–33.

Smith, Paul Julian, and Emilie Bergman, eds. *¿Entiendes?* Durham: Duke University Press, 1995.

Stoll, Anita K., and Dawn L. Smith, eds. *Gender, Identity, and Representation in Spain's Golden Age.* Lewisburg: Bucknell University Press, 2000.

al-Subki, Taj al-Din. *Mu'id al-ni'am wa-mubid al-niqam.* Edited by Muhammad 'Ali al-Najjar et al. Cairo: Maktabat al-Khanji, 1993.

———. *Tabaqat al-Shafi'iyya al-kubra.* 11 vols. Edited by Mahmud Muhammad al-Tanahi and 'Abd al-Fattah Muhammad al-Hulw. Cairo: Dar Ihya' al-Kutub al-'Arabiyya, 1964–1976.

Subramanyam, Sanjay. "Persians, Pilgrims, and Portuguese: The Travails of Masulipatnam Shipping in the Western Indian Ocean, 1590–1655." *Modern Asian Studies* 22 (1988): 503–30.

Sweet, Michael, and Leonard Zwilling. "The First Medicalization: The Taxonomy and Etiology of Queers in Classical Indian Medicine." *Journal of the History of Sexuality* 3, no. 4 (1993): 590–607.

Szkilnik, Michelle. "The Grammar of the Sexes in Medieval French Romance." In *Gender Transgressions: Crossing the Normative Barrier in Old French Literature,* edited by Karen J. Taylor, 61–88. New York: Garland, 1998.

Taussig, Michael. "Maleficium State Fetishism." In *The Nervous System.* New York: Routledge, 2001.

al-Tawhidi, Abu Hayyan. *Akhlaq al-Sahib wa-bn al-'Amid,* edited by Muhammad b. Tawit al-Tanji, 1965, republished Beirut: Dar Sadir, 1992. Also commonly titled *Mathalib al-Wazirayn.*

al-Tha'alibi. *Tatimmat al-Yatima.* Edited by Mufid Muhammad Qamiha. Beirut: Dar al-Kutub al-'Ilmiyya, 1983; 1947. Another edition edited by 'Abbas Iqbal. Tehran, 1934.

Traub, Valerie. "The Joys of Martha Joyless: Queer Pedagogy and the (Early Modern) Production of Sexual Knowledge." In *Renaissance Culture and the New Millenium,* edited by Leonard Barkan, Bradin

Cormack and Sean Keilen. New York: Palgrave Macmillan, forthcoming 2008.

———. "Mapping the Global Body." In *Early Modern Visual Culture: Representation, Race, and Empire in Renaissance England,* edited by Peter Erickson and Clark Hulse, 44–97. Philadelphia: University of Pennsylvania Press, 2000.

———. "The Present Future of Lesbian Historiography." In *Companion to Lesbian, Gay, Bisexual, Transgender, and Queer Studies,* edited by George Haggerty and Molly McGarry. London: Blackwell, 2007. pp. 124–45.

———. "The Psychomorphology of the Clitoris; Or, the Reemergence of the Tribade in English Culture." In *The Renaissance of Lesbianism in Early Modern England,* 188–228.

———. *The Renaissance of Lesbianism in Early Modern England.* Cambridge: Cambridge University Press, 2002.

al-Tunakabuni, Muhammad Mu'min al-Husayni. *Tuhfat al-muminin,* Bibliotheque Nationale (manuscript Persan Supp. 1287).

Tusi, Shaykh. *al-Nihaya fi Mujarrad al-Fiqh wa'l Fatawa,* Malik Library (manuscript Majmu'a 3624).

'Ubyd Zakani, Nizam al-Din. *Collected Works.* Edited by Mohammad-Ja'far Mahjoub. New York: Bibliotheca Persica Press, 1999.

Uebel, Michael. "Re-Orienting Desire: Writing on Gender Trouble in Fourteenth-Century Egypt." In *Gender and Difference in the Middle Ages,* edited by Sharon Farmer and Carol Braun Pasternack, 230–57. Minneapolis: University of Minnesota Press, 2003.

Usama b. Munqidh. *Kitab al-I'tibar.* Edited by Philip Hitti. Princeton: Princeton University Press, 1930. Translated by Philip K. Hitti, *An Arab-Syrian Gentleman and Warrior in the Period of the Crusades: Memoirs of Usamah Ibn-Munqidh.* Princeton: Princeton University Press, 1929.

Van Gelder, G. J. *The Bad and the Ugly: Attitudes towards Invective Poetry (Hija') in Classical Arabic Literature.* Leiden: Brill, 1988.

Vanita, Ruth, ed. *Queering India: Same-Sex Love and Eroticism in Indian Culture and Society.* New York: Routledge, 2002.

Véguez, Roberto A. "*Don Quijote* and 9-11: The Clash of Civilizations and the Birth of the Modern Novel." *Hispania* 88, no. 1 (2005): 101–13.

Velasco, Sherry. *The Lieutenant Nun: Transgenderism, Lesbian Desire and Catalina de Erauso.* Austin: University of Texas Press, 2000.

Warner, Michael. *The Trouble with Normal: Sex, Politics, and the Ethics of Queer Life.* New York: Free Press, 1999.

Watt, Diane. "Behaving Like a Man? Incest, Lesbian Desire, and Gender Play in *Yde et Olive.*" *Comparative Literature* 50, no. 4 (1998): 265–85.

———. "Read My Lips: Clippying and Kyssyng in the Early Sixteenth Century." In *Queerly Phrased: Language, Gender and Sexuality,* edited by Anna Livia and Kira Hall, 167–77. New York: Oxford University Press, 1997.

Weever, Jacqueline de. "The Lady, the Knight, and the Lover: Androgyny and Integration in *La Chanson d'Yde et Olive.*" *Romanic Review* 81, no. 4 (1991): 371–91.

Wittig, Monique. "The Straight Mind." *Feminist Issues* 1, no. 1 (1980): 103–11.

Wright, J. W., and Everett Rowson, eds. *Homoeroticism in Classical Arabic Literature.* New York: Columbia University Press, 1997.

Yarshater, Ehsan. "Love-Related Conventions in Sa'dī's Ghazals." In *Studies in Honour of Clifford Edmund Bosworth.* Vol. 2, *The Sultan's Turret: Studies in Persian and Turkish Culture,* 420–438. Leiden: Brill, 2002.

Yarsheter, Ehsan, and Ahmad Ashraf, eds. *Encyclopaedia Iranica.* New York: Encyclopaedia Iranica Foundation, 1985–.

Yde et Olive. In *Esclarmonde, Clarisse et Florent, Yde et Olive: Dreifortsetsungen der chansun von Huon de Bordeaux, nach der einzigen Turiner handschrift.* Edited by Max Schweigel. Marburg: Elwert, 1889.

Yde et Olive. In *"Esclarmonde, Clarisse et Florent, Yde et Olive I, Croissant, Yde et Olive II, Huon et les Géants,* Sequels to *Huon de Bordeaux,* as Contained in Turin MS L.II.14, an Edition." Edited by Barbara Anne Brewska. PhD dissertation, Vanderbilt University, 1977.

Yde et Olive. In *Les Prouesses et faictz du trespreux noble et vaillant Huon de Bordeaux, pair de France et Duc de Guyenne.* Edited by Benoist Rigaud. Fols. 116v–178r. Lyon, 1587. Accessed electronically at the Bibliothèque Nationale in Paris (http://www.bnf.fr).

Ze'evi, Dror. "Changes in Legal-Sexual Discourses: Sex Crimes in the Ottoman Empire." *Continuity and Change* 16, no. 2 (2001): 219–42.

———. *Producing Desire: Changing Sexual Discourse in the Ottoman Middle East 1500–1900.* Berkeley: University of California Press, 2006.

About the Authors

Sahar Amer is associate professor of Asian and international studies at the University of North Carolina–Chapel Hill. She specializes in medieval French literature and the relations between Arabs and French, Muslims and Christians, from the Middle Ages to the present. She is interested in the status of Arabs and Muslims in contemporary France, as well as in questions of Orientalism, postcolonialism, sexualities, and cross-cultural encounters. In addition to articles on various aspects of medieval and contemporary French and Francophone literatures, she has written *Esope au féminin: Marie de France et la politique de l'interculturalité* (Rodopi, 1999) and *Crossing Borders: Love between Women in Medieval French and Arabic Literatures* (2008).

Kathryn Babayan is associate professor of Iranian history and culture at the department of Near Eastern studies, University of Michigan. She specializes in the cultural and social histories of early modern Iran. She is the author of *Mystics, Monarchs and Messiahs: Cultural Landscapes of Early Modern Iran* (Harvard, 2003) and a coauthor (with Sussan Babaie, Ina Baghdiantz-McCabe, and Massumeh Farhad) of *Slaves of the Shah: New Elites of Safavid Iran* (London: I.B. Tauris, 2004). She is currently working on the politics of eros and friendship in early modern Iran.

Brad Epps is professor of Romance languages and literature and chair of studies of women, gender, and sexuality at Harvard University. He has published over seventy articles on modern literature, film, art, architecture, and immigration from Spain, Latin America, Catalonia, and

365

France and is the author of *Significant Violence: Oppression and Resistance in the Narratives of Juan Goytisolo* (Oxford University Press, 1996); *Spain Beyond Spain: Modernity, Literary History, and National Identity* (with Luis Fernández Cifuentes) (Bucknell University Press, 2005); and *Passing Lines: Immigration and Sexuality* (with Keja Valens and Bill Johnson González) (David Rockefeller Center of Latin American Studies/Harvard University Press, 2005). He is currently preparing three books: *All about Alomódovar* (with Despina Kakoudakim) (University of Minnesota Press); *The Ethics of Promiscuity*, on gay and lesbian issues in Latin America, Spain, and Latino cultures in the United States; and *Barcelona and Beyond*, on the transformations of the Catalan capital.

Dina Al-Kassim teaches British, American, French, Arabic, Anglophone, and Francophone modernisms, critical theory, and postcolonial studies in the comparative literature department at the University of California at Irvine. Al-Kassim's research interests include psychoanalysis, gender and queer theory, postcolonial critique, literary and political appropriations of psychoanalysis, nineteenth-century fin-de-siècle culture, colonial law and manipulations of kinship structures, postcolonial Islam, feminist philosophy, and theories of culture. Al-Kassim has published most recently in *Interventions, Public Culture and the Lesbian,* and the MLA's *Gay Studies Newsletter.* Forthcoming publications include *On Pain of Speech,* which addresses the problem of subjection in modernist literature, and *Repudiating the Law,* a comparative study of the phantom of kinship and impossible reparation in the postcolonial states of north and south Africa. Her publications include "The Face of Foreclosure," *Interventions: International Journal of Postcolonial Studies* 4, no. 2 (2002): 168–175; "Crisis of the Unseen: Unearthing the Political Aesthetics of Hysteria in the Archeology and Arts of the New Beirut," *PARACHUTE* 108, Special Issue on Beirut (2002): 147–154; and "The Faded Bond: Calligraphesis and Kinship in Abdelwahab Meddeb's Postcolonial Fiction," *Translation toward a Global Market,* Special issue of *Public Culture* 13 (2001): 113–138.

Frédéric Lagrange is maître de conférences in Arabic literature at the University of the Sorbonne in Paris. His research deals with three sometimes overlapping fields—modern Arabic literature; gay, lesbian, bisexual, and transgender studies applied to Arabic literature; and the ethnomusicology of the Middle East in the period 1850 to 1930. His publications include "Jughrafya Mahfuzistan: mukawwinat al-hara 'inda Nagib Mahfuz wa-dalalatuha al-ramziyya fi 'Awlad Haratina'," *Bulletin d'Etudes Orientales* 56, nos. 2004–2005 (2006): 233–58; "L'Obscénité du Vizir," *Arabica* 53 (2006): 54–107; "Sources and Methods for Research on Women and Islamic Cultures for the Disciplinary Fields of Sexualities and Queer Studies," *Encyclopaedia of Women and Islamic Cultures* (Leiden: Brill, 2003); "Une Egypte libertine: Taqatiq et chansons légères au début du XXe siècle," in *Paroles, Signes, Mythes, Mélanges offerts à Jamel Eddine Bencheikh,* edited by Floréal Sanagustin (IFEAD, 2001) 257–300; "Male Homosexuality in Modern Arabic Literature," in *Imagined Masculinities* edited by Mai Ghoussoub and Emma Sinclair-Webb (Saqi Books, 2000), 169–193.

Afsaneh Najmabadi teaches history and studies of women, gender, and sexuality at Harvard University. Her most recent book, *Women with Mustaches and Men without Beards: Gender and Sexual Anxieties of Iranian Modernity* (University of California Press, 2005) is a study of cultural transformations in nineteenth-century Iran centered on reconfigurations of gender and sexuality. The book received the 2005 Joan Kelly Memorial Prize from the American Historical Association. She is also an associate editor of *Encyclopedia of Women and Islamic Cultures* (Brill, vol. 1, 2003; vol. 2, 2005; vols. 3–4, 2006; vols. 5–6, 2007). She is currently working on a research project tentatively titled "Transing and Transpassing across Sex-Gender Walls in Contemporary Iran."

Everett K. Rowson received his PhD from Yale University in Arabic and Islamic studies. He has taught at Harvard and the University of Pennsylvania and is now associate professor in the department of Middle Eastern and Islamic studies at New York University. He has published extensively in the areas of Islamic philosophy, Arabic literature, and medieval Middle Eastern social history. He is currently completing a book on homoeroticism in premodern Arab cultures.

Leyla Rouhi (PhD, Harvard University, 1995) is professor and chair of Romance languages at Williams College. Her research focuses on the early modern period in Spain, especially interactions among Judaism, Christianity, and Islam. She is the author of *Mediation and Love: A Study of the Go-Between in Key Near Eastern and Western Texts* (Brill,

1999) and coeditor (with Cynthia Robinson) of *Under the Influence: Questioning the Comparative in Medieval Castile* (Brill, 2005).

Valerie Traub is professor of English and women's studies at the University of Michigan, where she directs the women's studies program. She is the author of *The Renaissance of Lesbianism in Early Modern England* (Cambridge University Press, 2002) and *Desire and Anxiety: Circulations of Sexuality in Shakespearean Drama* (Routledge, 1992). A new collection, *Gay Shame* (coedited with David Halperin) is forthcoming from the University of Chicago Press. She has published widely on the history of sexuality and early modern literature and historiography.

Index

HARVARD MIDDLE EASTERN MONOGRAPHS

1. *Syria: Development and Monetary Policy*, by Edmund Y. Asfour. 1959.

2. *The History of Modern Iran: An Interpretation*, by Joseph M. Upton. 1960.

3. *Contributions to Arabic Linguistics*, Charles A. Ferguson, Editor. 1960.

4. *Pan-Arabism and Labor*, by Willard A. Beling. 1960.

5. *The Industrialization of Iraq*, by Kathleen M. Langley. 1961.

6. *Buarij: Portrait of a Lebanese Muslim Village*, by Anne H. Fuller. 1961.

7. *Ottoman Egypt in the Eighteenth Century*, Stanford J. Shaw, Editor and Translator. 1962.

8. *Child Rearing in Lebanon*, by Edwin Terry Prothro. 1961.

9. *North Africa's French Legacy: 1954-1962*, by David C. Gordon. 1962.

10. *Communal Dialects in Baghdad*, by Haim Blanc. 1964.

11. *Ottoman Egypt in the Age of the French Revolution*, Translated with Introduction and Notes by Stanford J. Shaw. 1964.

12. *The Economy of Morocco: 1912-1962*, by Charles F. Stewart. 1964.

13. *The Economy of the Israeli Kibbutz*, by Eliyahu Kanovsky. 1966.

14. *The Syrian Social Nationalist Party: An Ideological Analysis*, by Labib Zuwiyya Yamak. 1966.

15. *The Practical Visions of Ya'qub Sanu'*, by Irene L. Gendizier. 1966.

16. *The Surest Path: The Political Treatise of a Nineteenth-Century Muslim Statesman*, by Leon Carl Brown. 1967.

17. *High-Level Manpower in Economic Development: The Turkish Case*, by Richard D. Robinson. 1967.

18. *Rebirth of a Nation: The Origins and Rise of Moroccan Nationalism, 1912-1944*, by John P. Halsted. 1967.

19. *Women of Algeria: An Essay on Change*, by David C. Gordon. 1968.

20. *The Youth of Haouch El Harimi, A Lebanese Village*, by Judith R. Williams. 1968.

21. *The Problem of Diglossia in Arabic: A Comparative Study of Classical and Iraqi Arabic,* by Salih J. Al-Toma. 1969.

22. *The Seljuk Vezirate: A Study of Civil Administration,* by Carla L. Klausner. 1973.

23. and 24. *City in the Desert,* by Oleg Grabar, Renata Holod, James Knustad, and William Trousdale. 1978.

25. *Women's Autobiographies in Contemporary Iran,* Afsaneh Najmabadi, Editor. 1990.

26. *The Science of Mystic Lights,* by John Walbridge. 1992.

27. *Political Aspects of Islamic Philosophy: Essays in Honor of Muhsin S. Mahdi,* by Charles E. Butterworth. 1992.

28. *The Muslims of Bosnia-Herzegovina: Their Historic Development from the Middle Ages to the Dissolution of Yugoslavia,* Mark Pinson, Editor. 1994.

29. *Book of Gifts and Rarities: Kitāb al-Hadāyā wa al-Tuḥaf.* Ghāda al Hijjāwī al-Qaddūmī, Translator and Annotator. 1997.

30. *The Armenians of Iran: The Paradoxical Role of a Minority in a Dominant Culture: Articles and Documents,* Cosroe Chaqueri, Editor. 1998.

31. *In the Shadow of the Sultan: Culture, Power, and Politics in Morocco,* Rahma Bourqia and Susan Gilson Miller, editors. 1999.

32. *Hermeneutics and Honor: Negotiating Female "Public" Space in Islamic/ate Societies,* Asma Afsaruddin, editor. 1999.

33. *The Second Umayyad Caliphate: The Articulation of Caliphal Legitimacy in al-Andalus,* by Janina M. Safran. 2000.

34. *New Perspectives on Property and Land in the Middle East,* Roger Owen, editor. 2001.

35. *Mystics, Monarchs, and Messiahs: Cultural Landscapes of Early Modern Iran,* by Kathryn Babayan. 2003.

36. *Byzantium Viewed by the Arabs,* by Nadia Maria El Cheikh. 2004.

37. *The Palestinian Peasant Economy under the Mandate: A Story of Colonial Bungling,* by Amos Nadan. 2006.

38. *The Moral Resonance of Arab Media: Audiocassette Poetry and Culture in Yemen,* by W. Flagg Miller. 2007.

39. *Islamicate Sexualities: Translations across Temporal Geographies of Desire,* Kathryn Babayan and Afsaneh Najmabadi, editors. 2008.